AGRICULTURAL PRICES AND COMMODITY MARKET ANALYSIS

AGRICULTURAL PRICES AND COMMODITY MARKET ANALYSIS

John N. Ferris
Michigan State University

♾ The paper used in this publication meets the minimum requirements of ANSI/NISO Z39.48-1992 (R 1997) (Permanence of Paper).

Michigan State University Press
East Lansing, Michigan 48823-5245

1998 edition originally published by WCB McGraw-Hill, Boston 0-07-021728-9
2005 edition published by Michigan State University Press 0-87013-751-4

Printed and bound in the United States of America.

11 2 3 4 5 6 7 8 9 10

The Library of Congress has catalogued the 1998 edition as follows:
Ferris, John N.
Agricultural prices and commodity market analysis / John N. Ferris. —1st ed.
p. cm.
Includes index.
ISBN 0-07-021728-9
1. Commodity exchanges—United States. 2. Agricultural prices—United States—Forecasting. 3. Farm produce—United States—Marketing. I. Title.
HG6049.F467 1997
332.64'41'0973—dc21 97-22841
CIP

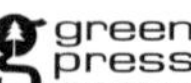
Michigan State University Press is a member of the Green Press Initiative and is committed to developing and encouraging ecologically responsible publishing practices. For more information about the Green Press Initiative and the use of recycled paper in book publishing, please visit *www.greenpressinitiative.org*.

Visit Michigan State University Press on the World Wide Web at: *www.msupress.msu.edu*

ABOUT THE AUTHOR

John N. (Jake) Ferris is a professor emeritus in the Department of Agricultural, Food, and Resource Economics at Michigan State University. His MSU responsibilities have blended extension, teaching, and research, including international assignments and two with the federal government in Washington, D.C. His professional focus has been on price analysis, outlook, and marketing strategies. Dr. Ferris has authored over a thousand articles, bulletins and staff papers, contributing regular outlook articles to a national livestock publication and the *Michigan Farmer.* He directed several multidisciplinary futuring projects on the long-range prospects and potential for Michigan agriculture, natural resources and the food industry. Professor Ferris developed AGMOD, an innovative econometric model of U.S. and world agriculture which generates year-to-year projections on major commodities. He developed commodity marketing courses for both graduate and undergraduate students that emphasized the application of forecasting tools. He has received a number of recognitions, including a "Distinguished Extension Program Award" and several "Premiere Forecasting Awards" from the American Agricultural Economics Association, the "1996 Distinguished Service to Agriculture Award" from the Michigan Farm Bureau and the 2007 "Certificate of Distinction" for outstanding service to agriculture from the Purdue Agricultural Alumni Association.

CONTENTS

PREFACE xvii

1 Introduction 1

SECTION I THEORETICAL CONCEPTS AND EMPIRICAL MEASUREMENT OF DEMAND AND SUPPLY 5

2 Theoretical Concepts of Demand and Supply 7

DEMAND 8
- Demand as a Composite 8
- Demand Shifters 10
- Irreversibility 10

FORMULATION OF DEMAND EQUATIONS 11

FARM SUPPLY 15

PRICE SPREADS, DERIVED DEMAND, AND PRICE FORMATION 16
- Price Spreads 16
- Implications of Fixed Spreads 18

SUMMARY 19

QUESTIONS FOR STUDY 19

3 Measuring Demand for Domestic Consumption 21

SINGLE DEMAND EQUATIONS 21
- Price 23
- Population 23
- Adjusted Population Variable 24
- Income 25
- General Inflation 26
- Other Demand Factors 26
- Quarterly and Monthly Demand Equations 29

DEMAND ELASTICITIES, FLEXIBILITIES, AND IMPACT MULTIPLIERS 30
- Demand Elasticity 31
- Demand Flexibility 31

Impact Multipliers 31
Point Elasticities and Flexibilities 31
Relationship Between Elasticities and Flexibilities 33
Role of These Measurements 34
DEMAND SYSTEMS 34
Conditions 35
Empirical Example 35
Pros and Cons 36
CONDITIONAL REGRESSION 39
SUMMARY 40
QUESTIONS FOR STUDY 40

4 **Measuring Demands for Storage, Speculation, and Exports** 42

DEMAND FOR STORAGE AND SPECULATION 42
Current and Expected Prices 43
Storage Costs and Availability 44
DEMAND FOR EXPORTS 44
Prices and Exchange Rates 46
Population and Purchasing Power 49
Foreign Production and Carryover 49
Trade Policies 50
Transportation Costs 50
Livestock Feed 51
Concluding Comment 51
SUMMARY 51
QUESTIONS FOR STUDY 51

5 **Measuring Price Spreads and Derived Demand for Agricultural Products and Inputs** 53

PRICE SPREADS AND DERIVED DEMAND FOR AGRICULTURAL PRODUCTS 54
Formulation at Equilibrium 54
USDA Retail-Farm Price Spreads 55
U.S. Marketing Costs and Profits 58
Direct Forecasting of Retail Food Prices 59
PRICE SPREADS RELATED TO QUALITY DIFFERENCES 61
Government Grades 61
Modeling Grades and Close Substitutes 62
Wholesale Beef Market Example 63
Processed Feed Market Example 65
DEMAND FOR AGRICULTURAL INPUTS 67
Income and Equity 68
Prices, Costs, Government Programs, and Productivity 68
Replacement Demand 69
Enterprise Profit and Risk 69

Technical Requirements and Structure 69
Deflation 69
SUMMARY 70
QUESTIONS FOR STUDY 70

6 **Measuring Farm Supply** 72

EXPECTATIONS 73
Geometric Distributed Lags 75
Polynomial Distributed Lags 78
Rational Expectations 82
RISK AND ITS MEASUREMENT 85
GROSS MARGINS AND RATIOS 87
Formulation 88
Costs of Production 90
Gross Margin on Corn 91
Pros and Cons 94
INTEGRATED SUPPLY MODELS 95
SUMMARY 96
QUESTIONS FOR STUDY 96

SECTION II GENERATION OF ECONOMETRIC/SIMULATION MODELS 97

7 **Recursive and Simultaneous Supply-Demand Models** 99

RECURSIVE MODELS 100
Price Dependent Demand 100
Quantity Dependent Demand 103
Geometric Lags 105
More Complex Lag Structures 107
Observation of Large Models 111
Why Cycles Persist in Agriculture 111
SIMULTANEOUS MODELS 112
Identification Problem 114
Two-Stage Least Squares 118
Relevance of Simultaneity 119
SUMMARY 119
QUESTIONS FOR STUDY 120

8 **Building Econometric/Simulation Models** 121

GAUSS-SEIDEL ALGORITHM 122
GUIDELINES FOR MODEL BUILDING 124
THE BALANCE SHEET 128
EXAMPLES OF ECONOMETRIC/SIMULATION MODELS 129

Livestock 129
Dairy 131
LARGE-SCALE ECONOMETRIC MODELS 133
SWOPSIM 134
AGMOD 136
Dynamic Generation of Elasticities and Flexibilities 138
SUMMARY 140
QUESTIONS FOR STUDY 141

9 Forecast Evaluation 142

ASYMMETRIC ERRORS 143
MEASURES OF TOTAL ERROR 144
MEASURES OF BIAS ERROR 145
THEIL'S INEQUALITY COEFFICIENTS 145
STANDARDS FOR COMPARISON 146
Short-range (Period-to-Period) Forecasting Evaluation 147
Long-range Forecasting Evaluation 147
DOUBLE EXPONENTIAL SMOOTHING (DES) 149
HANDLING EXOGENOUS VARIABLES 150
EX-ANTE AND EX-POST 152
HANDLING THE RANDOM ERROR 152
SUMMARY 153
QUESTIONS FOR STUDY 153

10 Stochastic Modeling 154

SCOPE OF THE PROBLEM 154
HOW TO PROCEED 157
CROP YIELD DISTRIBUTIONS AND NORMALITY TESTS 158
AGGREGATION OF COUNTRIES OR REGIONS 160
DISTRIBUTIONS AND CORRELATIONS 161
AN EXAMPLE WITH MICROTSP 162
SUMMARY 166
QUESTIONS FOR STUDY 166

SECTION III LONG-TERM PROJECTIONS AND APPLICATIONS 169

11 Generating Long-Term Projections and Forecasts 171
QUANTITATIVE APPROACH 172
Demand 173
Supply 178
Prices 181
COMBINING SUBJECTIVE WITH QUANTITATIVE METHODS 182
Scenario Writing 183

Delphi 184
Nominal Group Technique 186
Example of Long-range Outlook Projects 186
SUMMARY 187
QUESTIONS FOR STUDY 187

12 Spatial Commodity Analysis and Trade 189

REPRESENTATIVE PRICES 190
PRICE SURFACES 190
MARKET DIVISION 191
SIMPLE TRADE MODEL 192
INTERREGIONAL ANALYSIS 196
INTERREGIONAL ANALYSIS EXPANDED 198
SHIFT-SHARE ANALYSIS 200
PLANT LOCATION 202
SUMMARY 206
QUESTIONS FOR STUDY 206

13 Application of Models to Long-Range Planning and Policy Analysis 208

FARMERS AND AGRIBUSINESSES 209
POLICY ANALYSIS 210
Policy Instruments 210
Modeling Decision Makers and Modifying Policy Assumptions 212
NEW CHALLENGES 212
Dynamic vs. Static 213
Stochastic Impacts 214
Implications to Producers, Consumers, and Taxpayers 214
Impacts on Types of Farms by Regions 215
Implications to Total Food System and Economy 215
Evaluation of Research and Education 215
SUMMARY 216
QUESTIONS FOR STUDY 216

SECTION IV SHORT-TERM FORECASTING, FUTURES MARKETS, AND SOURCES OF MARKET INFORMATION 217

14 Seasonals 219

GENERATING A SEASONAL PRICE PATTERN 220
EXAMPLE ON HOGS 222
FITTING SEASONALS TO DECISION MAKING 225

SUMMARY 231
QUESTIONS FOR STUDY 232

15 Commodity Futures and Options Markets 233

WHAT ARE FUTURES MARKETS? 234
Description 234
How Futures Prices Are Quoted 235
Who Participates 236
What Commodities Are Traded, Where, and Why? 236
Economic Functions 237
Concepts About Futures Not Easily Understood 239
OPTIONS ON FUTURES 240
Factors Affecting Premiums 241
How Options Prices Are Quoted 242
PROFIT PATTERNS DIAGRAMMED 243
PRICING OPTIONS 245
Black/Scholes Model 246
Delta Formulas 248
SUMMARY 248
QUESTIONS FOR STUDY 249
GLOSSARY 249

16 Forward Pricing with Futures and Options 253

SELLING A CASH PRODUCT 253
Simple Storage Hedge 254
Storing Soybeans and Buying Puts 257
Forward Pricing Alternatives for a New Crop 259
EMERGING RULES 268
MORE EXOTIC FORWARD PRICING SCHEMES 271
BUYING A CASH PRODUCT 271
BASIS—A KEY TO EFFECTIVE FORWARD PRICING 273
New Crop Basis 275
Storage Basis 275
HEDGE RATIOS 278
SUMMARY 280
QUESTIONS FOR STUDY 280

17 Technical Analysis 282
PRICE DISCOVERY AND MARKET EFFICIENCY 282
VERTICAL BAR CHARTS 284
Formations 284
Trend Lines 287

Continuation Formations 290
Reversals 292
Gaps 293
MOVING AVERAGES AND STOCHASTICS 295
Moving Averages 295
Stochastics 297
VOLUME, OPEN INTEREST, AND PRICE 298
RELATIVE STRENGTH INDEX 299
NET TRADER POSITIONS 300
OTHER TECHNICAL TOOLS 300
Point and Figure Charting 300
Cycles 302
Japanese Candlesticks 302
EVALUATION 302
SUMMARY 304
QUESTIONS FOR STUDY 304

18 Time Series Models 305

STATIONARITY 306
White Noise 307
Dickey-Fuller Test 308
Engle-Granger Co-integration Test 311
APPLYING AR, MA, AND ARMA MODELS TO A DEMAND EQUATION ON HOGS 311
Correcting for Serial Correlation in Residuals with AR(1) 313
Autoregressive Models (AR) 314
Moving Average Models (MA) 316
Autoregressive Moving Average Models (ARMA) 316
Application of ARMA to Residuals in OLS Equations 317
INTEGRATED AUTOREGRESSIVE MOVING AVERAGE MODELS (ARIMA) 318
UNIVARIATE FORECASTING WITH TIME SERIES MODELS 322
SUMMARY 328
QUESTIONS FOR STUDY 328

19 Sources of Agricultural Data and Market Analysis 330

MONITORS IN AGRICULTURE AND FOOD 332
Crop and Livestock Estimates, General Farm Statistics 332
Applying the Census and Other Non-annual Data 333
Market News 336
Macro, Other Data Related to Agriculture and Food 336
International Statistics 337
INTERPRETERS (ANALYSTS) IN AGRICULTURE AND FOOD 337
ELECTRONIC TRANSMISSION 338

SUMMARY 338
QUESTIONS FOR STUDY 338

APPENDIX A Glossary of Statistical Terms 341
APPENDIX B A Note on Indices 345
REFERENCES 347
AUTHOR INDEX 355
SUBJECT INDEX 357

PREFACE

This book is about the "nitty-gritty" of commodity analysis and forecasting. While the focus is on agricultural commodities and food, the principles apply to other commodities as well. The forecast horizon ranges from the intra-day activity of scalpers on futures markets to monthly and quarterly time frames, to the year-by-year projections of econometric/simulation models, and to the very long-range concerns about world food supply-demand balances. The book also extends forecasting into decision making and policy analysis.

The emphasis is on applied econometrics. The reader would be best prepared having completed courses in intermediate economic theory and introduction to econometrics. Most essential is an understanding of college algebra and multiple regression, and familiarity with microcomputer software programs in statistics. However, readers without formal courses in econometrics should be able to comprehend most of the material with extra reading on linear regression in introductory econometric texts.

References in the text are to MicroTSP from Quantitative Micro Software. This program has been replaced by EViews, the Windows version.

This book evolved from lecture notes in a graduate course in agricultural economics, designed to prepare students for some of the more common tasks in market analysis as undertaken by professionals in industry, government and academic institutions. Each student has been required to estimate the structural parameters of an econometric/simulation model, evaluate it and solve the model for a 10-year projection period. With this term problem as a focus, students have the incentive to test the procedures suggested in the text.

While the emphasis is on agriculture and the food system in the United States, increased globalization of markets dictated that the subjects be applicable throughout the world. Even futures markets, which have been a major institution in U.S. agriculture, are expanding globally. The rationale and role of these markets are treated in some detail.

While the book is organized in a logical sequence, the reader could enter at any point to explore particular subjects of interest. In a sense, the book is intended to cover the salient aspects of modeling and forecasting, and to provide readers with a conceptual idea on topics deserving closer inspection. Hopefully, the book will encourage readers to pursue such subjects more intensively.

The book reflects 40 years of experience of the author as an on-campus teacher of graduates and undergraduates, as an extension specialist and as a researcher. The research in recent years has focused on the development and application of large econometric/simulation models. Having forecasts published regularly forces analysts to sharpen their tools and sort out the important from the unimportant. This book contains what this author believes is particularly relevant in forecasting and where additional refinement in these procedures is needed.

ACKNOWLEDGMENTS

This book is dedicated to my wife, Maxine, who supported me in this endeavor as well as my entire professional career. This she did while handling family obligations and launching her own career in academia.

Special credits go to a superb secretary, Nancy Creed, who saw this manuscript through class notes stages and countless revisions as a textbook. Graduate students provided valuable feedback on what to include and how to present the material. Reviewers of early drafts quickly revealed to me that I had not written the "perfect text." I am indebted to those persons and have kept their comments and suggestions in mind as the manuscript was revised and restructured. As noted in Chapter 18, my colleague, Robert Myers, was particularly helpful in a review of that chapter.

Other reviewers instrumental in assisting the author through the revision process include:

James J. Ahern Jr., California Polytechnic State University
Peter Barry, University of Illinois
Andrew Barkley, Kansas State University
James Eales, Purdue University
Darrel Good, University of Illinois
Henry Kinnucan, Auburn University
Patricia Lindsey, Oregon State University

As usual, I assume responsibility for errors of omission and commission.

John N. (Jake) Ferris

AGRICULTURAL PRICES AND COMMODITY MARKET ANALYSIS

1

INTRODUCTION

The extensive public and private resources devoted to measuring, monitoring, analyzing, and forecasting commodity supplies, demands, and prices attest to the importance of these activities to the world economy. Food, being an especially precious commodity, draws extra attention. Impending food shortages and high prices make headlines. Also, food surpluses and low prices, creating stress on the farm, garner action through government programs.

Decision-making at many levels depends on reasonably accurate assessments of future developments in the commodity scene. In the agriculture and food sector, this ranges over inventory decisions of farm equipment manufacturers, farmers' allocation of land in spring planting, developing marketing programs by producer associations, positioning rail cars at harvest, designing special promotions at the retail store, forward contracting wheat for export, designing the next farm bill, etc.

The U.S. Department of Agriculture (USDA), in cooperation with state departments of agriculture, sets the pace by generating crop and livestock estimates and monitoring market prices. So important is this task that the private sector is also involved. These organizations not only gather such information, but also have extensive programs in disseminating commodity news.

Analysis and forecasting are major functions of the Economic Research Service of the USDA and an inter-agency unit known as the World Agricultural Outlook Board. Land Grant Universities and many private firms also devote considerable resources to this activity.

Citations could be made of similar programs in other nations and particularly international organizations such as the Food and Agriculture Organization (FAO) of the United Nations, the Organization for Economic Cooperation and Development (OECD), and the World Bank.

Data valuable for commodity analysis extend well beyond the standard production, stocks, use, and price statistics. Household consumption surveys, cost of production studies, financial statistics such as interest rates, descriptive studies of industries, and technical conversion rates all contribute to comprehensive commodity market research. The *Census of Agriculture* of the U.S. Department of Commerce (before 1997) and U.S. Department of Agriculture (since 1997) provides key benchmark data to identify structural changes on the farm.

While market analysts often feel constrained by voids in the data base, agriculture is blessed with a vast statistical resource compared to many other industries. This rich database may reflect the long-term traditional role of the public sector in agricultural data collection and dissemination beginning in the mid 1800s at the federal level in the U.S.

In the 1950s, when the field of econometrics was in its infancy, market analysts were restricted to electro-mechanical desk calculators and large, slow main-frame computers. These large computers speeded up in the 1960s and, at that time, the smaller desktop and then the hand-held electronic calculators appeared on the scene. The expansion in availability and use of the microcomputer, which began in the 1970s, accelerated in the 1980s. The capacity of these machines was enlarged in the 1990s as they dominated hardware for econometricians and others.

Also, during the 1980s and early 1990s, evolution in software programs allowed market analysts to pursue more ambitious and comprehensive projects. Possibly one of the most valuable contributions of these programs was to provide faster feedback to the analyst as econometric/simulation models were being developed. The process of exploring alternative formulations became more efficient.

Improved computer hardware and software may shorten the distance between the decision maker and the modeler. Some decision makers may become modelers, or will have personnel closeby who can tap computer models for answers to questions requiring a quick response.

Moreover, the process of modeling is a rich learning experience. One might say, "Modeling is too important to leave to specialized modelers." The point is that analytic activity can become more decentralized with a role for those who, in the past, have applied the output of large econometric models, but have not plugged directly into the operation and development of the model itself. At the same time, economists specializing in modeling continue to improve the capability of these analytical tools.

Considering (1) the extensive agricultural database, (2) an expanding analytic capacity with new computer hardware and software programs, and (3) the importance of food in world economic development, agricultural economists can demonstrate how to transform agricultural statistics into useable information for decision makers. As nation after nation shifts from centrally directed economies to a market orientation, commodity market analysis will become more relevant. Agricultural products and other raw materials are important to the economies of these nations. Also, the poorer countries are heavily dependent on products of farms, forestries, and mines for foreign exchange to initiate economic development.

Implementation of the North American Free Trade Agreement (NAFTA), the Uruguay Round of the General Agreement on Tariffs and Trade (GATT) and subsequent agreements under the World Trade Organization (WTO) will also challenge commodity analysts and political scientists to evaluate the consequences for the producer, consumer, and government expenditure sectors. In many nations, highly structured price-setting mechanisms will give way to volatile markets, upon which the commodity futures industry thrives.

This book is divided into four sections. Chapters 2 through 6 in Section One extend theoretical concepts of demand and supply to agriculture and the food system and prescribe empirical procedures for analysis. In Section Two, chapters 7 through 10 integrate demand-and-supply relationships in constructing and evaluating econometric/simulation models designed to generate dynamic forecasts of agricultural variables. How to deal with risk such as the weather effect on crop yields is also covered.

While Section Two concentrates on methodology relevant for intermediate-term forecasting, say the next one to five years, Section Three (chapters 11 through 13) addresses the challenge of projecting ahead beyond five years when structural change and new technology must be taken into account. A perspective on interregional adjustments, international trade, and plant location is included in this section. Application of these projections for decision making and policy making is also presented.

Finally, Section Four relates more to short-term forecasting, that is, less than a year into the future. This includes seasonals, technical analysis, time series models, and descriptions of futures and options markets and their functions. These institutions are important elements in U.S. and world commodity markets. Sources of agricultural data and market analysis are enumerated in the concluding chapter.

SECTION ONE

THEORETICAL CONCEPTS AND EMPIRICAL MEASUREMENT OF DEMAND AND SUPPLY

2

THEORETICAL CONCEPTS OF DEMAND AND SUPPLY

POINTS:

1. Total demand as a composite of domestic consumption, storage and speculation, and exports.
2. How changing storage and speculation demands trigger price volatility.
3. Ceteris paribus assumptions challenge empirical demand analysis.
4. Identifying demand shifters.
5. Formulating and interpreting an ordinary least squares equation.
6. Price and profit expectations in supply analysis.
7. Interaction of farm supply, retail, and derived farm demands.
8. Measurement problems with retail demand.
9. The farm-retail price spread as the equilibrium between supply and demand for marketing services and materials.

Empirical demand and supply analysis should proceed with a strong theoretical framework in economics and statistics. Such background is invaluable in assisting researchers in identifying the relevant variables to include and the statistical tools that are appropriate. Even so, analysts must be prepared for unexpected and counter-intuitive results. But rather than rejecting theory in those cases, they may often be able to refine and enlarge upon the concepts that help to explain and forecast human behavior.

DEMAND

A book on marketing appropriately presents a lead section on demand. This is a subtle reminder that production should be oriented to buyers' requirements, including the tastes and preferences of the ultimate consumer and also characteristics deemed important by marketers, processors, exporters, etc.

The theory of demand is covered lightly in this chapter. For an introduction to this subject, read Chapter 2 in *Economics of Resources, Agriculture and Food* (Seitz, Nelson and Halcrow, 1994). Demand is also extensively treated in textbooks on introductory and intermediate economic theory.

Demand is defined as the schedule of amounts that buyers will purchase given a set of prices (Marshall, 1920). The "law of demand" states that the higher the price, the less of a given good will be purchased. For the ultimate buyer of food, demand could relate retail prices to amounts that will actually be consumed within a given time frame. Utility maximization is the focus. (See Chapter 3 for a review of demand elasticities and flexibilities.)

Demand as a Composite

Purchases essentially reflect the demand for immediate consumption *and* the inclination of consumers to restock their shelves or fill their freezers when prices are particularly attractive or reduce inventories when prices are high. Consumers, of course, consider prices as "attractive" or "high" based upon anticipated prices. Purchases, then, reflect a demand for immediate consumption and a demand for storage and speculation.

In agricultural markets, the ultimate consumer is not the only actor on the demand side. On highly perishable items, the consumer may predominate; but on storable products and items such as inputs into livestock feeding, other forces may be very influential. Demands to fill storages and provide dependable flows of feed to livestock facilities may prominently influence price. Food processors have similar demands for dependable supplies. On such commodities, demands for both storage and speculation may even override the ultimate demand for consumption in explaining wide swings in farm, wholesale, and retail prices.

Demands for storage and speculation strongly reflect *expectations.* These expectations are determined by anticipated utilization and product availability, and future changes in other market factors such as agricultural policies. Changing estimates of next year's crop may strongly influence current prices, even though current crop year availabilities and utilization levels remain constant.

Demands for immediate consumption, and storage and speculation could apply to a domestic market isolated from the rest of the world. More typically, most nations participate in an international market and face an export demand. At high prices, the amount demanded of the domestic product drops sharply at the level of price that attracts imports (negative exports). At low levels of price, the domestic product may become competitive in foreign markets. Therefore, the demand for such a product may be decomposed into demands for:

1 Domestic consumption (by the ultimate consumer).
2 Storage (at various levels in the marketing chain).

3 Speculation (at various levels in the marketing chain).
4 Exports.

The Marshallian approach involves ceteris paribus assumptions that incomes, prices of substitutes, prices of complements, storage costs, etc., *and* expected future prices on the given product are held constant. Given these assumptions, these four elements of demand and this summation are graphically presented in Figure 2-1. Under the ceteris paribus assumptions, total demand may be relatively elastic (amount demanded [Q] is highly responsive to price [P]) at high and low prices even though demand for domestic consumption may be inelastic throughout.

Given some level of expected price, storers and speculators would want to buy as much as they could handle at low current prices, which would assure profits. This is indicated in Figure 2-1, as the curve flattens out to the positive side on quantity. On the other hand, high current prices encourage sales out of storage and the curve flattens out to the negative side.

Given some level of international prices, domestic prices might vary within a range which would neither attract imports nor facilitate exports (Figure 2-1). But at some lower price, exports would become profitable, making the *demand for exports* quite elastic. At the other extreme, domestic prices rising above some level would attract substantial imports.

FIGURE 2-1 Demand Components for a farm product.

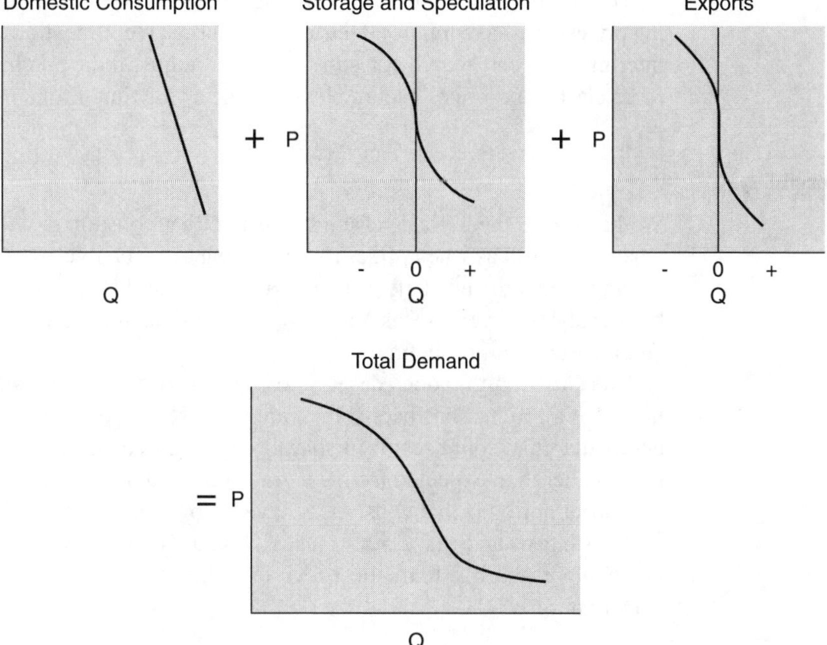

Obviously, if the nation is a major participant in international markets, prices within the nation will influence prices abroad invalidating the assumption that international prices remain constant. Also, changes in expected prices will strongly influence current prices of a storable product. These circumstances do not invalidate the theory, but prevent analysts from observing relationships at extreme values.

Demand Shifters

Multiple forces cause these demand schedules to shift to the right or left. An increase in domestic income would tend to shift the *demand for immediate consumption* to the right unless it is an "inferior" good. An increase in the price of a substitute would shift the *demand for immediate consumption* to the right; an increase in the price of a complement, to the left. Increases in real incomes of foreign consumers would tend to shift the *demand for exports* to the right. An increase in expected future prices relative to current prices would shift the *demand for storage and speculation* to the right. An increase in storage costs shifts the *demand for storage and speculation* to the left.

The *export demand* can be shifted by a complex set of factors. An increase in prices in foreign markets or competing export regions would shift the *export demand* to the right. Similarly, a decline in the value of the domestic currency, vis-a-vis the foreign market country or the competing exporter, will shift the *export demand* for the product to the right. International trade policies may be important as well, such as the European Union's (EU's) use of export restitutions and the U.S.'s implementation of the Export Enhancement Program, which subsidize exports.

The definition of demand implies a specified time period. In the very short-run, changing prices may have minor effects on utilization. Over time, however, consumers and the interim users can search for substitutes and adjust their purchases. Demands become more elastic and prices become less volatile as the time frame increases.

Irreversibility

We have little theoretical reason to assume that consumers will follow the same path when prices fall as when prices rise, implying a "reversible" demand curve. Yet, very little empirical demand analysis deals with irreversibility as illustrated in Figure 2-2. Perhaps analysts regard this as a minor aspect of demand and concentrate on more important measurement problems.

One situation that does deserve testing for irreversibility is a case in which the demand for a product has been expanding consistently over time. Sharply reduced product availability could result in sharply higher prices in the relatively short-run—to a level higher than expected from existing empirical demand measurements (Figure 2-2). The presumption is that consumers have become accustomed to an increasingly higher level of intake and that prices must rise sharply to ration out the reduced supplies—much more sharply than the previous price declines which encouraged increased consumption.

FIGURE 2-2 An irreversible demand curve.

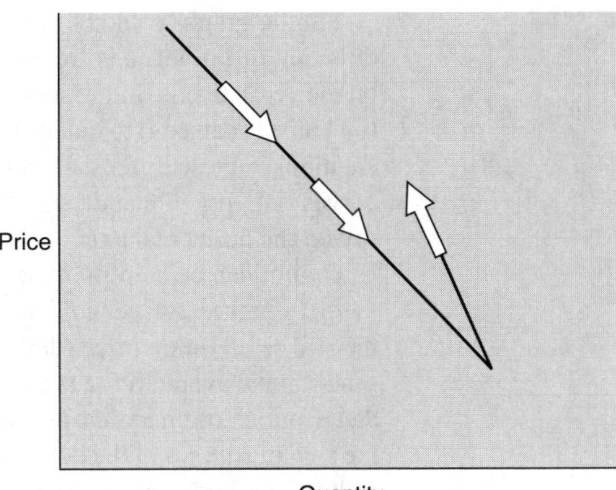

FORMULATION OF DEMAND EQUATIONS

While the illustration of demands for immediate consumption, storage and speculation, and exports is helpful to conceptualize the relationship between price and utilization of a product, the role of the demand shifters is reduced. Of course, the impact of demand shifters on utilization could also be illustrated. For example, the impact of consumer income on immediate consumption with all other factors constant (including price) could be drawn as in Figure 2-3.

FIGURE 2-3 Independent effect of consumer income on consumption.

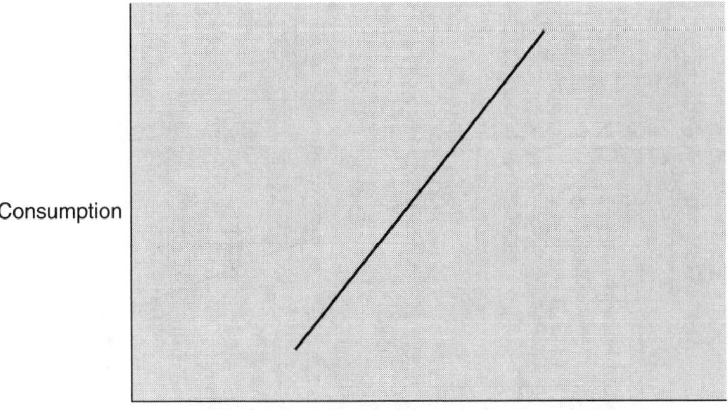

Assumption: All other influences are constant.

Similar graphs could be drawn for other demand shifters. Note that in Figure 2-3, the direction of influence is from consumer income on the horizontal axis to consumption on the vertical axis. In Figures 2-1 and 2-2, the cause–effect relationship was from price (on the vertical axis) to quantity or utilization (on the horizontal axis). The different orientations in these figures are purely arbitrary. Traditionally, in drawing standard demand curves (i.e., price-quantity relationships), price is placed on the vertical axis and quantity on the horizontal axis.

Graphs can be helpful in measuring demand relationships as well as conceptualizing them. In Figure 2-4, per capita consumption of fresh onions in the U.S. is plotted against the real retail onion price (deflated by the Consumer Price Index). The database represents annual averages for 1980 to 1994. The line in the graph represents the fitting to the data from an ordinary least squares regression procedure. The line is positioned so that the sum of squares of the horizontal deviations from the line is minimized (why this procedure is called "least squares"). As expected, the consumption is inversely related to price.

Price is not the only influence on consumption as shown by the deviations from the demand line. Economic theory suggests that consumer income could also be a factor. To test this theory, the horizontal deviations from the demand line were plotted against real disposable income (Figure 2-5). In this case, the deviations or residuals were plotted on the vertical scale and real disposable income per capita on the horizontal scale. Similar to demand, the line in Figure 2-5 is generated by the ordinary least squares procedure.

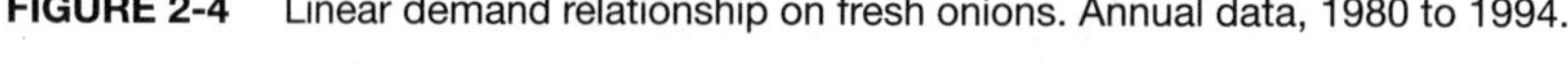

FIGURE 2-4 Linear demand relationship on fresh onions. Annual data, 1980 to 1994.

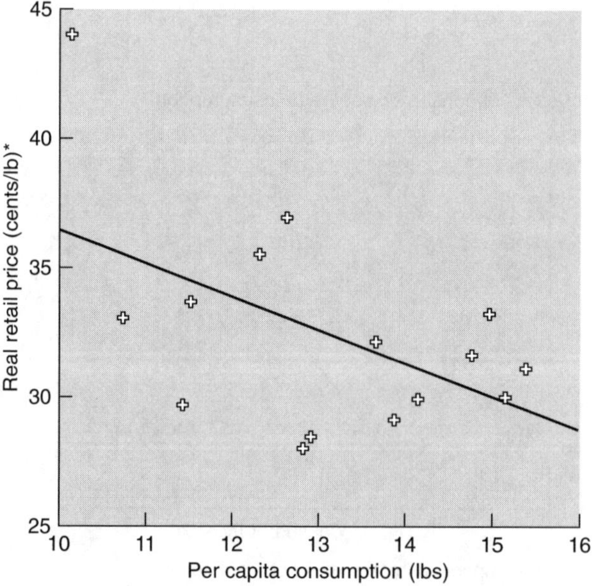

*Retail price divided by the Consumer Price Index (1982 - 84 = 100%).

FIGURE 2-5 Effect of real disposable income on the residuals in the demand relationship between onion prices and consumption.

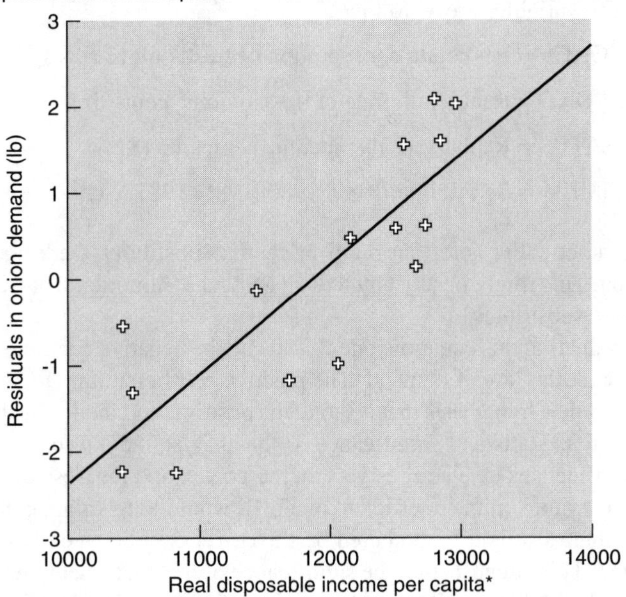

*Disposable income per capita divided by the CPI (1982 - 84 = 100%).

From Figure 2-5, an analyst would conclude that per capita consumption of onions is positively related to consumer income after price effects were taken into account. Also apparent from Figure 2-5 is the conclusion that retail onion prices and consumer income do not explain all of the variation in fresh onion consumption. Additional factors affecting onion demand need to be explored.

An analyst might have hypothesized that the demand for fresh onions is related to a number of trends including away-from-home eating, particularly in fast-food restaurants. These trends may be, in part, related to higher incomes, but more to living styles. Without better measures of "living styles," the researcher may simply have introduced a variable called "serial time." This variable had the value of 1980 in 1980, 1981 in 1981, etc. Using ordinary least squares (OLS), the addition of serial time resulted in the following equation:

$$\text{CONC} = -\ 603.8 - \underset{(-3.02)}{.05987} * \text{RPOND} + \underset{(.69)}{.0001757} * \text{DICD}$$

$$+ \underset{(5.76)}{.31037} * \text{TIME}$$

$R^2 = .98 \quad \bar{R}^2 = .97$

Standard error of the regression = 2.1 percent of the mean of the dependent variable.

Figures in parentheses are *t* values.

The variables are as follows:

CONC = Per capita consumption of fresh onions (lbs.)

RPOND = Real retail price of fresh onions (cents/lb.)

DICD = Real disposable income per capita ($).

TIME = Serial time. 1980=1980, 1981=1981, etc.

Parenthetically, note that retail prices on substitutes were not incorporated in the equation. This might be attributed to an a priori assumption that fresh onions have no or few close substitutes.

In evaluating this equation, one would cite the negative coefficient on RPOND as consistent with the law of demand. The positive coefficient on DICD may not be strongly supported by a hypothesis that it should be positive, and the *t* value being less than 2 casts doubts on its statistical significance. If the analyst had a priori reasoning that a collection of influences labeled lifestyles increased demand for fresh onions, the positive sign and 5.76 *t* value on the coefficient of TIME would help validate the hypothesis.

The analyst might be bothered by the correlation between DICD and TIME, which was .953. This suggests that the significance of the coefficient on TIME might be partly attributed to DICD and not truly a trend apart from DICD. This problem, known as collinearity in this case, or more generally as multicollinearity, denies the researcher an accurate reading of the separate impacts of the independent variables. The analyst would be obliged to search for other variables in place of TIME to reduce this problem. With 15 years of observations (1980–1994), however, there would be limitations of how many additional variables could be added since degrees of freedom would become restrictive.

The R^2 indicates that 98 percent of the variation in the dependent variable was associated with the equation; slightly less with $\bar{R}^2$ which adjusts for degrees of freedom. The standard error of the regression is 2.1 percent of the mean value of the dependent variable. The equation performs well by these statistical measures. (See section on "Glossary of Statistical Terms" in Appendix A for a review of regression analysis.)

Generally, statisticians regard *t* values with absolute values of about 2 or greater as the standard for significance, denoting that the coefficient is different from zero with a probability of 95 percent or more. The *t* value of .69 on the coefficient of DICD might be reason to omit that variable from the equation. However, if the analyst had strong a priori reason to believe that DICD was an appropriate explanatory variable and carried the expected sign, the equation could remain as specified. If the coefficient on any independent variable, significant or not, carried the "wrong" sign, that variable should be eliminated. The analyst needs to formulate a strong rationale for the variables included in any demand equation and be prepared to respecify equations after evaluating the statistical properties. This applies to supply and other behavioral equations as well.

Utilization of most farm and food products depends upon multiple factors too numerous to measure precisely. The analyst must draw from economic theory and an understanding of consumer behavior to establish the most important determining variables and how to formulate them in measuring demand. A similar approach is required in measuring supply.

FARM SUPPLY

Farm supply is defined as the schedule of amounts farmers would be willing to produce at various levels of *expected* prices for the product, all other factors being constant. This definition is parallel to the definition of demand that relates prices to purchases assuming all other influences on purchases are at a constant level. While demand theory holds that consumer purchases are inversely related to price, supply theory strongly proposes that production (or amounts supplied to the market) is directly related to price. Profit maximization is the focus.

A major difference between demand and supply analysis on agricultural products is the distinction between current prices and expected prices. While *expected* prices are relevant in the demand for storage and speculation, *current* prices are predominant in the demand for immediate consumption and exports. Because of the biological lag in agricultural production, *expected* prices predominate in farm supply analysis. This does not have to be the case because futures markets and forward contract markets do provide farmers with the opportunity to establish prices at the time the initial production decision is made. Even so, this alternative either has not been extensively used or has not been available.

The basic farm supply relationship is diagrammed in Figure 2-6 with the direction of dependence from expected prices on the vertical axis to total production on the horizontal axis. The heavy line denotes a "reversible" supply schedule and the light line at the lower end of the solid line suggests the possibility of "irreversibility." The derivation of industry supply relationships from the cost curves of individual firms would reveal the possibility of irreversibility particularly if fixed costs were high relative to total costs. Indeed, this attribute of agriculture (i.e., high fixed costs) is a major contributor to the "farm problem" (Johnson, 1972). Firms would enter the industry if expected prices were above the minimum of the average *total* cost curve, but would not exit unless expected prices dropped below the minimum of the average *variable* cost curve. (For the derivation of supply functions from the theory of the firm, see Seitz,

FIGURE 2-6 Diagram of farm supply.

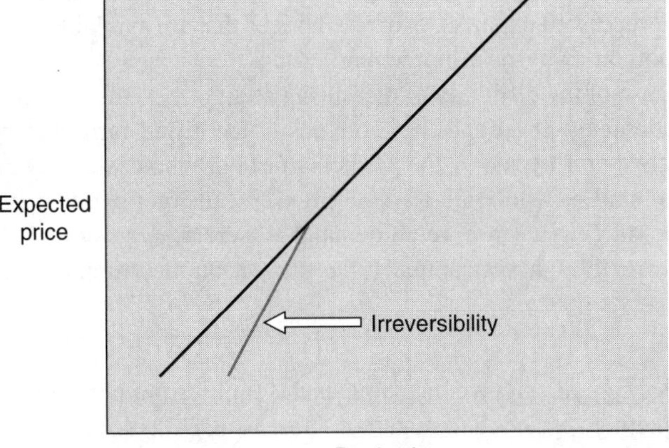

et al., chapters 3, 4 and 5.) This "supply trap" prolongs periods of economic stress as farmers are slow to respond to prices that do not cover average total costs per unit of output. Eventually, of course, the higher cost producers would exit if unable to cover their average total costs.

Underlying the farm supply schedule are assumptions that prices on competing and complementary farm products are constant as are prices on inputs in the production process. The technology in converting inputs into farm products is also presumed to be static. Changes in such prices and/or technology will shift the farm supply curve to the right or left. Higher prices on competing products would shift the curve to the left; higher prices on complementary products would shift the curve to the right. Increased prices on inputs would move the curve to the left, and improved technology on the given product would tend to shift the curve to the right; improved technology on competing products would tend to move the supply schedule to the left.

Because of the role of expectations and lagged response to those expectations, the time frame being considered is particularly important in supply analysis. This is true to a much lesser extent in demand analysis. In the short-run—less than one production period—supply is perfectly inelastic; that is, a change in price expectations will not affect the amount available. For that reason, supply analysis incorporates a minimum time frame of one production period. The complexity of how expectations are formulated and the importance of asset fixity in agriculture dictate that farmers respond to changing prices beyond one production period. The longer the time frame, the greater the supply elasticity.

This response, known as "distributed lags" in supply, will be discussed in detail in Chapter 6. For purposes of illustration, the price formation process covered in the remainder of Chapter 2 will be restricted to a one-period time frame.

PRICE SPREADS, DERIVED DEMAND, AND PRICE FORMATION

The total demand for a typical farm product illustrated in Figure 2-1 is primarily derived from retail demands for domestic consumption and wholesale-level demands for storage and speculation and for exports. How to measure this derivation, however, presents some challenges. Farm products may lose their identity at retail, having been converted into product mixtures such as pizzas, pies, sandwiches, etc. Similar problems arise with value added (processed) exports. Also, retail prices that are available are for stores and exclude the important away-from-home market.

Because of the difficulty of measuring retail prices, the preferred approach is often to orient the analysis around the more easily identified farm or wholesale prices. Retail prices are then forecast by the predicted farm or wholesale prices plus some measure of farm-to-retail or wholesale-to-retail price spreads on the raw materials contained in the retail product. In a sense, retail demand is thereby *derived* from farm or wholesale demand, even though, conceptually, the focus is on the ultimate consumer.

Price Spreads

The price spread can be considered as the equilibrium between the supply and demand for marketing services and materials (Sorenson, ed., 1964). The supply and demand for

FIGURE 2-7 Diagrams of the supply and demand for a food product and its price spread.

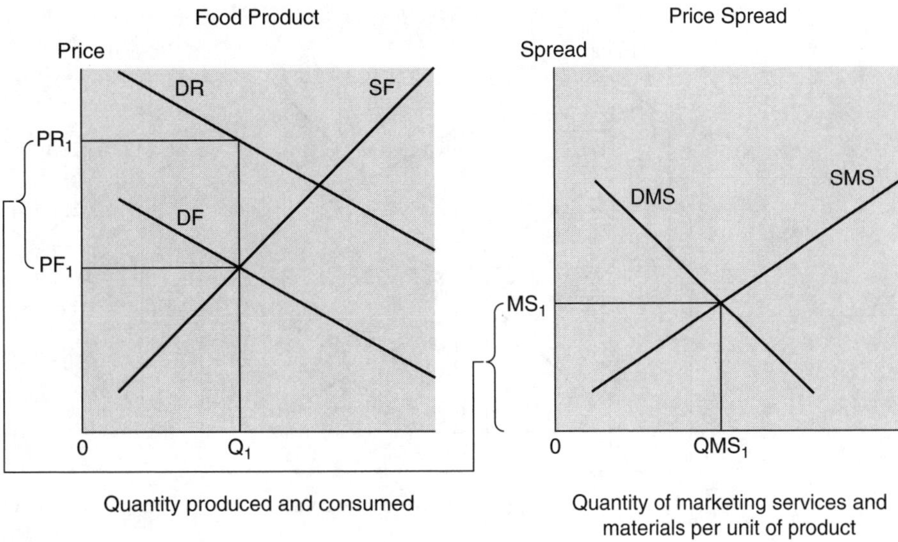

the basic farm product and the supply and demand for the marketing services and materials *per unit* of that product can be diagrammed as shown in Figure 2-7.

The price at the farm is determined by the intersection of the farm supply (SF) and farm demand (DF) curves, i.e., PF_1 with production at Q_1. This is an equilibrium position in that a higher price would encourage farmers to bring forth in the next production period an amount that would exceed the amount demanded—and prices would fall. A lower price would result in production below amount demanded and prices would rise. Given the production level at Q_1, the retail price as defined by the retail demand curve (DR) is PR_1. The spread between the farm demand curve and the retail demand curve is defined by the equilibrium between the supply curve for marketing services and materials (SMS) and the demand curve for marketing materials and services (DMS).

Note that the supply-demand diagram for marketing services and materials relates to price spreads *per unit* of the farm product. These supply and demand relationships will shift just as the supply and demand curves for the basic farm product are affected by numerous influences that impinge on the farm market.

Conceptually, analysts may find Figure 2-7 helpful in thinking through the effects of abrupt and secular changes on the equilibrium position of both the supply and demand for the farm product and the price spread. This is illustrated in Figure 2-8 in which an increase in marketing costs per unit of product is traced from an initial equilibrium position to the subsequent equilibrium. Note that this change shifts the supply of marketing services and materials (SMS) to the left, but has no effect on the demand for these items (DMS) and the farm supply (SF) and retail demand (DR) for the basic farm product. The increased marketing costs also shift the farm demand (DF) to the left. Other effects are decreased marketing services and materials supplied and demanded, increased market-

FIGURE 2-8 Diagrams of the supply and demand for a food product and its price spread

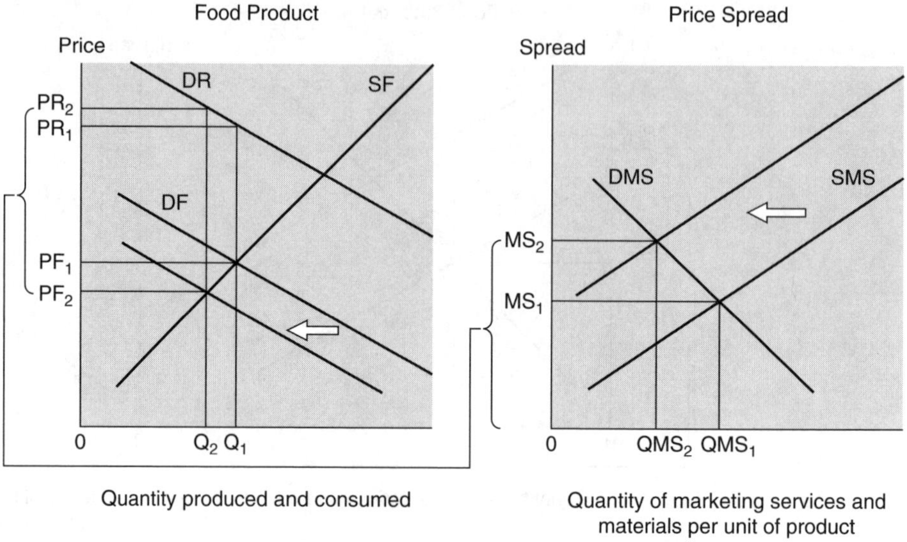

Food Product | Price Spread

Price: PR_2, PR_1, PF_1, PF_2 — DR, SF, DF — Quantity produced and consumed: 0, Q_2 Q_1

Spread: MS_2, MS_1 — DMS, SMS — Quantity of marketing services and materials per unit of product: 0, QMS_2 QMS_1

ing spread, increased retail price, lower farm price, and reduced quantity of the product supplied and demanded.

In Figures 2-7 and 2-8, the retail demand and farm demand are drawn as parallel lines. This implies that the amount of product on the market has no effect on the marketing spread—a general pattern observed, but not necessarily the case. Possibly, at higher levels of production, processing and marketing firms could realize economies to scale that would reduce their unit costs. These economies, in turn, would reduce spreads in a competitive market, and the retail and farm demands would tend to move closer together. On the other hand, increased production could push these firms to higher levels on their average variable and total cost curves, and widen the spreads.

Empirical observation indicates that processing and marketing firms are normally operating in a production range where the cost curves are relatively flat, and common changes in the availability of supplies have little effect on costs. A caveat, however, is that sharp and unexpected changes in supplies in the short run may upset plans in such a way that marketing spreads are affected. For example, in meat packing, slaughterers tend to widen margins in periods of unexpected gluts in the markets. In periods of unanticipated shortages, they tend to bid aggressively for supplies and the margins are squeezed. In the longer run context, however, farm and retail prices tend to move in tandem, widening out with secular increases in marketing costs.

Implications of Fixed Spreads

The relatively fixed price spreads have important implications to farm price instability—a perennial farm problem. This is indicated by the following elasticity formulas. (See Chapter 3 for derivation of elasticities.)

Price elasticity of demand at retail = $(\Delta Q/\Delta P) * (PR/Q)$

Price elasticity of demand at farm = $(\Delta Q/\Delta P) * (PF/Q)$

where: $(\Delta Q/\Delta P)$ is the inverse of the slope of both the retail demand and the farm demand, PR is the retail price and PF the farm price with production at Q.

Since the only difference in the two formulas is PR and PF, and since $PF < PR$, the price elasticity of demand at the farm level is less than at the retail level at each level of consumption. The greater the difference between PF and PR, i.e., the wider the price spread, the lower the price elasticity at the farm relative to the price elasticity at retail.

The demand for most food products at retail tends to be inelastic. This inelasticity translates to even more inelasticity at the farm level. With price flexibility of demand being nearly inverse to elasticity, this means that small changes in farm production are accompanied by very sharp variations in farm prices. This is compounded by the difficulty farmers have in matching output to demands—difficulties that can be traced to biological lags in putting products on the market and to uncontrollable forces such as weather and pests.

SUMMARY

Total demand for farm products is a composite of demands for domestic consumption, storage and speculation, and exports. Volatility in these commodity markets can often be attributed to shifts in demands for storage and speculation. Lags in forming expectations and responses to those expectations generate supply functions with increased elasticity over time. Equilibrium farm prices and quantities in the framework of one production period to the next are established by the interaction of the farm-supply curve and derived farm-demand curve. The farm-retail price spread, established by the interaction of the demand and supply of marketing services and materials, provides the means to forecast retail prices. The relatively fixed farm-retail price spread renders the demand at the farm level more inelastic than at the retail level.

QUESTIONS FOR STUDY

1 Marshallian demand relationships are primarily academic and not easily amenable to empirical measurement. Explain.

2 What might cause "irreversibility" in a demand curve?

3 Select a food commodity with which you are familiar. Plot the annual average Consumer Price Index of that product for the past 15–20 years on the vertical axis of a graph and annual per capita consumption on the horizontal axis. Connect the successive years with straight lines. Draw a line that you think would be a representative demand curve for the commodity. Is it straight? Does it conform with what you would expect?

4 In question 3, select what you think would be the most important demand shifter. Plot the horizontal deviations from your demand curve on the vertical axis of another chart against your demand shifter on the horizontal axis. By inspection, is the result what you expected? Why or why not?

5 Changing demands for storage and speculation may be the major reason behind short-term fluctuations in prices of certain agricultural commodities. Explain.
6 The U.S. is a major exporter of corn. Theoretically, the export demand would be highly price elastic. Why is this not likely the case?
7 An agricultural enterprise with high fixed costs relative to total costs may exhibit irreversibility in supply. Explain.
8 Explain what happens to farm and retail prices from equilibrium-to-equilibrium when the demand for marketing services increases, assuming no effect on the demand for the farm product at the retail level.
9 Why don't price spreads rise and fall as farm prices rise and fall?
10 Why is the demand for eggs at retail more elastic than the demand for eggs at the farm?

3

MEASURING DEMAND FOR DOMESTIC CONSUMPTION

POINTS:

1 How to formulate empirical demand equations for domestic consumption.
2 Techniques to conserve on degrees of freedom and reduce multicollinearity.
3 Measurement of trends, structural shifts, and anomalies.
4 Calculations of elasticities, flexibilities, and impact multipliers.
5 Conceptualization of the demand system approach.
6 Application of conditional regression.

This chapter on demand for domestic consumption illustrates the application of econometric and mathematical tools for estimation by single equations and by systems of equations. The procedures could also be applied to other demands and to supply as well, but will not be covered in the same detail in those chapters. The material on elasticities, flexibilities, and impact multipliers is also relevant to subsequent chapters.

SINGLE DEMAND EQUATIONS

Empirical demand analysis is not completely an application of the science of economics, but also entails the artful eye of an econometrician. Some "trial and error" efforts are inevitable, but strong logic is paramount in approaching demand measurement. Following are some guidelines for measuring domestic demand for a given product (Table 3-1). This table and similar tables in succeeding chapters list possible independent variables for

TABLE 3-1 GUIDELINES FOR FORMULATING DEMAND EQUATIONS FOR DOMESTIC CONSUMPTION (DOMESTIC CONSUMPTION IS THE DEPENDENT VARIABLE.)

Independent Variable	Formulation
1. Price of the product	Retail price deflated by the CPI[a].
2. Price of substitutes	Retail price deflated by the CPI[a].
3. Price of complements	Retail price deflated by the CPI[a].
4. Population	Divide the domestic consumption by the population.
5. Special demographic effects such as age, sex, urbanization, race or ethnic orientation, region, etc.	Percent of population in a particular classification; generation of a population variable adjusted for shifts in a particular classification.
6. Income	Convert to per capita and deflate. Transform as appropriate or possibly to disposable (after-tax) income or discretionary income (after tax and necessities taken into account). Data limitations may require use of GDP or total consumer expenditures per capita.
7. Income distribution	Procedures similar to 5.
8. General inflation	Divide by deflator such as CPI, GDP implicit price deflator, etc.; alternatively, employ as a separate variable. Deflate all variables if any are deflated.
9. Other	
Tastes	Serial time, i.e., variables with values corresponding to successive years, such as 1, 2, 3, 4, . . . , etc., or 1960, 1961, 1962, etc.
Living patterns	Serial time.
Nutrition, diet health concerns	Dummy variable, serial time.
New technology	Dummy variable, serial time.
Occupation shifts	Serial time.
Education shifts	Serial time, school years completed, etc.
Size of household, and other household characteristics	Average number of persons per household, age of head of household, etc.
Promotion	Dummy variable, promotion expenditures.
Product innovation	Dummy variable, serial time.
Irreversibility	Dummy variable.
Major event not likely to be repeated	Dummy variable.
10. Within-year analysis	
Season	Dummy variable for each quarter, separate quarterly equation.
Weather	Temperature, rainfall.

[a]Farm or wholesale prices can also be employed in combination with variables representing the retail-farm or retail-wholesale marketing spreads.

the indicated equations. All of the listed variables cannot be incorporated, so the analyst must select the most relevant subset.

Price

Obviously, the prices consumers face are at retail and this level in the marketing chain is the appropriate choice. However, farm or wholesale prices may be used if:

1. Retail prices are unavailable.
2. Measurement errors are large for retail prices relative to farm or wholesale prices.
3. The product cannot be readily identified at retail.
4. The margin between farm or wholesale and retail prices is quite small.

Measurement errors for retail prices are a common problem. The Consumer Price Indexes for individual food items in the U.S. do not properly account for merchandising programs such as use of "specials." While "special" prices may be included in the sampling, the fact that consumers buy more of the product at special prices than at regular prices is not tallied. Even more important, the CPI on individual foods applies only to food consumed at home. In recent years, consumers have spent 45 percent of their food dollars away from home.

Many agricultural products lose identification at retail. Measuring consumer demand for products like wheat flour or sugar requires attention to multiple products and the combinations of other raw materials involved in their processing and marketing. In such cases, focusing on the wholesale level for the component products is more realistic.

In many nations, large volumes of food products are sold through local farmers' markets or from farm-to-farm. In such situations, farm or wholesale prices may be reasonable proxies for retail.

If farm or wholesale prices are employed as proxies for retail when the marketing spread is significant, analysts need to account for that difference. Techniques to do this will be discussed in the section on price spreads in Chapter 5.

Population

As indicated in Table 3-1, population is normally incorporated in time series analysis by converting consumption and income to a per-capita basis. The rationale is that year-to-year changes in population would usually be accompanied by one-to-one changes in total consumption. Dividing consumption and consumer income by population implicitly captures this one-to-one relationship and saves degrees of freedom in the ordinary least squares (OLS) analysis.

The point is that population could be incorporated as a separate variable, but in doing so, a degree of freedom would be utilized. Incorporating population as a separate variable would be justified if the demographic characteristics of the population had changed noticeably over the period of analysis—characteristics that could not be measured. However, because population is generally monotonically (without reversal) increasing, it is strongly correlated with other time series variables. This adds problems of multicollinearity and consequently contributes to difficulties in measurement of the structural parameters.

An alternative procedure to handle changing demographics is to convert consumption and income to a per-capita basis and add a variable that captures the essence of the shift in the composition of the population. For example, the per-capita consumption of fluid milk is higher in the age group of 21 years and younger than in older age categories. If the percent of the population 21 years and younger had changed significantly in the analysis period, a demand equation for fluid milk could incorporate a variable, "percent of population 21 years and younger," to handle this demographic shift.

Adjusted Population Variable

If a characteristic of the population is singularly important to the demand for a product, techniques are available to handle that feature without additional variables. One technique is to calculate an "adjusted population variable." An example of this procedure is presented in Table 3-2.

Assume that, in 1990, per-capita consumption of a product was estimated to be 50 percent greater among those 40 years and over compared to those under 40 years. (Consumption of high bran cereal might be an example.) Such data might have been obtained from a Nationwide Food Consumption Survey conducted from time to time by the USDA.

In columns (4) and (5) in Table 3-2, the specific per-capita consumption levels for the younger and older segments were set at 10 and 15 pounds per capita, respectively, for 1990. No data are presumed available for the other years in the 1987–1995 database. Total population and numbers in the two age categories are tabulated in columns (1) to (3).

TABLE 3-2 AN EXAMPLE ON THE CALCULATION OF ADJUSTED POPULATION

	(1)	(2)	(3)	(4)	(5)	(6) [(2)×(4) + (3)×(5)] ÷ (1)	(7) (6) ÷ 12.64	(8) (1)×(7)
		Age		Consumption per Capita		Estimates are Consumption per Capita if 1990 Rates Apply		
Year	Total Pop.	< 40	≥40	< 40 lbs.	≥40	lbs.	Index 1990= 1.000	Adj. Pop.
1987	1000	500	500			12.50	.989	989
1988	1020	500	520			12.55	.993	1013
1989	1040	500	540			12.60	.997	1036
1990	1060	500	560	10	15	12.64	1.000	1060
1991	1080	500	580			12.69	1.004	1084
1992	1100	500	600			12.73	1.007	1108
1993	1120	500	620			12.77	1.010	1131
1994	1140	500	640			12.81	1.013	1155
1995	1160	500	660			12.84	1.016	1179

If the per-capita consumption levels of the two age groups were constant throughout the historical time period, per-capita consumption for the entire population would be calculated as in column (6). This calculation is performed by multiplying the per-capita consumption by the population for each age group and dividing the summation of the products by the total population. The assumed per-capita consumption of the total population is then converted to an index with 1990 = 1.000 as in column (7). The final step is to calculate an adjusted population variable by multiplying the index by the total population [column (8)].

The next step in the analysis is to divide the annual data on total consumption by the adjusted population variable. Note that adjusted population increased more rapidly in 1987–1995 than the actual population, as the older, higher consuming segment of the population increased while the numbers in the younger segment remained constant. The role of the adjusted population variable accounts for that fact.

If per-capita consumption of the product increased in 1987–1995 with the employment of adjusted population as a divisor, an analyst might conclude that the aging of the population was not the explanation. If there was no change in per-capita consumption with this formulation, one might conclude that the increase in per-capita consumption calculated with the actual population was, in fact, due to the increase in the older population.

Of course, underlying this approach is the assumption that the relationship between the per-capita consumption level of the younger and older populations was constant. The analysis would be improved if other data points were available from the Nationwide Food Consumption Survey and interim years could be interpolated. Again, the contribution of employing an adjusted population variable is to conserve on degrees of freedom.

This technique, as illustrated with age, could also be applied to other demographic shifts such as sex, urbanization, race or ethnic orientation, region of a country, etc. The procedure could also be applied to changes in the distribution of income. Known characteristics about the consumption habits of those in relatively high-income classifications could be factored into the population series to improve the predictive power of the income per-capita variable. Also, as with age, the proportion of the population in a particular income class could be entered as a separate variable.

Income

In most instances, conversion of total income to a per-capita basis and deflated will suffice in demand analysis. If possible, the income variable should be transformed to disposable (after-tax) income to properly account for amounts available for spending on food. To formulate equations for luxury food items, use of "discretionary" income might be advised. Discretionary income is calculated by subtracting expenditures on necessities (non-luxury foods, housing, clothing, and transportation) from disposable income.

A disposable income series for the U.S. is regularly calculated and published by the U.S. Department of Commerce. In nations where such data are not available, real Gross Domestic Product per capita would be appropriate. Some analysts have had to resort to total consumer expenditures as a proxy for income.

General Inflation

Recommendations for handling general inflation in time series analysis are similar to those for handling population. Routinely, analysts should consider dividing price and income variables by an index of consumer prices. Like population, consumer prices tend to increase monotonically over time and therefore are correlated with other variables in a demand equation. Including consumer prices as a separate variable rather than a deflator introduces problems of multicollinearity.

Another statistical reason, as pointed out by Tomek and Robinson, is to reduce the problem of heteroscedasticity (Tomek and Robinson, 1990). Heteroscedasticity refers to changing variance of the error term. Leaving variables in their nominal form tends to result in greater variance in the error term of the equation at higher levels of price and income.

In some cases, however, inclusion of an index of consumer prices as a separate variable may be appropriate. Following are some examples:

1 "Money illusion." Consumers react to a change in nominal price even though real prices may have remained the same.
2 The index of consumer prices is not an accurate measure. When dividing price and income variables by a deflator, the analysts are implicitly assuming equal weight to the numerator and the denominator. Measurement problems with the deflator would be amplified more in this formulation than with the index of consumer prices as a separate variable. As a separate variable, the contribution of the deflator can be explored directly.
3 The product being deflated is a major component of the deflator. Deflating the index of food prices by the index of all consumer prices would be inappropriate.

The choice of the appropriate deflator is somewhat arbitrary. A traditional deflator for the U.S. has been the Consumer Price Index (CPI) of the Bureau of Labor Statistics, U.S. Department of Labor. However, this index represents a fixed bundle of goods and services. While the weights are revised from time to time, short-term substitute effects are excluded. That is, when the price of a component item rises, consumers may cut back on its use and consequently its weight in the index is overvalued; and the opposite is true when the price on the item falls.

Some analysts have preferred the Implicit Price Deflator for Personal Consumption Expenditures (U.S. Department of Commerce) which has provided for shifting weights more frequently than has been applied to the CPI. (See section on "A Note on Indices" in Appendix B.) One way to decide on the most appropriate deflator may be to try both and observe the statistical results. In any case, all price and income variables should be deflated in the demand equation if one variable is deflated.

Other Demand Factors

As indicated in item 9 of Table 3-1, many other variables are candidates for inclusion in a demand equation on food. Changing tastes, fads, living patterns, concerns about health, technology, etc., may be important, either individually or collectively, in explaining what foods consumers purchase. Ideally, analysts should incorporate variables that measure those individual effects.

For example, the advent of the microwave oven has changed food-consumption patterns both at home and away from home. To measure this impact on, say, baked potato consumption, the analyst should incorporate microwave oven sales in the equation.

Data on microwave oven sales and other key variables appropriate to measure the various other factors affecting demand as listed in item 9 may not be available. In addition, a number of these factors may be relevant to the demand for a given product—too numerous to include in a demand equation. Individually, they may be of minor importance, but collectively impinge upon demand in a major way. The usual technique to handle these influences is to incorporate a "serial time" variable.

Some alternative formulations of serial time variables are presented in Table 3-3. Linear trend can be represented by a simple variable with 1-unit increments. As illustrated for a period from 1975 to 1995, the variable could arbitrarily begin with 1 for 1975, 2 for 1976, 3 for 1977, etc. More conveniently, the variable could have the value for the year, i.e., 1975=1975, 1976=1976, 1977=1977, etc.

TABLE 3-3 FORMULATION OF TIME AND DUMMY VARIABLES IN TIME SERIES ANALYSIS WITH ANNUAL DATA

	Example of Alternative Formulations					
Year	Linear Trend	Trend Squared	Linear Trend to 1985	Linear Trend after 1985	Dummy for Period Beginning with 1985	Dummy for 1985
1975	1	1	-10	0	0	0
1976	2	4	–9	0	0	0
1977	3	9	–8	0	0	0
1978	4	16	–7	0	0	0
1979	5	25	–6	0	0	0
1980	6	36	–5	0	0	0
1981	7	49	–4	0	0	0
1982	8	64	–3	0	0	0
1983	9	81	–2	0	0	0
1984	10	100	–1	0	0	0
1985	11	121	0	0	1	1
1986	12	144	0	1	1	0
1987	13	169	0	2	1	0
1988	14	196	0	3	1	0
1989	15	225	0	4	1	0
1990	16	256	0	5	1	0
1991	17	289	0	6	1	0
1992	18	324	0	7	1	0
1993	19	361	0	8	1	0
1994	20	400	0	9	1	0
1995	21	441	0	10	1	0

Trends may or may not be linear. To test this, an analyst may want to incorporate both a linear trend variable and squared trend variable. If, for example, the coefficient on linear trend is significantly negative and the coefficient on trend squared is significantly positive, indications would be that declining trend influences were leveling off.

Other functional forms of the time variable could be explored. Functional forms as a topic will be addressed in Chapter 11.

In the historical period covered in a time series analysis, trends may also remain fairly linear, but follow different rates of change or even be reversed. In the 1975–1995 period illustrated in Table 3-3, tests for shifting linear trends could be performed by incorporating time variables such as a combination of "Linear Trend to 1985" and "Linear Trend after 1985." Comparison of the coefficients on these two variables can establish whether trend influences have been consistent over the entire time period and, if not, how the trends have changed. Tests for determining whether trends are linear can also be conducted by smoothing techniques discussed in Chapter 9.

A variable such as "Linear Trend after 1985" might also be appropriate to capture the effect of an innovation with growing influence, such as the introduction of microwave ovens. This approach, of course, would be pursued only if data on microwave oven sales were unavailable.

The employment of so-called "dummy" variables may also handle a number of situations where data are scarce or unavailable. In Table 3-3, the "Dummy for Period Beginning with 1985" (with zero values up to 1984 and values of 1 from 1985 onward) is an example of how to measure several possible events that might have occurred in 1985.

1 The Surgeon General issued a warning that this product might injure your health.
2 A major processor introduced a "new, improved" product and promoted it heavily.
3 "60 Minutes" broadcast a negative image on cultural practices related to the product.
4 A major fast-food restaurant chain added this product to their menu.

If the event had a significant impact on demand that lingered throughout the late 1980s and early 1990s, the *t* value on the coefficient of this dummy variable would so indicate. If the effect trailed off after a few years, the analyst might modify the dummy variable by returning its value to zero in the early 1990s.

The "Dummy for 1985" in Table 3-3 is an example of a "general purpose" type variable for addressing several circumstances. Its major role is to handle anomalies—situations that may develop in a given year, but are unlikely to reoccur. At least, such events cannot be anticipated and as such incorporated in a model designed for forecasting.

The negative news about the use of Alar on apples (1989) or the poison scare on Chilean grapes (1988-89) are examples. These events were damaging in the short-run, but not necessarily beyond a year or two.

Dummy variables might be used in a demand equation to test for irreversibility. This might be accomplished by placing a value of 1 in each year that per-capita consumption declined from the previous year and zero otherwise. A positive and significant coefficient on this dummy variable would signify that demand was more inelastic in years of declining consumption than in years of increasing consumption.

Errors in the data or specification of a demand equation may generate "outliers" in the residuals from an OLS fit to the data. If due to specification errors, the analyst should proceed to attempt to account for the discrepancy. If this fails or if there is a data error, the outlier may be handled by adding a dummy variable for that year as is shown for 1985 in Table 3-3. The "rule of thumb" is to employ dummy variables for this purpose sparingly!

Quarterly and Monthly Demand Equations

The suggested formulations for demand equations based on annual data can also be applied to equations based on quarterly or even monthly data. A routine approach would be to incorporate constants for each quarter or each month. Such variables account for demand shifts that may be related to changing seasons.

The technique is fairly simple. In addition to the constant for the equation, dummy variables for three quarters for a quarterly model (or 11 months for a monthly model) are added. If the constant for the equation represents the first quarter, the coefficients for dummy variables for the other three quarters represent deviations from the constant for the first quarter. The dummy variables have the value of 1 for the respective quarter and zero for the other quarters (Table 3-4). Dummies would be similarly constructed for monthly models.

A refinement could be added for the major independent variable. In addition to quarterly dummies that establish the appropriate intercept for each quarter, different coefficients (slopes) for the major independent variable could be measured by forming four separate variables representing each quarter. The variable for quarter 1 would have the

TABLE 3-4 FORMULATIONS OF DUMMY VARIABLES IN TIME SERIES ANALYSIS WITH QUARTERLY DATA

	Constant Dummies			Coefficient (Slope) Dummies for Major Independent Variable[a]			
Year and Quarter	Quarter 2	Quarter 3	Quarter 4	Quarter 1	Quarter 2	Quarter 3	Quarter 4
1993.1	0	0	0	X	0	0	0
1993.2	1	0	0	0	X	0	0
1993.3	0	1	0	0	0	X	0
1993.4	0	0	1	0	0	0	X
1994.1	0	0	0	X	0	0	0
1994.2	1	0	0	0	X	0	0
1994.3	0	1	0	0	0	X	0
1994.4	0	0	1	0	0	0	X
1995.1	0	0	0	X	0	0	0
1995.2	1	0	0	0	X	0	0
1995.3	0	1	0	0	0	X	0
1995.4	0	0	1	0	0	0	X

[a]X denotes the values for the major independent variable for the respective quarter.

value for that quarter and zero in the other quarters (Table 3-4). The variable for quarter 2 would have the respective value for that quarter and zeros otherwise, etc. This formulation is not necessary for all quarterly demand equations, but may be useful if one independent variable has a particularly predominant impact on consumption. Otherwise, the coefficient on this variable would be the same for each quarter, which may be a constraint not warranted.

This approach might be extended to a second major independent variable. If all the independent variables were divided into four quarters, the formulation would be the same as having a separate demand equation for each quarter. There is no reason that a separate equation for each quarter should be avoided, except that degrees of freedom are lost. Experience suggests that such a step is generally not necessary.

A basic component for quarterly demand equations and monthly equations as well are constant dummies for quarters or months. Whether separate quarterly or monthly estimates are generated for the coefficients on the major independent variable(s) is a matter of judgment, but could be tested by determining whether the coefficients for each quarter or month are significantly different.

In monthly demand equations, more so than in quarterly equations, variables such as temperature might be incorporated. Such a variable would be relevant in demands for soft drinks, ice cream, etc.

Monthly demand equations involve special data problems. While retail, wholesale, and farm prices are usually available on a monthly basis, consumption figures are not. Even if consumption or disappearance figures were available, special problems arise in terms of the different days in the month, the number of weekends embraced by a particular month, the month in which Easter occurs, etc.

Standard econometric analysis can be applied to quarters in a manner similar to the methodology applied to annual data. One common difference is that the analyst is more likely facing problems of serial correlation in the residuals in quarterly models. The step to monthly demand equations is much more difficult than from annual to quarterly models. In addition to data problems, serial correlation in residuals is usually quite prominent in monthly equations. This problem is addressed in Chapter 18 on "Time Series Models."

If monthly forecasts are required, analysts will need to use some ingenuity in the modeling process. One approach may be to combine quarterly demand equations with procedures to allocate quarterly forecasts of consumption to the respective months within the quarter. This procedure could also be explored for a combination of annual and quarterly demand equations. The basic demand equation could be annual with allocations of consumption to quarters based on normal seasonal patterns.

DEMAND ELASTICITIES, FLEXIBILITIES, AND IMPACT MULTIPLIERS

The relationships between individual independent variables in a demand equation and the dependent variable can be classified as elasticities, flexibilities, and impact multipliers. The classical, and perhaps the most familiar, term is elasticity. Elasticity applies to demand equations in which the dependent variable is quantity purchased (or specific use such as consumption). Following are some key definitions.

Demand Elasticity

Demand elasticity is the ratio of *percent* change in *quantity purchased* relative to the *percent* change in an independent variable in the demand relationship. Own-price elasticity refers to the effect of the price of the given product on quantity purchased. Cross-price elasticity refers to the effect of the price of a substitute or complement on the quantity purchased of the given product. Income elasticity refers to the effect of consumer income on the quantity purchased. Other elasticities could be similarly defined.

The sign on own-price elasticities would be expected to be negative. The sign on cross-price elasticities for substitutes would be expected to be positive; on complements, negative. Income elasticities could be either positive or negative.

Demand Flexibility

An alternative formulation for a demand equation is to position price as the dependent variable and to include quantity purchased (alternatively quantity produced or available) as an independent variable. This is particularly appropriate if the quantity purchased is largely predetermined by the quantity produced or available which, in turn, is based on farmers' decisions in the previous period. In the U.S., this formulation fits livestock and perishable crops that predominate the domestic market and that must be consumed in the given production period (i.e., international trade and carryover stocks are minor).

Demand flexibility, more commonly called price flexibility of demand, is the ratio of the *percent* change in *price* relative to the *percent* change in an independent variable in the demand relationship. Reference can be made to price flexibility of demand with respect to (1) quantity purchased, produced, or available, (2) quantity of substitutes or complements purchased, produced, or available, (3) consumer income, and (4) other independent variables.

The sign on own-price flexibilities would be expected to be negative. The sign on cross-price flexibilities on substitutes would be expected to be negative; on complements, positive. As with elasticities, income flexibilities could be either positive or negative.

Impact Multipliers

Impact multipliers can be applied both to demand equations with quantity purchased dependent and price dependent.

Impact multipliers relate the *actual* (not percent) change in the dependent variable to a one-unit *actual* (not percent) change in an independent variable. In a linear demand equation, the coefficients on the independent variables are the impact multipliers. If the equation is linear in logs (log-log functional form), the coefficients are elasticities if the dependent variable is quantity purchased, and flexibilities if the dependent variable is price.

Point Elasticities and Flexibilities

The measurement of elasticities and flexibilities is somewhat arbitrary. Striking off two points on a demand curve and calculating the percent changes involved has the disadvantage of being somewhat imprecise. What base to use for calculating percentage can result in different answers. For this reason, "point" estimates are preferred.

The conceptualization is as follows for calculating own-price elasticity. To calculate a percent change in price, a base must be established and the change in price set. Let the base be P and the change in price ΔP. Given same base P, the demand relationship will provide the amount purchased, Q. The demand curve will also supply the change in the amount purchased, ΔQ, given ΔP. The equation for own-price elasticity is, then:

$$(\Delta Q/Q)/(\Delta P/P)$$

By transformation,

$$(\Delta Q/Q)/(\Delta P/P) = (\Delta Q/\Delta P) * (P/Q)$$

The term (ΔQ/ΔP) is equivalent to the coefficient on own price in the demand equation, i.e., the impact multiplier. This facilitates calculation of the elasticity of demand at the point on the demand line represented by the P and Q.

The point price flexibility of demand can be calculated by a similar procedure. In this case, the formula for the price flexibility of demand is:

$$(\Delta P/P)/(\Delta Q/Q)$$

By transformation,

$$(\Delta P/P)/(\Delta Q/Q) = (\Delta P/\Delta Q) * (Q/P)$$

The procedure can be visualized in Figure 3-1. Given point Q_1, P_1 on the demand curve, a tangent can be drawn that intersects the horizontal axis at Q_2 and vertical axis

FIGURE 3-1 Graphical illustration of calculation of own-price elasticity of demand and price flexibility of demand.

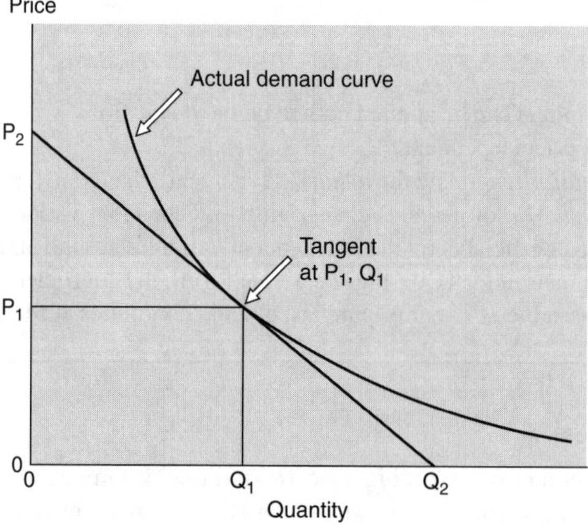

at P_2. The slope of the tangent is constant throughout and defines $\Delta Q/\Delta P$ or $\Delta P/\Delta Q$ at the point Q_1, P_1. The relationship $\Delta P/\Delta Q$ is the slope of the tangent and $\Delta Q/\Delta P$ is the inverse of the slope. The slope is equal to P_2/Q_2 and the inverse, Q_2/P_2.

The own-price elasticity equals:

$$(Q_2/P_2) * (P_1/Q_1)$$

The price flexibility of demand equals:

$$(P_2/Q_2) * (Q_1/P_1)$$

For a linear demand relationship as represented by the tangent in Figure 3-1, the slope and inverse of the slope are constant throughout. But for every point on the line, the P and Q will differ. Therefore, the elasticity and flexibility will differ at each point on the line. If the curvilinear demand relationship were linear in logs, the elasticity and flexibility would be constant throughout.

The advantage of elasticities and flexibilities is that they represent relationships between percentages and the specific units involved do not have to be known. With impact multipliers, units involved must be known, but if the demand relationship is linear, the position on the demand line will not affect their values. The following simple matrix summarizes these properties:

	Elasticities and Flexibilities	Impact Multipliers
Value depends on level of output	Yes*	No
Need to know units	No	Yes

*Except in log-log functions.

Relationship Between Elasticities and Flexibilities

The formulas for elasticities and flexibilities indicate that they are reciprocals of each other. However, in the measurement process with time series, this relationship may not hold. If own price and price of a substitute are independent variables in a regression equation with the *quantity purchased* dependent, these two independent variables are likely to be positively correlated. A decline (increase) in the price of a given product is likely to be accompanied by a decline (increase) in the price of the substitute. The coefficient on the price of the given product is not "cleanly" the total impact multiplier of that price relative to the quantity purchased.

Somewhat offsetting would be the effect of changing prices on the given product on the price of the substitute and that effect in turn on the quantity purchased. A decline in the price of a given product would tend to lower the price of a substitute, which in turn would tend to *increase* the quantity purchased of the substitute and *decrease* the quantity purchased of the given product. A rise in the price of a given product would have the opposite effect. Because of this cancelling effect of the price of the substitute, the coefficient on the own-price variable exaggerates the separate impact of that variable on the quantity purchased.

With *price* dependent in a regression equation and consumption or amounts available of the given product and its substitute as independent variables, the circumstances are different. Chances are that the quantities of the given product and its substitute are not correlated or only remotely so. Because of production lags, quantities of a product and its substitutes supplied to the market in a particular time period are not closely associated. Therefore, the coefficient on the quantity variable of the given product tends to carry the exact weight of that variable and does not have to offset counter-effects of substitutes. For that reason, the own-price elasticity of the demand for a product (from a regression equation with quantity dependent) tends to be greater than the inverse of the price flexibility (from a regression equation with price dependent).

For a product with one substitute, the price elasticity of demand relationship would be as follows:

Total-price elasticity = own-price elasticity

+ (cross-price elasticity of substitute)

* (percent change in price of substitute)

For example, if the own-price elasticity was –.30, the cross-price elasticity of the substitute was +.20 and the percent change in the price of the substitute was +.50 given a 1-percent change in the price of the product, the formula would apply as follows:

$$\begin{aligned}\text{Total price elasticity} &= -.30 + (.20 * .50)\\ &= -.30 + .10\\ &= -.20\end{aligned}$$

From this formula, it is clear that the own-price elasticity of –.30 is greater in absolute terms than the total-price elasticity of –.20.

Role of These Measurements

Elasticities, flexibilities, and impact multipliers should be regarded more as terms for communication rather than the objectives of empirical analysis even though much attention is given to these measurements in econometric work. They can provide a means to aggregate estimates from various sources into large global models as have been developed by the USDA. However, as will be discussed in Chapter 8, these measurements are very transitory and are subject to several restrictive assumptions. Econometric analysis and forecasting can proceed with no reference to these measurements of relationships. However, to relay certain key information to other analysts or clientele groups, carefully worded references to elasticities, flexibilities, and impact multipliers can be insightful.

Demand Systems

Conceptually, most food products have a number of substitutes and possibly a complement or two. The substitutes and complements may include non-food as well as food items. In time series analysis, measurement of these cross elasticities is restricted by degrees of freedom. With 20 to 30 years of observations, at best, cross elasticities with respect to only two or three substitutes can be estimated with single-equation techniques.

Conditions

For this reason, procedures have been developed to estimate matrices of own, cross, and income elasticities of demand by imposing certain conditions on the relationships. This approach can be termed "aggregate demand analysis" or "demand systems techniques." As discussed by Tomek and Robinson (1990), common sets of conditions include:

1 *Homogeneity.* The sum of own elasticity, cross elasticities, and income elasticity equals zero. Intuitively, a large income elasticity implies a large own-price elasticity. Also, a large number of substitutes or a few close substitutes implies a large own-price elasticity.
2 *Symmetry (sometimes called Slutsky's condition).* The cross-price elasticity of one good relative to another is proportional to its relative importance in consumer expenditures. Intuitively, a price change on a major item in food expenditures is likely to have a greater effect on consumption of a minor product than the price of a minor product on the consumption of a major product.
3 *Engle aggregation.* The sum of income elasticities of all items in consumers' budgets weighted by the relative importance of each item equals one. Intuitively, if consumers' income increases, total expenditures should increase proportionally. The change in expenditures on any given item is directly related to the level of expenditures on that item and its income elasticity.

These three conditions, expressed algebraically are as follows:

1. $Eii + Ei1 + \ldots + Eij + Eiy = 0$

2. $Eij = (Rj/Ri) * Eji + Rj * (Ejy - Eiy)$

3. $R1 * E1y + R2 * E2y + \ldots Rn * Eny = 1$

where: Eii = own-price elasticity for i

Eij = cross elasticity, effect of j on i

Eiy = income elasticity for i

Ri = expenditures on i as ratio to total

Empirical Example

To illustrate the application of these conditions in aggregate demand analysis, assume that the total system involves three commodities, designated as 1, 2, and 3. Also, assume that the own and income elasticities for the three commodities are known, as are the proportion each represents of total expenditures. The own-price elasticities for 1, 2, and 3 are −.8, −.6, and −1.2, respectively. The income elasticities are +.3, +.8 and +1.5, respectively. The ratio to total expenditures are .3, .2, and .5. With the amount of information available a priori, only two of the conditions need to be applied to solve the system of equations. Employing homogeneity and symmetry, the following set of equations can be constructed:

Homogeneity

$$-.8 + E12 + E13 + .3 = 0$$

$$E21 - .6 + E23 + .8 = 0$$

$$E31 + E32 - 1.2 + 1.5 = 0$$

Symmetry

$$E12 = (.2/.3) * E21 + .2 * (.8 - .3)$$

$$E13 = (.5/.3) * E31 + .5 * (1.5 - .3)$$

$$E23 = (.5/.2) * E32 + .5 * (1.5 - .8)$$

With six equations and six unknowns, the unknowns can be identified. The system can be solved by substitution or determinants. The cross elasticities are:

$$E12 = .067 \qquad E21 =- .049 \qquad E31 =- .100$$

$$E13 = .433 \qquad E23 =- .151 \qquad E32 =- .200$$

As discussed by Huang (1985, 1993), the entire set of elasticities can be measured directly by similar techniques without the a priori estimates for certain cells. Stepwise partitioning procedures with analysis of food aggregates seem appropriate based on Huang's endeavors. Tables 3-5 and 3-6 highlight the results of his 1993 work based on annual time series data for 1954 to 1990.

Table 3-5 presents the aggregated demand system and Table 3-6, an example of the detail within the aggregate, "meats and other animal proteins." These tables include the own- and cross-price elasticities among food products, expenditure elasticities that are similar to income elasticities, and a time trend denoted by the constant term (CONST). Table 3-5 also includes the demand elasticities related to the aggregate of non-food. These demand elasticities were estimated for 39 food categories plus non-food. The total matrix was solved with 35 observations for each of the items involved—clearly not possible without the imposition of several conditions.

Pros and Cons

Efforts continue to be directed toward improving estimation procedures for demand systems. At this stage, certain advantages and disadvantages can be enumerated:

TABLE 3-5 AGGREGATED DEMAND SYSTEM FOR FOOD GROUPS AND NON-FOOD

Food Group	Price									
	MEAT	STAPLE	FATS	FRUITS	VEGETA	PRO.FV	DESERT	N.FOOD	EXPEND	CONST
MEAT	-0.3611	–0.0004	0.0059	0.0107	–0.0060	–0.0097	–0.0333	–0.1219	0.5157	–0.0109
	(.0328)	(.0206)	(.0090)	(.0107)	(.0064)	(.0083)	(.0115)	(.0749)	(.0819)	(.0026)
STAPLE	.0300	–.1508	–.0330	–.0411	.0241	.0314	.0007	.0202	.1186	–.0045
	(.0383)	(.0649)	(.0259)	(.0266)	(.0191)	(.0261)	(.0226)	(.0901)	(.0918)	(.0028)
FATS	.0632	–.1311	–.0674	–.0239	–.0710	.1090	–.0098	–.1081	.2391	.0014
	(.0640)	(.0997)	(.0820)	(.0536)	(.0493)	(.0603)	(.0484)	(.1506)	(.1556)	(.0048)
FRUITS	.1773	–.2016	–.0270	–.1954	.1694	–.1571	.2276	.3908	–.3840	.0064
	(.1083)	(.1452)	(.0759)	(.1069)	(.0567)	(.0780)	(.0632)	(.2649)	(.2680)	(.0083)
VEGETA	.0660	.1502	–.1267	.2043	–.1348	–.0811	.0062	–.3599	.4079	–.0036
	(.0781)	(1292)	(.0863)	(.0701)	(.0989)	(.0877)	(.0545)	(.1776)	(.1932)	(.0057)
PRO.FV	.0506	.0859	.0879	–.0979	–.0383	–.2876	–.0514	–.0821	.4341	.0091
	(.0485)	(.0832)	(.0499)	(.0456)	(.0414)	(.0744)	(.0338)	(.1112)	(.1148)	(.0035)
DESERT	.0784	–.0106	–.0053	.0538	.0014	–.0227	–.1049	–.2281	.3947	–.0168
	(.0317)	(.0335)	(.0184)	(.0171)	(.0118)	(.0156)	(.0225)	(.0937)	(.0995)	(.0031)
N.FOOD	.0606	–.0420	–.0114	–.0081	–.0073	–.0108	–.0303	–.9794	1.1500	–.0015
	(.0035)	(.0029)	(.0013)	(.0016)	(.0009)	(.0012)	(.0016)	(.0101)	(.0102)	(.0005)
WEIGHT	.0773	.0417	.0109	.0077	.0062	.0132	.0293	.8137	NA	NA

Note: For each pair of estimates in the table, the upper part is the estimated elasticity, and the lower part (in parentheses) is the standard error. The notations are MEAT (meats and other animal proteins), STAPLE (staple foods), FATS (fats and oils), FRUITS (fresh fruits), VEGETA (fresh vegetables), PRO.FV (processed fruits and vegetables), DESERT (desserts, sweeteners, and coffee), N.FOOD (nonfood), EXPEND (expenditure), CONST (constant term), WEIGHT (expenditure weight), and NA (not applicable).

TABLE 3-6 DISAGGREGATED DEMAND SUBSYSTEM FOR MEATS AND OTHER ANIMAL PROTEINS

	Price										
Food Category	BEEF.V	PORK	O.MEAT	CHICKN	TURKEY	FISH	C.FISH	EGGS	CHEESE	EXPEND	CONST
BEEF.V	−0.6212 (.0572)	0.1143 (.0275)	0.1072 (.0460)	0.0183 (.0171)	0.0041 (.0114)	−0.0064 (.0112)	0.0005 (.0117)	0.0230 (.0101)	−0.0257 (.0125)	0.3923 (.1240)	−0.0001 (.0083)
PORK	.1922 (.0488)	−.7281 (.0424)	.0795 (.0482)	.0126 (.0206)	.0127 (.0122)	.0252 (.0124)	.0099 (.0131)	.0024 (.0114)	−.0061 (.0139)	.6593 (.1461)	−.0231 (.0098)
O.MEAT	.8180 (.3350)	.3550 (.1991)	−1.8739 (.5480)	.2800 (.1366)	−.0560 (.1191)	−.0241 (.1397)	.0232 (.1314)	−.1694 (.0956)	.3576 (.1409)	−.5737 (.4802)	.0321 (.0296)
CHICKN	.1030 (.0863)	.0470 (.0585)	.1914 (.0944)	−.3723 (.0560)	−.0226 (.0294)	−.0135 (.0287)	.0178 (.0316)	.0791 (.0258)	−.0389 (.0327)	.0769 (.1884)	.0286 (.0123)
TURKEY	.0887 (.1988)	.1410 (.1203)	−.1358 (.2845)	−.0767 (.1017)	−.5345 (.1217)	.0380 (.0978)	.1354 (.0955)	−.0728 (.0672)	.2218 (.1002)	−.1267 (.3449)	.0437 (.0218)
FISH	−.1132 (.1955)	.2559 (.1225)	−.0619 (.3335)	−.0485 (.0990)	.0370 (.0977)	.1212 (.1606)	.0144 (.1168)	.0005 (.0727)	.0113 (.1196)	.4290 (.3076)	−.0187 (.0188)
C.FISH	.0093 (.2033)	.1037 (.1290)	.0512 (.3136)	.0593 (.1090)	.1345 (.0954)	.0145 (.1167)	−.3715 (.1486)	−.2384 (.0764)	.1291 (.1163)	.3942 (.3621)	−.0113 (.0219)
EGGS	.0918 (.0387)	.0120 (.0246)	−.0925 (.0504)	.0585 (.0196)	−.0167 (.0148)	.0004 (.0161)	−.0521 (.0169)	−.1103 (.0172)	.0088 (.0183)	.2865 (.0816)	−.0223 (.0053)
CHEESE	−.2268 (.1090)	−.0259 (.0686)	.4228 (.1679)	−.0690 (.0563)	.1099 (.0500)	.0057 (.0597)	.0645 (.0581)	.0189 (.0415)	−.2472 (.0833)	.4181 (.1934)	.0119 (.0118)
WEIGHT	.0316	.0180	.0043	.0062	.0018	.0018	.0018	.0082	.0036	NA	NA

Note: For each pair of estimates in the tables, the upper part is the estimated elasticity, and the lower part (in parentheses) is the standard error. The notations are BEEF.V (beef and veal), PORK (pork), O.MEAT (other meats), CHICKN (chicken), TURKEY (turkey), FISH (fresh and frozen fish), C.FISH (canned and cured fish), EGGS (eggs), CHEESE (cheese), EXPEND (expenditure), CONST (constant term), WEIGHT (expenditure weight), and NA (not applicable).

Advantages

1. Comprehensive.
2. Elusive cross elasticity effects measured.
3. Budgetary effects can be introduced.

Disadvantages

1. Demanding of data and resources.
2. Constant elasticities assumed.
3. Retail prices reflect only at-home consumption. Important away-from-home consumption excluded.
4. Effects of structural change, trends in preferences, tastes, etc., not carefully examined in most such studies.

CONDITIONAL REGRESSION

Nevertheless, some of the concepts gleaned from the systems approach can be helpful for single equation demand analysis. For example, application of cross-sectional studies can be combined with time series analysis as was discussed in generating "age-adjusted" population data. Another technique of value to shore up time series is to incorporate income elasticities from household consumption studies (or from other sources).

Suppose a regression equation generated an income elasticity that was either not significant or that carried the "wrong" sign, a priori. Say the sign was insignificant and negative when substantial evidence from periodic surveys of food consumption in households indicated that high-income households consumed more of the product per capita than the low-income households. The income elasticity from the household consumption study could be made explicit in the formulation of the demand equation and the other parameters of the equation estimated by ordinary least squares.

The procedure is illustrated with a log-log demand equation on beef in which the coefficients are the elasticities.

$$\text{Log DCBFC} = b1 + b2 * \text{Log RPBFD} + b3 * \text{Log RPPKD} + k * \text{Log DICD}$$

where: DCBFC = Per capita consumption of beef

RPBFD = Retail price of beef deflated

RPPKD = Retail price of pork deflated

DICD = Disposable income per capita deflated

bi = Coefficients estimated by OLS

k = Income elasticity derived from a household consumption survey

To formulate the equation for the OLS analysis, position k * Log DICD on the left side as follows:

$$(\text{Log DCBFC} - k * \text{Log DICD}) = b1 + b2 * \text{Log RPBFD} + b3 * \text{Log RPPKD}$$

This creates a new dependent variable, and in this form the OLS procedure will generate values for the bi, with the constraint that the income elasticity is k.

This "conditional regression" approach to single-equation demand analysis can be applied in several ways. A broad application is in aggregation. Suppose in a price-dependent demand equation, an analyst is dealing with a product with many substitutes—too many to measure separate cross-price flexibility relationships. With careful attention to common denominators in measurement of the availability of these products, the econometrician could combine the separate products into one or two classifications. For example, in a price dependent demand equation on pork, the meat substitutes for pork—beef, veal, poultry, meat and fish—could be combined into one variable by converting each to a boneless, trimmed equivalent.

Aggregation, of course, constrains the cross-effects to the relative weight of each product in the substitute variable. Attention to aggregating similar products is important. In the above example, the specifications of the demand for pork equation might be improved by separating the substitute variable into red meat (beef and veal) and white meat (poultry and fish).

SUMMARY

As indicated in this chapter, the domestic consumer demand for a farm product is a function of many factors, too numerous to measure independently by OLS. The task of the econometrician is to introduce conditions that will conserve on degrees of freedom, reduce multicollinearity and still meet certain a priori beliefs about demand. Conversion of prices and incomes to real terms, consumption to a per-capita measure, and substitutes to a single variable are examples of transformations that achieve those objectives. Some form of a time variable can also capture secular forces that are not measurable individually. Dummy variables can enhance the statistical properties of a demand equation for special events and abrupt demand shifts, but should be used sparingly.

If resources permit, a system approach allows the researcher to apply a number of conditions in order to estimate a more complete set of demand parameters than possible with the single-equation procedure. Such past studies, however, have revealed several weaknesses.

QUESTIONS FOR STUDY

1 Why deflate prices and incomes? Give two reasons why dividing by a deflator such as the CPI is preferable over entering the deflator as a separate variable.
2 In single-equation demand analysis, why focus on farm or wholesale prices rather than retail prices?
3 Why and when should a "serial time" variable be incorporated in a demand equation?
4 Under what circumstances is calculating an "adjusted population variable" based on age justified?
5 Calculate the price elasticity of demand if the slope of the demand curve is –3, the level of price is 10, and the level of quantity is 8.

6 Explain why price flexibility of demand may *not* be the inverse of the price elasticity of demand.

7 Explain why a large income elasticity for a good might be associated with a large own-price elasticity.

8 Under what circumstances might you undertake a demand study using the system approach? When might you limit yourself to a single-equation approach?

9 Using the six-equation example illustrating homogeneity and symmetry, can you solve for the cross elasticities?

10 Describe in narrative form what "conditional regression" involves and where it is appropriate.

4

MEASURING DEMANDS FOR STORAGE, SPECULATION, AND EXPORTS

POINTS:

1. How to formulate empirical demand equations for storage.
2. Components of storage costs.
3. Effect of anticipated low stocks.
4. How to formulate empirical export demand equations.
5. Calculation of indices of exchange rates in competing nations and in importing nations.
6. Measurement of transmission elasticities.

Demands by storers and speculators for a commodity can be an important source of volatility in commodity markets. This is particularly true in short-run variability in prices when no discernable change in demands from domestic or foreign consumers is evident. Export demand includes both demands for consumption and for storage and speculation outside the exporting nation.

DEMAND FOR STORAGE AND SPECULATION

As indicated in Chapter 2, the demand for storage and speculation is a combined variable with an important shifter—expected prices. Given some level of expected prices, the demand curve would register the effect of various levels of current prices on a change in stocks.

Current and Expected Prices

Demand for storage and speculation is more difficult to identify than demand for consumption because of the important role of expectations. The choice of current prices depends upon the location of storage. If storage is on the farm, farm prices would be relevant. If in commercial storage facilities, some wholesale level price is appropriate. And, of course, to the extent that consumers do accumulate and release stocks, retail prices could also be the focus.

Once the analyst determines what storage operation is to be researched and the appropriate price series to use, the major challenge is to introduce price expectations into the demand equation. One approach for commodities actively traded on futures exchanges is to presume that storage operators expect cash prices to be equal to some futures contract less normal "basis" with respect to that cash market (Table 4-1). Basis is simply the difference between a given futures price and a selected cash price. Basis patterns are fairly consistent and predictable. An example of a reasonable predictor for basis is to apply a moving average of basis for, say, the past three years, or an olympic average of the past five years (drop the high and low and average the remaining three years).

In fact, the ability to hedge effectively long positions (holding the cash commodity) in the cash market by selling futures provides a fairly secure gross margin for storage operators. Gross margin is the selling price less the purchase price of the commodity.

One can conceptualize that the product demand for storage and speculation is really a function of expected gross margins. The higher the expected gross margin, the more product will be demanded by storers. If the total amount available is fixed or perfectly

TABLE 4-1 GUIDELINES FOR FORMULATING DEMAND EQUATIONS FOR STORAGE AND SPECULATION (ADDITION TO OR RELEASE FROM STORAGE IS THE DEPENDENT VARIABLE.)

Independent Variable	Formulation
1. Current price	Farm or wholesale price deflated by the CPI[a]
2. Expected price	Futures price less normal basis Government price supports or controls Past prices Authoritative forecasts "Rational expectations"
3. Storage costs	Commercial storage rates Cost of construction and maintenance of storage facilities
4. Interest cost on stored product	Short-term interest rates (Treasury Bills, Farm Credit Service, banks) times the price of the product
5. Storage availability	Peak stocks as a percent of capacity

[a]To the extent that consumers participate in storage activities, retail prices may be relevant.

inelastic (as is typical in the short-run), the storers bid the product away from consumers or exporters, which, in turn, tends to drive up the current price and reduce the expected gross margin. In a competitive market, the new equilibrium price will depend on how increased amounts in storage affect the cost of storage per unit of product.

In addition to futures prices, other methods may provide some indication of price expectations. For some commodities, government price supports or controls may predominate the outlook. Recent past prices may be influential in expectation formation. Forecasts from authoritative sources, such as the USDA, may guide the thinking of storage operators. Large and successful storers and speculators may have "rational expectations." That is, they are able to integrate supply, demand, and other information in formulating forecasts much in the same way as professional price forecasters do. This subject will be treated in more depth in Chapter 6.

If the carryover of the end of the crop year is anticipated to be unusually low, demands for storage and speculation may accelerate as the situation develops. Market prices increase sharply to ration out limited supplies and protect a "pipeline carryover." A pipeline carryover can be defined as the amount needed to assure processors, exporters, livestock producers, consumers, etc., that their day-to-day requirements between crop years will not be interrupted.

Storage Costs and Availability

Other shifters can be identified in the demand for storage and speculation. In the grain trade, the term "carrying costs" is used to denote commercial storage rates plus interest tied up in the grain. An analyst wanting time series data on costs outside of foregone interest on the grain could obtain published rates from elevators or perhaps derive estimates from costs for construction and maintenance of storage facilities. The interest cost on the stored product could be derived by multiplying short-term interest rates times the price of the stored product. Short-term rates could be represented by such instruments as Treasury Bills or loans by the Farm Credit Services or local banks.

In the short-run, storage availability may affect the demand for storage. If excess storage is available even at the peak of supplies, current prices will be bid up relative to future prices, (i.e., the demand shifts upward and expected gross margins are squeezed). Tight storage situations depress current vis-a-vis future prices. Data in the U.S. have been collected on storage capacity and may be useful in forecasting prices, particularly at the peak of harvest. A variable such as "peak stocks as a percent of capacity" might be explored.

DEMAND FOR EXPORTS

Forecasting export demand is also challenging in part due to trade policies in both importing and exporting nations and foreign food aid programs of developed nations. For a description of these policies, see chapters 9 and 10 in *Food and Agricultural Policy, Economics and Politics* (Halcrow, Spitze and Allen-Smith, 1994). While some of the same factors pertaining to domestic demand may be relevant, other determinants may be overriding. Major guidelines are presented in Table 4-2.

TABLE 4-2 GUIDELINES FOR FORMULATING DEMAND EQUATIONS FOR EXPORTS (QUANTITY EXPORTED FROM A GIVEN NATION IS THE DEPENDENT VARIABLE.)

Independent Variable	Formulation
Price in exporting country	Border price in exporting country denominated in a prominent international currency such as dollars or EU, converted to real prices
Price in competing exporting countries	[Index of real exchange rates (denominated in $ or EU) weighted by relative importance of exports] × real price of the product in the given exporting nation
Price in importing countries	[Index of real exchange rates (denominated in $ or EU) weighted by relative importance of imports] × real price of the product in the given exporting nation
World market price	Price in freely traded market with substantial volume; standard quality and widely publicized information
Population	Divide consumption by population in importing nations
Purchasing power	Aggregate real per capita incomes (denominated in $ or EU) in importing nations Real export earnings less debt service obligations (particularly for developing nations) Foreign exchange
Production in importing nations	Same variable
Demands for inventory	Projected ending stocks as a percent of use in major importing countries
Consumption maintenance (price inelastic) demand	Production in importing nations less "forecast" consumption in importing nations
Border protection policies	Extent of quotas, duties, and levies on imports
Export subsidies from competing exporting nations	Subsidy rate per unit of exports
Transportation costs	Truck, rail, and ocean shipping rates
Livestock numbers (for feed demand)	Index of grain- and high-protein-consuming animal units

Economic theory suggests that the price in the given exporting nation compared to other exporting nations and the translation of those prices to the importing nations would be important considerations. These prices, in combination with the population and purchasing power of the market, should explain the major variations in export demand for a product of a given nation—that is, in absence of major changes in trade policies. The prices in importing nations, plus their population and purchasing power, would establish the size of the pie. Relative prices between exporting nations would help determine how the pie would be divided among the nations.

In practice, derivation of empirical export demand relationships often compromises theory. Price spreads among the major exporting nations tend to be minimized by competition and therefore do not provide measurement opportunities, particularly with annual data. Importing nations often have their own domestic production of a given commodity with regulated prices and may not respond readily to changing world prices generated by exporting nations.

Prices and Exchange Rates

For this reason, the numerous price variables may be collapsed into two variables such as: (1) the price in a given exporting nation translated into an average price for the importing nations and (2) the price in a given exporting nation translated into an average price competing exporting nations face. With (1), the purpose is to estimate product prices importing nations face. With (2), the purpose is to evaluate the competition represented by the prices at which these other exporting nations could sell. To average several nations together, a strong, broad-based currency becomes the common denominator such as the U.S. dollar or the Euro (EU).

The linking variable is the weighted real exchange rate. The real exchange rate for an individual country is calculated as follows relative to U.S. dollars:

$$IRXR_i = (\text{Exchange rate in local currency of country i/U.S. dollar}) \times (\text{Index of inflation in U.S./Index of inflation in the given country i})$$

For example, assume that the Canadian dollar is trading at C$1.20 relative to the U.S. $ and that the Canadian CPI is 160 (1980=100) and the U.S. CPI is 150 (1980=100). The real exchange rate could be:

$$(C\$1.20/\$1.00) \times (150/160) = 1.2 \times .94 = 1.125$$

If U.S. wheat prices are about $3.00 per bushel, the real price of U.S. wheat in the U.S. is $2.00 (3.00/150%). The real price of U.S. wheat in Canada is $2.25 ($2.00 × 1.125). Given some level of Canadian wheat prices denominated in U.S. dollars, U.S. wheat could become more competitive if:

1. U.S. wheat prices declined.
2. The Canadian dollar strengthened (dropped) relative to the U.S. dollar.
3. The U.S. inflation rate declined relative to the Canadian inflation rate. This indicates the U.S. cost of production declined relative to Canada's.

This relationship is particularly important on wheat relative to Canada, a major competing exporter. Similar comparisons could be generated with importers. Rather than enhancing the U.S. competitive position relative to *exporters,* the three developments listed above would lower the real price to *importers.* In both instances, the rise or decline in the real price of U.S. wheat abroad would tend to reduce or increase U.S. wheat exports.

To create a variable that accounts for the array of importing nations, a weighting scheme must be devised. On wheat, the USDA has based the weights on the dollar value of U.S. exports of wheat to the respective countries in 1983–1985 (U.S. Department of Agriculture, Agricultural Outlook, 1988). They were as follows for 30 countries:

Country	Share of U.S. Exports of Wheat	Country	Share of U.S. Exports of Wheat
Japan	.145	Indonesia	.030
Belgium	.003	South Korea	.080
France	.002	Philippines	.035
West Germany	.001	Portugal	.013
Italy	.022	Egypt	.065
Netherlands	.024	Iraq	.037
United Kingdom	.002	Israel	.019
Norway	.001	Saudi Arabia	.009
Algeria	.031	Brazil	.102
Morocco	.048	Chile	.030
Nigeria	.065	Colombia	.025
South Africa	.001	Peru	.019
Tunisia	.017	Venezuela	.036
Bangladesh	.028	Taiwan	.029
Hong Kong	.005		
India	.048	Total	1.000

With this set of weights, the USDA derives a time series on the real trade-weighted dollar exchange rates for U.S. markets for wheat. A base period is selected, the most recent series being 1985=100. (A base period is an arbitrary year or other period for which indices are assigned the value of 100 percent.) The formula would be for a variable defined as the "Index of Real Trade-Weighted Dollar Exchange Rates for U.S. Wheat Markets" (USDA, Agricultural Outlook, various issues).

$$\text{IRWXRM} = \left(\sum_{i=1}^{30} \text{IRXR}_i \text{ x weight of country i} \right) / \text{ value of this variable in 1985}$$

To capture the price of U.S. wheat faced by *competitors,* the USDA proceeded in a similar way. The weights for competing exporters, based on non-U.S. shares in total dollar value of 1983–1985 world trade, are as follows:

Country	Share of Wheat Exports from 4 Major Exporting Nations
Canada	.401
France	.256
Australia	.203
Argentina	.140
	1.000

The formula for this index would be:

$$\text{IRWXRC} = \left(\sum_{i=1}^{4} \text{IRXR}_i \text{ x weight of country i} \right) / \text{ value of this variable in 1985}$$

To repeat, we would calculate:

IRWXRM = Index of real trade weighted exchange rate for wheat in traditional markets.

IRWXRC = Index of real trade weighted exchange rate for wheat in countries that are major competitors to the U.S.

The next step might be to multiply these indices by the real border price for U.S. wheat (such as on the Gulf of Mexico, Atlantic ports, or Pacific Northwest ports). These variables could be incorporated in a demand equation for U.S. wheat exports, i.e.,

Price of U.S. wheat in importing nations

$= \text{IRWXRM} \times \text{PWHD}$

Price of U.S. wheat faced by competing export nations

$= \text{IRWXRC} \times \text{PWHD}$

where: PWHD is the real U.S. price of wheat in terms of dollars at U.S. ports.

The negative impact on U.S. exports of higher U.S. wheat prices to importers would be observed in the same crop year that prices rose. The negative impact on U.S. exports of higher U.S. wheat prices to competitors could be observed not only in the same year, but in later years as well, as foreign wheat producers responded with delay to the rising market. Also, since some wheat may be produced in the importing nations, those producers too may expand output over time.

In review, higher real U.S. wheat prices confronting importers and exporters could be due to: (1) higher domestic wheat prices in the U.S., (2) increases in local currency exchange rate relative to the dollar (i.e., the dollar becomes stronger), (3) increases in the inflation rate in the U.S. relative to other nations, or (4) some combination of the above three factors.

The obvious question at this point is, "Why not compare the implicit U.S. wheat price faced by both importers and competing exporters with their own domestic wheat price, i.e., the price being received by their own wheat producers?" This would be in the tradition of Marshall, treating the U.S. price as it affected the amount exported, all other conditions, including foreign producers' prices, being held constant. This approach may be impractical for empirical measurement because: (1) world market forces almost simultaneously determine the price for both the U.S. and the foreign nations or (2) border protection isolates the local markets. In (1) the substitution elasticity of U.S. wheat for other wheat would approach infinity. In (2) the substitution elasticity of U.S. wheat for other wheat would be low or near zero. The term used to describe how U.S. wheat prices affect prices in individual nations is "price transmission elasticities." More generally, price transmission elasticities refer to the impact of "world" prices on prices in individual nations, i.e., the percent change in a product's price in a given nation divided by a percent change in the world price. Because the U.S. is predominant in world wheat markets, relationships between prices in the U.S. and other nations would correlate strongly with price transmission elasticities based on world markets.

As a general approach on all commodities, an exporting nation might evaluate global export prospects from the world price in combination with relevant exchange rates and inflation rates relative to its own performance in fulfilling those demands over time. Transportation costs would be particularly relevant.

Some may be skeptical as to whether world prices are really relevant. A study for the World Bank by Mundlak and Larson in 1990 established that price transmission elasticities were relatively high (Mundlak and Larson). This was true even in highly protected markets such as the EC. Their analysis was based on annual data for 58 countries in 1968–1978 (Table 4-3).

Population and Purchasing Power

Factors other than price will likely be even more important in measuring net export demand. Of course, population and purchasing power are likely to be the most important variables over time. As with domestic demand, the preferred approach to handle population is to divide consumption by the population in the importing nations.

Purchasing power can be tallied in several ways. One would be similar to domestic demand analysis. For each importing nation or aggregation of nations, per capita real incomes denominated in dollars or EU could be calculated. Particularly for developing nations, real export earnings less debt service obligations would be a relevant indicator of the ability to import. Stock of foreign exchange would also be a variable to consider. Such data are available from the World Bank.

Foreign Production and Carryover

Key to forecasting net export demand is to determine the level of production of a given commodity and its substitutes in the importing nations. Often importing nations do have

TABLE 4-3 TRANSMISSION ELASTICITIES OF PRODUCER PRICES WITH RESPECT TO WORLD PRICES, 1968–1978

Product	Transmission Elasticity	R^2	Number of Countries
Rice	.692	.83	45
Barley	.770	.87	49
Maize	.820	.86	58
Rye	.810	.89	39
Oats	.796	.88	51
Millet	.853	.89	34
Sorghum	.858	.82	45
Wheat	.693	.85	58
Rubber	.518	.82	10
Sugar	.199	.87	54

Source: Mundlak, Yair, and Donald F. Larson, *On the Relevance of World Agricultural Prices,* International Economic Department, The World Bank, WPS 383, March 1990.

their own domestic industry. Prices may be regulated and also the government may establish what imports will be allowed, based on domestically available supplies.

In this regard, carryover levels into a crop or calendar year may have an effect on imports more pronounced, ton for ton, than anticipated production. Government authorities are sensitive about food supplies and tend to respond quickly if availability is in question. Demands for inventory could be measured by such variables as beginning stocks as a percent of utilization or even projections of ending stocks as a percent of use. The latter variable would be a combination of beginning stocks, forecast production, and consumption.

Lack of data or even failures in obtaining reasonable estimates of net export demand from the traditional independent variables may force researchers to turn to simpler, less sophisticated procedures. Production and consumption data are widely available on many agricultural products for major nations. An analyst might explore generating a domestic demand equation with per-capita consumption as a function of real per-capita income and perhaps another variable or two such as serial time. The net import demand (per capita in this case) could be a simple function of the difference between the *forecast* per-capita *consumption* and the actual per-capita *production.* Some, but usually not all, of a change in shortfall would likely be accompanied with a change in imports.

Trade Policies

Border protection policies and export subsidies hamper the process in measuring net export demand. The problem is not unsurmountable. Analysts may have to resort to traditional market shares. Encroachment on another nation's share may invite retaliation so that in the final analysis, year-to-year changes in shares may be limited. The analysts' attention turns to forecasting the size of the total export pie. In some cases, a formula sets the total imports and the task is to predict the outcome of that formula.

Analysts may have to turn to modeling decision makers, taking into account past behavior, the economic conditions, political situation, and the power of producers versus consumers. How do these decision makers respond to changing conditions in setting quotas, duties on imports, export subsidies, etc.?

Transportation Costs

Analysts formulating net export demand equations for a given product of a given nation often will first focus on the total world market, then how much imports will represent of that market, and finally what the given nation's share will be of that trade. Very detailed analysis may involve sorting out the transportation costs from the exporting nations to the importing nations. This information, in combination with assumptions about government trade policies, would provide insights into the prospective market share.

Such detail is not often addressed in standard time series analysis. In theory, rising real transportation costs would tend to lower net export demand as domestic producers in the importing nations would benefit relative to producers in the exporting nations. The year-to-year impacts from this source, however, would be expected to be relatively minor.

Livestock Feed

Analysis of net export demands would, of course, be tailored to the particular product. For coarse grain and by-product feeds in particular, attention would be given to livestock numbers and normal consumption rates. Studies of least cost feed formulations under alternative prices for livestock and the respective feeds might be quite insightful in generating such demand models.

Concluding Comment

The emphasis in the preceding discussion was on analyzing and forecasting exports from a given nation. If the task is to forecast trade flows among nations, identifying the amounts shipped from given nations or regions to given nations or regions, the assignment is much more complex and challenging. Methodology for such research is not included in detail in this book although more reference to this subject is contained in Chapter 12.

SUMMARY

The expected price is the key shifter of the demand for storage and speculation, but difficult to establish accurately. Commercial storage operators rely on hedging in futures to provide price and profit protection. Speculators in cash and futures market have to rely on their acumen for forecasting prices. Emerging projections for a low carryover may result in current prices accelerating upward to ration out supplies and keep the carryover from dropping below pipeline levels.

Trade and domestic policies and variable exchange rates complicate measuring export demand. Otherwise the procedure resembles that for analyzing demand for domestic consumption, storage, and speculation. With indexes of exchange rates and a prominent international currency as a base, empirical analysis can proceed and nations can be aggregated. However, compromises in application of trade theory will often be necessary.

QUESTIONS FOR STUDY

1 Changing demands for storage and speculation may be the major reason behind short-term fluctuations on prices of certain agricultural commodities. Explain.
2 What is meant by "pipeline carryover" and what would you anticipate if projections pointed to stocks dropping below this level?
3 If the exchange rate of a local currency increases relative to the U.S. dollar, i.e., a dollar can fetch more of the local currency, the value of the dollar has increased. How would this impact U.S. exports to that nation?
4 Describe what happens if the exchange rate doesn't change, but inflation in the U.S. is greater than in the importing nation.
5 What is meant by "price transmission elasticities"?
6 What particular considerations should be given to import demands from developing nations?
7 How do increased transportation costs affect export demand?

8 How are indices constructed for "real trade-weighted exchange rates" for competing nations?

9 Plot the U.S. wheat prices received by farmers and the exchange rate for the Japanese yen (¥/$). Discuss the impact on the demand for U.S. wheat in Japan.

10 How would you forecast the total utilization of high-protein livestock feed (from all sources, domestic and foreign) in Japan?

5

MEASURING PRICE SPREADS AND DERIVED DEMAND FOR AGRICULTURAL PRODUCTS AND INPUTS

POINTS:

1. How to formulate equations to forecast farm–retail price spreads and retail food prices.
2. Calculations of farm–retail price spreads.
3. Factors affecting the farmers' share of retail prices on U.S. foods.
4. U.S. marketing costs and profits.
5. How to formulate equations to forecast prices on different grades and close substitutes.
6. Role of government grades.
7. How to formulate empirical demand equations for agricultural inputs.
8. Role of farm income and equity in input demand.

As mentioned in Chapter 2, farm level demand can be considered as derived from retail demand. The farm–retail price spread is equal to the equilibrium of demand and supply of marketing services and materials per unit of product. Similarly, farmers' demands for an input are derived from the farm level demand for the product and costs of other inputs.

This chapter focuses on forecasting the farm–retail price spread, price spreads between grades, and farmers' demands for inputs. The subjects embrace two common tasks of commodity analysts: (1) forecasting retail and wholesale food prices and (2) forecasting sales of inputs into agriculture.

PRICE SPREADS AND DERIVED DEMAND FOR AGRICULTURAL PRODUCTS

Price spreads, whether farm–retail, farm–wholesale, or wholesale–retail, can be considered as a function of variables representing demand and supply for the marketing services and materials per unit of the product marketed. The unit could be the retail weight, wholesale weight, or farm weight. Generally retail weights are used. The top section of Table 5-1 lists some variables that are candidates to explain the price spreads.

Formulation at Equilibrium

In practice, however, measurement of the quantities of marketing services and materials as functions of price spreads is not often accomplished because of lack of data. Instead, the focus is on the price spread at equilibrium. The rationale for this approach is that the structure of processing and marketing farm products is such that increased costs are quickly passed on to consumers and/or back to farmers. As the industry meets increased demands for marketing services and materials, any increased costs involved are built into the price spreads. For this reason, formulation of the sector for the supply and demand for marketing services and materials may be aggregated, requiring one equation incorporating variables from both supply and demand.

TABLE 5-1 GUIDELINES FOR FORMULATING DEMAND AND SUPPLY EQUATIONS FOR MARKETING SERVICES AND MATERIALS (PRICE SPREAD PER UNIT OF PRODUCT IS THE DEPENDENT VARIABLE.)

Formulation	Independent Variable
Variables representing demand	
Income	Disposable income per capita
Living patterns, etc.	Serial time
Variables representing supply	
Marketing costs	Wage rates in marketing firms
	Price of materials used in marketing the product (packaging materials, joint products, etc.)
	Transportation rates
	Consumer Price Index as a proxy for the above costs
	Cost of taxes, regulations
New technology	Dummy variable, serial time
Structural changes	Serial time
System shocks	Dummy variable
Key variables representing equilibrium demand and supply	
Income	Disposable income per capita
Marketing costs	Consumer Price Index
Trends	Serial time

By setting the price spread as the dependent variable, measurement of quantities of marketing services and materials is unnecessary, simplifying the procedure. The independent variables may include a selection from the listing in the top section of Table 5-1 or similar items. For a number of purposes, some combination of the three variables listed at the bottom of Table 5-1 may be sufficient. In fact, some measure of general inflation such as the Consumer Price Index may be all that needs to be incorporated.

A major reason for predicting price spreads is to forecast food prices. This can be accomplished in a two-step process:

Price spread = f (factors affecting the supply and demand for marketing services and materials)

Retail price = Farm price + price spread

Alternatively, a regression analysis could be conducted with the retail price as the dependent variable:

Retail price = f (farm price and factors affecting the supply and demand for marketing services and materials)

If no retail price series is available, an analyst might explore the following formulation to represent retail demand with consumption per capita as the dependent variable:

Consumption per capita = f (farm price and factors affecting the supply and demand for marketing services)

The factors represent proxies for the price spread.

While the farm price was listed in the above example formulations, a similar procedure could be used with wholesale prices if the analysis focused on that level in the food chain. Centering the analysis on farm or wholesale prices may be advisable, particularly when the product at retail differs significantly from the product at the farm or wholesale level. If appropriate retail prices are available, some measurement of the marketing spread may be needed.

USDA Retail–Farm Price Spreads

A procedure of the U.S. Department of Agriculture to calculate price spreads is as follows:

1. Determine the conversion factor between the farm weight and retail weight. The U.S. Department of Agriculture publishes a set of these factors for major products (USDA, Weights, 1992).
2. Calculate the farm price in retail weight equivalent, termed the gross farm value. This is equal to the farm price times the conversion factor which represents the ratio of the farm weight to the retail weight.
3. Estimate any by-product values in terms of the retail weight of the principal product.
4. Deduct by-product values from gross farm value to compute the "net farm value."

5 Subtract the net farm value from the retail price to calculate the price spread.

An example of the procedure is shown below on beef prices for 1995:

	Cents/lb.
Live steer price	66.26
x Conversion factor*	2.4
= Gross farm value	159.0
- By-product allowance	20.6
= Net farm value	138.4
Retail price	284.4
-Net farm value	138.4
= Farm-retail spread	146.0
Farmer's share = 138.4/284.4 = 49%	

* Farm weight/retail weight

The U.S. Department of Agriculture estimated that the average price received by farmers for steers in 1995 was about $66.26 per cwt., equivalent to 66.26 cents per pound. About 2.4 pounds of live steer are required to furnish one pound of beef at retail. The product of 2.4 times 66.26 is 159.0, the gross farm value, which represents the market value to producers of 2.4 pounds of live animal, equivalent to one pound of retail cuts. The by-product allowance of 20.6 cents represents the portion of the gross farm value attributed to edible and inedible by-products (mostly hides and tallow). Subtracting the by-product allowance from the gross farm value yields the net farm value that then can be directly compared to the retail price of beef.

Subtracting the net farm value from the retail price generates the farm–retail spread on beef (i.e., 146.0 cents per pound). Dividing the net farm value by the retail price gives the farmer's share of the retail price of beef which was 49% in 1995.

A selection of commodities for which the USDA calculates price spreads and farm value share of the retail price is presented in Table 5-2. The retail prices relate to grocery stores and do not include away-from-home consumption. Note the wide differences among the products, from eggs for which farmers received 60% of the retail price to bread and corn flakes for which the farmers received only 6%-8% of the retail price. The farmers' share in no way is indicative of the profitability of producing the commodity. In fact, an aggressively marketed product may require large expenditures for processing and promotion and may still be among the more profitable enterprises even though the farmers' share may be small.

Inspection of the list in Table 5-2 reveals some of the reasons for the differences in the relative importance of marketing and in the farmers' share. Highly processed products (i.e., cereals, canned, and frozen items) have wide price spreads. A number of the fresh fruits and vegetables have wide price margins because of their perishability and high transportation costs. In the U.S., a high percentage of these fresh items are produced in the far West and in Florida—areas at distance from the major consuming centers.

Another element that affects marketing spreads, not apparent in Table 5-2, is price

TABLE 5-2 RETAIL PRICE, FARM VALUE, AND FARM VALUE SHARE FOR SELECTED FOODS, 1995*

Food	Retail Price 1995	Farm Value 1995	Farm Value Percentage of Retail Price 1995
Animal products:			
Eggs, Grade A large, 1 doz.	0.93	0.56	60
Beef, Choice, 1 lb.	2.84	1.38	49
Chicken, broiler, 1 lb.	.92	.49	53
Milk, 1/2 gal.	1.43	.58	41
Pork, 1 lb.	1.95	.67	34
Cheese, natural cheddar, 1 lb.	3.39	1.16	34
Fruit and vegetables:			
Fresh			
Lemons, 1 lb.	1.14	.30	26
Apples, red delicious, 1 lb.	.84	.21	25
Potatoes, 10 lbs.	3.79	.80	21
Oranges, California, 1 lb.	.62	.12	19
Grapefruit, 1 lb.	.55	.10	18
Lettuce, 1 lb.	.80	.18	23
Frozen			
Orange juice concentrate, 12 fl. oz.	1.21	.48	40
Broccoli, cut, 1 lb.	1.19	.22	18
Corn, 1 lb.	1.09	.14	13
Peas, 1 lb.	.96	.14	15
Green beans, cut, 1 lb.	1.00	.11	11
Canned and bottled			
Peas, 17 oz. can	.45	.11	24
Corn, 17 oz. can	.40	.11	28
Applesauce, 25 oz. jar	1.05	.16	15
Pears, 29 oz. can	1.22	.23	19
Peaches, cling, 29 oz. can	1.13	.16	14
Apple juice, 64 oz. bottle	1.45	.26	18
Green beans, cut, 17 oz. can	.39	.06	15
Tomatoes, whole, 17 oz. can	.54	.04	7
Dried			
Beans, 1 lb.	.63	.25	40
Raisins, 15 oz. box	1.64	.40	24
Crop products:			
Sugar, 1 lb.	.38	.13	34
Flour, wheat, 5 lbs.	1.23	.43	35
Shortening, 3 lbs.	2.66	.80	30
Margarine, 1 lb.	.83	.23	28
Rice, long grain, 1 lb.	.53	.11	21
Prepared food:			
Peanut butter, 1 lb.	1.80	.48	27
Pork and beans, 16 oz. can	.40	.08	20
Potato chips, regular, 1 lb. bag	1.95	.35	18
Chicken dinner, fried, frozen, 11 oz.	1.17	.17	15
Potatoes, french fried, frozen, 1 lb.	.86	.12	14
Bread, 1 lb.	.79	.06	8
Corn flakes, 18 oz. box	1.75	.10	6
Oatmeal, regular, 42 oz. box	2.56	.18	7
Corn syrup, 16 oz. bottle	1.63	.06	4

**Source:* USDA, ERS.

risk. The greater the risk of an unfavorable price movement during the period a processor or marketing agency is carrying title to a product, the wider the farm–retail spread. This is particularly true on perishable items and those commodities for which there is no futures market. Futures markets enable marketers to protect themselves against price risk.

U.S. Marketing Costs and Profits

The USDA does not publish detailed cost data by commodities, but does calculate the aggregate costs and profits for domestically produced farm foods. This information is illustrated in Figure 5-1 which shows the allocation of the consumers' food dollar in 1994.

FIGURE 5-1 Allocation of the Consumers' Food Dollar in 1994*

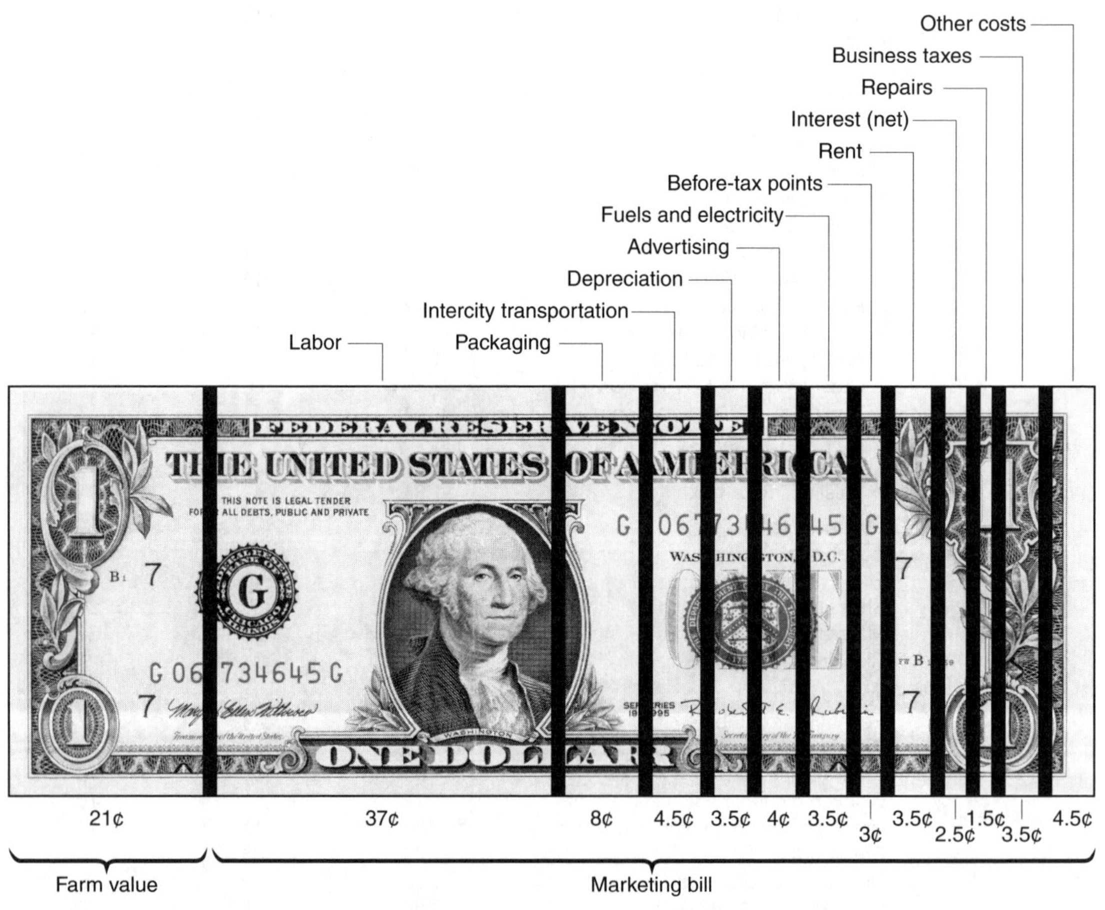

Notes: Calculated by ERS from government and private sources.
Includes food eaten at home and away from home. Other costs include property taxes and insurance, accounting and professional services, promotion, bad debts, and many miscellaneous items.

*Source: USDA, ERS, *Food Cost Review, 1995*, Agricultural Economics Report No. 729, April 1996.

This breakdown refers to total expenditures on domestically produced farm foods, for consumption at home, and away from home.

Of total food expenditures, farmers received 21 cents of the consumers' food dollar. Of the balance of 79 cents, 37 cents went for labor (i.e., 47 percent of the cost of marketing food was labor). Packaging was a relatively significant 8 cents and the balance fairly evenly divided over intercity transportation, depreciation, advertising, fuels and electricity, rent, interest, repairs, and other. Before-tax profits represented 3 cents of the U.S. consumers' food dollar.

Profits have not been large in food marketing in terms of sales. After-tax profits of food processing firms have averaged around 4 percent and retail food stores have been at 1 percent or less (USDA, *Food Marketing Review,* 1996). A more relevant measure is return on stockholders' equity which has been around 15 to 20 percent for food processors and about 13 percent for food retailers.

The point is that costs are over-riding factors determining price spreads and variation in profits is minor. While competition appears quite strong, the structure of the food marketing industry is such that in the short term, price spreads may not reflect costs. In periods of declining farm prices, retailers may be reluctant to reduce their regular prices. Part of the rationale is that consumers are particularly sensitive to *rising* prices so that retailers resist lowering prices if they feel they would have to increase them in the future. Often, rather than lowering regular prices, they run specials more frequently than usual.

Analysts working with short-term data such as weekly or monthly farm and retail prices will have to account for a lagging response at retail to changing farm prices. However, over the longer run—on an annual basis—retail prices do tend to reflect farm prices and marketing costs.

Direct Forecasting of Retail Food Prices

If data on farm–retail price spreads are available, the analyst could generate equations to predict those spreads. Most likely, some measure of inflation would predominate in forecasting spreads as illustrated in the following OLS equation on the farm–retail spread on beef, based on annual data for 1970–1995:

$$\text{FRSPBF} = 9.66 + \underset{(12.00)}{85.73} * \text{CPI} + \underset{(3.95)}{.660} * \text{AR}(1)$$

$R^2 = .982 \qquad \bar{R}^2 = .980$

Standard error of the regression = 4.9 percent of mean of the dependent variable.

Figures in parentheses are *t* values.

where:

FRSPBF= Farm–retail price spread on beef (¢/lb.).

CPI = Consumer Price Index (1982–1984 = 1.000).

AR(1) = First order autoregressive error specification to correct for serial correlation in the residuals. (See Chapter 18.)

As can be noted, CPI in combination with AR(1) "explains" about 98 percent of the variation in the farm–retail spread on beef. Other independent variables could be explored, but would have limited effect on improving the equation. Adding the forecast of FRSPBF to a forecast of the net farm value of beef would provide the forecast for the retail price of beef.

Alternatively, the retail price of beef could be forecast directly as a function of steer prices and the CPI as follows:

$$\underset{}{RPBF = 14.27 + \underset{(11.00)}{2.02 * PSR} + \underset{(9.80)}{88.91 * CPI} + \underset{(4.59)}{.687 * AR(1)}}$$

$R^2 = .995 \quad \bar{R}^2 = .995$

Standard error of the regression = 2.1 percent of the mean of the dependent variable.

Figures in parentheses are *t* values.

where:

RPBF = Retail price of beef (¢/lb.).

PSR = Slaughter steer price, Choice 2–4, Nebraska direct, 1100–1300 lbs. ($/cwt.).

While a calculation of by-product allowances was omitted in this equation, its inclusion would have added little to the explanatory power of the equation. This is not to suggest that PSR should not have been converted to a net farm value, but that analysts should determine whether the extra precision is worth the effort. Also, the USDA calculates and publishes by-product allowances only for a limited number of products.

The USDA does not calculate retail food prices and farm–retail price spreads for all food items. A much more complete coverage of retail food prices is published monthly as Consumer Price Indices of the U.S. Department of Labor. Also, weights are available in terms of the relative importance of each of the food classifications for at-home consumption. For this reason, analysts wanting to forecast selected food prices and/or aggregates of food prices such as "food at home" might well focus on the CPI series.

For example, an OLS equation based on 1970–1995 data generated the following results for the CPI on beef and veal:

$$CPIBFVL = -.04 + \underset{(8.99)}{.008167 * PSR} + \underset{(12.15)}{.539 * CPI} + \underset{(4.08)}{.702 * AR(1)}$$

$R^2 = .996 \quad \bar{R}^2 = .995$

Standard error of the regression = 2.3 percent of mean of the dependent variable.

Figures in parentheses are *t* values.

where:

CPIBFVL = Consumer Price Index for beef and veal (1982–84 = 1.000).

As expected, the statistical properties were quite strong as was the case with RPBF as the dependent variable. Similar equations could be estimated for other foods and the indices of their retail prices could be aggregated using the relative weights computed by the U.S. Department of Labor.

PRICE SPREADS RELATED TO QUALITY DIFFERENCES

Unlike manufactured products, for which specifications can be met with very close tolerances, farm products come off the production line carrying a spectrum of quality. Public and private programs are continuing to assist farmers to produce to specification, but the vagaries of Mother Nature will often interface and thwart those efforts. In any case, federal and state governments have been involved in developing grades and standards to help buyers and sellers in the marketing chain communicate quality among themselves and back to producers.

Government Grades

Government has been involved in establishing grades and standards under the presumption that the communication system is more effective with the consistency such a program provides, rather than having each firm tout its own grades. This continues to be something of an issue between the public and private sectors.

Tomek and Robinson discuss, in some detail, what is involved in establishing a grading system (Tomek and Robinson, 1990). Among other considerations, quality attributes and defects should be identified that are economically important to buyers and measurement costs should be minimal, i.e., benefits of grading should exceed costs.

Any such government grading system should be relatively fixed in the short-run, but subject to modifications in the long-run. A classic example of a problem in the U.S. relates to the most important crop, corn. While there have been changes in the long-term history of government grades, the current system reflects the markets of many years ago when a very high percent of the corn crop was fed to livestock within the U.S.

For that reason, U.S. No. 2, the predominant grade for corn, allows 3 percent broken kernels and foreign material. For domestic livestock feeding, this amount has been no particular problem. But in recent years, only about two-thirds of the crop has been fed domestically and the remainder exported or processed for industrial use. Broken kernels contribute to deterioration in quality in long trips by ship to foreign markets. The dry milling industry also has specific requirements not compatible with current government grades (Hill et al., 1991).

Whatever the system, multiple uses for many products stretch the ability of a single set of grades to fit the requirements for all the buyers and sellers. Grading systems essentially represent compromises.

Since demands change over time, grades and standards must change. Perhaps a multiple system is needed as major new uses come into the picture. In the corn example, not only are there different requirements for exporting versus domestic livestock feeding, but also the expanding use in dry and wet milling is accompanied by their own separate quality requirements.

Inadequate as some government grades have become, they still play a predominant role in U.S. commodity marketing. They certainly add understanding to market price quotations with grade designations over systems that simply report a range or an average price for all receipts on a particular day. Prices quoted by grade allow econometricians to be more precise with spatial models as well as tracking pure price movements over time.

The question to be addressed is, "How do you incorporate grades and standards into econometric analysis?" This subject might be viewed in a somewhat broader context of dealing with relatively close substitutes.

Modeling Grades and Close Substitutes

Econometricians should select prices that are representative of the entire nation or the particular region they are examining. Clearly, the USDA's compilation of average prices received by farmers would be representative. However, more precision can be gained by selecting a particular location or center and a predominant grade as the key price series. A deficiency of average prices received by farmers is that changes in the quality of what farmers produce are reflected in the price. The analyst is usually looking for a pure price effect separate from quality.

For example, those dealing with the spring wheat crop in Northern Plains states need a more sophisticated model than one that generates the average price received by U.S. wheat farmers. That price would not be entirely irrelevant, but they would want to know what might change the relationship between prices on spring wheat and the U.S. average.

Moreover, they would want to monitor prices in terms of both government grades and protein content at specific sites—country elevators, the Gulf, Duluth, etc. Much of this pricing is also done in terms of futures prices on the Minneapolis Grain Exchange (MGE). Analysts have reason to want to compare hard spring futures at MGE with futures in other classes, such as at the Kansas City Board of Trade (KCBT) or Chicago Board of Trade (CBT). Futures contracts are in terms of specific grades and standards. Hard red spring wheat futures at the MGE are traded with the base grade of U.S. No. 2 Northern Spring Wheat, 13.5 percent protein or higher. The grading system then is essential to monitor pure price changes over time and for spatial price analysis as well.

The various grades of a given agricultural product can be considered close substitutes in demand. As such, they could be modeled in ways similar to the methods suggested in Chapter 2 on "Theoretical Concepts of Demand and Supply." However, rather than setting the utilization of some particular grade as a function of own price and prices of the other grades, a more feasible approach would be to formulate demand equations with price dependent, as described in Chapter 3 on "Measuring Demand for Domestic Consumption."

There are two good reasons to proceed in this manner: (1) prices on the various grades would tend to be highly correlated, which complicates the measurement of the separate price effects; and (2) little information is available in detail on the amounts sold in each of the grade classifications. The agricultural commodity analyst is left with little choice, but to look at demand by grades with prices dependent.

TABLE 5-3 GUIDELINES FOR FORMULATING DEMAND EQUATIONS FOR GRADES AND CLOSE SUBSTITUTES
(PRICE OF THE GRADE OR CLOSE SUBSTITUTE IS THE DEPENDENT VARIABLE.)

Independent Variable	Formulation
	Alternative No. 1
Price of a key grade	Same (select a grade that is most representative of the product)
Availability of the product in the grade being analyzed (different from the key grade)	Percent of total product in the grade being analyzed
	Alternative No. 2
"Basic market value" of the close substitute	Derive an assumed market value based on the components of the product and market prices of the components
Availability of the product being analyzed	Percent of the total product in the collection of close substitutes
	Alternatives No. 1 and No. 2
Trends	Serial time
Anomalies	Dummy variable

In Table 5-3 are guidelines for formulating such equations, with Alternative No. 1 relating to grades. The suggestion is to identify the most prominent grade of the product as the major independent variable to forecast prices of other grades. Prices on this key grade might also be the focus of the basic demand analysis for the product. A second variable might well be the supply of the grade being analyzed relative to the combination of all the grades. This availability could be the percent of the total supply of the product represented by the grade in question.

Alternative No. 2 in Table 5.3 addresses the situation of a set of close substitutes that does not involve grades. While an approach similar to Alternative No. 1 could be pursued, another avenue might be explored. By breaking the commodities down into their component parts, an analyst could generate values based on those components times their respective prices. For example, feeding values for concentrate feeds could be derived from energy and protein content and prices. Nutrient values for fertilizer could be derived from content and prices on nitrogen, potassium, and phosphate.

As with Alternative No. 1, a second variable could account for the relative supply of the product being analyzed. In Alternatives No. 1 and No. 2, additional variables may be required as suggested in the bottom section of Table 5-3.

To illustrate some possible techniques to address the measurement of demands by grade or demand among close substitutes, two examples are presented, one on the wholesale beef market and one on modeling processed livestock feeds. Consider first the wholesale beef market.

Wholesale Beef Market Example

It happens that the wholesale beef market is one in which we have a good idea of how much product moves within each of the grades. About 95 percent of all U.S. steer and heifer beef is federally graded. Roughly, of the federally graded steer and heifer beef, two-thirds is Choice and one-fourth is Select. The balance is Prime (top grade) and Standard (lowest grade). The difference between Choice and Select is relatively small. The principal characteristic distinguishing USDA Choice from USDA Select beef is the amount of marbling in the rib eye muscle between the 12th and 13th ribs, with Select having less marbling than Choice. USDA Select scores lower than Choice in total calories, fat, and saturated fatty acids (no difference in cholesterol), but because of consumer preferences for taste, Choice boxed beef sells for a higher price than Select.

Canner and Cutter cow beef is mainly for hamburger and ground beef. Even so, steer (and heifer) beef compete with low-quality cow beef because: (1) a good share of steer and heifer carcasses go into hamburger and ground beef and (2) excess fat from grain fed steers and heifers is mixed with lean cow beef to produce the desired flavor in hamburger and ground beef. Imported beef is also used in much the same way as domestically produced cow beef.

Depending on the purpose of the analysis, a suggested procedure to model these three wholesale grades of beef is to explore price relationships. Since the Choice grade is key, the analyst could develop a model to forecast prices on Prime, Select, Standard, and Canner and Cutter beef, using Choice beef prices as an independent variable.

Observe the relationships between wholesale prices in the central U.S. on Choice and Select steer beef and Canner and Cutter cow beef (Figure 5-2). As stated before, the federal government grade of Choice (steers and heifers) predominates the beef market.

FIGURE 5-2 Wholesale Beef Prices, Central U.S. Markets, Steer and Cow Beef, Annual Average, 1975–1993*

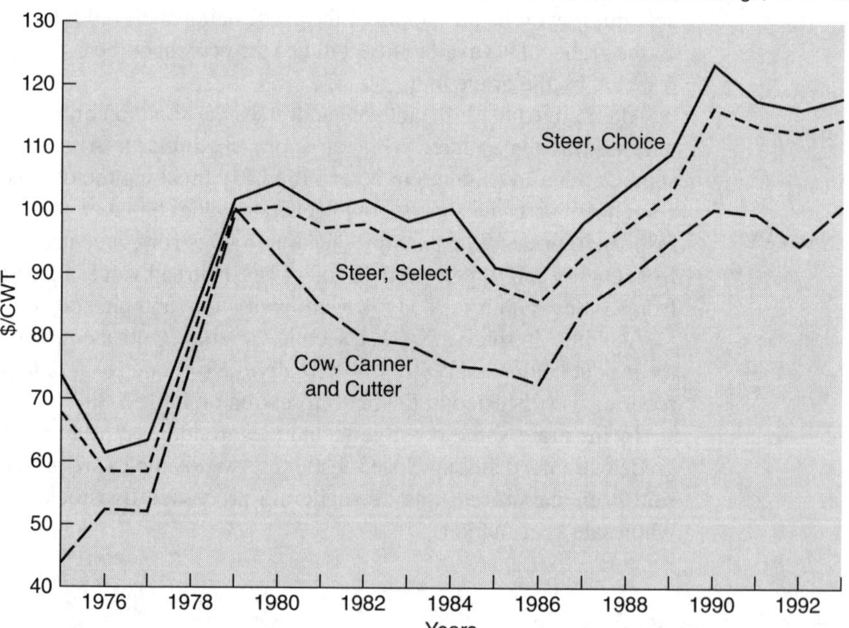

*Choice steer beef, 700–850 lb.; Select steer beef, 550–700 lb.

The less important grade of Select is a fairly close substitute as is apparent in the price pattern shown in Figure 5-2. Wholesale prices on cow beef of Canner and Cutter grade fluctuate in a somewhat parallel relationship with the steer grades, but with more departures than can be seen between Choice and Select steer beef.

A suggested approach to modeling this market is to concentrate on Choice steer beef. That price series could be the dependent variable in the basic demand equation which could include the per-capita availability of all beef, per-capita availability of substitutes, consumer income, and likely some trend variables. A refinement might be to differentiate fed beef from non-fed beef, including imports.

To forecast prices on Select steer beef, the analyst might be content to simply generate that price as a function of the price of Choice steer beef. For prices on Canner and Cutter cow beef, however, more information should be introduced. A priori, it would seem that a combination of the price on Choice steer beef and the relative importance of non-fed beef to total beef supplies should be explored.

The results of an OLS analysis for 1975–1993 were as follows:

$$\text{Price of Select Beef} = -3.44 + .990 * \underset{(66.2)}{\text{Price of Choice Beef}}$$

$R^2 = .996 \quad \bar{R}^2 = .996$

Standard error of the regression = 1.2 percent of mean of the dependent variable.

Figure in parenthesis is the *t* value.

$$\text{Price of Canner and Cutter Cow Beef} = 101.02 + .4705 * \underset{(5.13)}{\text{Price of Choice Beef}}$$

$$\underset{(-5.90)}{-356.12} * \text{Ratio of Non-fed Beef to Total Beef Supplies}$$

$R^2 = .952 \quad \bar{R}^2 = .946$

Standard error of the regression = 5.0 percent of mean of the dependent variable.

Figures in parentheses are the *t* values.

The statistical properties would be acceptable for most analysts, and the step-wise process to generate price forecasts on the Select steer beef and Canner and Cutter cow beef is fairly transparent. Alternative methods, of course, could be followed. The recommendation is to focus on the key grade and model price relationships for other grades or close substitutes around it.

Processed Feed Market Example

The processed feed market is composed of a number of relatively close substitutes. Among the oilseed meals, animal protein products, grain protein feeds, and other by-product feeds, the USDA keeps tabs on feeding of 19 different products (USDA, *Feed*

Situation and Outlook Report, various issues). While soybeans are produced mainly for the meal, most of the other feeds are by-products of processing operations where the main output is not feed. For that reason, the availability of the feed logically should be an independent variable in a demand equation and price should be dependent.

An obvious problem is how do you handle the 19 different products in some reasonable fashion. Not only does an analyst have to deal with the processed feeds, but also feed grains, feed wheat, and to a lesser extent, harvested forages and pasture. This example is introduced at this point to emphasize the importance of introducing a priori information as a means to make the task manageable.

The objective in this particular example was to forecast prices on the feed by-products of ethanol and high fructose corn syrup (HFCS) production. Both have been expanding. By 1992–1993, production of these feeds, which included corn gluten feed and meal and distillers' dried grains, represented over 15 percent of all processed feeds and about 40 percent processed feed excluding the high-protein feeds (oilseed meals and animal protein).

What this analyst did is only one of several alternatives, but was a logical process drawing heavily from books on the content and nutritional value of feeds (Ensminger and Olentine, 1980). First, a variable was constructed to represent the price of feed energy. Since corn is by far the major feed grain and source of energy in U.S. livestock rations, corn prices were the base for determining energy. The protein value in corn was deducted.

A principal source of protein is soybean meal. So the price of soybean meal less the value the energy component (based on corn prices) was removed. This procedure created two variables: one a hypothetical price of energy, and the other, the hypothetical price of protein. Of course, energy and protein represent the predominant value of any feedstuff.

The next step was to estimate the feed value of corn gluten feed, corn gluten meal, and distillers' dried grain (DDGS). Essentially, the price of protein was multiplied by the protein content of each feed, and the energy price was multiplied by the energy content of each feed to derive hypothetical feed values. These hypothetical feed values then became major independent variables in explaining the actual price of each feed.

Other independent variables in the price equation for these feeds were measures of total production relative to the total output of processed feeds. Reasoning that future price relationships would be closer to feed values, limits were placed on how far out of line with feed value these prices would be expected to go in the future. Rationale for this is that with expansion in availability of these feeds, farmers and feed suppliers will be inclined to adjust rations more readily as price relationships changed.

Models that provide the means to forecast corn and soybean meal prices may incorporate the impacts of the entire feed grain—processed feeds–forage complex in some way. One way might be to divide the feed sector into feed grain, high-protein, other processed feeds, and forage. Each component could be measured in metric tons. Alternatively, each sector could be converted to total energy (digestible or metabolizable) using some coefficient representing average calories among ruminant and non-ruminants. Similarly, digestible protein could be another common denominator, as estimated by authoritative animal nutritionists. (See Ensminger and Olentine, 1980.)

DEMAND FOR AGRICULTURAL INPUTS

Demands from the ultimate consumer, at home or abroad, extend back through retailing, wholesaling, processing, transportation, and other marketing channels to the farmer. The farmer, in turn, translates these demands back to the industries supplying inputs to agriculture. Farmers' demands for cash inputs represent an important market in the food chain. In the U.S., cash farm expenditures have increased relative to income; in 1995, farmers spent three-fourths of their gross cash farm income on cash input items. These items included manufactured inputs such as: fertilizer and lime, fuels and oils, electricity, and pesticides. Other costs included interest charges, repair and maintenance, contract and hired labor, and inputs of farm origin such as feed, livestock, and seed.

The approach to developing prediction equations for farm inputs could be applied at the national, regional, state, or local levels. The USDA regularly publishes income and balance sheet data for states as well as the nation. The Bureau of Economic Analysis of the USDC generates farm income data annually even for counties—using the 5-year Census of Agriculture as a base. County farm income can also be estimated from data generated by state departments of agriculture.

Table 5-4 provides suggestions on specifying demand equations for agricultural inputs. The USDA publishes aggregate data on farm income that could be key independent

TABLE 5-4 GUIDELINES FOR FORMULATING DEMAND EQUATIONS FOR AGRICULTURAL INPUTS (EXPENDITURES OR AMOUNTS PURCHASED ARE THE DEPENDENT VARIABLES.)

Independent Variable	Formulation
1. Farm income	Real net cash farm income
2. Wealth position	Real capital gains Real net equity position
3. Product prices	Real product price received by farmers
4. Price of input and prices of substitutes and complements	Real price of the input and prices of substitutes and complements
5. Government programs	Direct payments to farmers Restrictions on resource use, such as land
6. Productivity	Serial time; dummies
7. Environmental regulations	Serial time; dummies
8. Interest rates	Rates on government instruments, charges of Farm Credit Services, banks
9. Replacement demand	Average age of capital item Percent of capital item inventory over X years of age
10. Enterprise profit	Real gross margin over direct costs of production (can apply to input demand equations that are enterprise specific)
11. Risk	Variability of real net cash farm income Variability of real gross margins over variable costs in specific enterprises
12. Technical requirements	Livestock numbers, acreages, etc.
13. Structure of agriculture in terms of size of farms	Number of farms classified by acreage or gross income

variables in demands for inputs. Gross cash income is comprised primarily of cash receipts from crops, livestock, and direct government payments; deducting cash expenses results in net cash income. If demand for a major expenditure item is to be estimated, that item could be deducted from total cash expenditures to generate a variable that would purportedly represent farmers' purchasing power for the item in question. Routinely, the net income variables should be deflated.

Income and Equity

In a sense, net cash farm income can be considered as amounts farmers have available for purchasing capital items and meeting household expenses. Depreciation is not included in cash expenses. In the long-run, net farm income—basically net cash farm income plus (1) non-money income, (2) value of inventory change, and less (3) capital consumption (depreciation)—is a relevant variable particularly for estimating demand equations for capital items. Net farm income above the amount needed to meet household expenses would be available to replace and expand capital investment. This capital investment could be registered in terms of quantities of capital inputs, prices of capital inputs, or a combination of both, i.e., expenditures. Examples of such targets for analysis would include units of tractors sold, farmland prices, and expenditures on machinery.

Farmers' ability and inclination to buy are also conditioned by their wealth position. Capital gains in addition to income may be relevant in formulating demand for inputs. In a major way, improved equity enhances farmers' ability to obtain credit. For the benefit of those who might want to incorporate such information in measuring the demand for inputs, the USDA publishes balance sheets annually of the U.S. farming sector, tabulating assets, liabilities, and equity (USDA, *State Financial Summary,* 1993).

A suggested procedure would be to incorporate changes in capital gains and equity separate from income flow in formulating a demand equation for farm inputs. A reasonable assumption is that farmers would respond differently to variations in income than to changes in capital gains. Rising land values are often the major source of capital gains. Farmers' decisions in transforming these capital gains into increased input purchases is a more complex process than buying more inputs out of current income.

The application of both farm income and capital gains or equity considerations may involve long lags when applied to capital purchases. Buying capital items commits farmers to production over an extended period requiring long-range foresight. If stressful times have been experienced in recent years, inclination to buy may be attenuated. On the other hand, a succession of very profitable years accompanied by increased asset values and equity is often followed by buoyant expectations and above-normal spending patterns.

Prices, Costs, Government Programs, and Productivity

In the absence of income data, or for other reasons, analysts might rely on prices of the product(s) related to the input and the price of the input itself along with its substitutes and complements. If government payments are involved and/or restrictions placed on input use, this information may be relevant also. Changes in productivity that modify input-output transformations might be measured by a serial time variable or dummy variables. Similar variables might be appropriate to monitor the effect of environmental regulations, such as the banning of certain pesticides. Across a broad spectrum of inputs, particularly capital items, interest rates may be significant as an independent variable.

Replacement Demand

Analysts will have to draw on creativity to measure replacement demand for capital items. Relevant data such as the average age of the inventory of the capital item on farms or the percent of the inventory over X years of age may be difficult to obtain. Engineering data on the average life-span of a given piece of equipment may be useful information in combination with sales data. Everything else being equal, cycles in sales should be spaced in line with the normal life-span of the equipment.

Enterprise Profit and Risk

A more refined and targeted approach to demand analysis for inputs would be to organize the research around enterprises. Substantial data are available on input use by enterprise. For any given input, the major enterprises could be identified and gross margins from those enterprises would be the driving force in input demand. Input use in each enterprise could be aggregated into a total demand relationship. (See Chapter 6.)

A factor that may be important, but difficult to measure, is risk. Everything else being equal, the more risky an enterprise, the less the demand for an input. This might be measured by a separate variable such as variability or standard deviation of real gross margin over some recent period. (See Chapter 6.)

Technical Requirements and Structure

In deriving input demand equations, analysts may incorporate certain technical requirements that are relatively insensitive to price. Such requirements may be predominant factors. For example, the demand for feed grain may be determined primarily by the number of animals on farms modified by the livestock price, the price of feed grain, and the price of high-protein feeds. The demand for seed will likely depend almost exclusively on planted acres of a given crop modified by trends in seeding rates.

Input requirements vary substantially from farm to farm depending on size. Equipment needs on large farms are substantially different than on medium-sized or small farms. For example, to forecast sales of tractors over 100 horsepower, the number of farms with over 1,000 tillable acres might contribute to the analysis. Small-tractor sales may relate not only to the number of farms under 100 acres, but also estimates of nonfarm incomes in these households.

Deflation

While the Consumer Price Index (CPI) may be an appropriate deflator for variables in retail food demand equations, such a measure may not fit farmers' input demands. The

USDA does compute and publish Indices of Prices Paid by Farmers as well as Indices of Prices Received. The CPI is incorporated in the Prices Paid Index to represent the household sector, but would not necessarily match up with prices paid for inputs into the farm operation, particularly items like feed, fertilizer, and feeder livestock. Analysts may wish to construct special indices to include those prices farmers must pay for household items (CPI) and farm inputs other than the input that is being forecast.

The problem of designing an appropriate deflator is mitigated by the application of enterprise gross margins. The importance of various farm inputs is incorporated in the computation leaving the CPI or similar indicator of general inflation as an appropriate deflator.

SUMMARY

While conceptually, farm–retail price spreads would be analyzed as functions of demand and supply of marketing services and materials, the competitive structure of the industry and lack of data force researchers to concentrate on the spreads at equilibrium incorporating both demand and supply variables in single equations with the spread as the dependent variable. In fact, some measure of general inflation in marketing costs may be sufficient as an independent variable. While farm–wholesale and wholesale–retail price spreads do vary, competition at those levels tends to keep the spreads in line with marketing costs. If the purpose is to forecast retail food prices, a straight-forward procedure would be to estimate, by OLS, retail food prices as a function of farm prices and a measure of marketing costs.

In commodity market analysis, the econometrician must select a representative price series—a key grade or some average of various grades—to incorporate in supply-and-demand equations. At the same time, needs may remain for more precise price forecasts for given grades at given locations. With the key or average price series as an independent variable, prices on a given grade of the product could be forecast by OLS with the possible inclusion of other independent variables such as the relative supplies of the given grade. Alternatively, a commodity could be separated into component parts for which price series are available. From the relative importance of these components and their respective prices, an assumed basic market value could be derived. This value, along with relative supplies of the commodity, could be included as independent variables to forecast the price of the particular grade or close substitute in the product category.

Derived demand for farm inputs would logically depend greatly on real net farm income and the equity position of farmers. For capital items, interest rates and replacement demand may have special relevance.

QUESTIONS FOR STUDY

1 Why isn't the marketing spread on beef equal to the retail price less the farm price of cattle?

2 What are the major factors explaining the differences in the farm value share of the retail price for major food items?

3 What advantages might there be to incorporating Consumer Price Indexes of food products into demand analysis rather than dollar estimates of retail prices on those products?
4 Prices received by farmers for corn reflect a combination of all grades. Prices may decline in some years because of heavy discounting attributed to poor quality. Explain why this is a problem for econometric analysis and suggest ways it might be handled.
5 Why is it difficult to develop demand models with quantities of different grades of a product as the dependent variables?
6 Fertilizer is sold in many forms with different levels of N, P, and K. How might you proceed to develop a model to forecast fertilizer prices by components?
7 Why should net cash or net farm income be a separate independent variable from capital gains in forecasting input purchases?
8 Suggest ways that replacement demand might be measured for a capital item.
9 How would you forecast the demand for the services of a veterinarian?
10 How would you formulate a demand equation for used farm equipment?

6

MEASURING FARM SUPPLY

POINTS:

1. How to formulate empirical farm supply equations.
2. How to measure expected prices and adjustment to those expectations with distributed lags.
3. Conceptualizing "rational expectations."
4. Introduction of risk into supply equations.
5. Importance and pros and cons of gross margins in supply analysis.
6. How to introduce government programs in supply analysis.

In Chapter 2, farm supply was defined as "the schedule of amounts farmers would be willing to produce at various levels of *expected* prices for the product, all other factors being constant." However, most empirical farm supply analysis will focus on dependent variables other than production. The reason is that production includes effects beyond the farmers' control—influences such as weather and, to some extent, pests.

Analysts should select, as dependent variables, key indicators of farmers' intentions. On annual crops, for example, planted area and not production would be appropriate. Planted area reflects the farmers' response to expected prices. Production reflects not only planted area, but also weather and pest infestation. To some extent, farmers can enhance yields per acre or hectare if expected prices are encouraging, but this impact may be minor relative to weather. In any case, separate equations should be established—one for planted area (and possibly harvested area as a function of planted area) and one for yields as follows:

Area planted = f (expected prices, other independent variables).
Area harvested = f (area planted, weather/pest variable).

Yield per harvested acre = f (serial time, weather/pest variable).

Production = area harvested * yield per harvested acre.

Area harvested will normally be highly correlated with area planted and the weather/pest effect may be omitted since it can't be forecast very far in the future anyway. Yields as a function of serial time reflect improved technology and cultural practices. While a weather/pest variable could be highly significant in explaining yields, it might be eliminated since weather/pests are hardly predictable a year in advance. Of course, every effort should be made to measure weather/pest effects on area harvested and yields to improve the model specification. However, modeling such effects is often beyond the reach of available resources. (The yield function will be discussed in more detail in chapters 9 and 10.) Production, then, becomes simply the product of area harvested times yield.

In addition to planted area, examples of other major indicators of farmer response to expected prices would be:

1 Number of beef (dairy) cows on farms.
2 Number of beef (dairy) heifers for replacement on farms.
3 Number of cattle placed on feed.
4 Number of sows farrowing.
5 Number of broiler-type (egg-type) pullets placed in hatchery supply flocks.
6 Number of broiler-type (egg-type) eggs in incubators.
7 Number of non-bearing apple trees.

The supply analysis then proceeds adding the necessary linking equations needed to derive the desired production data—beef, milk, pork, broilers, eggs, apple production, etc. These additional equations may also reflect farmer price expectations. But generally, one equation will be the predominant supply relationship. A suggested formulation of the independent variables for this central supply equation is presented in Table 6-1.

The application of serial time and dummy variables to account for technical change, structural change, irreversibility and anomalies is similar to the procedures explained for demand. A weather variable could be a complex combination of rainfall, temperature, degree days, sunlight, etc., in a crop development simulation model. Anomalies and pests might be handled with a dummy variable. The other independent variables listed in Table 6-1 will be discussed in some detail.

EXPECTATIONS

A challenge to econometricians is to measure expectations. Perhaps the most naive expectation model is to employ the price in the most recent past period as a proxy for expected price. This implies a relatively short memory by producers and a lack of understanding about what supply and demand factors are likely to impinge on price formation in the coming period. An improvement on this model would be some measurement of the

TABLE 6-1 GUIDELINES FOR FORMULATING FARM SUPPLY EQUATIONS (KEY INDICATOR OF FARMERS' RESPONSE TO EXPECTED PRICES IS THE DEPENDENT VARIABLE.)

Independent Variable	Formulation
Expected	
Price of product Price of substitutes Price of complements Price of major inputs	Values in previous period, distributed lags, futures, rational expectations
Technical conversion rates	Serial time, exponential smoothing
Risk	Measure of variability
Structural changes—gradual	Serial time
Structural changes—abrupt	Dummy variable
Government policy variables	
Non-recourse loan	Value
Direct payments	Value
Area set-asides	Value
Irreversibility	Dummy variable
Weather	Rainfall, temperature at planting time, degree days, days of sunlight
Anomalies, pests	Dummy variable

role of prices over several past periods in generating expectations. This is called the "distributed lag" approach to expectation formulation.

Assume that prices on a given product have been as follows:

Year	Price
t-3	1
t-2	4
t-1	3

The simple one-period model would set the expected price E(P) for year *t* at 3. An alternative would be to apply a simple average to the three years and generate:

$$E(P) = (3+4+1)/3 = 2.67$$

Considering that memory is a declining function of time, another alternative would be to assume declining weights such as:

$$E(P) = .5 * 3 + .3 * 4 + .2 * 1 = 2.9$$

Economic theory provides little basis for determining what the proper weights should be or how many periods back should be incorporated in expectation formulation. In absence of behavioral theory to provide guidance, statistical analysis can be instrumental in providing some answers.

In line with the above example, weights could be derived by the following OLS equation:

$$Q_t = a + b_1 * P_{t-1} + b_2 * P_{t-2} + b_3 * P_{t-3} + b_4 * Z$$

where: Q_t = output, P_{t-i} are lagged prices, and Z represents other relevant independent variables.

An analyst might "hunt" for the appropriate lag length by introducing additional lagged P_{t-i} until the coefficients are not significant or turn negative. Two problems emerge in this process: (1) multicollinearity and (2) loss of degrees of freedom.

Geometric Distributed Lags

These problems can be reduced by the application of geometric distributed lags, procedures attributed to Nerlove and earlier, Koyck (Nerlove, 1958), (Koyck, 1954). Consider the following general form of a supply equation in which production is a function of past prices:

$$Q_t = \alpha + \sum_{i=1}^{\infty} \beta_i P_{t-i} \; where \; \beta_i = \beta\lambda^i; \; 0 < \lambda < 1 \; ; i = 1, 2 \ldots \infty$$

This means that the β_i are a declining function of the time lag.

A. $Q_t = \alpha + \beta\lambda P_{t-1} + \beta\lambda^2 P_{t-2} + \ldots + \beta\lambda^\infty P_{t-\infty}$

B. $Q_{t-1} = \alpha + \beta\lambda P_{t-2} + \beta\lambda^2 P_{t-3} + \ldots + \beta\lambda^\infty P_{t-\infty}$

Multiply Equation B by λ

C. $\lambda Q_{t-1} = \lambda\alpha + \beta\lambda^2 P_{t-2} + \ldots + \beta\lambda^\infty P_{t-\infty}$

Subtract C from A

D. $Q_t - \lambda Q_{t-1} = \alpha - \lambda\alpha + \beta\lambda P_{t-1}$

E. $Q_t = \underbrace{(1-\lambda)\alpha}_{a} + \underbrace{\lambda}_{b_1} Q_{t-1} + \underbrace{\beta\lambda}_{b_2} P_{t-1}$

α, β, and λ can be identified from the coefficients (a, b_1 and b_2) of an OLS analysis.

Impact Multipliers:

1-year lag	$\beta\lambda$
2-year lag	$\beta\lambda + \beta\lambda^2$
Long run	$\beta\lambda/(1-\lambda)$

Proof of Long-run Impact Multiplier:

In long run: $Q_t = Q_{t-1}$

$Q_t = (1-\lambda)\alpha + \lambda Q_t + \beta\lambda P_{t-1}$

$Q_t - \lambda Q_t = (1-\lambda)\alpha + \beta\lambda P_{t-1}$

$(1-\lambda)Q_t = (1-\lambda)\alpha + \beta\lambda P_{t-1}$

$Q_t = \alpha + [\beta\lambda/(1-\lambda)]P_{t-1}$

Elasticities:

1-year lag $\beta\lambda*(P_{t-1}/Q_{t-1})$

2-year lag $(\beta\lambda + \beta\lambda^2)*(P_t/Q_t)$

Long run $[\beta\lambda/(1-\lambda)]*(P_{t+\infty}/Q_{t+\infty})$

where P_i and Q_i refer to the base values.

To illustrate this procedure, consider the following situation:

An OLS equation was estimated as follows:

$Q_t = (1-\lambda)\alpha + \lambda Q_{t-1} + \beta\lambda P_{t-1}$

with the result

$Q_t = 2 + .6Q_{t-1} + 6P_{t-1}$

Solving for α, β, and λ,

$(1-\lambda)*\alpha = 2$

$\lambda = .6$

$\beta*\lambda = 6$

$\beta *.6 = 6$

$\beta = 6/.6 = 10$

$(1-.6)*\alpha = 2$

$.4*\alpha = 2$

$\alpha = 2/.4 = 5$

Given: $P_{t-1} = 4$; $Q_{t-1} = 50$

Hold P_{t+i} at 4; $i = -1$ to ∞

<u>Year</u>

t $Q_t = 2+.6 * 50 + 6 * 4 = 56$

t+1 $Q_{t+1} = 2+.6 * 56 + 24 = 59.6$

t+2 Q_{t+2} = 2+.6 * 59.6+24 = 61.76

.

.

.

t+∞ $Q_{t+\infty}$ = 5+(6/.4) * 4 = 5+15 * 4 = 65

Raise P_{t+i} to 5, i.e., by 1

t Q_t = 2+.6 * 50 +6 * 5 = 62

t+1 Q_{t+1} = 2+.6 * 62 +30 = 69.2

t+2 Q_{t+2} = 2+.6 * 69.2+30 = 73.52

.

.

.

t+∞ $Q_{t+\infty}$= 5+(6/.4) * 5 = 5 + 15 * 5 = 80

With the above results, the impact multipliers and elasticities would be calculated as follows:

Year	Impact Multiplier	Elasticity
t	+6.00	+6.00 * (4/56.00) = +.43
t+1	+9.60	+9.60 * (4/59.60) = +.64
t+2	+11.76	+11.76 * (4/61.76) = +.76
.		
.		
.		
t+∞	+15.00	+15.00 * (4/65.00) = +.92

The results from this example emphasize that supply elasticities tend to increase over time. Models that employ fixed elasticities of supply are suspect. Whenever single-valued supply elasticities are quoted, the time frame must be specified. Obviously, a time frame of infinity is not relevant. The above example can be interpreted to mean that the supply elasticity is about +.76 in a time frame of a couple of years and approaches +.92 after a few more years.

Also obvious is the recognition that supply elasticities cannot be measured with the precision indicated. In this example, prices were held constant over the time frame and then increased and held constant at the higher level. Such conditions rarely are duplicated in the real world as other influences throw markets into flux. This phenomenon will be discussed in Chapter 8, and alternatives will be explored on how to measure both supply and demand elasticities in dynamic markets.

An additional conundrum in applying the geometric distributed lag to represent expectations is whether it is really a lag between changing prices and price expectations or a lag between changing price expectations and adjustment to those expectations. In the literature, references are made to "adaptive expectation" and "partial adjustment" or "stock adjustment" models (Pindyck and Rubinfeld, 1991). The former focuses on lags in forming expectations and the latter on adjustments to expectations. Granted, in agricultural production there are both.

Particularly in relatively free and volatile markets, farmers change their expectations only after a new price level has been clearly ascertained—and this may take some time. Once expectations have been modified, response may be delayed because of the biological lag and also because of fixity in capital inputs. Farmers wanting to cut back may be trapped for some time with assets that have to be depreciated. Farmers wanting to expand in line with optimistic expectations may not have the necessary capital or credit to invest immediately. The problem is, statistically, that the relationship between changes in realized prices and output cannot be easily separated into expectation lags and adjustment lags.

Polynomial Distributed Lags

An alternative to geometric lag formulations is a procedure in which the weights or coefficients on the lagged price variables are constrained to specified polynomial functions. Rather than a lag structure that transcends infinity as in geometric lags, the polynomial distributed lags (PDL) cover some finite specified period, i.e.:

$$(1)\quad Q_t = \alpha + \sum_{i=0}^{N} \beta_i P_{t-i}$$

The restriction placed on the coefficients is:

$$(2)\quad \beta i = \theta_0 + i\theta_1 + i^2\theta_2 + \ldots + i^M\theta_M$$

$$= \sum_{m=0}^{M} i^m \theta_m;\ \mathrm{i} = 0, 1, 2 \ldots, \mathrm{N};\ \mathrm{M} < \mathrm{N}$$

where: N = specified finite lag length

M = degree of polynomial

The degree of the polynomial must be less than the number of terms in the polynomial lag minus one. Otherwise, there will be no reduction in the number of parameters to be estimated.

Substituting (2) into (1) gives:

$$(3)\quad Q_t = \alpha + \sum_{m=0}^{M} \theta_m \left[\sum_{i=1}^{N} i^m P_{t-i}\right]$$

As an example, assume that N = 5 and M = 3.

$$(1) \quad Q_t = \alpha + \beta_o P_t + \beta_1 P_{t-1} + \beta_2 P_{t-2} + \beta_3 P_{t-3} + \beta_4 P_{t-4}$$

$$\beta_o = \theta_o$$

$$\beta_1 = \theta_0 + \theta_1 + \theta_2 + \theta_3$$

$$\beta_2 = \theta_0 + 2\theta_1 + 4\theta_2 + 8\theta_3$$

$$\beta_3 = \theta_0 + 3\theta_1 + 9\theta_2 + 27\theta_3$$

$$\beta_4 = \theta_0 + 4\theta_1 + 16\theta_2 + 64\theta_3$$

$$(2) \quad Q_t = \alpha + \theta_0 P_t + (\theta_0 + \theta_1 + \theta_2 + \theta_3) P_{t-1}$$
$$+ (\theta_0 + 2\theta_1 + 4\theta_2 + 8\theta_3) P_{t-2}$$
$$+ (\theta_0 + 3\theta_1 + 9\theta_2 + 27\theta_3) P_{t-3}$$
$$+ (\theta_0 + 4\theta_1 + 16\theta_2 + 64\theta_3) P_{t-4}$$

$$(3) \quad Q_t = \alpha + \theta_0 (P_t + P_{t-1} + P_{t-2} + P_{t-3} + P_{t-4})$$
$$+ \theta_1 (P_{t-1} + 2P_{t-2} + 3P_{t-3} + 4P_{t-4})$$
$$+ \theta_2 (P_{t-1} + 4P_{t-2} + 9P_{t-3} + 16P_{t-4})$$
$$+ \theta_3 (P_{t-1} + 8P_{t-2} + 27P_{t-3} + 64P_{t-4})$$

Equation (3) immediately above can be solved by OLS and the parameters, θ_i, estimated. Then from those values, the β_i can be identified.

The MicroTSP software provides alternatives for (1) number of periods to be lagged, (2) the degree of the polynomial, and (3) four options on constraining the end points. Both the beginning and end periods can be constrained to zero; the near end point can be constrained to zero; both ends can be so constrained; and both ends can be unconstrained.

In Figure 6-1 are representations of the geometric lag distribution and alternative PDLs of two degrees with different constraints. As can be noted, the geometric lag is one of declining weights over past periods at successively smaller levels. A feature of the PDL is that it can assume multiple forms, such as allowing for increasing as well as declining weights over the past. At polynomial degrees higher than two, the distribution may even be bi-modal, tri-modal, etc. However, only in extreme cases would degrees beyond two be reasonable.

The advantage of the existing software programs incorporating PDL is that alternative assumptions can be made quickly about the period of lags, degrees of the polynomial, and form of the constraints. Trial-and-error procedures provide the analyst insights into producer response patterns. Even so, an understanding of the industry being analyzed is imperative in using this tool effectively.

An advantage in application of PDL is that it is more general and flexible than geometric lags. Also, the error term obeys the classical assumptions for OLS. A disadvantage is that the lag period and degree of the polynomial must be specified. Also, PDLs

FIGURE 6-1 Effect of feeder prices on beef cow numbers.

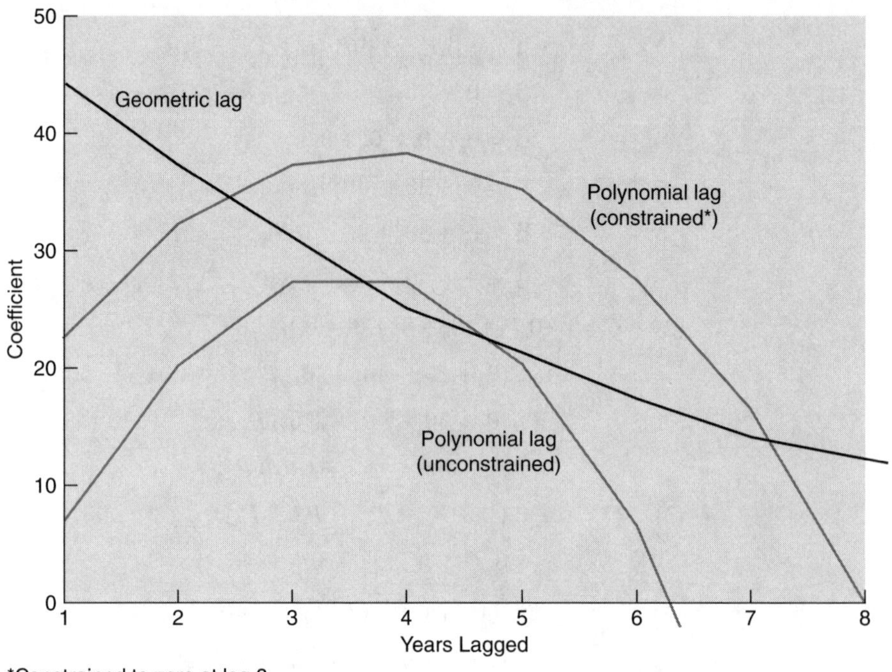

*Constrained to zero at lag 8.

generally reduce the number of observations of the dependent variable in time series analysis relative to implementation of geometric lags. At the minimum, a geometric lag supply equation would require only a one-period lag.

In some cases, analysts may combine features of geometric lags and PDLs in the same equation. An example of this is presented in Table 6-2 for a set of alternative equations for predicting the number of beef cows on U.S. farms on January 1. All four equations included the lagged dependent variable as an independent variable.

The long biological process in the beef cattle industry suggests implementing a distributed lag analysis in supply. The simple geometric lag format shown in Table 6-2 required only three independent variables—the number of beef cows lagged one year [NCWBF(−1)], the deflated annual average price of feeder calves lagged one year [PFCVD(−1)], and the deflated price of farm land lagged one year [PLND(−1)]. The signs on the independent variables were as expected, the *t* values were statistically significant, and the R bar square was an acceptable .92.

However, with 29 years of observations, an analyst would feel compelled to examine the lag structure in more detail. The geometric lag formulation was modified by adding PFCVD(−2) and PFCVD(−3). This revealed that the simple geometric lag structure was inappropriate. Rather than declining weights to PFCVD over the past, PFCVD(−2) was more influential in generating response from cow-calf operators than was PFCVD(−1).

TABLE 6-2 STATISTICAL RESULTS FROM FOUR DISTRIBUTED LAG FORMULATIONS FOR PREDICTING THE NUMBER OF BEEF COWS ON FARMS, JANUARY 1, ANNUAL DATA FROM 1964 TO 1992

	Geometric Lag				Polynomial Distributed Lag			
Variable	Simple		Modified		6-Year Lag 3rd Degree No Constraints		4-Year Lag 2nd Degree Far End Constrained to 0	
	Coefficient	*t-value*	*Coefficient*	*t-value*	*Coefficient*	*t-value*	*Coefficient*	*t-value*
NCWB(–1)	.954	16.5	.890	28.6	.873	21.9	.858	21.6
PFCVD(–1)	44.6	4.4	14.3	2.1				
PFCVD(–2)			51.0	6.2				
PFCVD(–3)			7.3	1.0				
PDL1					20.5	5.5	26.0	9.5
PDL2					–14.5	–3.4	–7.4	–2.0
PDL3					–2.5	–1.4		
PDL4					1.7	1.6		
Lag Distribution of PFCVD(–1)								
0					26.0	4.1	32.9	6.5
1					30.8	7.1	26.0	9.5
2					20.5	5.5	18.2	5.0
3					5.1	1.3	9.5	3.1
4					–5.3	–1.2		
5					–.9	–.2		
Sum					76.2	6.4	86.6	9.5
PLND(–1)	–1.65	–2.7	–1.53	–5.2	–1.41	–3.9	–1.34	–3.66
R^2	.920		.981		.979		.972	

Also, this formulation resulted in an improved R bar square, at .981. In addition, these results would strongly suggest that a PDL procedure should be implemented.

As indicated in Table 6-2, the first step was to examine a long lag with the flexibility of a third-degree polynomial and no constraints on either the near point nor the far point of the range. Since obviously PFCVD in the current year has no effect on the January 1 inventory of beef cows, the focus for the PDL was on PFCVD(–1). The coefficients on the PDLi have no particular meaning except as they provide the means for estimating the coefficients on PFCVD(–i). The results confirm the outcome of the modified geometric lag equation that the impact of PFCVD(–2) is greater than PFCVD(–1) and that the weights do diminish for periods earlier than t–2. The negative and insignificant coefficients for the lag distribution of PFCVD(–1) of 4 and 5 (actually, *t*-5 and *t*-6), indicate that the arbitrarily selected period for this PDL was probably too long.

For that reason, the next step was to select a four-year lag, a second-degree polynomial, and constrain the far end of the range to zero (Table 6-2). In this formulation, PFCVD(–1) became the most influential variable in predicting NCWB (although PFCVD[–2] had a higher *t* value) with the weights declining almost linearly for *t*-2, *t*-3, and *t*-4. All the coefficients on PFCVD(–i) were significant and the R bar square, at .972, was near that of the longer PDL formulation. The cumulative effect of PFCVD(–i), at 86.6, was noticeably above the 76.2 of the alternative PDL. However, an analyst might well continue to explore other modifications of the PDL procedure to achieve even stronger statistical properties.

While this methodology may appear somewhat arbitrary and ad hoc, such a process is appropriate when a theoretical base and/or a priori information are not readily available, if available at all. The philosophy being expounded here is to use statistical analysis to tell you what you do not know or cannot find out from other sources. At the same time, the analyst should exploit all available information about an industry relevant to modeling before turning to econometrics.

Rational Expectations

What do economists mean by "rational expectations"? This term applies to the process by which decision makers formulate their beliefs about the future, taking all relevant information into account. In a sense, decision makers become economists or econometricians specializing in forecasting. An early proponent, John Muth, explained the approach as follows:

> Expectations, since they are informed predictions of future events, are essentially the same as the predictions of the relevant economic theory (Muth, 1961).

This hypothesis implies well informed decision makers and basically refutes the assumption that expected prices or profits are based solely on past values. Clearly, lagged and distributed lagged price and profit expectation models would label decision makers as naive. On the other hand, to presume that decision makers can integrate supply-and-demand information and accurately forecast prices is also unrealistic. Even the best of the econometricians have difficulty accomplishing that.

The logic of the rational expectations hypothesis is compelling, just the same, and analysts should be prepared to test its validity. Several methods are available to incorporate rational expectations into econometric models:

1. Modification of standard models
2. Implicit rational expectations econometrics
3. Surveys of industry decision makers
4. Authoritative forecasts
5. Application of futures prices
6. Combination of futures and lagged cash prices
7. Combinations of above alternatives

Forms of rational expectations have routinely been incorporated in econometric models. Government loan rates on grains that have set lower bounds on market prices commonly appear in supply equations on these products. Contract prices with growers of processed vegetables form the expected price in econometric models of this industry. In many nations, farm prices are rigidly controlled. The task of the analyst in these cases is to model the Minister of Agriculture, food processor management, etc.—those decision makers who set the prices—employing not only economic theory, but also in some cases political and social considerations.

To illustrate the implicit rational expectations hypothesis, the following simple two-equation model can serve as an example:

Demand $P_t = a_0 - a_1 Q_t + a_2 I_t$

Supply $Q_t = b_0 + b_1 P_{t-1} - b_2 C_{t-1}$

where: P_t = price

Q_t = production

I_t = consumer income

C_t = production cost per unit

This is a recursive supply-demand model in that expected values for P_t and C_t are based on lagged values.

In the view of an econometrician, the logical expected price for period t is:

Expected price $P_t{*} = a_0 - a_t (b_0 + b_1 P_{t-1} - b_2 C_{t-1}) + a_2 I_t$

formed by substituting the equation for Q_t in the equation for P_t. Assume that I_t is forecast exogenously from an authoritative source.

The rational expectation model (assuming a recursive supply-demand model prevails), then, is:

$$Q_t = b_0 + b_1 [(a_0 - a_1 b_0) - a_1 b_1 P_{t-1} + a_1 b_2 C_{t-1} + a_2 I_t] + b_2 C_{t-1}$$

$$= (b_0 + b_1 a_0 - b_1 a_1 b_0) - a_1 b_1^2 P_{t-1} + (b_1 a_1 b_2 + b_2) C_{t-1} + b_1 a_2 I_t$$

$$P_t = a_0 - a_1 Q_t + a_2 I_t$$

The major difference from the structural equations is that enlightened farmers using rational expectations respond negatively to prices in t-1 and positively to production costs in t-1. They also respond positively to the forecast of consumer income. This system works for enlightened farmers as long as most farmers respond positively to past prices and negatively to past costs. Of course, as more farmers shift to rational expectations, the advantage dissipates and enlightened farmers are forced to a new expectation model. When *all* farmers become enlightened, the expected prices and costs are equal to the actual prices and costs (except for random disturbances), and the final model solution conforms to the rational expectation hypothesis. This is a rather simplistic example of rational expectation econometrics, but demonstrates the complexities.

While it may be presumptuous to believe that decision makers act as econometricians, they certainly have access to publications that carry outlook information. Authoritative forecasts could be used as proxies for decision makers' expectations. This approach was incorporated in a study on farmers' response to price conducted in the early 1960s (Lerohl,

1965). In that project, outlook statements released from the U.S. Department of Agriculture were transformed into reasonable price expectations of farmers. This, of course, was predicated on the assumption that farmers were aware of these forecasts and believed them.

Another approach is to incorporate surveys of industry decision makers about their expectations. Unfortunately, time series data from surveys are limited.

A very pragmatic approach to simulating price expectations for the year ahead is to apply futures prices. Analysts could identify the critical periods of the year in which production decisions are made, tabulate the prices on futures contracts for the upcoming production period and generate reasonable expectations for farm prices. This can easily be done with analysis of the normal "basis" between futures prices and the relevant cash prices. Since futures prices are available on each business day and widely quoted, this source has promise in simulating farmers' price expectations.

Considering the complex process farmers go through in formulating expectations, a reasonable assumption is that some *combination* of the aforementioned approaches is the logical choice as an expectation model. As a test, one might explore alternatives with a standard distributed lag model as a base. An option might be to weight distributed lags by 50 percent and an expected cash market based on futures by 50 percent and observe the statistical properties relative to the distributed lag model. This procedure appears arbitrary, but reflects the lack of a strong theoretical underpinning of how expectations are formulated.

A number of other combinations might be explored. In any case, such models should be specified in a way to allow for shifts in expectation formulations over time. The trend to fewer and more specialized farm operations would likely be accompanied by changes in the forces impinging on expectations. Most probable is that the naive lag models would give way to more sophisticated rational expectation models. Incorporation of time variables could help account for these shifts.

The lesson from the rational expectation hypothesis (REH) is that analysts need to monitor their traditional approach (using lagged prices and profits) and explore a more information-based process. At the same time, the weaknesses of REH should be recognized.

1 Unrealistic to presume that decision makers:
  a Have comprehensive information at critical decision-making times.
  b Know how to use effectively what information they do have.

2 Their accurate response to rational expectations would tend to negate the forecasts if most farmers responded to rational expectations. The false reading would discredit this approach and REH would fall into disrespect.

3 Authoritative forecasting carries a large error term.

4 Persistence of cycles in recent years tends to refute REH.

5 Difficulties in generating forecasts more than one year ahead with REH.

The industry most likely to exhibit REH is poultry meat. This is a highly integrated system with decision making in the hands of relatively few large processors. Evidence that REH is operating is that forecasts of red meat production appear to influence output of poultry meat. The presence of REH in poultry meat is also indicated in other studies (Aradhyula and Holt, 1989).

On the other hand, limited research on corn and soybeans by this author questions whether REH is prevalent in other agricultural sectors. Substituting harvest futures prices at planting less normal harvest basis (normal difference between futures and cash farm prices) for lagged farm prices in supply equations on corn and soybeans resulted in weaker statistical properties (Ferris, 1986).

RISK AND ITS MEASUREMENT

Based on economic theory, given the same expected price, response would be greater to a fairly assured price versus a very uncertain price. This can be illustrated by observing responses to changes in price in Figure 6-2.

In Figure 6-2 are two price series normalized for the first 10 years to a base of zero and increased by 20 percent in years 11 to 20. The means for both series in the first 10 years are the same and in the second 10 years are also the same. Series A is a free market price and Series B is a regulated price. The response to a 20-percent increase in price in Series B would likely be much more rapid than the response to Series A because of less confidence that the increase in level of price would be permanent with Series A.

This is an extreme case between controlled and uncontrolled prices. Similar conclusions could be reached in two free markets in which the prices on one commodity were much more volatile than on another commodity. Given the same commodity over time,

FIGURE 6-2 Hypothetical Pattern of Prices on Two Commodities in Percent Change from a Base Year.

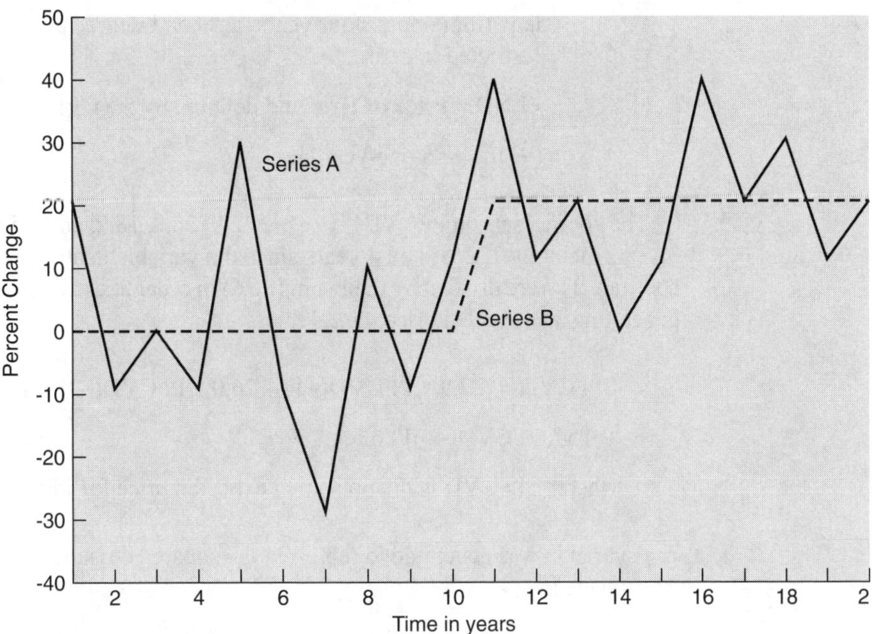

the elasticity of supply would tend to decline as the volatility of price increased and rise as volatility declined.

Various methods have been employed to handle risk empirically. Generally, some variable to measure the difference between expected prices and actual prices has been introduced in standard supply equations (Just, 1975; Behrman, 1968; Traill et al., 1978; and Hurt, 1982). Traill et al. used an iterative procedure in which an equation was estimated with distributed lags, omitting a risk variable. The estimated coefficients were used to formulate a first-round estimate of expected price. Deviations of actual price from this expected price series formed the risk variable.

Variables that strictly measure differences between expected and actual prices do not properly account for risk. Unexpectedly low prices have much more serious consequences for producers than unexpectedly high prices. For this reason, refined econometric supply analysis incorporating risk employs asymmetric variables, i.e., the left-hand tail of an appropriate probability distribution is emphasized. This effect might be incorporated with a dummy variable with the value of one for years following a significant departure on the low side from expected returns; zero, otherwise.

As an example of how risk can be incorporated in a supply analysis, the following PDL equation was estimated by least squares (as presented in Table 6-2):

NCWB = f [NCWB(−1), PDL (PFCVD(−1),3,2,2), PLND(−1)]

where: NCWB = Number of beef cows on farms, January 1

PDL (PFCVD,3,2,2) is a MicroTSP polynomial distributed lag function on the coefficients of the price of feeder calves deflated by the CPI, with lags from one to four years, a second-degree polynomial, and the far end restricted to zero.

PLND = Price of farmland deflated by the CPI

(−1) = a one-year lag

The coefficients on PFCVD(−1) were 32.9, 26.0, 18.2, and 9.5 for lags of 0, 1, 2, and 3 years (actually 1, 2, 3, and 4 years since the variable itself is lagged one year). These coefficients were divided by their sum (86.6) in order to establish reasonable weights for generating an expected price, i.e.,

EPFCVD = [32.9 * PFCVD(−1) + 26.0 * PFCVD(−2) + 18.2 * PFCVD(−3)
+ 9.5 * PFCVD(−4)]/86.6

where: EPFCVD is the presumed expected price for PFCVD in year *t*

A variable was generated to represent the squared deviations of the actual price from the expected:

$$SEPFCVD = (PFCVD - EPFCVD)^2$$

RMSEPFC4 = (.25 * (SEPFCVD(−1) + SEPFCVD(−2) + SEPFCVD(−3) +SEPFCVD(−4)))^.5

where: RMSEPFC4 = root mean squared error of the actual price from the expected for the previous four years

The variable, RMSEPFC4, was then added to the original supply equation to measure the impact of risk. The coefficient on the variable carried the correct negative sign from this expanded least squares analysis with a t value of −1.63. The adjusted R^2 was slightly higher. While not a strong argument for incorporating a risk variable, this example illustrates the process.

GROSS MARGINS AND RATIOS

As in demand analysis, econometricians are limited in terms of how many independent variables they can incorporate in ordinary least squares supply equations. In addition to product prices, prices on substitutes, input prices, and measurement of technological change, complex lag structures may have to be considered as well as risk. Also, government programs may be prominent elements in how farmers formulate production decisions and must be incorporated.

With 20 to 30 observations of annual data, analysts cannot realistically expect to capture the impact of more than five or six independent variables. Even with 40 years of observations, one might be reluctant to add variables due to problems of multicollinearity. Also, with structural change as a common phenomenon, the early part of a 40-year data span would not likely be very representative of a forecast period and may need to be discarded.

A convenient solution to this problem is to combine variables into gross margins or ratios and work with a shorter database of around 20 to 30 years. Price ratios have been frequently used in supply equations. An example is the "hog–corn" ratio, simply the price of hogs divided by the price of corn. This measurement of the profitability of the hog enterprise has been an effective leading indicator of changes in swine production.

The value of the hog–corn ratio relates to the importance of corn in the cost of producing hogs. However, other feed, primarily high-protein meal, is also important in hog rations as are non-feed costs. The major deficiency in ratios, such as the hog–corn ratio, is that the denominator is given the same weight as the numerator. Clearly, corn costs are much less important than gross receipts from sales when tallying hog budgets.

A more promising alternative is to generate enterprise gross margins over direct costs or even over total costs. With this procedure, each cost item enters the gross margin variable in relation to its importance in the enterprise.

In the hog example, the impact of changing corn prices on hog production can still be measured through the gross margin variable. This would be transmitted through the coefficient on the gross margin variable times the price of corn times the bushels of corn needed to produce a hundredweight of live hog. Price elasticities of supply can also be derived by multiplying this "impact multiplier" by a given ratio of price to quantity and measured by distributed lag procedures described earlier in this chapter.

Formulation

Gross margin variables can be formulated in various ways. On livestock, a preference is to establish gross margins in terms of units of output such as hundredweight of live hogs or cattle, hundredweight of milk, dozen eggs, etc. Alternatively, returns per sow, cow, 1,000 layers, pounds of broilers or turkeys at wholesale, etc., could also be estimated. On crops, the preference is to calculate gross margins in terms of area (acres or hectares) rather than bushels, hundredweight, M.T., etc. The reason is that cost data are more stable on a per-unit-of-area basis than on a product basis. Costs per unit of product vary substantially from year-to-year due to volatility in yields from weather effects, a factor of much less importance in livestock production.

On crops, a compelling reason to employ gross margins may be to incorporate parameters of government programs. The complexities of such programs preclude separate statistical measurements of these parameters in many cases.

The gross margin for a farm enterprise would be amounts available to pay for other costs (not explicitly covered in the cost component of the gross margin) and family living. As such, gross margins should be deflated by an index representing these other costs and family living expenses. To the extent that other enterprise costs are correlated with general inflation (and clearly family living costs are correlated with general inflation), a Consumer Price Index would suffice.

Following is an illustration of how a supply equation for an annual crop could be formulated with gross margin variables.

Dependent variable

AP = Area planted

Independent variables

PP = Price of product

PC = Price of a competing product

PFTP = Price of fertilizer for the product

PCMP = Price of chemicals for the product

PFUP = Price of fuel for the product

PSDP = Price of seed for the product

PFTC = Price of fertilizer for the competing product

PCMC = Price of chemicals for the competing product

PFUC = Price of fuel for the competing product

PSDC = Price of seed for the competing product

CPI = Consumer Price Index

YP = Yield per acre for the product

YC = Yield per acre for the competing product

TIME = Serial time to measure technical change

GVP = Variable related to government programs on the product

DVI = Dummy variable to account for irreversibility

Obviously, with 20 to 30 years of observations, measuring the separate impact of these variables would not be plausible, statistically. However, application of a priori information about the industry, and particularly costs of production, allows the analyst to take each of the variables into account. Assuming a geometric-type lag structure, area planted could be made a function of: (1) lagged area planted, (2) expected real gross margin per acre on the product, (3) expected real gross margin per acre on the competing crop, (4) serial time to handle structural/technological change, (5) a government program variable, and (6) a dummy variable designed to account for irreversibility. This procedure reduces the number of independent variables from 16 to 6.

This could be accomplished in several ways. A suggested procedure is to transform the long list of independent variables as follows:

EGMPD = expected real gross margin per acre on the product

$$= [PP_{t-1} * EYP - (k\ PFTP_{t-1} + 1\ PCMP_{t-1} + m\ PFUP_{t-1} + n\ PSDP_{t-1})] / CPI_{t-1}$$

EGMCD = expected real gross margin per acre on the competing crop

$$[PC_{t-1} * EYC - (p\ PFTC_{t-1} + q\ PCMC_{t-1} + r\ PFUC_{t-1} + s\ PSDC_{t-1}] / CPI_{t-1}$$

where: EYP = trend yield on the product (likely some function of TIME)

k,l,m,n = amounts of the respective inputs applied to the product per acre

EYC = trend yield on the competing crop (likely some function of TIME)

p,q,r,s = amounts of the respective inputs applied to the competing crop per acre

Trend yield rather than lagged yield would be the more representative of expectations. Unusually high or low yields in a given year would not likely generate anticipation of similar yields in the following year.

The supply equation would then be formulated as:

$$AP_t = f\,(AP_{t-1}, EGMPD, EGMCD, TIME, GVP, DVI)$$

Alternative formulations could be explored. The government policy variable (GVP) might be incorporated in the expected gross margin variables (EGMPD and EGMCD). The dummy for supply irreversibility (DVI) could be formulated with a "zero, one" variable, zero if AP_t declined, and one if AP_t increased for each year. Very likely, the coefficients of input use (k, l, m, n, p, q, r, s) are not constants and need to be adjusted to reflect past values and projected possibly as some function of TIME or a more complex specification.

Certainly, the application rate on fertilizer has typically changed over time and could be expected to change in the future. The analyst might decide that the rate has been and will be strongly related to trends and can be measured with a time variable. Alternatively, k and p could be forecast as a function of, say, (1) the expected gross margin excluding fertilizer costs and (2) the price of fertilizer. This would make k and p endogenous. Further refinements might include:

1 Employing production functions on fertilizer use from experimental data.
2 Separating composite fertilizer application rates and representative prices into N, P, and K.
3 Modifying projections on application rates to account for political pressures related to the environment.

The degree of sophistication desirable in supply analysis depends, of course, on the data available. In some nations, application rates and prices on fertilizer may be the only input data available. If fertilizer is the major cash cost of the farmers, generating expected real gross margins over fertilizer costs may be sufficient. Even a step to generate expected real gross returns (i.e., lagged price times expected yield divided by an index of inflation) that involves no explicit costs may be preferable to lagged real price alone.

Costs of Production

Fortunately, many nations have been generating enterprise cost data over a sufficient number of years to be useful for time series analysis of supply. In the U.S., the Agriculture and Consumer Protection Act of 1973 and subsequent legislation mandated that the USDA annually estimate costs of producing wheat, feed grains, cotton, milk, rice, peanuts, sugarbeets, sugarcane, and tobacco (USDA, ERS, ECIFS 12-3, 1994).

Costs of production on most crops for the U.S. as a whole and selected regions date back to 1975; sugarbeet and sugarcane costs commenced in 1981. Costs of production on livestock have been expanded to include not only milk, but also cow-calf operations, cattle feeding, farrow-to-finish swine operations, feeder pig production, feeder pig finishing, and sheep production (USDA, ERS, ECIFS 12-3, 1994). Data for these enterprises have been published for all sizes of operations beginning in 1972. In recent years, costs of livestock production have been tabulated for selected regions of the nation and by size of operation.

The USDA costs of production reflect actual levels of input use, production practices, yields, and prices as measured by surveys of producers and suppliers. These costs include estimates of both cash expenditures and non-cash costs. Cash expenditures are incurred when factors of production are purchased or rented. Non-cash costs occur when factors are owned. Owned factors are priced at their opportunity costs (what they would earn in the closest alternative employment). Cash expenditures are divided into variable and fixed.

For supply models geared to forecasting ahead about one to five years, calculation of gross margins over *variable* cash costs should be sufficient. Fixed costs, both cash and non-cash, could also be incorporated, but would not be relevant to farmers' decisions on output for a relatively short-term planning horizon.

Cost of production data are always suspect because of the wide variation from farm to farm or firm to firm. The variation, however, tends to be more in the fixed costs than the variable costs. This is another reason why expected real gross margins over *variable* costs may be a preferred formulation for expected profits. Also, such data are more generally available or can be calculated.

In nations where official cost of production data are not available, techniques can be used to generate such a time series. One approach is to locate farm management handbooks published regularly with suggested costs for partial budgeting analysis. For state analysis in the U.S., land grant institutions publish farm account data on a regular basis. In Michigan, the Department of Agricultural Economics publishes annual crop and livestock cost estimates on nearly 100 enterprises (Nott et al., 1992).

In some nations or states, cost of production estimates by enterprise may not be available annually. Analysts still have options to generate yearly time series data through interpolation. Data points can be constructed for each year by assuming some monotonic transition process between sporadic cost of production estimates. Such a database precludes a detailed analysis of year-to-year variation in input application, but can still simulate a reasonable secular cost structure for an enterprise, valuable for estimating producers' response to profit expectations.

Gross Margin on Corn

Illustrative of how a time series supply analysis can be constructed with gross margins is the procedure followed with AGMOD on corn (Ferris, "A Description of 'AGMOD' . . . ," 1989). AGMOD, an econometric model of U.S. agriculture, is described in Chapter 8.

The USDA's estimate for the national average cost of production on corn for 1992 was as shown in Table 6-3 (USDA, ERS, ECIFS, 12-3, 1994). Such information provides the modeler with guidelines on which cost areas should receive the most attention. Most important variable cash costs are seed, fertilizer, chemicals, and fuels, lubrication, and electricity. For long-run projections, attention to cash fixed costs, capital replacement, land costs, and unpaid labor may be required.

To forecast costs of production, variable cash costs were divided into: (1) seed, (2) energy-related inputs, and (3) other. This classification was based on the presumption that prices on these inputs, while correlated, will change at different rates. Seed corn costs per acre were made a function of: (1) lagged farm corn prices, (2) the general price level (proxy for costs for processing seed corn), and (3) time (proxy for improved technology in producing seed corn). As expected, the signs on (1) and (2) were positive, and on (3), were negative.

A collection of the direct cost variables related to energy prices included fertilizer and lime, chemicals, and fuels, lubrication, and electricity. This combination of costs was regressed against the Producer Price Index on Fuels and Related Products and Power and

TABLE 6-3 COST OF PRODUCTION ON CORN, U.S., 1992[a]

Cash		Economic (Full Ownership)	
Item	*$/Acre*	*Item*	*$/Acre*
Variable		*Total*	
Seed	22.10	Variable cash expense	139.52
Fertilizer, lime	43.16	General farm overhead	10.58
Chemicals	23.46	Taxes and insurance	18.41
Custom operations	9.54	Capital replacement	30.19
Fuel, lubrication and electricity	18.29	Operating capital	2.49
Repairs	14.83	Other non-land capital	11.86
Hired labor	7.74	Land	64.29
Miscellaneous	.40	Unpaid labor	24.99
Total	139.52	Total:	302.33
Fixed			
General farm overhead	10.58		
Taxes and insurance	18.41		
Interest	14.74		
Total	43.73		
Total Cash Expenses	183.25		

[a]*Source:* USDA, ERS, ECIFS 12-3, 1994.

CPI of the Bureau of Labor Statistics, U.S. Department of Labor. Other variable cash costs were regressed on CPI. This combination of OLS equations provided the means to generate total cash variable costs, labeled VCCN.

The generation of expected real gross margins per acre from corn was a very simple identity:

$$\text{EGMCND} = (\text{FPCN}(-1) * \text{EYCN} - \text{VCCN}) / \text{CPI}$$

where: FPCN = Farm price of corn

EYCN = Trend yield in corn per acre

VCCN = Variable cash cost per acre

CPI = Consumer Price Index

(−1) = One-year lag

This formulation was based on the assumption that the farmer did not participate in the Feed Grain Program. However, most of the U.S. corn land has been in the program in years prior to 1996, rendering this formulation as insufficient to measure corn farmers' response to expected profits.

Modeling the expectations of a potential participant in the program was more of a challenge. However, the procedure was similar to budgets developed in educational programs with farmers to help them decide whether to participate. In past Feed Grain

Programs, farmers were assigned a corn base derived from historical plantings and often had to remove part of that base from production to be in compliance. The variable for expected profits was calculated in terms of a "base acre" as follows:

$$EGMPCN = (1\text{-}DRCN) * EMCN + [(1\text{-}DRCN\text{-}.15) * (TIME > 1990)] * [(TPCN\text{-}FPCN(\text{-}1)) * (FPCN(\text{-}1) >= LRCN) * (FPCN(\text{-}1) < TPCN) + (TPCN - LRCN) * (FPCN(\text{-}1) < LRCN)] * PYCN - VCDA * DRCN$$

$$EGMPCND = EGMPCN / CPI$$

$$EMCN = EFPCN * EYCN - VCCN$$

$$EFPCN = (FPCN(\text{-}1) >= LRCN) * FPCN(\text{-}1) + (FPCN(\text{-}1) < LRCN) * LRCN$$

where: DRCN = Percent of base that must be set aside

TPCN = Target price on corn in $/bu

LRCN = Government loan rate on corn in $/bu

PYCN = Program yield assigned to the farmer in bu/A (based on farm history)

VCDA = Cost for maintaining cover crop on set-aside acreage in $/A

While this formulation appears complex, it is simply a series of logical statements simulating expected gross margins over variable costs *per base acre* in the Feed Grain Program. The equations state that expected real profit equals the sum of:

1 Expected gross margins over variable costs on the proportion of the base that can be planted. Expected price of corn is the higher of last year's price or this year's government loan rate.
2 An expected deficiency payment that is (1) the difference between the lagged farm price and the target price if the lagged farm price is equal to or above the government loan rate *or* (2) the difference between the target price and the loan rate if the lagged farm price is below the loan rate. This payment is on the allowable plantings except that after 1990, 15 percent of the base was removed from eligibility for payment (in addition to the set-aside requirement). The deficiency payment is calculated on an assigned program yield rather than the actual yield.

Deducted from the sum of (1) and (2) is a cost for maintaining cover crops on the set-aside acres. The nominal values for expected profit are then deflated by the CPI. Other elements in the farm program were incorporated in this formulation, but not shown here for purposes of exposition.

While this formulation provided a means to capture expected gross margins for participating in the Feed Grain Program prior to 1996, the farm program applying to the 1996–2002 crop years invalidated this approach. Under the "Federal Agricultural Improvement and Reform Act" of 1996, called FAIR, farmers had much more flexibility in how they allocated their plantings to major crops. They had no restrictions except some limitations apply to planting fruits and vegetables on program acres. Participants received direct payments on feed grain, wheat, cotton, and rice at fixed rates in 1996–2002, regardless of market prices. Under previous programs, the deficiency payments declined as prices increased and were eliminated entirely if U.S. market prices exceeded the target prices.

In FAIR, there were no target prices or deficiency payments based on target prices. There were no set-asides. With such a dramatic change in the farm program, how would an analyst construct the variable, EGMPCN? One could simply bracket the equation previously described and multiply by (TIME < 1996), then adding an equation representing the new farm bill, i.e.:

$$\begin{aligned}
\text{EGMPCN} = {} & (\text{Previous equation}) * (\text{TIME} < 1996) \\
& + (\text{EMCN} + (\text{APR96} * (\text{TIME} = 1996) \\
& + \text{APR97} * (\text{TIME} = 1997) + \text{APR98} * (\text{TIME} = 1998) \\
& + \text{APR99} * (\text{TIME} = 1999) * \text{APR00} * (\text{TIME} = 2000) \\
& + \text{APR01} * (\text{TIME} = 2001) + \text{APR02} * (\text{TIME} = 2002)) \\
& * \ \text{PYCN}) * (\text{TIME} => 1996) * (\text{TIME} =< 2002)
\end{aligned}$$

where: APRi = Annual Payment Rate per bushel as established by FAIR in year i.

Again, the advantage of using gross margins is that changing parameters of agricultural legislation can be incorporated directly. Other considerations might have been explored in the total analysis since, for example, FAIR entailed a different risk component than previous farm programs. A dummy variable for the period beginning with 1996 could test for a supply shift.

The purpose of this example is to illustrate the process of constructing a comprehensive variable that incorporates several other variables. Each of the component variables contributes in a way that is logical and in line with its relative importance.

Pros and Cons

Application of gross margins in time series analysis does involve compromises. Analysts will have to weigh the pros and cons. Gross margins:

PRO:

1 Facilitate the introduction of a priori information.
***2** Facilitate the introduction of more independent variables by collapsing profit-related variables into one.

*Generally relates to use of product price:input price ratios as well as gross margins.

3 Simulate a form of profit variable familiar to farmers, i.e., partial budgeting, enterprise costs, farm program analysis.

***4** Reduce problem of multicollinearity; conserve degrees of freedom.

5 Provide a diagnostic tool for checking long-range projections. Consistency in real gross margins in the past provides a guideline to test the reasonableness of projected real gross margins and their components.

6 Provide the means to monitor changing profit levels for an enterprise. In models, this variable would be formulated as *realized* gross margin rather than *expected* gross margin.

CON:

***1** Force all components into a set response pattern proportionate to how they are established in the gross margin. Expectations and adjustment lags of prices on the product and its inputs cannot be differentiated. For example, in gross margins on hogs, differences in how farmers respond to hog prices versus corn prices cannot be refined.

2 Require more information. Cost data may not be available.

***3** Often result in lower adjusted coefficients of determination ($\bar{R}^2$) for supply equations than formulations with separate statistical measurements on the component variables.

INTEGRATED SUPPLY MODELS

In this particular example, how a supply equation on corn could be formulated is not obvious. The more attractive the government program, the higher the level of participation and the lower the planted acreage, especially if set-asides were required. An approach that has general application to modeling crop acreages is to generate an expected profit variable that is a composite of all crops that compete with each other, i.e., corn, other feed grains, soybeans, and wheat in this example. This "expected profit per acre on crops" would be the key variable to explain the entire area devoted to these crops *including the required set-aside acreage.*

A second set of equations allocates the projected total crop area to the competing crops and the set-asides. On corn, measurement of the attractiveness of participation in the government program generates the base area in the program. The set-aside requirements determine the planted acreage on participating farms. Of course, beginning with 1996, no set-asides would be required. On non-participating farms, plantings are allocated more on market price and yield expectations between corn and competing crops.

As would be anticipated, the equation generating the aggregate crop acreage would involve relatively long lags and would be constructed to accommodate this assumption. The shifts in planted acres within this aggregate, however, would happen in a much shorter time frame. The advantages of this two-step procedure in deriving supply equations are:

*Generally relates to use of product price:input price ratios as well as gross margins.

(1) separate lag functions can be measured and (2) bounds can be directly applied on total acreage. In this latter case, projections of total acreage can be monitored and adjusted to fit a priori estimates of available cropland.

SUMMARY

Analysts need to identify key variables that reflect farmers' price expectations when designing supply equations. Because production often incorporates influences beyond farmers' control—primarily weather—other variables such as planted acres are appropriate dependent variables. Production becomes a function of other equations linking to the primary supply equation.

How farmers form expectations and adjust output to them are normally measured by distributed lags. The changing structure of agriculture may change this response, possibly in the direction of "rational expectations." Also, changing risk levels in agriculture may modify supply elasticities.

To adequately measure the complex supply response process, a strong recommendation is to convert prices, costs, technical conversion rates, government program parameters, etc., into gross margin variables. Not only does this conserve on degrees of freedom and reduce multicollinearity problems, but allows the analyst to incorporate more relevant a priori information.

QUESTIONS FOR STUDY

1. Why are expectations of particular importance in supply analysis?
2. How would you formulate a supply equation for some annual crop familiar to you, such as potatoes, onions, broccoli, etc.?
3. Develop a complete set of equations that would allow you to forecast production of the crop you chose in question 2. If possible, locate the relevant data and estimate your supply model.
4. What distinguishes polynomial distributed lags from geometric distributed lags?
5. How would you introduce "rational expectations" into the supply model you developed for question 2?
6. How would you introduce risk into the supply model you developed for question 2?
7. Explain why implementation of gross margins in supply equations is a preferred approach. What are the weaknesses?
8. Suppose you have substantial research data from a field trial on fertilizer response on a major crop. How would you incorporate such information in a supply equation?
9. Price elasticities of supply can be calculated from the coefficient(s) on the gross margin variable (and the lagged dependent variable in a geometric type lag). Explain how this could be accomplished.
10. Supply elasticity for the total area planted to major crops is less than area planted to a given major crop. Explain.

SECTION TWO

GENERATION OF ECONOMETRIC/ SIMULATION MODELS

7

RECURSIVE AND SIMULTANEOUS SUPPLY-DEMAND MODELS

POINTS:

1 How supply and demand interact in generating prices.
2 Reasons why recursive models are prevalent in agriculture.
3 The "Cobweb Theorem" and market stability.
4 Dynamic properties of second-order difference equations.
5 Why livestock production and prices tend to be cyclical.
6 The identification problem in simultaneous models.
7 Converting simultaneous models to reduced form to measure structural parameters.
8 Application of two-stage least squares.

In the preceding chapters, the focus was on estimating separate demand-and-supply relationships. The following chapters deal with the interaction of demand and supply in establishing prices.

Whether price is determined in a relatively free market by the interaction of supply and demand or administratively determined, its role is key in guiding production and in allocating quantities to consumers. In a free market with attributes of "perfect competition" (i.e., many buyers and sellers, complete knowledge, homogenous product, and no price discrimination), a price at any given point in time could be considered at equilibrium. The amount supplied to the market just equals the amount purchased for domestic consumption, storage, or export—brought into balance by price.

If an administratively established price is too high, the government may have to accumulate the surplus. If the price is too low, late shoppers will be left out.

If we relax the "complete knowledge" assumption of perfect competition, a process known as price discovery emerges. Price at any given time will not likely be at a stable equilibrium while market participants search for balance. If the price is too high, unwanted inventories accumulate. If the price is too low, stocks are depleted and sales are missed.

The biological lag in agriculture, coupled with the unpredictable impacts of weather, disease, and pests, often keeps amounts supplied out of line with farmer's intentions. Price in any given period usually is not in equilibrium in the context of several periods. Reaction to this disequilibrium occurs in the subsequent period(s).

RECURSIVE MODELS

The prevalence of the biological lag in agriculture suggests that recursive econometric models are most appropriate. Following are some simple examples of recursive models with price dependent demand, illustrating the dynamics of such models.

Price Dependent Demand

(1) Demand $P = a_0 + a_1 Q$

(2) Supply $Q = b_0 + b_1 P(-1)$

Assuming the sign on a_1 is negative and on b_1 is positive,

If $|a_1 b_1| < 1$, the model is convergent.

If $|a_1 b_1| > 1$, the model is divergent, explosive.

If $|a_1 b_1| = 1$, the model will display oscillations of equal amplitude.

Because of the patterns generated on a price-quantity graph, this model is a representation of the classical "Cobweb Theorem" which helps to explain why cycles persist in agricultural production and prices. This theorem requires that:

1 Producers' price expectations are based on past prices.
2 A lag exists between the time production plans are made and output is realized.
3 Prices are primarily determined by the amount produced.

Clearly, much of agriculture fits those requirements with some reservations as expressed in the section on "Rational Expectations" in Chapter 6.

Consider the following model:

(3) $PA = 50 - 3 * QA$

(4) $QA = 8 + .2 * PA(-1)$

In this case, a_1 = -3 and b_1 = .2 and |-3 * .2| = .6 and is < 1. Therefore, the model is convergent.

The process can be followed in Table 7-1 and Figure 7-1. Starting from a disequilibrium in Period 1, with PA at 10 and QA at 13.33 (P_1, Q_1 in Figure 7-1), farmers would respond according to the supply curve by reducing production to 10 units in Period 2 which would result in a price of 20 as described by the demand curve (P_2 Q_2 in Figure 7-1). This price (P_2) being attractive, farmers would increase production in Period 3 to 12 units as indicated by the supply curve—an amount that would fetch a price of 14 as indicated by the demand curve (P_3, Q_3 in Figure 7-1).

Note that the expansion in Period 3 was to a level less than the original output in Period 1, and prices did not drop so low as in Period 1. The process would continue in subsequent periods with damped oscillation in both price and quantity. Prices would converge to 16.25 and quantity would converge to 11.25.

Another simple Cobweb model is:

(5) PB = 50 – 3 * QB

(6) QB = 8 + .4 * PB(-1)

In this case, a_1 = -3 and b_1 = .4 and |-3*.4| = 1.2 and is > 1. This means the model is divergent as illustrated in Figure 7-2 and calculated over 10 periods in Table 7-1.

Starting at Period 1 where the price is 10 units and the quantity is 13.3 (P_1, Q_1), producers respond by cutting back to 12 units in Period 2, which brings a price of 14 (P_2, Q_2). This was followed by an expansion to 13.6 in Period 3 resulting in a price drop to 9.2 (P_3, Q_3). As can be traced in Figure 7-2 and Table 7-1, the pattern is for ever-increasing amplitude in the oscillations for price and quantity.

The stable Cobweb model is represented by the following equations:

TABLE 7-1 TABULATION OF THE SEQUENCE OF PRICES AND QUANTITIES IN CONVERGENT, DIVERGENT AND STABLE COBWEB MODELS

	Convergent		Divergent		Stable	
Period	Price (PA)	Quantity (QA)	Price (PB)	Quantity (QB)	Price (PC)	Quantity (QC)
1	10.00	13.33	10.00	13.33	10.00	14.00
2	20.00	10.00	14.00	12.00	16.00	11.00
3	14.00	12.00	9.20	13.60	10.00	14.00
4	17.60	10.80	14.96	11.68	16.00	11.00
5	15.44	11.52	8.05	13.98	10.00	14.00
6	16.74	11.09	16.34	11.22	16.00	11.00
7	15.96	11.35	6.39	14.54	10.00	14.00
8	16.42	11.19	18.33	10.56	16.00	11.00
9	16.15	11.28	4.00	15.33	10.00	14.00
10	16.31	11.23	21.20	9.60	16.00	11.00

FIGURE 7-1 Convergent cobweb model.

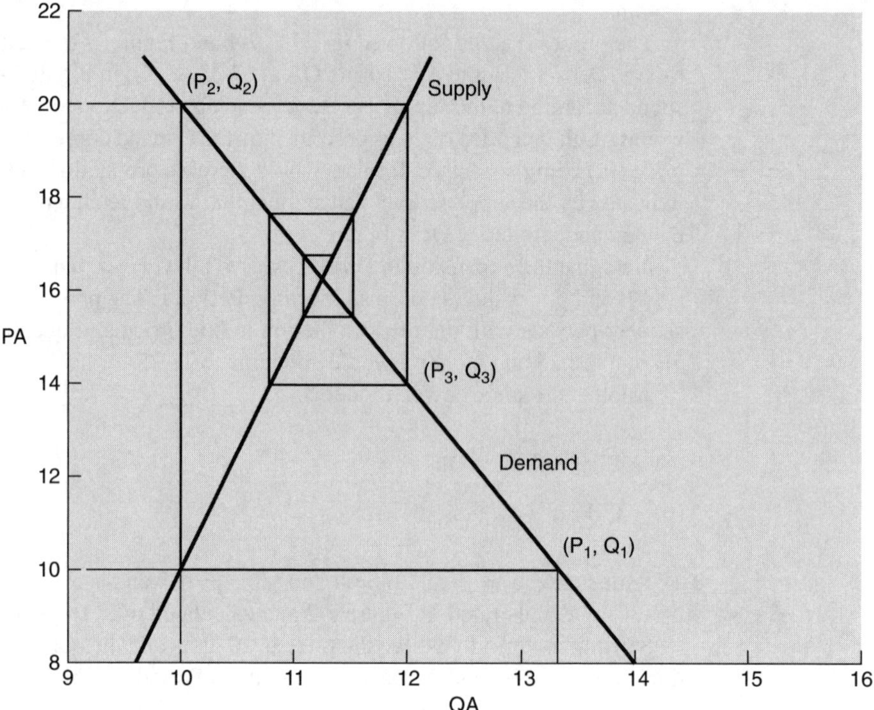

(7) PC = 38 - 2 * QC

(8) QC = 6 + .5 * PC(-1)

With a_1 = -2 and b_1 = .5, |-2*.5| = 1, which is the condition for oscillations with constant or stable amplitudes. This is illustrated in Figure 7-3 and tabulated for 10 periods in Table 7-1. Prices vary from 10 to 16 and quantities from 14 to 11 units.

These cases, while quite simplistic, can help students understand more complex dynamics of commodity markets. Certainly, the credibility of the divergent or explosive cases can be called into question. This case draws attention to the assumption of linearity in the supply-and-demand relationships postulated in these examples. While divergent cases may exist in the neighborhood of the equilibrium, non-linearity in supply-and-demand curves at extreme points will constrain oscillations in price and quantity.

This more-likely situation is illustrated in Figure 7-4. In the region around the equilibrium, the slopes of the supply-and-demand lines are the same as in the divergent case of Figure 7-2. However, outside that range, the demand curve was assumed to be more elastic than in Figure 7-2, and became perfectly elastic around PB = 9. Note that the expanding oscillations reached a limit beginning in the fifth period.

FIGURE 7-2 Divergent cobweb model.

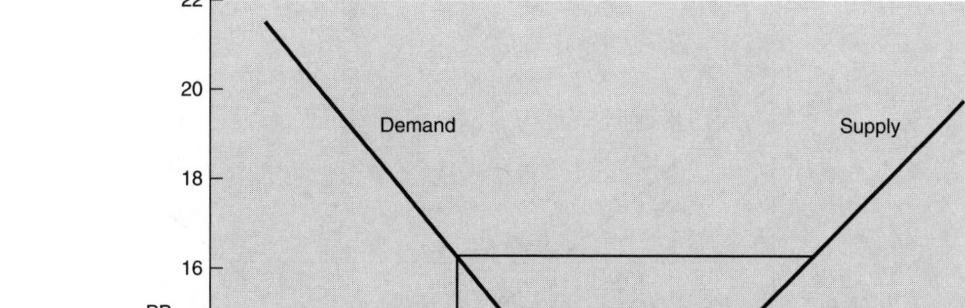

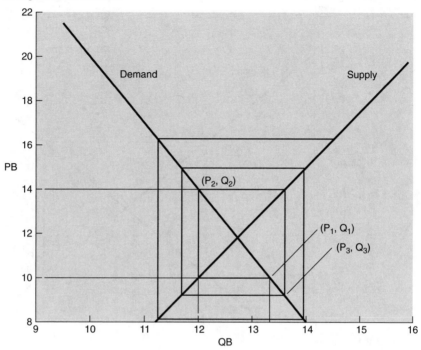

The message to modelers is that the assumption of linearity is convenient, but may not be appropriate in certain cases and particularly at extremes in supply and demand.

Quantity Dependent Demand

Similar procedures can be developed for evaluating the stability characteristics of other models. A general procedure is to convert recursive models into difference equations. Consider the following model in which quantity is dependent in a demand equation.

(9) Demand $QD = a_0 + a_1\ P$

(10) Supply $QS = b_0 + b_1\ P(-1)$

If stocks, exports, and imports are negligible,

$$QD = QS$$

$$a_0 + a_1\ P = b_0 + b_1\ P(-1)$$

$$a_1\ P = - a_0 + b_0 + b_1\ P(-1)$$

$$P = 1/a_1\ (- a_0 + b_0) + (b_1/a_1)\ P(-1)$$

FIGURE 7-3 Stable cobweb model.

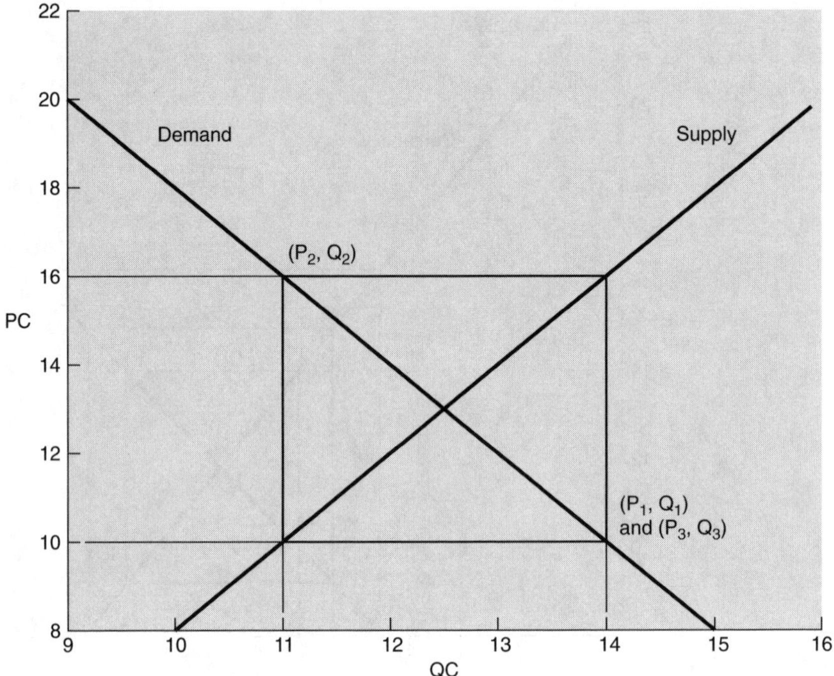

If $|b_1| < |a_1|$, the model is convergent.

If $|b_1| > |a_1|$, the model is divergent, explosive.

If $|b_1| = |a_1|$, the model will display oscillations of equal amplitude.

The key to whether a model is convergent, divergent, or exhibiting oscillations of equal amplitude depends on whether the coefficient on the lagged price variable is less than, greater than, or equal to "one" in the single equation on prices alone. This also holds true in the examples of models with price dependent in demand. Equations (1) and (2) can be converted into equations with price alone or quantity alone, i.e.,

$$\text{(11)} \quad P = a_0 + a_1\,(b_0 + b_1\,P(-1))$$
$$= (a_0 + a_1\,b_0) + a_1\,b_1\,P(-1)$$

$$\text{(12)} \quad Q = b_0 + b_1\,(a_0 + a_1\,Q(-1))$$
$$= (b_0 + b_1\,a_0) + b_1\,a_1\,Q(-1)$$

The evaluation for the stability of the model depends on the product of a_1 and b_1 in either equation (11) or (12). Assuming that a_1 is negative and b_1 is positive, the model will generate oscillating patterns unless the initial conditions happen to represent the

FIGURE 7-4 Divergent cobweb model stable at extremes.

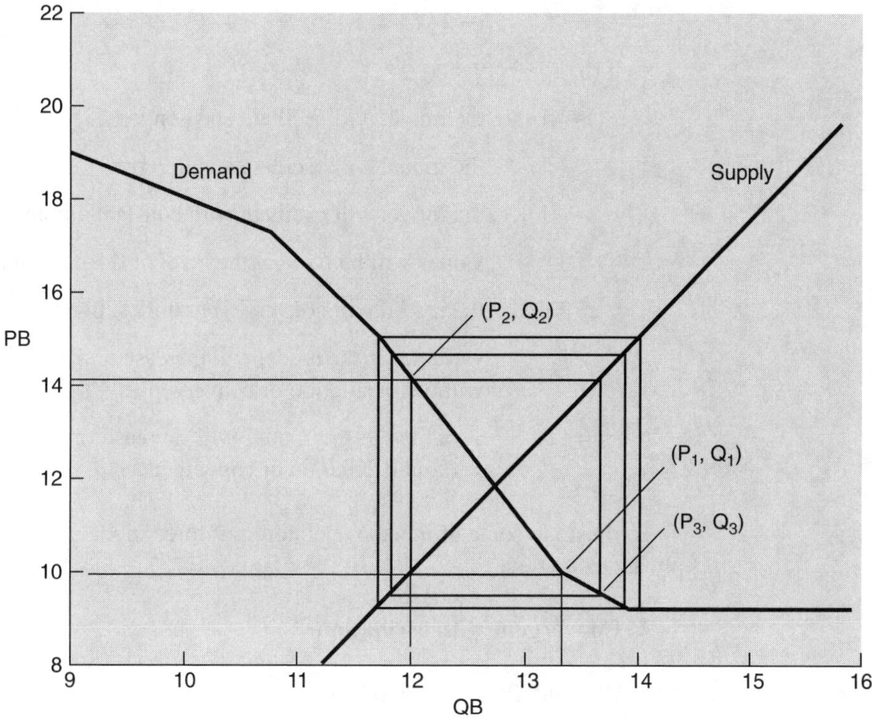

equilibrium. Note that all of the examples illustrated in Figures 7-1 through 7-4 and Table 7-1 started at disequilibrium positions. As with the example with quantity dependent in demand, the model is convergent if $|a_1 b_1| < 1$, divergent if $|a_1 b_1| > 1$, and with stable oscillations if $|a_1 b_1| = 1$.

Geometric Lags

The stability of models with geometric lag structures can be evaluated with similar procedures. Consider the following two-equation model with a geometric lag in supply,

(13) Demand $P = a_0 + a_1 Q$

(14) Supply $Q = b_0 + b_1 P(-1) + b_2 Q(-1)$

The model can be expressed either as a univariate equation in P or Q. Converted to Q,

$$Q = b_0 + b_1 (a_0 + a_1 Q(-1)) + b_2 Q(-1)$$

$$Q = (b_0 + b_1 a_0) + b_1 a_1 Q(-1) + b_2 Q(-1)$$

$$Q = (b_0 + b_1 a_0) + (b_1 a_1 + b_2) Q(-1)$$

Since $(b_1\ a_1 + b_2)$ can be either positive or negative, an additional set of conditions apply.

If $(b_1\ a_1 + b_2)$:

$> -1 < 0$, the model will oscillate and converge.

< -1, the model will oscillate and diverge.

$= -1$, the model will oscillate with constant amplitude.

$= 0$, values will be fixed at the level of the constant.

$> 0 < 1$, the model will converge, but not oscillate.

> 1, variables in the model will increase or decrease at an accelerated rate without oscillation or convergence.

$= 1$, variables in the model will increase or decrease at a constant rate without oscillation or convergence.

To illustrate some of the above conditions, three models with geometric lags in supply are examined:

A. Convergent with oscillation

Demand $PA = 50 - 2\ QA$

Supply $QA = 7 + .4\ PA(-1) + .2\ QA(-1)$

$QA = 7 + .4\ (50 - 2\ QA(-1)) + .2\ QA(-1)$

$QA = 7 + 20 - .8\ QA(-1) + .2\ QA(-1)$

$QA = 27 - .6\ QA(-1)$

B. Divergent with oscillation

Demand $PB = 50 - 2\ QB$

Supply $QB = 7 + .6\ PB(-1) + .1\ QB(-1)$

$QB = 7 + .6\ (50 - 2\ QB(-1)) + .1\ QB(-1)$

$QB = 7 + 30 - 1.2\ QB(-1) + .1\ QB(-1)$

$QB = 37 - 1.1\ QB(-1)$

C. Convergent without oscillation

Demand $PC = 50 - 2\ QC$

Supply $QC = -10 + .3\ PC(-1) + 1.1\ QC(-1)$

$$QC = -10 + .3\,(50 - 2\,QC(-1)) + 1.1\,QC(-1)$$

$$QC = -10 + 15 - .6\,QC(-1) + 1.1\,QC(-1)$$

$$QC = 5 + .5\,QC(-1)$$

As can be noted, the coefficients on QA(−1), QB(−1), and QC(−1) in the final derivation of the equations in quantity alone match the classification for the dynamics of the models. The paths over 10 time periods for quantities in the three models are graphed in Figure 7-5. The initial conditions for the models were set at the same level for periods 1 and 2.

More Complex Lag Structures

The indicated rules for stability are convenient for simple lag models involving only one past period or geometric lag. However, rules for more complex lag structures such as encompassed in polynomial distributed lags cannot so easily be evaluated. The procedures outlined thus far have related to a set of models that can be reduced to "first-order difference equations." To determine the dynamic characteristics of "second-order" or higher difference equations, analysts need more advanced tools.

In agricultural supply equations, appropriate lags may encompass several years. In applying polynomial distributed lag procedures, typically three or more past years may be relevant. Even evaluating a second-order difference equation requires alternative

FIGURE 7-5 Dynamics of the quantity variable over 10 periods generated by three models with geometric lags in supply.

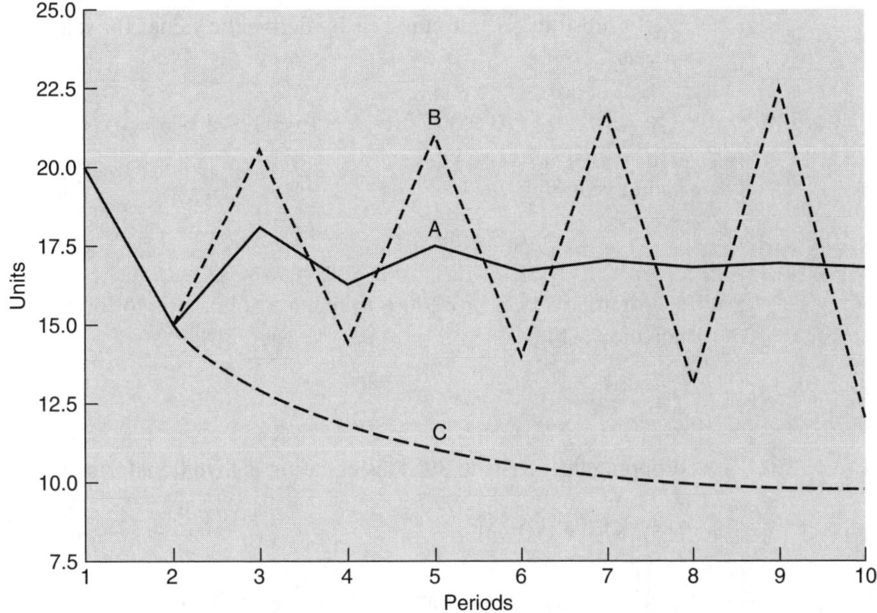

approaches. An example with a second-order difference equation will serve to illustrate the process for higher order difference equations. For detailed explanations, refer to W.J. Baumol's *Economic Dynamics* (Baumol, 1970).

Difference equations can be expressed as functions of the roots of "characteristic equations." For a second-order difference equation, the characteristic equation would be a quadratic. Conceptually, such representations are appropriate because of the cumulative effects of difference equations over time.

The procedure for a model with two period lags in the supply equation would be as follows:

Demand $PD = 50 - 2\ QD$

Supply $QD = 9 + .5\ PD(-1) + .1\ PD(-2)$

Formulating a single equation for quantity (QD)

$$QD = 9 + .5\ (50 - 2\ QD(-1)) + .10\ (50 - 2\ QD(-2))$$

$$QD = 9 + 25 - QD(-1) + 5 - .2\ QD(-2)$$

(15) $$QD = 39 - QD(-1) - .2\ QD(-2)$$

Assume that the initial values for QD in the first two years were as follows:

t=0 QD = 15

t=1 QD = 20

By substitution, one could easily derive the values for years 2, 3, 4, etc. For example, in year 2,

$$QD = 39 - 20 - .2 * 15 = 39 - 20 - 3 = 16$$

and in year 3,

$$QD = 39 - 16 - .2 * 20 = 39 - 16 - 4 = 19$$

Alternatively, a procedure to reach a solution is to formulate an approximation for equation (15),

$$x^t =- x^{t-1} - .2\ x^{t-2}$$

dropping the constant, 39. This equation is then transformed into a quadratic,

(16) $x^2 + x + .2 = 0$

The roots for a quadratic ($ax^2 + b\ x - c = 0$) are:

$$x1,\ x2 = \frac{-\ b \pm \sqrt{b^2 - 4ac}}{2a}$$

Applying this formula to equation (16):

$$x1 = \frac{-1 + \sqrt{1 - .8}}{2} = -.5 + .224 = -.276$$

$$x2 = \frac{-1 - \sqrt{1 - .8}}{2} = -.5 - .224 = -.724$$

To compute the representative equation using the roots, the format is as follows:

(17) $QD = a\,(x_1)^t + b\,(x_2)^t + z$

where: a and b are coefficients on the respective roots raised to the t power and z is a constant for the equation.

The term z must provide the means to reproduce the constant in equation (15) when t = 0 in the quadratic (equation 16), and is computed as follows:

$$z + z + .2\,z = 39$$

$$2.2\,z = 39$$

$$z = 17.73$$

To solve for a and b, set equation (17) equal to the initial values for QD in $t = 0$ and t = 1, i.e.,

$$QD(0) = a\,(-.276)^0 + b\,(-.724)^0 + 17.73 = 15$$

$$QD(1) = a\,(-.276)^1 + b\,(-.724)^1 + 17.73 = 20$$

which is:

(18) $QD(0) = a + b + 17.73 = 15$

(19) $QD(1) = -\ .276\,a - .724\,b + 17.73 = 20$

Solving equations (18) and (19) for a and b,

$$a = .66$$

$$b = -\ 3.39$$

The solution, then, is,

(20) $QD(t) = 17.73 + .66\,(-.276)^t - 3.39\,(-.724)^t$

The result can be verified,

$QD(0) = 17.73 + .66 - 3.39 = 15$

$QD(1) = 17.73 - .18 + 2.45 = 20$

$QD(2) = 17.73 + .05 - 1.78 = 16$

$QD(3) = 17.73 - .01 + 1.29 = 19$

etc.

The value of solving difference equations in this manner is that the roots provide an indication of the stability characteristics of the system. For second-order difference equations, the rules are as follows:

Real roots, both positive (or zero)

Both < 1:	The model will converge, but not oscillate.
One $= 1$, other < 0:	The model will converge, but not oscillate.
Either > 1:	The model will diverge, but not oscillate.

Real roots, both negative

Both > -1 and < 0:	The model will oscillate and converge.
One $= -1$, other > -1 and < 0	The model will oscillate and converge to a lower amplitude.
Either < -1:	The model will oscillate and diverge.

One root positive and the other negative

The larger root (in absolute value),

> 0 and < 1:	The model will converge and not oscillate.
$= 1$:	The model will converge and not oscillate.
> 1:	The model will diverge, but not oscillate.
> -1 and < 0:	The model will oscillate and converge.
$= -1$	The model will oscillate and converge to a lower amplitude.
< -1:	The model will oscillate and diverge.

Another set of solutions to difference equations involves complex roots. This is the result if $b^2 < 4\,ac$. Such a solution points to oscillation. Baumol provides guidelines for evaluating the stability in such cases (Baumol, 1970). If the real part is labeled f and the imaginary component g i, i.e., f + g i and f – g i, the rules are as follows:

If $\sqrt{f^2 + g^2} > 1$, the model diverges.

If $\sqrt{f^2 + g^2} = 1$, the model exhibits oscillations with constant maximum amplitude.

If $\sqrt{f^2 + g^2} < 1$, the model converges.

To derive solutions for third-order difference equations, roots of cubic equations must be identified. Higher order systems require even more advanced mathematical tools. In any case, stability and convergence would be indicated if there is no root in the characteristic equation, real or complex, with an absolute value greater than or equal to one.

Observation of Large Models

Because lag structures in agricultural modeling often transcend three or more years, and also because models are not easily reduced to univariate equations, these procedures for identifying stability may not be very practical. Also, even if the stability characteristics could be evaluated, lack of stability may not be a particular problem for the time period being forecast. Add the increased complexities from non-linearity in models, and you may have a nearly impossible task for mathematical analysis.

A much easier approach is to simply solve the model over the historical data period and generate projections. By observation, the modeler can determine whether the model is tracking well and reproducing patterns consistent with the past. Software with solution algorithms such as Gauss-Seidel provide a convenient procedure for such diagnostics. (See Chapter 8.)

In all of the cases described, the constants in the structural equations determine the level of the solutions, but not the stability characteristics of the models. Similarly, if exogenous variables were added to the structural equations, those variables would modify the equilibrium position of the endogenous variables, but would not affect the model's stability in the long run. Exogenous variables are those that values are established externally, and the endogenous variables are those that values are determined within the system itself. The exogenous variables will affect the time path of the endogenous variables, but will not, in turn, be affected by the endogenous variables.

However, the introduction of repeated external "shocks" can keep a convergent model from reaching an equilibrium. For any given set of values for exogenous variables, long-run equilibrium levels could be established for the endogenous variables in a convergent model. If random shocks are introduced, the endogenous variables may tend to move toward an equilibrium, but would not converge to it.

Why Cycles Persist in Agriculture

Shocks from the effects of weather, pests, plant and animal diseases, war, embargoes, farm programs, etc., are quite common in agriculture. Such developments tend to keep even convergent systems in oscillation—popularly known as cycles. The impact of weather on crop yields is one of the most destabilizing forces in agriculture. While long-run weather forecasting is not reliable, probability distributions on weather can be introduced into models. This would render equilibrium solutions to models as probability statements. Such modeling procedures are discussed in Chapter 10.

The length of the cycles generated by recursive models in agriculture depends on the biological process. On annual crops, the minimum length would be two years. The actual length would depend on the lag between realized prices or profits and changes in expectations of those prices or profits. Tree fruits would exhibit very long cycles. In livestock, response in broilers is a matter of quarters of a year; on eggs, the minimum cycle is about two years; on hogs, about four years; and on beef cattle, the length could span 10 to 15 years. Biological lags in several sectors of the livestock industry are diagrammed in Figure 7-6.

The dynamics of expansions and contractions in livestock numbers contribute to the persistence of cycles. To expand the cattle herd, cows and heifers are held back from slaughter for breeding purposes. This reduces beef production and enhances cattle prices. Higher cattle prices, in turn, encourage further expansion, more withholding of heifers, reduced slaughter, and even higher prices. The expansion proceeds well beyond the level warranted by consumer demand, and as increased beef supplies finally reach the market, cattle prices fall to unprofitable levels.

As contraction gets underway, more cows and heifers than normal are sold for slaughter, further depressing prices. This triggers further liquidation and numbers of cattle on farms and ranches are trimmed excessively. The pattern of slaughter of breeding stock in the expansion and liquidation phases of the cattle cycle can be observed in Figure 7-7. Production of cow and bull beef is relatively low at the early stages of expansion in cow numbers and high at the beginning of liquidation.

Similar relationships are characteristic of hogs and other livestock enterprises. The retention and liquidation of breeding stock can be termed "positive feedback" in the dynamics of livestock cycles. A positive feedback contributes to instability in contrast to a "negative feedback" which provides a dampening effect. Eventually, prices and profits provide the needed negative feedback.

SIMULTANEOUS MODELS

Econometricians have given considerable attention to simultaneity in supply-demand interaction. This may have originated from efforts to model the macro economy and certain non-agricultural industries. Also, the lack of short-period data such as weekly or monthly statistics may have prompted efforts to deal with responses not captured by quarterly or annual data.

A basic model exhibiting simultaneity would be:

Demand $P = a_0 + a_1 Q + u$

Supply $Q = b_0 + b_1 P + v$

where: price (P) and quantity (Q) are in terms of the current time period and u and v are error terms for each equation

While the demand relationship is the same as assumed in recursive models discussed thus far, the supply equation postulates that current prices determine amounts supplied. The econometric problem this presents is called "identification," i.e., how to measure the parameters of demand and supply.

FIGURE 7-6 Biological lag in production of beef, pork, and chicken.

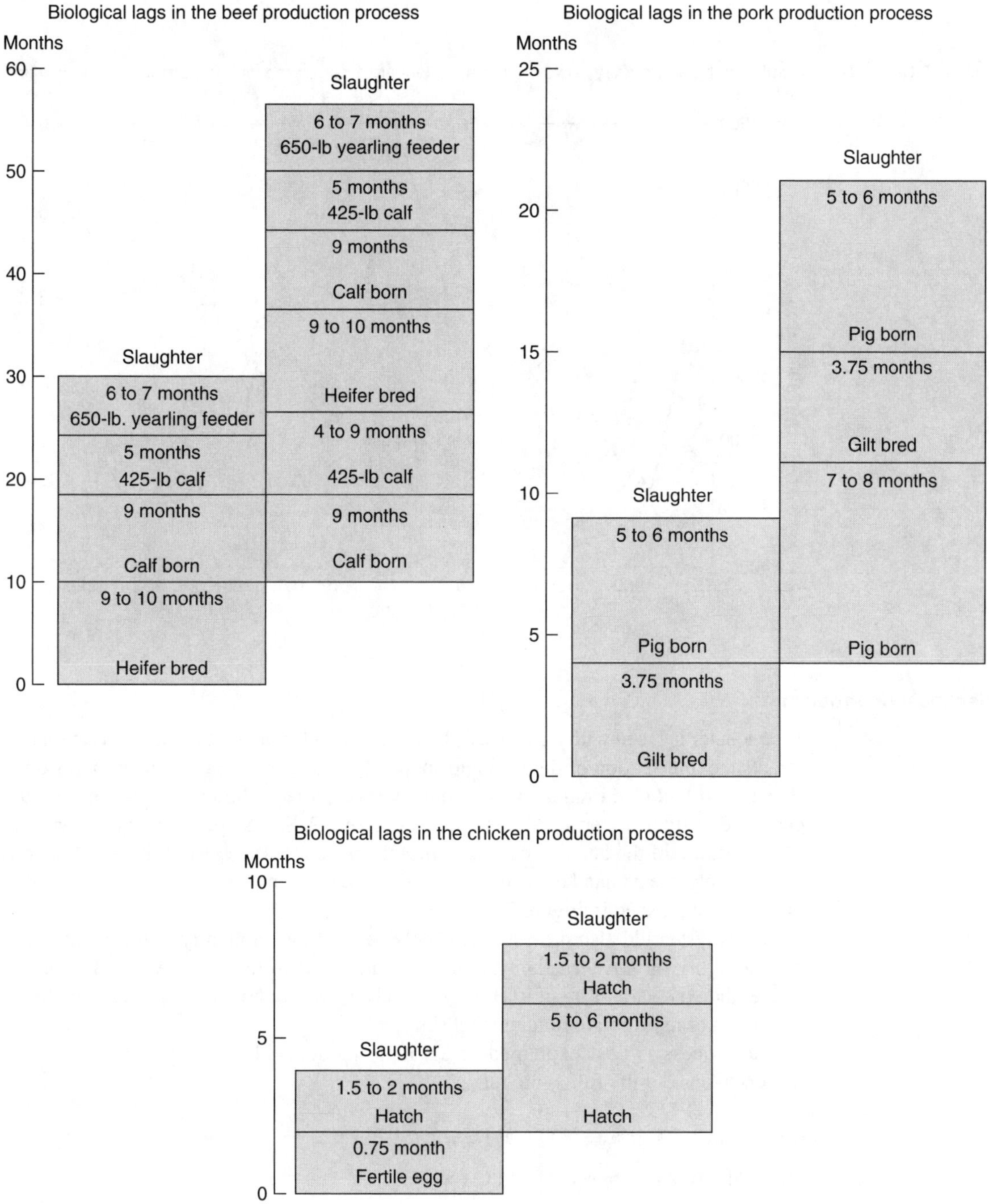

Biological lags in the beef production process
Months
60
50
40
30
20
10
0
Slaughter
6 to 7 months
650-lb yearling feeder
5 months
425-lb calf
9 months
Calf born
9 to 10 months
Heifer bred
4 to 9 months
425-lb calf
9 months
Calf born
Slaughter
6 to 7 months
650-lb. yearling feeder
5 months
425-lb calf
9 months
Calf born
9 to 10 months
Heifer bred
Biological lags in the pork production process
Months
25
20
15
10
5
0
Slaughter
5 to 6 months
Pig born
3.75 months
Gilt bred
7 to 8 months
Pig born
Slaughter
5 to 6 months
Pig born
3.75 months
Gilt bred
Biological lags in the chicken production process
Months
10
5
0
Slaughter
1.5 to 2 months
Hatch
5 to 6 months
Hatch
Slaughter
1.5 to 2 months
Hatch
0.75 month
Fertile egg

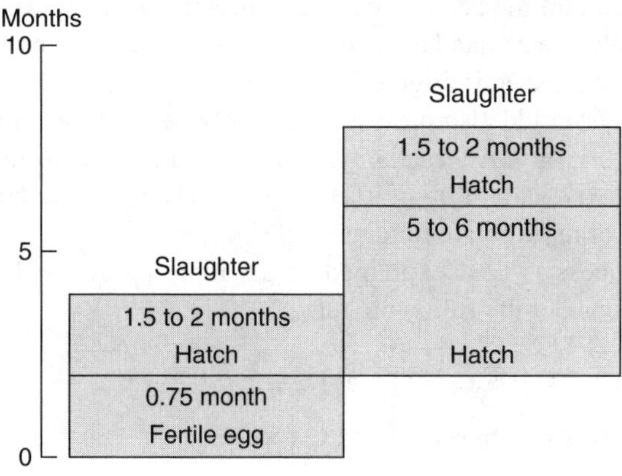

Source: Stillman, Richard, *A Quarterly Model of the Livestock Industry,* Technical Bulletin No. 1711, ERS, USDA, December 1985.

FIGURE 7-7 Number of beef and dairy cows on farms on January 1 compared with the production of cow and bull beef.

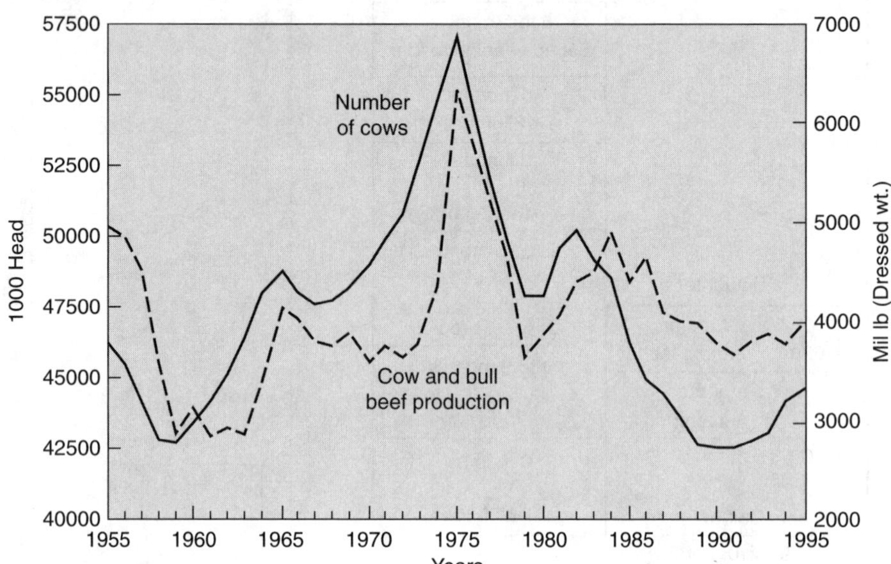

Identification Problem

The modeler is faced with a two-way plot as shown in Figure 7-8. Each observation represents the intersection of demand and supply, but there is no way to determine slopes. However, if included in the model is some type of demand shifter, the slope of the supply curve could be ascertained as shown in Figure 7-9. Shifts upward and/or downward in the position of the demand curve outlines the pattern that describes the supply curve. Alternatively, the demand curve could be identified if the model included a supply shifter as can be established in Figure 7-10.

An analyst could also measure the supply curve if the variability of u is greater than the variability of v. Alternatively, demand could be identified if the variability of v is greater than the variability of u. However, analysts would more correctly rely on the introduction of appropriate fundamental shifters.

The process is best explained in a simple model with both demand-and-supply shifters. Consider the following model:

(21) Demand $P = a_0 + a_1 Q + a_2 DI + u$

(22) Supply $Q = b_0 + b_1 P + b_2 C + v$

Ignoring constants and error terms,

(23) $P = a_1 Q + a_2 DI$

(24) $Q = b_1 P + b_2 C$

FIGURE 7-8 Observations from simultaneous model.

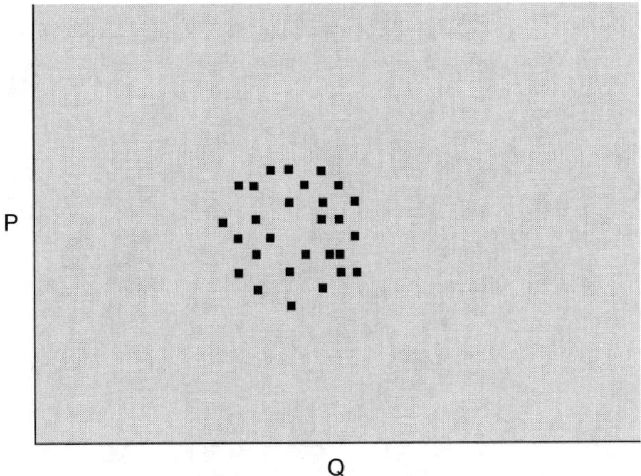

FIGURE 7-9 Observations from simultaneous model supply identified.

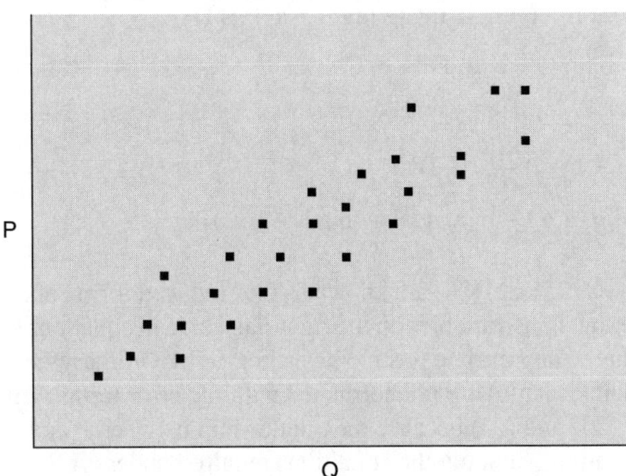

where: DI represents consumer income and C represents producers' costs of production.

By substitution, the endogenous variables, P and Q, can be made functions of the exogenous variables, DI and C, as follows:

$$P = a_1 b_1 P + a_1 b_2 C + a_2 DI$$

$$P - a_1 b_1 P = a_1 b_2 C + a_2 DI$$

FIGURE 7-10 Observations from simultaneous model demand identified.

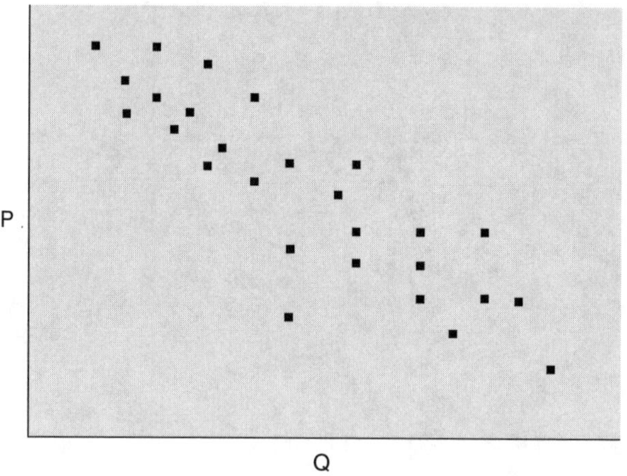

$$P\,(1 - a_1\, b_1) = a_1\, b_2\, C + a_2\, DI$$

(25) $$P = [a_1\, b_2/(1 - a_1\, b_1)]\, C + [a_2/(1 - a_1\, b_1)]\, DI$$

$$Q = b_1\, a_1\, Q + b_1\, a_2\, DI + b_2\, C$$

$$Q - b_1\, a_1\, Q = b_1\, a_2\, DI + b_2\, C$$

$$Q\,(1 - b_1\, a_1) = b_1\, a_2\, DI + b_2\, C$$

(26) $$Q = [b_1\, a_2/(1 - b_1\, a_1)]\, DI + [b_2/(1 - b_1\, a_1)]\, C$$

Equations (25) and (26) are known as the "reduced form" of equations (23) and (24). With the exogenous variables on the right-hand side in equations (25) and (26), the equations are in the appropriate form to be estimated by Ordinary Least Squares (OLS). The independent variables are not correlated with the error terms. This was not the case for equations (23) and (24) because the relationship between P and Q in each equation implies correlation, violating the conditions required under OLS.

Estimation of the coefficients by OLS for equations (25) and (26) establishes the following four equations with RF_i representing the reduced form coefficients:

$$RF_1 = a_1\, b_2/(1 - a_1\, b_1)$$

$$RF_2 = a_2/(1 - a_1\, b_1)$$

$$RF_3 = b_1\, a_2/(1 - b_1\, a_1)$$

$$RF_4 = b_2/(1 - b_1\, a_1)$$

With four equations and four unknowns, values for a_1, a_2, b_1, and b_2 can be derived, i.e., identified. This is a case in which the model is said to be "just identified."

For systems of equations, rules for identification have been established. The notation for such rules are as follows:

System

ES = number of endogenous variables (or equations)

XS = number of exogenous variables

TS = ES + XS

Equation

EE = number of endogenous variables

XE = number of exogenous variables

TE = EE + XE

The rules that apply to any equation in the system are:

a. Just identified $TS - TE = ES - 1$

b. Over identified $TS - TE > ES - 1$

c. Under identified $TS - TE < ES - 1$

Applying these rules to the system described by equations (21) and (22),

	TS – TE	ES – 1	Result
Demand	4 – 3 = 1	2 – 1 = 1	Just identified
Supply	4 – 3 = 1	2 – 1 = 1	Just identified

Cases of over or under identification may arise. Consider the following equation set:

(27) Demand $P = a_0 + a_1 Q + u$

(28) Supply $Q = b_0 + b_1 P + b_2 C + v$

where: C is cost of production, an exogenous variable

	TS – TE	ES – 1	Result
Demand	3 – 2 = 1	2 – 1 = 1	Just identified
Supply	3 – 3 = 0	2 – 1 = 1	Under identified

If the equation is under identified, the problem is unsolvable. In the above example, an exogenous variable must be added to the demand equation (equation 27).

A case of over identification is established in the following example:

(29) Demand $P = a_0 + a_1 Q + a_2 DI + u$

(30) Supply $Q = b_0 + b_1 P + b_2 C + b_3 T + v$

where: DI is consumer income, C is cost of production, and T represents a technology variable, all exogenous variables.

	TS – TE	ES – 1	Result
Demand	5 – 3 = 2	2 – 1 = 1	Over identified
Supply	5 – 4 = 1	2 – 1 = 1	Just identified

Two-Stage Least Squares

With over identification, alternatives are available such as "Two-Stage Least Squares" (2SLS). To illustrate the 2SLS process for equations (29) and (30), the constants will be dropped for expository purposes. The reduced form is calculated as follows:

$$P = a_1 (b_1 P + b_2 C + b_3 T + v) + a_2 DI + u$$

$$P = a_1 b_1 P + a_1 b_2 C + a_1 b_3 T + a_1 v + a_2 DI + u$$

$$P - a_1 b_1 P = a_1 b_2 C + a_1 b_3 T + a_1 v + a_2 DI + u$$

$$(31)\quad P = [a_1 b_2/(1 - a_1 b_1)] C + [a_1 b_3/(1 - a_1 b_1)] T + [a_2/(1 - a_1 b_1)] DI + (a_1 v + u)/(1 - a_1 b_1)$$

Following a similar procedure for Q,

$$(32)\quad Q = [b_1 a_2/(1 - b_1 a_1)] DI + [b_2/(1 - b_1 a_1)] C + [b_3/(1 - b_1 a_1)] T + (b_1 u + v)/(1 - b_1 a_1)$$

Note that there are six coefficients and five unknowns in equations (31) and (32). The procedure used to identify the coefficients in the structural equations in the just identified model (equations 23 and 24) cannot be applied. A system of n linear equations in (n – 1) unknowns has a unique common solution only under very restrictive conditions. Another approach must be pursued.

Note also that P as the dependent variable in equation (31) is correlated with the error term v which would cause a problem if equation (30) were estimated by OLS. Likewise, Q as the dependent variable in equation (32) is correlated with the error term u, which would cause a problem in equation (29) if that equation were estimated by OLS.

However, OLS estimates of P and Q in the reduced form equations (equations (31) and (32)) are linear combinations of exogenous variables and uncorrelated with u and v. If the fitted values from equations (31) and (32) were substituted for the actual values in the structural equations, equations (29) and (30), the following equations would result (omitting constants):

$$(33)\quad P = a_1\hat{Q} + a_2 DI + \{u + a_1 [(b_1 u + v)/(1 - b_1 a_1)]\}$$

$$(34)\quad Q = b_1\hat{P} + b_2 C_t + b_3 T + \{v + b_1 [(a_1 v + u)/(1 - a_1 b_1)]\}$$

The second stage then is to apply OLS to equations (33) and (34). This should provide unbiased estimates of the structural parameters since the error term is uncorrelated with the independent variables, and also follows the other classical assumptions for OLS.

More advanced estimation methods are available such as "Three-Stage Least Squares" (3SLS) and "Seemingly Unrelated Regression" (SUR). For discussion of these tools, refer to standard econometric texts.

Relevance of Simultaneity

There is a philosophical question surrounding the determination of whether recursive or simultaneous approaches are the most relevant. In other words, is the world really recursive or simultaneous? One argument is that the decision process is really recursive as actions are taken in response to certain stimuli. Simultaneous equation systems are only relevant because our database cannot capture the very short lags that may be involved in certain situations.

A model of the U.S. broiler industry based on annual data would exhibit simultaneity not because current supplies are affected by current prices, but because annual data are inappropriate. With quarterly data, a recursive model should be able to measure supply response.

Even in industries in which a biological lag is not present and in which effective information systems are in place, lags exist in the decision process. However, the resources required to obtain key short-run indicators of such actions may be prohibitive in costs. For this reason, tools to handle simultaneity problems may still be needed.

In the macroeconomic scene, actions of the Federal Reserve Board in controlling the money supply and interest rates may be an example of decision making that borders on simultaneity. Responding quickly to a broad base of economic indicators and acting in a somewhat covert manner, this body's actions may not be easily captured by recursive modeling with short time frame databases. But even here, outside analysts are constantly predicting the Fed's actions as government reports are released from week to week.

The guideline implied is to first attempt to develop models with short time units, i.e., weeks, months or quarters, before resorting to simultaneous estimating procedures. In spite of the attention given to simultaneity by econometricians, other problems of estimation, particularly accuracy of data, loom large in comparison. Also, the complexity of large, comprehensive models preclude estimation of structural parameters by conversion to reduced form or application of Two-Stage Least Squares. If the major purpose of the model is for forecasting, estimation of structural parameters may not even be necessary.

SUMMARY

Because of the biological lag in agriculture, recursive-type econometric models are standard. Many enterprises fit the classic Cobweb model which requires that (1) producers' price expectations are based on past prices, (2) a lag exists between the time production plans are made and output is realized, and (3) prices are primarily determined by the amount produced. These characteristics, in combination of shocks originating with weather/pests, tend to keep farm prices and production oscillating over time in a pattern called cycles. In absence of shocks, the models can be evaluated in terms of their dynamics, i.e., whether and how they converge. For livestock, sale and retention of breeding stock introduces positive feedback which contributes to market instability.

Simultaneity is also present to some degree in agricultural markets, and techniques, such as conversion to a reduced form and application of two-stage least squares, are available to allow estimation of structural parameters on relatively simple models. In some cases, simultaneity problems can be handled by converting data to a higher frequency to form recursive models.

QUESTIONS FOR STUDY

1 Plot a supply-demand chart in which expected price is equal to last year's price. Starting from disequilibrium, illustrate a convergent model. Do the same illustrating a divergent model.
2 Identify an agricultural commodity that has the characteristics required for the "Cobweb Theorem" to apply. Plot the annual price and the key indicator of supply response (planted acres, farrowings, etc.) against time. Can you establish whether or not cycles exist and their length?
3 In question 2, can you find years in which the model was "shocked"? Can you determine the reasons, if any?
4 What characteristics of hog enterprises generate cyclical patterns of production and price?
5 What is meant by "positive" feedback in livestock models?
6 Describe how to evaluate the stability of a model that contains a supply equation with a geometric lag.
7 In an empirical model in which prices and production are determined simultaneously, a shifter in the demand equation may be needed to identify the supply equation. Explain.
8 Define "reduced form."
9 Why is the "two-stage least squares" procedure needed?
10 Existence of simultaneity problems in estimating parameters for econometric models may be related to the frequency of the data. Explain.

8

BUILDING ECONOMETRIC/SIMULATION MODELS

POINTS:

1 How large models are solved.
2 Techniques for formulating supply-demand models.
3 Use of balance sheets.
4 Examples of models.
5 Reference to major large-scale models.
6 Structure of AGMOD, model of U.S. agriculture.
7 Dynamic generation of elasticities and flexibilities.

Rather than estimating relatively small models as discussed in Chapter 7, this chapter reviews techniques to build and solve relatively large econometric/simulation models in agriculture. The terms econometric and econometric/simulation are often used interchangeably in describing models. Econometric refers to statistically measured relationships. Most models include equations that are transformations, technical relationships, etc., not statistically derived—and so the term "simulation" is added. Examples of these large models will be presented in this chapter.

To illustrate modeling, this chapter and later chapters will draw heavily from MicroTSP (Hall et al., 1990). Other software programs are available to accomplish similar purposes, but MicroTSP can provide an excellent introduction into the modeling process.

In addition to the standard procedures in regression and time series analysis, MicroTSP facilitates model development, solving, and evaluation. Because complex models are difficult or impossible to solve in an exact, mathematical sense, MicroTSP incorporates a fairly common algorithm known as Gauss-Seidel.

GAUSS-SEIDEL SOLUTION ALGORITHM

Traditional approaches to solving a set of linear equations for the purpose of forecasting have involved inverting large matrices. The problem, however, is that most systems involve non-linear relationships (Heien et al., 1973). Even certain simple identities could not be incorporated, such as: (1) price times quantity = gross revenue, (2) income divided by population divided by the Consumer Price Index = real per-capita income, or (3) area harvested times yield = total production. Other non-linear relationships such as Engle curves were also difficult to handle.

Several attempts were made to overcome this disadvantage. One was to apply linear approximations of non-linear relationships by the Taylor's series expansion. By the early 1970s, large-scale model builders turned to Gauss-Seidel, a technique that had been known for some time as a procedure for solving linear and non-linear systems of equations.

The procedure is a fairly simple one and involves a step-wise trial-and-error method to achieve an approximate solution. This can be illustrated with the following two-equation model.

$$\text{ESTCN} = 5 - 1.0\ \text{FPCN}$$

$$\text{FPCN} = 3 - .25\ \text{ESTCN}$$

where: ESTCN = ending stocks of corn in billion bushels.

FPCN = farm price of corn in dollars per bushel.

Because this is a linear system, the solution can be found by matrix inversion or simply by substitution, i.e.,

$$\text{ESTCN} = 5 - 1.0\ (3 - .25\ \text{ESTCN})$$

$$= 5 - 3 + .25\ \text{ESTCN}$$

$$.75\ \text{ESTCN} = 2$$

$$\text{ESTCN} = 2/.75 = 2.67$$

$$\text{FPCN} = 3 - .25 \times 2.67 = 3 - .67 = 2.33$$

The Gauss-Seidel approach would be as follows:
Assume some arbitrary value for FPCN such as \$1.00 per bushel:

Iteration #1

$$\text{ESTCN} = 5 - 1.0 \times 1 = 4$$

$$\text{FPCN} = 3 - .25 \times 4 = 2$$

Iteration #2

$$ESTCN = 5 - 1.0 \times 2 = 3$$

$$FPCN \quad = 3 - .25 \times 3 = 2.25$$

These first two iterations can be shown graphically in Figure 8.1.

Iteration #3

$$ESTCN = 5 - 1.0 \times 2.25 = 2.75$$

$$FPCN \quad = 3 - .25 \times 2.75 = 2.3125$$

Iteration #4

$$ESTCN = 5 - 1.0 \times 2.3125 = 2.6875$$

$$FPCN \quad = 3 - .25 \times 2.6875 = 2.3281$$

Iteration #5

$$ESTCN = 5 - 1.0 \times 2.3281 = 2.6719$$

$$FPCN \quad = 3 - .25 \times 2.6719 = 2.3320$$

The percent changes between successive iterations were as follows:

FIGURE 8-1 Illustration of Gauss-Seidel algorithm.

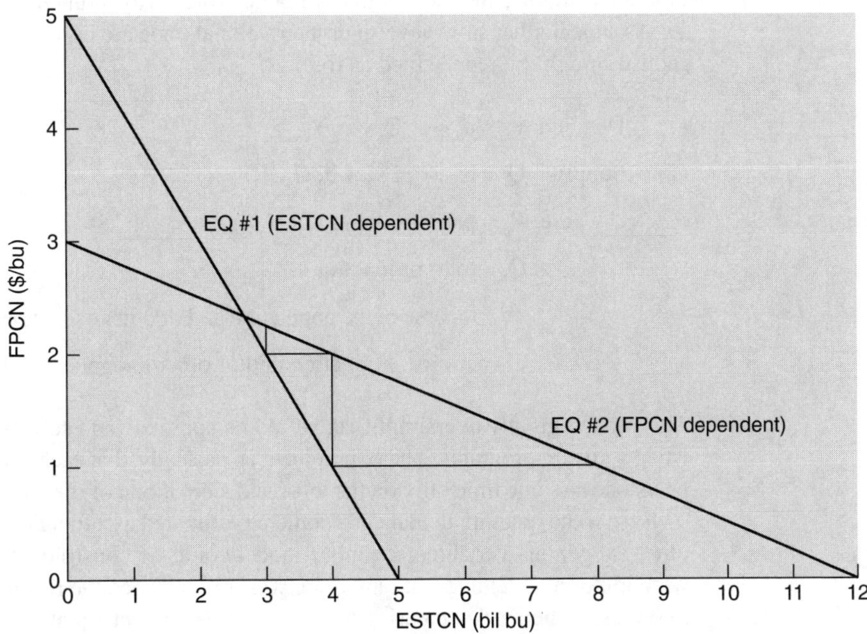

Iteration	ESTCN	FPCN
	% Change	
#1 to #2	−25.0	+12.5
#2 to #3	−8.3	+2.8
#3 to #4	−2.3	+.7
#4 to #5	−.6	+.2

If the program for Gauss-Seidel were set to declare a solution when the percent changes in the values for the endogenous variables from one iteration to the next were less than 1 percent, the process would end at Iteration #5. In MicroTSP, the default value for ending the program is 1/2 percent. This parameter, called CONVERGE, can be set at higher or lower values. At higher values, the solution would be reached more rapidly. As pointed out in the *MicroTSP Users Manual,* there is no strict relation between the percent change in a variable from one iteration to the next and the accuracy of the solution.

In addition to CONVERGE, the SOLVE command also includes some maximum number of iterations. Called MAXIT, this is set at a default value of 100, but can be adjusted up or down depending on the user's preference.

Given the possibility to solve complex linear or non-linear systems of equations, how should such a model be constructed?

GUIDELINES FOR MODEL BUILDING

To estimate the structural equations and linkages in standard econometric models, and construct the total system, analysts must establish the characteristics of the industry. A most convenient system to model is one in which price is primarily determined by the amount available, and the amount available is primarily a function of past prices or profits. Assume neither stock levels nor international trade are important in this industry. This industry might be represented as follows:

(1) Demand $P_t = a_0 + a_1 Q_t + a_2 Y_t$

(2) Supply $Q_t = b_0 + b_1 P_{t-1} + b_2 C_t$

where: P_t = price of the product

Q_t = total production

Y_t = income of the population and/or other exogenous variables in demand

C_t = cost of production and/or other exogenous variables in supply

This model, greatly oversimplified, would be complete and solvable as written with existing software programs. The requirement is, basically, that each endogenous variable appears one and one time only on the left-hand side of one of the equations in the program.

Even if the quantity demanded should be estimated as a function of price, income, and other exogenous variables, a similar model could be constructed if: (1) stock changes were minor and (2) international trade was minor. Since the resulting price would have to represent the market clearing level, a price dependent equation could be fashioned as follows:

$$\text{Demand } QD_t = a_0 + a_1 P_t + a_2 Y_t$$

$$\text{Supply } QS_t = b_0 + b_2 P_{t-1} + b_2 C_t$$

At equilibrium each year, $QD_t = QS_t$
Therefore,

$$\text{Demand } -a_1P_t = -QS_t + a_0 + a_2Y_t$$

$$P_t = -\frac{a_0}{a_1} + \frac{1}{a_1} QS_t - \frac{a_2}{a_1} Y_t$$

This transforms the demand equation into the same formulation as in equation (1) with price as a function of production (pre-determined) and income and/or other exogenous variables. In this formulation, the system could be solved similarly to the model with equations (1) and (2).

A more general model could be illustrated with the following structural equations, with quantity demanded dependent and with stock levels and international trade as substantive components.

(3) Domestic demand $QDD_t = a_0 + a_1 P_t + a_2 Y_t$

(4) Export demand $QED_t = b_0 + b_1 P_t + b_2 YE_t$

(5) Ending stocks demand $QEST_t = c_0 + c_1 P_t + c_2 IR_t$

(6) Production $Q_t = d_0 + d_1 P_{t-1} + d_2 C_t$

(7) Balance sheet $QEST_t = QEST_{t-1} + Q_t - QDD_t - QED_t$

(8) Lower bound on ending stocks $QEST_t \geq K$

where: QDD_t = domestic demand

QED_t = export demand

YE_t = income in nations receiving the exports (exogenous)

$QEST_t$ = ending stocks

IR_t = interest rate (exogenous)

K = lower bound on $QEST_t$. This prevents ending stocks from becoming excessively low or even negative.

This formulation, which appears to be reasonable, cannot be solved with conventional software procedures for two reasons:

1 The same dependent variable, $QEST_t$, appears in three equations. Such duplication would preclude solution.
2 The endogenous variable, P_t, does not appear as a dependent variable.

Several alternatives can be explored to transform this model into one that can be solved. One is to convert the ending stocks equation, (5), into a price dependent equation and modify the combination of (7) and (8). The ending stock equation, (5), could be reformulated using the estimates of the structural parameters as follows:

(5a) Ending stock demand

$$-c_tP_t = -QEST_t + c_0 + c_2\, IR_t$$

$$P_t = -\frac{c_0}{c_1} + \frac{1}{c_1}\, QEST_t - \frac{c_2}{c_1}\, IR_t$$

A preferred formulation to (5a) would be to express the ending stocks as a ratio to total utilization as follows:

Ending stock demand

$$RQEST_t = c_0 + c_1\, P_t + c_2\, IR_t$$

with the conversion to a price dependent equation resulting in:

(5b) Ending stock demand

$$P_t = -\frac{c_0}{c_1} + \frac{1}{c_1}\, RQEST_t - \frac{c_2}{c_1}\, IR_t$$

where:

$$RQEST_t = QEST_t/(QDD_t + QED_t)$$

This transformation accounts for the presumption that amount of stocks demanded is related not only to prices, but also to the level of utilization. The greater the domestic and export disappearance, the greater the need for a certain "pipeline" carryover. By "pipeline" carryover, we mean the minimum amount of product needed at the end of a season to ensure that the channels for immediate consumption are filled enough to prevent any interruption in the flow of the product to domestic and foreign consumers.

Finally, equations (7) and (8) must be combined so that only one equation remains with the dependent variable, $QEST_t$, on the left-hand side. Using the operators available in MicroTSP, this could be accomplished as follows:

(9) (7 & 8 combined) Balance sheet with lower bound on ending stocks

$$\begin{aligned} QEST_t = {} & (QEST_{t-1} + Q_t - QDD_t - QED_t) \\ & * ((QEST_{t-1} + Q_t - QDD_t - QED_t) \geq K) \\ & + ((QEST_{t-1} + Q_t = QDD_t - QED_t) < K) * K \end{aligned}$$

If the equation for the balance sheet generates ending stocks greater than or equal to some lower bound K, the term $((QEST_{t-1} + Q_t - QDD_t - QED_t) \geq K)$ has the value of 1 and $((QEST_t + Q_t - QDD_t - QED) < K)$ becomes 0. This sets the value of $QEST_t$ at the level prescribed by the balance sheet equation. If $(QEST_{t-1} + Q_t - QDD_t - QED_t)$ is less than K, the operators will generate $QEST_t = K$.

Of course, if the estimates of ending stocks from the model persistently generate stocks below K or even below zero, the model would need to be respecified. Equations (5) or (5b) would likely receive the most attention. Abnormally low or negative ending stocks would likely be a symptom that prices had not been pushed up enough to ration amounts going into domestic and export markets. Quite possibly, the actual relationship between ending stocks and price is not linear.

Consider a model composed of equations (3), (4), (5b), (6), (7), and

(9b)	$RQEST_t$ with a lower bound	$RQEST_t = (QEST_t/(QDD_t + QED_t)) *((QEST_t/(QDD_t + QED_t)) \geq L) + ((QEST_t/(QDD_t + QED_t) < L)* L$

This formulation retains the balance sheet equation (7), but puts a lower bound L on the *ratio* of ending stocks to total utilization; it does not put a lower bound on $QEST_t$. In this model, one can monitor $QEST_t$ and respecify the price equation (5b) if necessary. Should the model persistently generate abnormally low or negative $QEST_t$, alternative functional forms for (5b) could be explored. Such functions would appropriately be designed to generate a more inelastic demand for stocks at low stock levels than at higher stock levels; or in flexibility terms, higher price flexibility relative to stocks at low levels than at high levels.

Examples of such a formulation would be to substitute ($1/RQEST_t$) or log of $RQEST_t$ for $RQEST_t$ in (5b). One would hope that such a reformulation, along with the inclusion of (9b), would: (1) improve the statistical properties of equation (5b) and (2) keep estimates of $RQEST_t$ from persistently hitting the lower bound L in solutions to the model, and certainly keeping estimates of $QEST_t$ from moving to extremely low or negative levels.

In MicroTSP, separate variables would have to be generated for OLS procedures, such as:

Inverse of $RQEST_t$	$INVRQEST_t = 1/RQEST_t$
or	
Log of $RQEST_t$	$LRQEST_t = \log (RQEST_t)$

With this particular non-linear formulation of equation (5b), solutions to the model could not be reached with Gauss-Seidel if $RQEST_t$ were zero. This is another reason for incorporating a lower bound on this variable above zero. Because of the range over which the Gauss-Seidel procedure operates with individual variables, the value zero might be crossed even though the equilibrium solution might have turned out positive.

This is a general guideline for the construction of a model with MicroTSP. Any variable that appears as a denominator or in a log form should be protected from becoming zero. If zero values are plausible, boundaries a fraction above zero should still be employed.

Alternative formulations can be analyzed. Salathe et al. prefer the incorporation of an equation with ending stocks as a function of current real price. Real price, then, is a function of an inverse of the combination of beginning stocks plus the supply function minus the demand function minus the ending stock function (Salathe et al., 1982).

THE BALANCE SHEET

Equation (7) was defined as the "balance sheet." This is an identity very much like an accounting form with the beginning stocks plus production plus imports equalling total supply. Deducting total domestic use and exports left ending stocks that became beginning stocks in the subsequent year.

Heading the balance sheet form can be the relevant data set on supply. For crops, this would be planted and harvested areas, yields per unit area, and any government program that might establish set-aside areas. An example of a typical balance sheet is presented in Table 8-1 on U.S. corn.

The reasons special attention is given to this form are: (1) characteristics of supply and demand can be portrayed over recent years and analyzed for the coming years in presentations to a lay audience and (2) econometric/simulation models are commonly designed to generate tables like this. In this particular table, projections for utilization, ending stocks, and prices are displayed as published by World Agricultural Outlook Board of the U.S. Department of Agriculture.

TABLE 8-1 SUPPLY/DEMAND BALANCE SHEET FOR CORN

	1991–92	1992–93	1993–94	Est. 1994–95	Proj. 1995–96
			(Million Acres)		
Acres Set-Aside and Diverted	7.4	5.3	10.9	2.4	6.2
Acres Planted	76.0	79.3	73.2	79.2	75.3
Acres Harvested	68.8	72.1	62.9	72.9	68.5
Bu./Harvested Acre	108.6	131.5	100.7	138.6	125.6
			(Million Bushels)		
Beginning Stocks	1521	1100	2113	850	1581
Production	7475	9477	6336	10,103	8600
Imports	20	7	21	10	10
Total Supply	9016	10,584	8470	10,963	10,198
Use:					
Feed and Residual	4877	5296	4704	5650	5400
Food, Seed, and Ind. Uses	1954	1511	1588	1700	1800
Total Domestic	6332	6813	6292	7350	7200
Exports	1584	1663	1328	2025	2000
Total Use	7915	8471	7620	9375	9200
Ending Stocks	1100	2113	850	1588	998
Ending Stocks, % of Use	13.9	24.9	11.2	16.9	10.8
Regular Loan Rate	$1.62	$1.72	$1.72	$1.89	$1.89
U.S. Season Average Farm Price, $/Bu.	$2.37	$2.07	$2.50	$2.20–$2.30	$2.30–$2.70

Source: USDA, World Agricultural Outlook Board, May 11, 1995.

EXAMPLES OF ECONOMETRIC/SIMULATION MODELS

The specification for a model depends on the analyst's a priori view of the world. This could be a strictly recursive type model or one with simultaneity.

Livestock

Figure 8-2 displays a recursive model on livestock. While FCCT, FCHG, FCBR, and FCTK (which are feed costs per unit of output) are generated by the model, they are functions of exogenous variables and thereby classified as exogenous. All the variables with codes ending in "F" are endogenous; that is, generated within the model. The remaining variables are exogenous. Typical of all types of models, the number of transformations (identities) will often exceed the number of behavioral equations.

In lines 1 through 4, feed costs for cattle on feed, hogs, broilers, and turkeys are generated as functions of the price of corn and soybean meal. These feed costs per hundredweight of output are deflated by the CPI in lines 5 through 8. In lines 9 through 12, production of beef, pork, broilers, and turkeys are converted to per-capita amounts, with additional coefficients on beef and pork to transform carcass weights to retail weights. In lines 13 through 16, total meat substitutes for each of the major red meat and poultry meat items were calculated. In line 17, total meat availability per capita was computed. Gross margins over the costs of feed, in real terms, were calculated in lines 18 through 20 for hogs, broilers, and turkeys.

The behavioral equations for supply and demand are portrayed in lines 21 through 30. In MicroTSP, the incorporation of OLS equations is relatively simple. Once the equations have been estimated in the work file, they can be stored, and then in the construction of the edit file, they can be fetched and added to the program.

The supply equations in lines 21 through 25 are relatively simple for demonstration purposes and not represented as the most sophisticated. In line 21, the number of beef cows on farms in year *t* is a function of the number on farms the year before and the real price of feeder calves over the previous three years. Line 22 links beef cow numbers to total beef production two years later with a positive trend. Production of pork, broilers, and turkeys are generated by geometric lag supply functions in lines 23 through 25.

In the demand equations in lines 26 through 30, real prices on steers, barrows and gilts, broilers, turkeys, and feeder calves, respectively, are the dependent variables. On steers, barrows and gilts, broilers, and turkeys, the demand format is similar—with availability per capita of the respective product, availability per capita of the substitutes, real disposable income, and trends as the independent variables. The demand for feeder calves was postulated in line 30 to be a function of the price of slaughter steers, the price of feeder calves the year before, and the cost of feed in cattle feeding—all in real terms.

Finally, prices were converted to nominal terms in lines 31 through 35. This is primarily for the benefit of those who are familiar with actual prices and are not familiar with the representation of prices in real terms.

While the livestock model portrayed in Figure 8-2 may appear complex, it is really a very straight-forward recursive model with past prices and profits generating the availability of the product which, in turn, generates prices and profits that determine next

FIGURE 8-2 Recursive model on livestock, price dependent in demand.

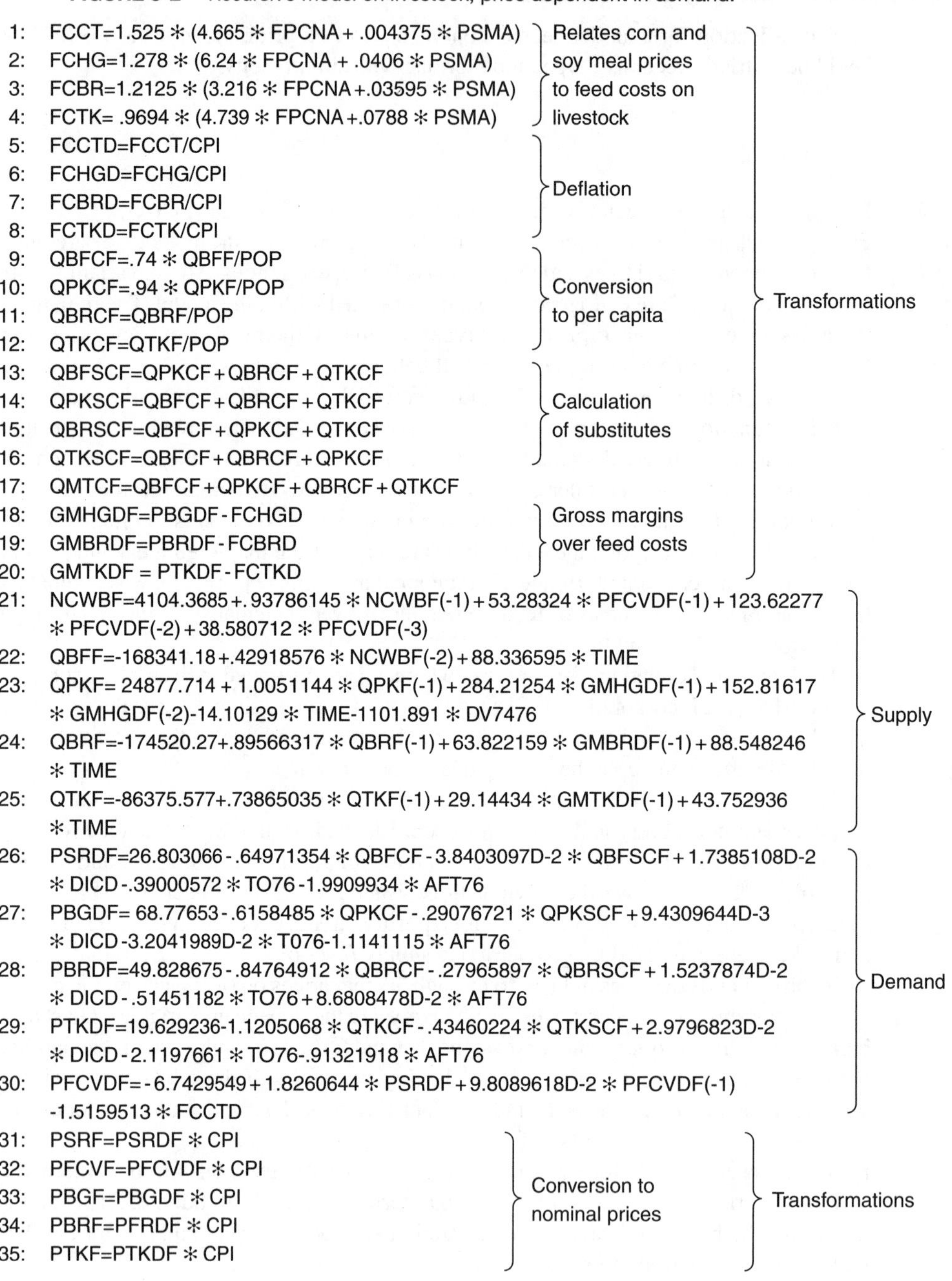

```
1:  FCCT=1.525 * (4.665 * FPCNA + .004375 * PSMA)
2:  FCHG=1.278 * (6.24 * FPCNA + .0406 * PSMA)
3:  FCBR=1.2125 * (3.216 * FPCNA +.03595 * PSMA)
4:  FCTK= .9694 * (4.739 * FPCNA+.0788 * PSMA)
        } Relates corn and soy meal prices to feed costs on livestock
5:  FCCTD=FCCT/CPI
6:  FCHGD=FCHG/CPI
7:  FCBRD=FCBR/CPI
8:  FCTKD=FCTK/CPI
        } Deflation
9:  QBFCF=.74 * QBFF/POP
10: QPKCF=.94 * QPKF/POP
11: QBRCF=QBRF/POP
12: QTKCF=QTKF/POP
        } Conversion to per capita
13: QBFSCF=QPKCF + QBRCF + QTKCF
14: QPKSCF=QBFCF + QBRCF + QTKCF
15: QBRSCF=QBFCF + QPKCF + QTKCF
16: QTKSCF=QBFCF + QBRCF + QPKCF
        } Calculation of substitutes
17: QMTCF=QBFCF + QPKCF + QBRCF + QTKCF
18: GMHGDF=PBGDF - FCHGD
19: GMBRDF=PBRDF - FCBRD
20: GMTKDF = PTKDF - FCTKD
        } Gross margins over feed costs
    } Transformations (1-20)
21: NCWBF=4104.3685 +. 93786145 * NCWBF(-1) + 53.28324 * PFCVDF(-1) + 123.62277
    * PFCVDF(-2) + 38.580712 * PFCVDF(-3)
22: QBFF=-168341.18 +.42918576 * NCWBF(-2) + 88.336595 * TIME
23: QPKF= 24877.714 + 1.0051144 * QPKF(-1) + 284.21254 * GMHGDF(-1) + 152.81617
    * GMHGDF(-2)-14.10129 * TIME-1101.891 * DV7476
24: QBRF=-174520.27+.89566317 * QBRF(-1) + 63.822159 * GMBRDF(-1) + 88.548246
    * TIME
25: QTKF=-86375.577+.73865035 * QTKF(-1) + 29.14434 * GMTKDF(-1) + 43.752936
    * TIME
    } Supply
26: PSRDF=26.803066 - .64971354 * QBFCF - 3.8403097D-2 * QBFSCF + 1.7385108D-2
    * DICD -.39000572 * TO76 -1.9909934 * AFT76
27: PBGDF= 68.77653 - .6158485 * QPKCF - .29076721 * QPKSCF + 9.4309644D-3
    * DICD -3.2041989D-2 * T076-1.1141115 * AFT76
28: PBRDF=49.828675 - .84764912 * QBRCF - .27965897 * QBRSCF + 1.5237874D-2
    * DICD - .51451182 * TO76 + 8.6808478D-2 * AFT76
29: PTKDF=19.629236-1.1205068 * QTKCF - .43460224 * QTKSCF + 2.9796823D-2
    * DICD - 2.1197661 * TO76-.91321918 * AFT76
30: PFCVDF= - 6.7429549 + 1.8260644 * PSRDF + 9.8089618D-2 * PFCVDF(-1)
    -1.5159513 * FCCTD
    } Demand
31: PSRF=PSRDF * CPI
32: PFCVF=PFCVDF * CPI
33: PBGF=PBGDF * CPI
34: PBRF=PFRDF * CPI
35: PTKF=PTKDF * CPI
        } Conversion to nominal prices
    } Transformations
```

year's output. Of course, values for the exogenous variables must be forecast for the projection period including the Consumer Price Index (CPI), corn prices (FPCNA), soybean meal prices (PSMA), population (POP), and real per-capita disposable income (DICD). This model would be solved very quickly with Gauss-Seidel because of its recursive nature and no simultaneous relationships.

Dairy

In Figure 8-3 is the edit file on a dairy model that incorporates simultaneity, and consumption is dependent in demand. Line 1 is the principal supply equation with the number of milk cows on farms on January 1 as a function of a long lag of real gross margins per cow over the cost of feed. In line 2, the milk production per cow is a function of trend (TIME), and the deflated prices of milk, corn, and soybean meal. Total milk production in line 3 is the product of milk cow numbers and milk production per cow.

Note in line 9 and then line 13 that QMKF affects the price of milk and in lines 2 and 3 the price of milk affects QMKF. In this situation, we have simultaneity.

Gross margins per cwt. and per cow are generated in lines 4 and 5. In line 6, per-capita commercial consumption of dairy products in milk equivalent is a function of the retail price of dairy products (CPIDPDF), real disposable income per capita, and trend. Disappearance from government stocks in line 8 is a function of beginning government stocks (ESTGDPF(−1)) and the ratio of commercial disappearance to production. The rationale for this latter variable is that the greater the commercial disappearance, the less that the government needs to release stocks for consumption.

In lines 9 through 12 are key relationships, all ratios, which contribute to the explanation of other endogenous variables in the model. The principal price equation is line 13 in which the real farm price of milk is a function of the real support price, the ratio of government ending stocks to total ending stocks, the ratio of commercial disappearance to production, and trend.

In line 15, the Consumer Price Index on Dairy Products is a function of the farm price of milk and the CPI, which is a proxy for the cost of marketing and processing milk. The ending stock equation in line 17 is designed to put a lower bound on these stocks at 3.4 percent of commercial disappearance. Also included in the model are equations to generate government ending stocks and purchases, in lines 18 and 19.

This model is presented as a general example of the modeling process, incorporating simultaneity, government programs, and lower bounds on stocks. The dairy model happens to be a sector in a much larger model (AGMOD) which encompasses major enterprises in U.S. agriculture including international trade in those products. The dairy sector could be designed to solve independently, in which case the prices of corn and soybean meal would become exogenous, joining the existing exogenous variables—Consumer Price Index, real disposable income per capita, population, and the government support rate.

One way to proceed in building models such as AGMOD is to develop each sector independently. In that way the diagnostic checking can be more easily managed. When the modeler is satisfied that each sector is performing satisfactorily, then the sectors can be joined and the total model tested.

FIGURE 8-3 Simultaneous model on dairy: consumption dependent in demand.

Supply

1: NCWMF= 7241.249 - 140.8388 * DV85 + 402.7365 * DV86 + 2.471721
* GMMCDF(-3) + 6.55397 * GMMCDF(-4) + 7.635682
* GMMCDF(-5) + 5.716859 * GMMCDF(-6) + .7975007 * GMMCDF(-7)
+ [AR(1)=.8637826] Number of dairy cows on farms, January 1

2: QMKCWF=465.0631 + .2407911 * TIME + 4.63898D-02 * FPMKDF - .132049
* FPCNDF(-1) - 4.845075D-04 * PSMDF(-1) Milk production per cow.

3: QMKF=NCWMF * QMKCWF Total milk production

Farm price of corn (FPCNDF) — Price of soybean meal (PSMDF)

Profit (Gross margin over feed costs)

4: GMMKDF=FPMKDF - FCMKDF Per cwt. of milk

5: GMMCDF=GMMKDF * QMKCWF Per cow

Demand (Milk Equivalent) — Population (POP); Real disposable income per capita (DICD)

6: CDMKCF =6126.934-99.56094 * CPIDPDF + 1.83795D-02 * DICD-2.868296 *TIME — Commercial disappearance per capita

7: CDMKF=CDMKCF * POP Commercial disappearance

8: GDDPF=54058.05 + .568884 * ESTGDPF(-1)-52772.23 * RCDQMKF + [AR(1)=.6106284]
Disappearance from government stocks

Key Relationships

9: RCDQMKF=CDMKF/QMKF Ratio of commercial disappearance to production

10: RFPMKSPF=FPMKDF/SPMKD Ratio of farm milk prices to the support price

11: RESGTDPF=4.104072 + .3368222 * RESGTDPF(-1) - 2.948307 * RCDQMKF
-.8902022 * RFPMKSPF — Ratio of government ending stocks to total ending stocks

12: RESTDPF=ESTDPF/CDMKF — Ratio of ending stocks to commercial disappearance

Price Equations — Support price deflated (SPMKD)

13: FPMKDF= 259.5267 + .8193213 * SPMKD-2.157285 * RESGTDPF+ 5.348588 * RCDQMKF
-1310915 * TIME + 1.173786 * DV89 + 1.07 * (TIME> 1990) Farm price of milk deflated

14: FPMKF=FPMKDF * CPI Nominal farm price of milk

15: CPIDPF=7.542613D-02+ 2.996298D-02 * FPMKF+ .5350569 * CPI-1.704171D-02
* DV73 +[AR(1)=.53085522] CPI for dairy products

16: CPIDPDF=CPIDPF/CPI CPI for dairy products deflated

Stock Equations and Government Purchases

17: ESTDPF=(ESTDPF(-1) + QMKF- CDMKF- GDDPF) * (((ESTDPF(-1) + QMKF
-CDMKF- GDDPF)/CDMKF)= >.034) + .034 * CDMKF * (((ESTDPF(-1) + QMKF
-CDMKF- GDDPF)/CDMKF)<.034) — Total ending stocks with lower bound equal to 3.4% of commercial disappearance

18: ESTGDPF=ESTDPF * RESGTDPF Government ending stocks

19: GPURDPF= ESTGDPF- ESTGDPF(-1) +GDDPF Government purchases

LARGE-SCALE ECONOMETRIC MODELS

A number of large-scale models of the macro-economy have emerged over the years. Prominent among these are the WEFA Group, Data Resources, Inc. (DRI), Georgia State, and the University of Michigan's Research Seminar in Quantitative Economics (RSQE). Over 50 macro forecasting units have been reporting to Eggert Economic Enterprises, Inc., which has been publishing their key prognostications about the U.S. economy in *Blue Chip Economic Indicators* (Eggert). The extent to which these entities use substantial econometric models is not known, but most would combine quantitative tools with experience and judgment in generating forecasts.

In agriculture, development of large-scale econometric models has proceeded for some time in international organizations, the U.S. Department of Agriculture, Land Grant Universities, and in private firms. While many of these models continue to undergo metamorphosis, their identities can be fairly well established at the moment. In the category of standard econometric simulation models would be the WEFA Group (Bala Cynwyd, PA), FAPSIM (USDA), FAPRI (Iowa State University, University of Missouri-Columbia), Sparks Companies, Inc. (Memphis, TN), AGSIM (Auburn University), POLYSIM (Oklahoma State University), COMGEM (Texas A&M University), and AGMOD (Michigan State University). Some of these models have particularly unique features. AGSIM focuses on a regional crop sector (Taylor et al., 1993). COMGEM includes an extensive macro sector. POLYSIM focuses on policy analysis and is oriented around a baseline derived exogenously for the most part. Many parameters are also drawn from outside sources.

A model called "The Basic Linked System" (BLS) is a set of national and regional models designed to analyze world food and agricultural policies. This system was developed by the International Institute for Applied Systems Analysis (IIASA) in Laxenburg, Austria in cooperation with the Centre for World Food Studies (SOW) in Amsterdam, the Netherlands. The model incorporates not only producer profit and consumer utility maximization, but also considers the behavior of national governments reaching policy goals (Taylor et al., 1993). The modeling activity for the U.S. and Canada is located in the USDA and the Center for Agricultural and Rural Development (CARD) at Iowa State University. Two other organizations heavily involved in long-run analysis of the world food situation are the United Nations (with "Project Link" and FAO program in Rome, Italy) and the International Food Policy Research Institute (IFPRI) in Washington, D.C.

The Center for Agricultural and Rural Development (CARD) at Iowa State University operates a national linear programming model directed at long-range forecasting and policy analysis (Taylor et al., 1993). This model has extensive detail on crop and livestock production in various regions of the U.S. and can address many questions not answerable in standard econometric/simulation models. Some of the limitations to the CARD LP model are being overcome by linkage to other systems including FAPRI.

A number of other Land Grant Universities, government agencies, and private firms are involved in forecasting and generating long-term projections. For example, the Congressional Budget Office regularly projects balance sheets and federal expenditures on major farm commodities. These programs, however, may not rely strictly on large-scale models, but reflect a substantial amount of judgment and experience in addition to the application of more directed quantitative tools.

SWOPSIM

Of particular note is a modeling framework in the USDA known as "Static World Policy Simulation" (SWOPSIM). This model differs from most of the models previously mentioned because it is not designed to generate year-by-year projections. The "Static" part of SWOPSIM indicates that the procedure will "calculate the implications of policy reform or other economic shocks after full model adjustment, but will not give the time path of adjustment" (Roningen et al., 1992).[1]

However, the modeling framework of SWOPSIM has appeal in that it is fairly transparent, is flexible, and can serve as a coordinating mechanism for modeling activities. Efforts have proceeded to develop this framework for major nations and regions of the world.

The focus for SWOPSIM has been to measure distortions in international trade and the impacts of removing assistance to agriculture in industrial market economies. This has involved developing a comprehensive database on Producer Subsidy Equivalents (PSE's) and Consumer Subsidy Equivalents (CSE's) with a methodology developed by the Organization for Economic Cooperation and Development (OECD). (See Chapter 13 on "Application of Models to Long-range Planning and Policy Analysis.")

The country models in SWOPSIM can best be described as matrices of supply-and-demand elasticities as illustrated for the U.S. in Figure 8-4. The demand system approach, as presented in Chapter 3, was applied to both demand and supply. A world market clearing mechanism solves world trade for each product, generating a world price. Producer and consumer subsidies for each nation are also introduced.

The elasticities are normally generated econometrically, but are not limited to that process. The time frame for the projection period in SWOPSIM is about five to seven years.

Another USDA modeling effort incorporates the Computable General Equilibrium (CGE) approach (Robinson et al., 1990). While basically a model of the U.S. economy, it emphasizes agriculture and international trade. As stated by Robinson,

> A CGE model simulates the working of a market economy in which prices and quantities adjust to clear markets for products and factors. The model specifies the behavior of optimizing consumers and producers in the market economy. It also includes the government as an explicit agent (although not an optimizer) and captures all transactions in the circular flow of income.

This type of model can address macroeconomic issues domestically and internationally not easily handled by the agriculture sector models. Optimization is possible, which

[1]Since the construction of SWOPSIM, the Economic Research Service of the USDA has developed a model-building framework that does allow users to trace out time paths (Roningen, 1992). Called DWOPSIM (for Dynamic World Policy Simulation), this model requires users to provide all of the structure, specification, and parameters for the equations.

FIGURE 8-4 Supply and demand elasticity matrices from SWOPSIM.

Supply	BF	PK	ML	PM	PE	DM	DB	DC	DP	WH	CN	CG	RI	SB	SM	SO	OS	OM	OO	CT	SU	TB	SUM
BF	.65	-.01	--	--	--	.02				--	-.09	-.02			-.01			--					.54
PK	-.02	1.00	--	-.01	--	--				--	-.25	-.05			-.07			--					.59
ML	--	--	.80	--	--	--				--	-.38	-.08			--			--					.34
PM	--	-.02	--	.65	-.02	--				-.02	-.11	-.02			-.09			--					.37
PE	--	--	--	-.02	.55	--				--	-.08	-.01			-.03			--					.40
DM	.03	--	--	--	--	.50				--	-.06	-.01			--			--					.44
DB						-.20	.50	.75	.50														.05
DC						-.33	-.13	.64	-.13														.05
DP						-.19	.48	-.72	.48														.05
WM										.60	-.25	-.06	--	.05			-.03			--	-.01	--	.31
CN										-.09	.48	--	--	-.07			--			--	--	--	.31
CG										-.10	-.03	.60	--	-.09			-.05			--	--	--	.33
RI										--	--	--	.40	--			--			--	--	--	.40
SB										.03	-.12	-.03	--	.60			--			-.11	--	-.01	.36
SM														-.38	.30	.13							.05
SO														-.38	.30	.13							.05
OS										-.09	--	-.08	--	--			.55			-.08	--	--	.30
OM																	-.69	.30	.44				05
OO																	-.69	.30	.44				.05
CT										--	--	--	--	-.54			-.08			.74	--	--	.12
SU										-.09	--	--	--	--			--			--	.50	--	.41
TB										--	--	--	--	-.05			--			--	--	.25	.19

← ANIMAL PRODUCT SUPPLY ELASTICITIES

← ANIMAL PRODUCT FEED COST ELASTICITIES

← TWO-DIGIT PRODUCT CODES

Sum = SUM OF ALL OWN PRICE AND CROSS PRICE ELASTICITIES IN A ROW →

← DAIRY PRODUCT SUPPLY ELASTICITIES

OWN PRICE ELASTICITIES ARE IN THE DIAGONAL OF THE MATRICES, CROSS PRICES ARE OFF-DIAGONAL. CROSS PRICE RELATIONSHIPS ARE GOVERNED BY SYMMETRY CONDITIONS. DUALITY RELATIONSHIPS GOVERN FEED COST RELATIONSHIPS, DIARY PRODUCT SUPPLY RELATIONSHIPS AND OILSEED CRUSHING DEMAND ELASTICITY RELATIONSHIPS. ROW SUMS INDICATE HOMOGENEITY CONDITIONS.

CROP SUPPLY ELASTICITIES →

← SOYMEAL AND SOYOIL SUPPLY ELASTICITIES

OTHER MEAL AND OTHER OIL SUPPLY ELASTICITIES →

← DEMAND ELASTICITY SYSTEM

Demand	BF	PK	ML	PM	PE	DM	DB	DC	DP	WH	CN	CG	RI	SB	SM	SO	OS	OM	OO	CT	SU	TB	SUM
BF	-.70	.05	--	.03	--	--	--	--	--	--	--	--	--	--	--	--	--	--	--	--	--	--	-.62
PK	.08	-.86	--	.03	--	--	--	--	--	--	--	--	--	--	--	--	--	--	--	--	--	--	-.74
ML	--	.37	-.70	--	--	--	--	--	--	--	--	--	--	--	--	--	--	--	--	--	--	--	-.33
PM	.09	.06	--	-.56	--	--	--	--	--	--	--	--	--	--	--	--	--	--	--	--	--	--	-.42
PE	--	--	--	--	-.35	--	--	--	--	--	--	--	--	--	--	--	--	--	--	--	--	--	-.35
DM	--	--	--	--	--	-.17	.01	.12	.01														-.02
DB	--	--	--	--	--	--	-.63	--	--	--	--	--	--	--	--	--	--	--	--	--	--	--	-.63
DC	--	--	--	--	--	--	--	-.60	--	--	--	--	--	--	--	--	--	--	--	--	--	--	-.60
DP	--	--	--	--	--	--	--	--	-.65	--	--	--	--	--	--	--	--	--	--	--	--	--	-.65
WH	--	--	--	--	--	--	--	--	--	-.35	.15	.10	--	--	--	--	--	--	--	--	--	--	-.10
CN	--	--	--	--	--	--	--	--	--	.04	-.21	.05	--	--	.02	--	--	--	--	--	.01	--	-.09
CG	--	--	--	--	--	--	--	--	--	.12	.25	-.47	--	--	--	--	--	--	--	--	--	--	-.10
RI	--	--	--	--	--	--	--	--	--	--	--	--	-.25	--	--	--	--	--	--	--	--	--	-.25
SB	--	--	--	--	--	--	--	--	--	--	--	--	--	-.42	.26	.11	--	--	--	--	--	--	-.05
SM	--	--	--	--	--	--	--	--	--	--	.09	--	--	--	-.31	--	--	.05	--	--	--	--	-.17
SO	--	--	--	--	--	--	--	--	--	--	--	--	--	--	--	-.37	--	--	.15	--	--	--	-.22
OS	--	--	--	--													-.32	.10	.14	--	--	--	-.09
OM	--	--	--	--	--	--	--	--	--	--	--	--	--	--	.62–	--		-.90	--	--	--	--	-.28
OO	--	--	--	--	--	--	--	--	--	--	--	--	--	--	--	.33		--	-.69	--	--	--	-.36
CT	--	--	--	--	--	--	--	--	--	--	--	--	--	--	--	--	--	--	--	-.20	--	--	-.20
SU	--	--	--	--	--	--	--	--	--	--	.16	--	--	--	--	--	--	--	--	--	-.24	--	-.08
TB	--	--	--	--	--	--	--	--	--	--	--	--	--	--	--	--	--	--	--	--	--	-.20	-.20

← MANUFACTURING AND FLUID MILK DEMAND SYSTEM --

OILSEED CRUSHING AND FOOD DEMAND SYSTEMS →

is often not a part of econometric/simulation models of the U.S. On the other hand, the aggregation in CGE models has been such that important details in forecasting and policy analysis in agriculture are concealed.

AGMOD

As representative of a standard large-scale econometric/simulation model, a brief description of AGMOD is included here to provide more insight into this type of a model. Use of the model will also be discussed.

AGMOD is a microcomputer econometric model of U.S. agriculture developed at Michigan State University beginning in 1986, building on previous activities related to the MSU Agriculture Model that was established on a main-frame. The model is commodity specific and includes feed grain, soybeans, wheat, and the major livestock enterprises. Based on annual data since 1960, the model is designed to generate annual forecasts about 10 to 15 years into the future.

The model was developed with MicroTSP software and employs the Gauss-Seidel solution procedure. The current version has over 500 equations and 700 variables. The program incorporates about 100 statistically derived equations that are updated at least once each year.

Also, satellite models can be linked to AGMOD by running a program that stores values of variables from AGMOD, loads the satellite model, fetches the stored values, and solves. Such models draw from AGMOD, but are not needed to solve the core model. For example, one such model generates U.S. cash farm income, and another forecasts retail food prices. Another such use of AGMOD is to support a model of Michigan agriculture.

The model is primarily recursive as is indicated in Figure 8-5. Most of the behavioral equations are linear. Prices and incomes are deflated by the Implicit Price Deflator for Personal Consumption Expenditures and exchange rates are used to link U.S. prices to the international sector.

A feature of the model is that all the U.S. supply equations are driven by gross margin-type variables. These margins represent gross revenue less variable costs (crops) or less feed costs (livestock) and are calculated in terms of purchasing power, i.e., are deflated. Gross margins are key indicators of profits for individual enterprises.

The output of the model can be used for long-range planning and for examining the impact of alternative scenarios relative to the underlying assumptions. Another application of the model is to evaluate alternative farm policy decisions as they affect individual enterprises, total farm income, government costs, and consumer food prices.

The model solves for a 15-year projection period in a few seconds. By employing a random number generator, projections can be established stochastically. One application has been to project crop yields as distributions around trends. Since the impact of weather on crop yields is one of the important unknowns in agricultural forecasting, this technique can, at least, add a probability dimension to projections. Possibly as many as 500 or more iterations are needed to formulate reasonable approximations of these distributions, so that the speed of the solution process is a key consideration. (See Chapter 10.)

FIGURE 8-5

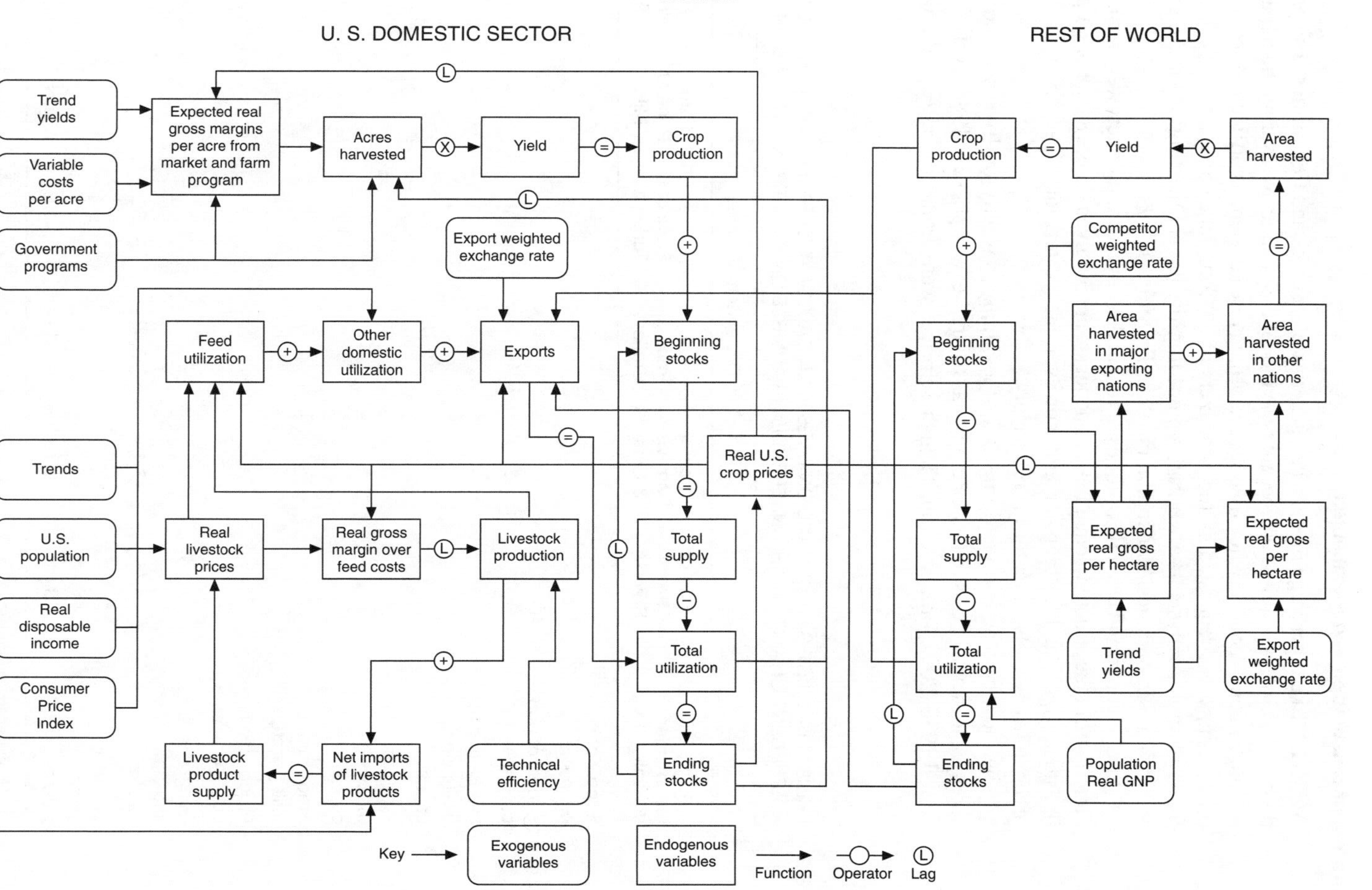

AGMOD
U. S. DOMESTIC SECTOR
REST OF WORLD
Trend yields
Variable costs per acre
Government programs
Expected real gross margins per acre from market and farm program
Acres harvested
Yield
Crop production
Export weighted exchange rate
Feed utilization
Other domestic utilization
Exports
Beginning stocks
Trends
U.S. population
Real disposable income
Consumer Price Index
Real livestock prices
Real gross margin over feed costs
Livestock production
Real U.S. crop prices
Total supply
Total utilization
Ending stocks
Livestock product supply
Net imports of livestock products
Technical efficiency
Crop production
Yield
Area harvested
Competitor weighted exchange rate
Beginning stocks
Area harvested in major exporting nations
Area harvested in other nations
Total supply
Expected real gross per hectare
Expected real gross per hectare
Total utilization
Trend yields
Export weighted exchange rate
Ending stocks
Population Real GNP
Key
Exogenous variables
Endogenous variables
Function
Operator
Lag

Dynamic Generation of Elasticities and Flexibilities

AGMOD, like other large models, can generate elasticities and flexibilities. The procedure is not always a simple one because the model is dynamic. Measuring the impact of a change in one variable, while holding everything else constant, is difficult. A set of such relationships was requested by the organizers of a "Conference on Large-scale Models for Economic Analysis"—a workshop preceding the annual meeting of the American Agricultural Economics Association in 1988 (Taylor et al., 1993).

Price, income, and cross flexibilities of demand on livestock products were measured directly from the structural equations, as no lags were involved (Table 8-2). For crop and livestock supply and for crop demand, however, lagged relationships were implicit. Irreversibility was also a factor in crop supply.

The most convenient way to measure the supply elasticity on livestock and both supply-and-demand elasticities on crops was to first set real prices at 1988 levels for the period 1988–2000 for a base run. Then these prices were arbitrarily raised and lowered

TABLE 8-2 PRICE FLEXIBILITIES OF DEMAND ON LIVESTOCK CALCULATED FROM AGMOD: EFFECT OF A 1 PERCENT CHANGE IN THE INDEPENDENT VARIABLE ON THE DEPENDENT VARIABLE

	Dependent Variable					
Independent Variable	Price of Choice Steers	Price of Barrows & Gilts	Price of Broilers	Price of Turkeys	Farm Price of Milk	Farm Price of Eggs
Supply of beef per capita	–2.70					
Supply of pork per capita		–3.40				
Production of broilers per capita			–2.75			
Production of turkeys per capita				–1.70		
Production of milk per capita					–.83	
Production of eggs per capita						–3.09
Supply of substitutes per capita[a]	–.15	–3.14	–3.43	–5.32	—	–2.23
Disposable income per capita	3.31	3.78	4.11	4.12	.55	1.11

Note: Based on forecast values for 1988.
[a]Other meat plus fish for meat items; all meat for eggs.

for subsequent runs. Tables 8-3 and 8-4 reflect the effects of changing the price 10 percent over and under the base run for 1988–2000, but tabulated in terms of a 1 percent change.

On livestock, the supply elasticity increased with additional time lags on all items except broilers and turkeys. A negative supply elasticity emerged on the supply of beef in the second year due to the withholding of female stock with rising prices and liquidation with falling prices. Irreversibility was significant only on crops. The apparent inconsistencies on the signs of supply elasticities on corn and wheat can be attributed to the application of farm programs in rising versus falling prices. AGMOD triggered increased set-asides if stocks increased or pulled land back into production if stocks reached pipeline levels.

In Table 8-4, the demand elasticities on crops carried the expected negative signs relative to price; also, the negative elasticities tended to increase as the time frame expanded.

This effort to measure flexibilities and elasticities with a model such as AGMOD revealed that such relationships depend on: (1) the extent of the change in the denominator of a flexibility or elasticity formula, (2) the direction of change in the denominator, (3) the length of time specified (how many periods into the future), and (4) the base period, i.e., the particular years being considered (in this case, 1988–2000). The point is that models employing constant elasticities and flexibilities may be very misleading for forecasting purposes.

In the process of constructing these large models, the analyst should be continually evaluating alternative formulations. Also, when the model is completed, a compelling

TABLE 8-3 SUPPLY ELASTICITIES ON LIVESTOCK AND CROPS CALCULATED FROM AGMOD: EFFECT OF A 1 PERCENT INCREASE IN PRICE ON THE DEPENDENT VARIABLE

		Year				
Dependent Variable	**Price**	**1988 %**	**1989 %**	**1993 %**	**1998 %**	**2000 %**
Supply of beef	Choice steers	NC	−.05	+.55	+1.45	+1.76
Supply of pork	Barrows & gilts	NC	+.13	+.76	+1.12	+1.19
Production of broilers	Broilers	NC	+0.07	+.11	+.10	+.10
Production of turkeys	Turkeys	NC	+0.08	+.09	+.08	+.07
Production of milk	Milk	NC	NC	+.39	+1.12	+1.14
Production of eggs	Eggs	NC	+.07	+.24	+.32	+.33
Production of feed grain	Corn					
Increase in price		NC	+.15	−.14	−.80	−.72
Decrease in price		NC	−.13	+.11	+.51	+.51
Production of soybeans	Soybeans					
Increase in price		NC	+.25	+1.10	+1.22	+1.14
Decrease in price		NC	−.25	−.47	−.71	−.46
Production of wheat	Wheat					
Increase in price		NC	+.23	−.61	−.25	+.07
Decrease in price		NC	−.23	+1.10	+.84	+1.08

Note: Both increase and decrease in price applied to crop production.

TABLE 8-4 DEMAND ELASTICITIES ON CROPS CALCULATED FROM AGMOD: EFFECT OF A 1 PERCENT INCREASE IN PRICE ON THE DEPENDENT VARIABLE

Dependent Variable	Price	Year 1988 (%)	1989 (%)	1993 (%)	1998 (%)	2000 (%)
Feed Grain	Corn					
Fed to livestock		−.16	−.20	−.40	−.59	−.65
Exports		NC	−.07	−.61	−1.03	−1.11
Total utilization		−.10	−.13	−.40	−.61	−.66
Soybeans	Soybeans, meal, and oil					
Fed to livestock (meal)		−.05	−.05	−.10	−.13	−.13
Crush		−.12	−.11	−.15	−.17	−.17
Exports		−.44	−.39	−.31	−.31	−.33
Total utilization		−.22	−.21	−.20	−.21	−.22
Wheat	Wheat					
Domestic consumption		NC	NC	NC	NC	NC
Fed to livestock		−.85	−1.55	−4.10	−5.86	−6.18
Exports		NC	−.12	−1.08	−2.47	−2.02
Total utilization		−.09	−.21	−.96	−1.76	−1.54

step is to measure its tracking performance, i.e., how close are the forecasts from the model to the actual level of the endogenous variables. Some of the more popular tools for forecast evaluation are described in Chapter 9.

SUMMARY

Large econometric/simulation models can be solved by an algorithm called Gauss-Seidel which provides approximate solutions to systems of equations. To accommodate Gauss-Seidel, certain techniques need to be followed in model building. Software programs such as MicroTSP provide convenient means to estimate structural equations, generate transformations, and compose and solve large models.

A number of large-scale models have been developed in both the public and private sectors. Michigan State University's AGMOD is fairly representative of econometric/simulation models—mostly recursive, commodity specific, and designed to generate year-to-year projections over a 10 to 15-year period. One model, SWOPSIM, substantially different from standard models, employs matrices of demand-and-supply elasticities by nations, enabling the USDA to evaluate trade policies.

In generating supply-and-demand elasticities and flexibilities, AGMOD revealed that these relationships depend on: (1) extent of change in the denominator of the formulas, (2) direction of change, (3) length of time, and (4) the particular base period for the measurement. The point is that elasticities and flexibilities are not constant.

QUESTIONS FOR STUDY

1. Why are so-called "econometric" models usually "econometric/simulation" models?
2. Why has Gauss-Seidel been a valuable tool for solving large econometric models?
3. How does the Gauss-Seidel approach differ from solving a linear system of equations with n equations and n unknowns?
4. Why incorporate a stock variable in terms of a ratio to total utilization? What functional form might be appropriate?
5. Why place lower bounds on variables such as ending stocks in the modeling process?
6. What is the difference between exogenous and endogenous variables?
7. Of what particular value are "balance sheets" in econometric modeling and the presentation of results?
8. What is meant by "satellite models"?
9. Compare SWOPSIM with AGMOD. What would you list as strengths and weaknesses of each?
10. Enumerate the factors affecting supply and demand elasticities and flexibilities. Describe why these factors may invalidate the assumption of constant elasticities and flexibilities as the time frame is expanded.

9

FORECAST EVALUATION

POINTS:

1. Selecting appropriate formulas to evaluate forecasts.
2. Sorting out bias and random errors.
3. Importance of asymmetry in forecast errors.
4. Standards to evaluate performance of econometric models.
5. Role of composite forecasts.
6. Ex-ante and ex-post evaluations.

Techniques for evaluating forecasts from econometric/simulation models or any other sources are related to those applied to single equations in regression analysis, but are more extensive. Measures such as: (1) the standard error of the regression as a percent of the mean of the dependent variable and (2) turning point errors in the period-to-period predictions versus the actual changes are examples of measures applied to individual regression equations that have parallel uses in general forecast evaluation.

A basic set of tools have been applied to agricultural forecasts by the United States General Accounting Office (USGAO, 1991). Their most recent analysis drew from a number of studies in addition to their own past programs (Armstrong, 1985; Ascher, 1978; Makridakis et al., 1984; Bretschneider, 1985). A forecast error, simply defined as:

Error = Actual Value – Forecast Value, or

E = A – F

has two components, a "random error" and a "bias error." With a sufficient number of observations, an analyst can begin to distinguish the random component from the bias component. The total error is the sum of the random error and the bias error.

A reason for sorting out the bias error is that an econometrician may be able to correct for that source of error, while having to live with the random component. Use of "add factors" to make such corrections is common in modeling. This merely involves placing a plus or minus value in an equation where the bias is evident. With unpredictable weather an important element in agriculture, the random component will remain prominent in most models.

ASYMMETRIC ERRORS

Since the total error values can be both negative or positive, a simple approach to measurement would be to add the total negative errors (forecasts were too high) and divide by the number of negative errors. Similarly, add the total positive errors (forecasts were too low) and divide by the number of positive errors. The modeler could then communicate with users the absolute average for erring on the high side versus erring on the low side and even provide the probability of negative or positive errors.

This differentiation may be important to the user. For example, the consequences to a farmer for prices turning out to be much lower than forecast could be very stressful while prices turning out to be higher than forecast could be euphoric.

While users could understand the meaning of absolute values, a preferred approach would be to calculate the errors in terms of *percent* of the actual values. Put in percentage terms, error measurements are more comparable over time on the same variable or among the endogenous variables in a model. The mean negative percentage error (MNPE) would be:

$$MNPE = \left[1/m \sum_{t=1}^{m} (NE_t/NA_t) \right] x\ 100$$

where: NE_t are the negative errors, NA_t are the actual values in the years (or other intervals) in which the error is negative, and m is the number of years (or other intervals) in which the error is negative.

The mean positive percentage error (MPPE) would be:

$$MPPE = \left[1/n-m \sum_{t=1}^{n-m} (PE_t/PA)_t \right] x\ 100$$

where: PE_t are the positive errors, PA_t are the actual values in the years (or other intervals) in which the error is positive, and n is the total number of years (or other intervals) in the evaluation period.

These measurements could be further refined in terms of the frequency with which positive or negative error terms were above a certain level. Turning back to the example of a farmer's concern about the error term on prices, small negative errors may be of little consequence. However, the probability of negative errors in forecasting prices that would spell bankruptcy for a farmer would be given particular attention.

The point is that forecast evaluation techniques should be designed with the user in mind and the purpose for which the exercise is being developed. Asymmetry in the design may be very important. While the techniques to be presented from here on are symmetric, they could be modified to fit particular decision-making frameworks.

MEASURES OF TOTAL ERROR

The USGAO has applied three measures of total error in evaluating forecasting accuracy (USGAO, 1991). The first is the same as MNPE and MPPE except that the signs of the error are not differentiated, i.e., absolute errors are computed in a formula for mean absolute percentage error (MAPE).

$$\text{MAPE} = \left[1/n \sum_{t=1}^{n} (|E_t|/A_t) \right] \text{x } 100$$

where: $|E_t|$ are the absolute errors and the other terms are as previously defined.

Somewhat of a deficiency with this formula is that any variable that has a lower bound, such as zero, but no upper bound, gets biased treatment. For a variable with a lower bound of zero, the low forecast can never be wrong by more than 100 percent, but the error on the high side has no limit.

To correct for this deficiency, USGAO has employed a formula called adjusted mean absolute percentage error (AMAPE).

$$\text{AMAPE} = \left[1/n \sum_{t=1}^{n} (|A_t - F_t|/.5\ (A_t + F_t)) \right] \text{x } 100$$

The sum of the absolute error, divided by half the actual plus the forecast, is then divided by the number of periods (and then multiplied by 100). This measure helps reduce the favor tendered to low forecasts in MAPE.

Probably the most common measure of forecast accuracy is the root mean squared percentage error (RMSPE).

$$\text{RMSPE} = \left[\left(\sqrt{1/n \sum_{t=1}^{n} E_t^2} \right) / \left(1/n \sum_{t=1}^{n} A_t \right) \right] \text{x } 100$$

Squaring the error term converts all observations to plus. Those squared errors are summed, with a square root taken of the sum divided by the total number of observations. That square root is then divided by the average of the actual values. The resulting figure is then multiplied by 100 to convert to percentage terms.

MEASURES OF BIAS ERROR

Bias error refers to consistent under- or overestimates from a forecasting scheme. To measure bias errors, signs on the errors are taken into account. One formula is mean percentage error (MPE).

$$\text{MPE} = \left[1/n \sum_{t=1}^{n} (E_t/A_t) \right] \text{x } 100$$

As with MAPE, this formulation favors underestimates that cannot exceed 100 percent on variables with a lower bound of zero.

A modification of MPE is trimmed mean percentage error (TMPE) defined as:

$$\text{TMPE} = \left[1/n-2 \sum_{t=1}^{n-2} (E_t/A_t) \right] \text{x } 100$$

where: the single most positive and single most negative errors are dropped.

This modification suppresses the dominating effect of an occasional large error that may be misleading in terms of the normal performance of the model.

A final formula to measure bias is called weighted mean percentage error (WMPE), defined as:

$$\text{WMPE} = \left[\left(\sum_{t=1}^{n} E_t \right) / \left(\sum_{t=1}^{n} A_t \right) \right] \text{x } 100$$

In this formula, the errors are summed and then divided by the sum of the actual values. This tends to diminish the effect of high individual percentage errors on the overall bias error.

THEIL'S INEQUALITY COEFFICIENTS

Procedures to evaluate forecasts have also been developed by H. Theil (Theil, 1966). Some debate has emerged in the profession on which formulation Theil intended. Three formulas have been applied, labeled U, U_1 and U_2, respectively.

$$U = \left[\sqrt{1/n \sum_{t=1}^{n} (F_t - A_t)^2} \Big/ \left(\sqrt{1/n \sum_{t=1}^{n} F_t^2} + \sqrt{1/n \sum_{t=1}^{n} A_t^2} \right) \right] \text{x } 100$$

$$U_1 = \left[\sqrt{1/n-1 \sum_{t=2}^{n} [(F_t - A_{t-1}) - (A_t - A_{t-1})]^2} \Big/ \right.$$

$$\left. \left(\sqrt{1/n-1 \sum_{t=2}^{n} (F_t - A_{t-1})^2} + \sqrt{1/n-1 \sum_{t=2}^{n} (A_t - A_{t-1})^2} \right) \right] \text{x } 100$$

$$U_2 = \left[\sqrt{1/n-1 \sum_{t=2}^{n} [(F_t - A_{t-1}) - (A_t - A_{t-1})]^2} \Big/ \right.$$

$$\left. \sqrt{1/n-1 \sum_{t=2}^{n} (A_t - A_{t-1})^2} \right] \text{x } 100$$

With "U," the comparisons are strictly between forecasts and actual values for a given time period, t, and do not involve the previous time period, t–1. A perfect fit would generate a U of 0 and with the extreme of a poor fit approaching a value of 1.

The formulas for U_1 and U_2 involve actual values for the previous time period, t–1. By inspection, one can discern that the numerators for all three formulations are the same except U_1 and U_2 have to drop the first period (t=1) in order to accommodate the lagged actual value. By collecting terms in the numerators of U_1 and U_2:

$$(F_t - A_{t-1}) - (A_t - A_{t-1}) = F_t - A_t$$

Notice that the numerators are root mean squared errors.

While all three formulations may be useful, Leuthold points out that U is seriously flawed because adding a constant to F_t and A_t will reduce the value of U, but not the correlation coefficient between the set of F_t's and A_t's (Leuthold, 1975). Leuthold claims Theil never meant U to be applied—only changes in F_t's from A_{t-1}'s and A_t's from A_{t-1}'s were to be considered.

The inequality coefficient U_1 is what Theil intended. Its values are not subject to the arbitrary nature of U. Like U, U_1 is bounded between 0 and 1, and for the same data series would have higher values than U.

The inequality coefficient, U_2, was later proposed by Theil as a modification to U_1, partly because the forecast did not appear in the denominator. This coefficient is also bounded at 0 for perfect forecasts, but has no upper limit. U_2 has the value of 1 if applied to a model where the forecast is equal to the actual value in t–1. The point is that U_2 can indicate whether a model generates forecasts that are *less* accurate as well as more accurate than simple naive models that establish a forecast as equal to the actual values for the previous period. Neither U nor U_1 can indicate to the analysts that their models can't even out-perform the naive model.

STANDARDS FOR COMPARISON

Alternative econometric/simulation models can be evaluated by the measures earlier discussed as applied to key endogenous variables. The modeler reviews these results and then selects the specification that provides the best overall performance. This, of course, involves considerable judgment and should be based on the purpose of the model and how it will be used.

In addition, as indicated in the discussion of the Theil inequality coefficients, a structural model would also be evaluated in comparison with other forecasting procedures. A weak challenger would be the naive model in which forecasts are simply actual values of the previous period. Another challenger might be trend or the prediction from techniques such as double exponential smoothing. Time series analysis, discussed in Chapter 18, could also generate empirical models for evaluating the tracking performance of a structural model.

Forecasts from other structural models, the USDA, surveys of economists, or other sources might also be introduced into the evaluation process. A very strong contender would be consensus forecasts from a collection of models and/or surveys of market analysts. The value of consensus forecasts in U.S. agriculture was documented in a study of responses to the Annual Outlook Survey of the American Agricultural Economics Association in 1983–1995 (Kastens et al., 1996). On prices, the futures market might provide a standard for testing the model. For example, can the model forecast cash prices a year in advance any better than futures prices over the same period (with some prediction scheme for basis, the difference between futures and cash price)?

If, as indicated in the discussion of Theil's U_2, analysts wanted to test a model against the naive model (using the last period's actual value), they should structure their model to incorporate all that is known in the previous period. For example, with a recursive model, they have a couple of alternatives on how to run the model over time.

1 If the model has lagged endogenous variables, make certain the solution process reads the actual value and not the forecast values on the lagged variables. Rather than have the model generate the lagged values of the endogenous variables over the test period, simply use the code for the actual variables for all the lagged endogenous variables on the right-hand side of each equation.
2 If the model has lagged endogenous variables, set them at the actual levels prior to the beginning period of the test run. Run the model over the test period with the model generating forecast values for the lagged endogenous variables.

Short-range (Period-to-Period) Forecasting Evaluation

In alternative 1, the model is geared to forecast one period ahead. Incorporating the known values of the lagged endogenous variables establishes the same situation for each period in the test that would be apparent to a forecaster. For example, if the price of hogs in years t–1 and t–2 affects hog production in t, why not use the known actual prices of hogs in t–1 and t–2 rather than the model's prediction of hog prices in the lagged years? In this form, Theil's U_1 and U_2 inequality coefficients can appropriately be applied.

An example of the application of the measures of error including U, U_1, and U_2 is shown in Table 9-1. This represents two simple hog models, testing whether a model with: (1) the hog–corn price ratio or (2) the separate variables lagged one and two years is the preferred specification for a supply equation. Error terms from "naive models" are also displayed.

For the short-range forecasts as compiled in the second two columns of Table 9-1, model 2 exhibited the better performance using mean errors, but slightly poorer on RMSPE. A slightly stronger bias was indicated with model 2 relative to model 1. Theil's inequality coefficients, U_1 and U_2, favored model 2. In comparison with naive models (first two columns of Table 9-1), equation (2) had the edge except for RMSPE relative to DES, the bias error registered in WMPE, and U.

Long-range Forecasting Evaluation

The long-range forecasting abilities of the models were evaluated in the final two columns of Table 9-1. The total period of 1973–1992 was included. Compared to the short-range forecasts, the performance of the long-range format for both models was weaker, for the most part, as expected—and for equation (2) even weaker than the naive

TABLE 9-1 FORECAST EVALUATION FOR PRICES ON BARROWS AND GILTS GENERATED FROM TWO HOG MODELS WITH A GEOMETRIC LAG IN THE SUPPLY EQUATION; NO. 1 WITH A TWO-YEAR LAG OF THE HOG–CORN RATIO AND NO. 2 WITH A TWO-YEAR LAG ON HOG PRICES AND THE PRICE OF CORN, 1973–1992

	Naive Models		Actual Lagged Values in Supply		Initialized in 1971–1972	
	Forecast in t = Actual in t-1 %	Forecast Based on Double Exponential Smoothing %	Equ. 1 %	Equ. 2 %	Equ. 1 %	Equ. 2 %
Error Measurement						
Total Error						
MNPE	–15.7	–13.6	–12.9	–10.6	–22.0	–18.2
MPPE	14.3	13.8	13.3	12.2	12.3	18.0
MAPE	15.2	13.7	13.1	11.4	15.7	18.1
AMAPE	14.8	13.2	13.4	11.8	15.8	18.8
RMSPE	20.6	18.7	19.5	19.8	20.6	23.9
Bias Error						
MPE	–5.2	–5.4	.2	.8	.3	1.7
TMPE	–5.9	–5.6	–*	–.1	.4	1.7
WMPE	–3.1	–1.4	2.9	3.6	3.1	2.1
Theil's Inequality Coefficient						
U	9.7	9.0	9.5	9.7	10.0	11.4
U_1	100.0	47.1	44.2	32.8	43.3	46.8
U_2	100.0	90.3	84.9	69.2	93.2	103.4

*Less than .1%.

models for U_2. However, the test against these naive models is unfair for long-range forecasting.

In long-range forecasting, the models are geared to forecast several periods ahead. Obviously, the models have to generate their own lagged endogenous variables beyond the initialization period. For example, if an annual database on hogs covered 1968–1992 and the analyst wanted to develop a model to forecast 10 years into the future, 1968 and 1969 would be the initialization years to test 1970–1979 (providing actual values of any lagged endogenous variables in 1968 and 1969). Then, to test 1971–1980, the lagged endogenous variables would be set at their actual values for 1969 and 1970. To test 1972–1981, lagged endogenous variables would be set at their 1970 and 1971 actual values. This procedure would continue until solving the models for 1983–1992, with lagged values set at their actual levels in 1981 and 1982.

After this process is completed, the analyst could generate the error term for each interval in the projection period. In the hog example, the error term would be calculated for each of the first through 10 years into the projection period. Since the solution process was by 14 different time segments, the analyst would have 14 observations for each year of a 10-year forecast period. The first year out would be identical to the results in alternative 1 (i.e., the one-year-ahead scheme). The expected result would be that the forecast errors increase as the years into the projection period move from 1 to 10.

All the tools for forecast evaluation could be applied to long-range as well as period-to-period type models. As constructed, Theil's inequality coefficient would not seem relevant to models designed for long-range forecasts. A possible modification would be to replace A_{t-1} in the numerators of U_1 and U_2 with F_{t-1}, and F_{t-1} for A_{t-1} in the first term of the denominator in U_1.

The reformulated U_1 and U_2 would be:

$$U_{1F} = \left[\sqrt{1/n-1 \sum_{t=2}^{n} [(F_t - F_{t-1}) - (A_t - A_{t-1})]^2} \Big/ \left(\sqrt{1/n-1 \sum_{t=2}^{n} (F_t - F_{t-1})^2} + \sqrt{1/n-1 \sum_{t=2}^{n} (A_t - A_{t-1})^2}\right)\right] \text{x } 100$$

$$U_{2F} = \left[\sqrt{1/n-1 \sum_{t=2}^{n} [(F_t - F_{t-1}) - (A_t - A_{t-1})]^2} \Big/ \sqrt{1/n-1 \sum_{t=2}^{n} (A_t - A_{t-1})^2}\right] \text{x } 100$$

Because of the long-term projection orientations of many econometric/simulation models, the pattern of the forecasts may be more important than how well the model performs from year-to-year. U_{1F} and U_{2F} evaluate how year-to-year changes in the forecasts compare with year-to-year changes in the actual values rather than how forecasts relative to the previous year's actual values compare with the year-to-year change in actual values. This provides more insight into longer-range patterns in which forecasts are built on previous year's forecasts rather than actual values. If positive or negative bias appears in the evaluation of the model over the historical period, techniques known as "add factors" can be supplied in the forecast period to adjust for this bias. For this reason, U_{1F} and U_{2F} may be relevant tools for evaluating how well models track movements over a period of years.

Procedures are not well developed for building naive models to test structural models forecasting beyond one period into the future. Conceivably, some type of univariate model could be devised with strict time series generation of each of the endogenous variables.

DOUBLE EXPONENTIAL SMOOTHING (DES)

One way to establish a naive model for a long-range forecasting model is simply to regress the endogenous variables on a time variable. If a model cannot generate forecasts more accurate than by plotting trends, the performance would be scored low.

Another technique to develop naive models for long-range projections is double exponential smoothing (DES). This procedure is described in Pindyke and Rubinfeld and in the *MicroTSP User's Manual* (Pindyke and Rubinfeld, 1991; Hall et al., 1990). This provides the analyst with a projection procedure in which more recent data can be given greater weight than the earlier data.

If, in the historical period prior to the estimation period, trends in the endogenous variables were not linear, extending past trends would not provide a very rigorous test for a structural model.

The formula for single exponential smoothing is:

$$F_t = \alpha A_{t-1} + (1-\alpha) F_{t-1}$$

The value of α is usually small (less than .1) and indicates how much weight to give to the most recent actual observation versus the forecast for the previous period. The term α is called a damping parameter. In MicroTSP, the analyst can either set the value of the damping parameter, or allow the program called "SMOOTH" to estimate it by finding the value that minimizes the sum of squared forecast errors within the sample.

In double exponential smoothing, the single smoothed data is smoothed again:

$$F'_t = \alpha F_{t-1} + (1-\alpha) F'_{t-1}$$

where: F'_t is the doubly smoothed forecasts.

MicroTSP's command for double exponential smoothing (SMOOTH(D)) includes a trend in the forecast.

The major difference between the forecasts from an equation in which the dependent variable is a linear function of time and the DES technique is that the latter gives more weight to observations just prior to the beginning of the test period. The projections from DES are linear.

This is only one example of the usefulness of DES for econometric simulation model building. Another application is to determine whether a variable is following a linear trend or not. Applying DES to a data set, the result will be the same as an OLS equation with the variable as a function of time if DES establishes that the relationship is essentially linear. In Figure 9-1, an examination of U.S. corn yields over 1955–1993, indicates leveling off in yields in this period.

Related to testing for linearity, DES provides a means for tracking certain variables over time in order to identify an underlying non-linear trend. This is illustrated on U.S. corn yields for 1900 to 1993 (Figure 9-2). The estimates from double exponential smoothing can establish the base for deriving the deviation from the underlying non-linear trend. As such, this procedure can be very useful in modeling crop yields stochastically, as well as other variables of this type.

HANDLING EXOGENOUS VARIABLES

Overlooked in this evaluation procedure for both the period-to-period and the long-term models is the handling of exogenous variables. Traditionally, analysts have assumed that these variables can be forecast without error. Truly, in all of the testing described, procedures designed for endogenous variables should be applied to exogenous variables. One reason this has not been done is that many exogenous variables are either

FIGURE 9-1 Yield of U.S. Corn in 1955 to 1993 tracked by a linear trend and DES.*

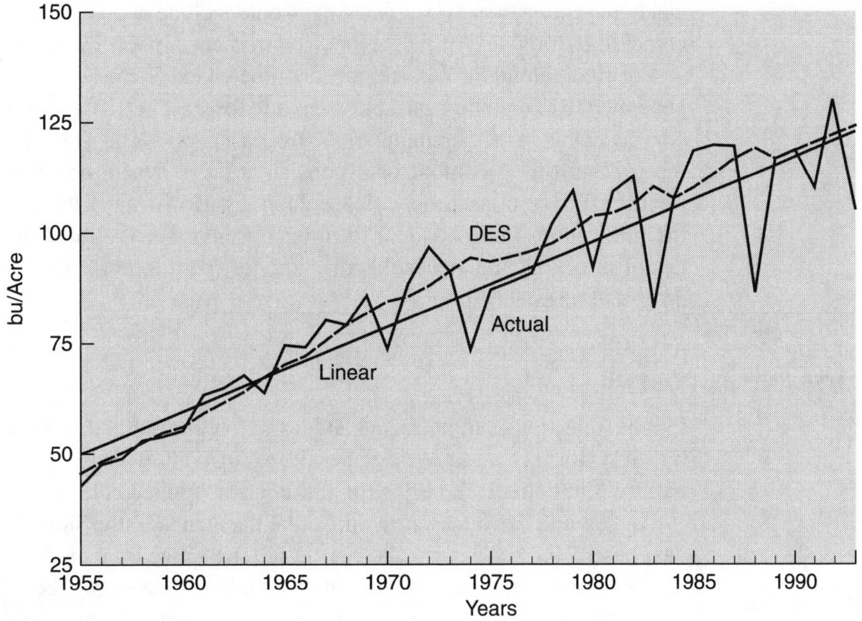

*Double Exponential Smoothing.

FIGURE 9-2 Yield of U.S. corn in 1900 to 1993 tracked by double exponential smoothing.

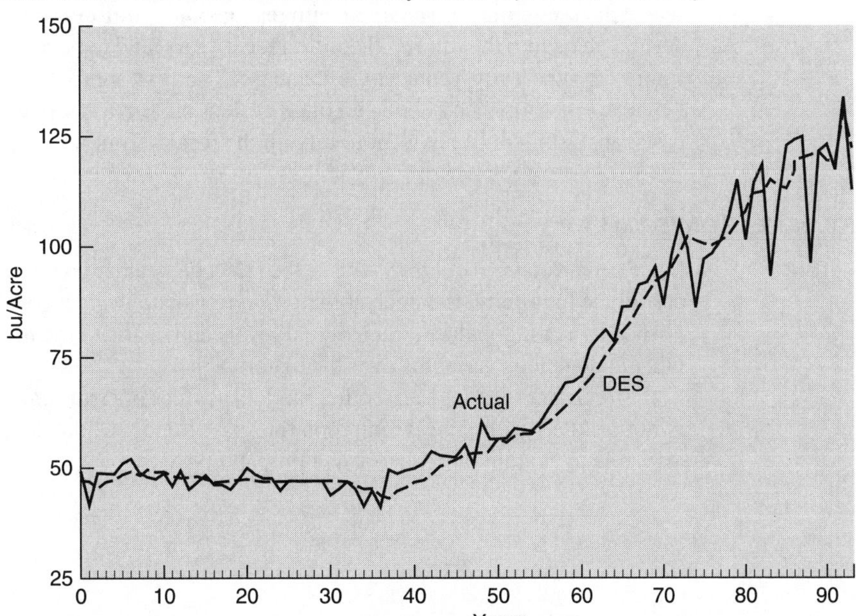

more predictable than the endogenous variables, or errors in their predictions are not crucial to the endogenous variables. This would include population, consumer disposable income, inflation rates, interest rates, government support rates, etc.

For rigor, an additional step needs to be taken. Some scheme needs to be applied to generate the exogenous variables for each forecast period assuming the level of knowledge available at the beginning of the forecast period. This could be based on expert opinion (difficult to document on a consistent basis over time), on-going macro models, trends, DES, or other time series techniques. However, if the purpose is to test strictly the endogenous mechanism of the model, analysts can rationalize employing actual values of the exogenous variables over the test period, but should recognize the forecast error will be underestimated.

EX-ANTE AND EX-POST

Finally, questions can be raised about the forecasting ability of a model based only on how it performs over an historic period, exclusively. This is termed as an "ex-post" evaluation. Alternatively, a very strong test can be applied called an "ex-ante" evaluation.

An "ex-ante" evaluation requires that the analysis stop short of the entire time series data base. Whether a period-to-period or long-range type model, the structural parameters are estimated from a time span that excludes the more recent years. The test period then is the span of actual observations beyond the time frame included in the model estimation. All the techniques covered previously could apply to the "ex-ante" period. This clearly is a more severe test for a model than an "ex-post" test.

Of course, an "ex-ante" test requires that important information be excluded from the analysis. Few econometricians readily give up the rich information contained in the most recent data set if they are charged with responsibility of forecasting the next year or next several years into the future. The most recent years tend to be more closely related to the future than the early years in the database. The best approach might be to explore an "ex-ante" performance as one part of an evaluation. But to properly prepare to issue forecasts, analysts will likely want to rely on the results from the entire database.

HANDLING THE RANDOM ERROR

Since certain sources of error, such as the effect of weather on crop yields, cannot be forecast in the long-term, the analyst may wish to isolate that source. This could be accomplished by setting yields at their actual levels and evaluate the model's performance on other endogenous variables over the historical period.

To *forecast* crop yields and other random sources of error *into the future,* the modeler is not saddled with simply extrapolating past trends. Chapter 10 introduces methods available to capture these errors in a probability sense.

SUMMARY

Errors in forecasts from econometric/simulation models contain random and bias components. Econometricians may be able to correct for bias errors and apply stochastic procedures to handle the random errors. Errors can be evaluated asymmetrically that could have special significance to decisions based on models.

Probably the most common measure of forecast accuracy is the root mean squared percentage error. Theil incorporates the root mean squared errors in the numerators of his formulas. Theil's U_2 is preferred in that it can evaluate whether a model can out-perform simple naive forecasts of no change from the previous period.

A weakness of Theil's formulas is the concentration on evaluating period-to-period forecasts. Other approaches are needed to evaluate the ability of models to capture longer-term patterns in endogenous variables. One way is to apply an ex-ante evaluation over several periods.

Other standards for evaluating models could include double-exponential smoothing, time series, futures markets, and consensus surveys.

QUESTIONS FOR STUDY

1 Why should evaluation of forecast errors be asymmetric?
2 What is meant by a "bias" error? How can it be corrected?
3 What is meant by "random" error? How can it be handled?
4 Why convert error measurements to percentage terms?
5 Why have a number of formulas included the summations and averaging of the square root of errors squared?
6 What is the advantage of Theil's U_2 over U_1?
7 Suggest standards for evaluating forecasts from a model other than simply comparing the forecasts with the actual values or changes from the previous period.
8 What is the difference between evaluation of models for short-run versus long-range forecasting?
9 Why is it difficult to evaluate forecasts of exogenous variables in a model?
10 Explain the difference between ex-ante and ex-post evaluations of forecasts from a model.

10

STOCHASTIC MODELING

POINTS:

1 Impact of weather/pests on crop yields.
2 Trends in crop yield variability.
3 Normality tests on crop yield variability.
4 Introducing stochastic components in an econometric model.
5 Consideration of the correlation of crop yield variability between crops.

Stochastic procedures can appropriately be applied to any equation in a model where the random error term is important and its distribution can be defined. Forecasters face major challenges on agricultural commodities because production depends so much on biological factors—particularly weather, but also disease and insects. From one year to the next, these important elements are virtually unpredictable. However, from observations of past fluctuations, probability distributions can be generated on the variables so affected. Crop yields represent the major target for this methodology.

SCOPE OF THE PROBLEM

The significance of these factors can be illustrated by the application of double exponential smoothing (DES) in tracking crop yields such as in Figures 9-1 and 9-2. This procedure provides a reasonable extension of past trends and is about as accurate as more sophisticated analytical tools in predicting yields a year ahead of harvest. Deviations of actual yields from the DES projections provide some measure of the inherent error in forecasting yields for the coming year.

These deviations were measured in terms of percent of trend for U.S. corn, soybeans, wheat, and coarse grain other than corn for 1955–1993. Histograms of these deviations are portrayed in Figures 10-1, 10-2, 10-3, and 10-4.

Viewing these histograms, one would conclude that trend forecasts of these yields would be off by 5 percent or more in about half of the years and off by 10 percent or more in about one year out of six (one year out of four for coarse grain other than corn). Crucial as this error term is in econometric forecasting, very few models make any allowance for these discrepancies.

For many years, agricultural economists have stressed the importance of generating probability distributions in forecasts (Teigen and Bell, 1978; Bessler and Moore, 1979; Nelson, 1979; Ikerd, 1979). Even so, the application of econometric models for this purpose has been quite limited. Nearly all agricultural econometric models incorporate trend yields or slight modifications based on expected crop prices relative to input prices. At best, these large models may be run with two or three alternative yield assumptions.

The major reasons modelers shy away from applying probability distributions in their methodology is the complexity involved and the presumption that users are primarily interested in the most likely path of the variables into the future. Even if generating probability distributions one year ahead were plausible, the large number of branches into following years requires many iterations in the solution process. Yet, with the advancement

FIGURE 10-1 Percent deviation of U.S. corn yields from trend established by DES, 1955–1993*.

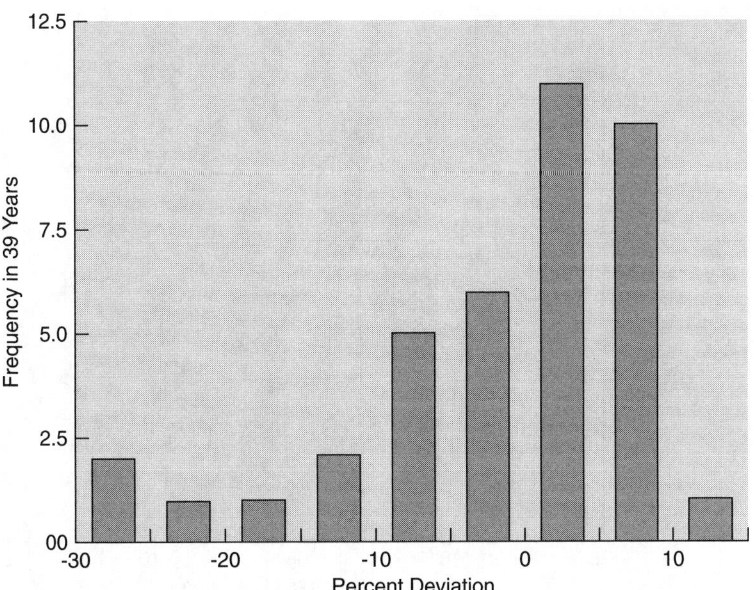

*Double Exponential Smoothing.

FIGURE 10-2 Percent deviation of U.S. soybean yields from trend established by DES, 1955–1993*.

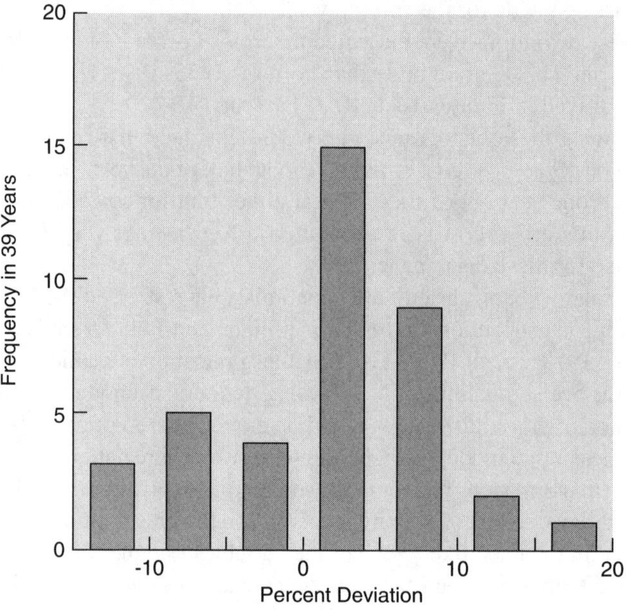

*Double Exponential Smoothing.

FIGURE 10-3 Percent deviation of U.S. wheat yields from trend established by DES, 1955–1993*.

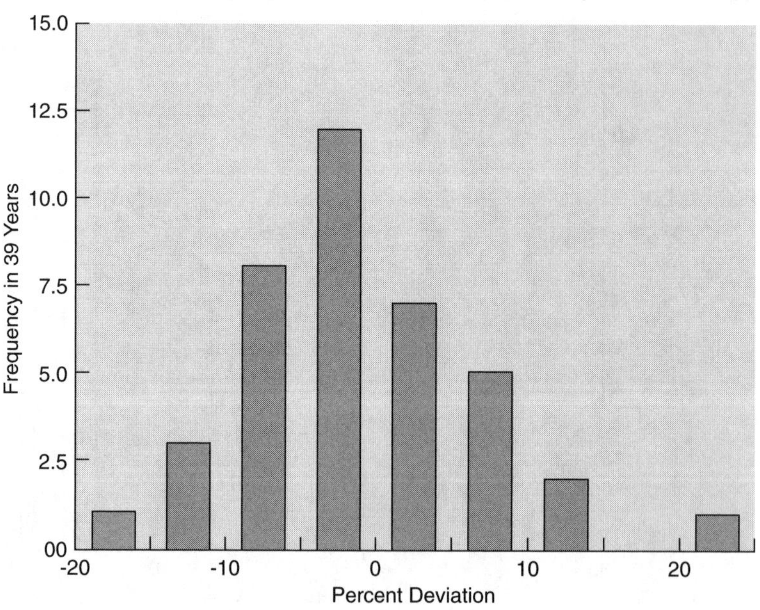

*Double Exponential Smoothing.

FIGURE 10-4 Percent deviation of U.S. yields of sorghum grain, barley, and oats from trend established by DES, 1955–1993*.

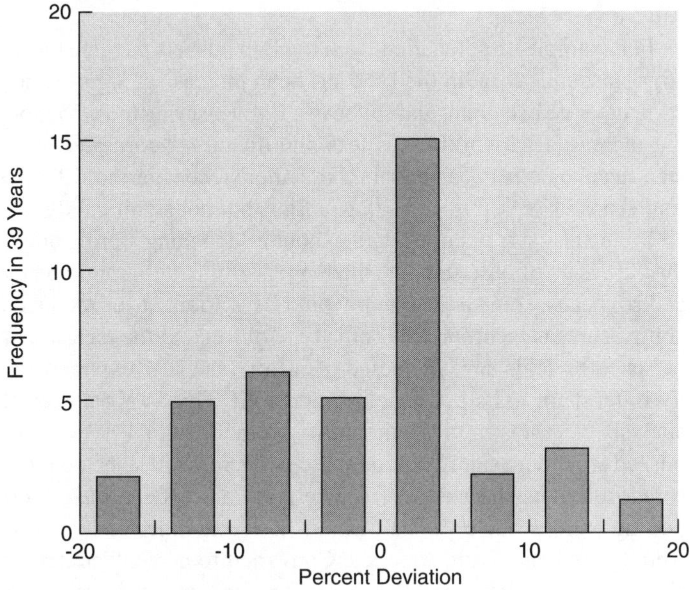

*Double Exponential Smoothing.

in computer technology and capacity, incorporating probability distributions in the forecasts is becoming feasible. This process is called stochastic modeling. Reliance on trend yields will continue and should be the baseline for econometric forecasting, but forecasts should also be presented with probability parameters.

Crop yields are one of many sources of error in econometric forecasts. Probabilities could be applied to any variables that are troublesome to predict as long as the error terms on these variables display stable distribution patterns. The focus on crop yields is appropriate, however, since they are not only the major source of year-to-year variability in domestic production, but in export demand as well.

HOW TO PROCEED

Deviations of crop yields from trends are primarily a function of weather. Year-to-year variability in weather follows a fairly random scheme, although some evidence of trends and cycles are present. Those who are compelled to introduce trends and cycles in weather could do so in stochastic modeling if they could relate such weather changes to yields. The stochastic part would be the deviations from the effects of trends and cycles in weather.

For large models, introducing stochastic modeling can open Pandora's Box. The process is more involved than assigning some probability distribution to deviations from single-valued forecasts of yields on various crops. Yield variability may be changing, requiring some modification of distributions estimated from historical patterns. Some attention to the selection of the historical period and how deviations are measured may help solve this problem.

For example, the deviation from trend in bushels per acre on corn, other coarse grain, soybeans, and wheat in the U.S. has been increasing, significantly so in 1955–1993 on corn, other coarse grain, and soybeans. By measuring the deviations in *percentage* terms, the increased variability was less significant on corn and soybeans and became insignificant on other coarse grain. For a more recent period, 1975–1993, variability for all four crops increased in percentage terms, but not significantly.

If the analyst is uncomfortable about establishing a probability distribution with less than 20 years of observations, the longer-term pattern might be the choice. But for corn and soybeans, some adjustment would be warranted for the increased percentage variability, such as incorporating some type of trend in the measure of dispersion.

As crop yields have increased over time, the U.S. experience has been that variability in terms of units per acre has increased. This is not universally true, however. An analysis of trends in yield variability from 1960 to 1993 on coarse grain, wheat, and oilseeds found no significant increase or decrease in selected regions of the world, measured in MT per hectare. For coarse grain and wheat, the regions were the major exporting nations, the European Union (EU) and other nations. For oilseeds, the regions were the EU and South America. Converted to percentage deviations, declines in variability were registered in all cases except for small insignificant increases in the fluctuations of EU coarse grain yields. Only for oilseeds (soybeans) in South America were the declines significant, however.

While there may be some preference for expressing yield deviations in terms of percentage of the trend, analysts will have to judge what measurement appears to be the most stable over time as well as what is the appropriate past period to include. Outlier years could be excluded, but only if the probability for such an occurrence is extremely unlikely in the forecast period (i.e., the year of a flood that happens only once in 500 years). But unless the period of observation is truncated, a general rule is to retain outlying years in the estimation of the probability distribution.

CROP YIELD DISTRIBUTIONS AND NORMALITY TESTS

If the deviations from trend yield approximated a normal distribution, simulating this distribution would be simplified using existing software programs. However, if this distribution is not normal, the analyst is then challenged to determine what the underlying pattern really is. If that can be determined, programs are available to incorporate non-normal distributions in the projection process.

Clearly, the variability of yield on U.S. corn is skewed to the left or low side (Figure 10-1). This means that the bad years are much worse than the good years are good. Yields were below trend by 10 percent or more in six years out of 39 and above trend by 10 percent or more in only one year. Because visualization of skewness is somewhat subjective, more precise measurements have been devised to assist analysts in evaluating distributions. Skewness can be measured as described by Jarque and

TABLE 10-1 VARIABILITY AND NORMALITY TESTS APPLIED TO YIELDS FOR SELECTED CROPS AND REGIONS OF THE WORLD, PERIODS WITHIN 1955–1993[A]

Crop and Region	Period	Standard Deviation	Skewness	Kurtosis	J-B Test[b]	Probability
		%				%
Coarse Grain						
Corn, U.S.	1955–93	9.9	−1.20	3.76	10.24	.60
Other, U.S.	1955–93	8.2	−.08	2.74	.15	92.87
All, U.S.	1955–93	9.1	−1.13	3.94	9.67	.80
Major Exporting Nations	1960–93	5.7	−.63	2.84	2.27	32.13
European Nations	1960–93	5.4	−.64	3.89	3.45	17.83
Rest of the World	1960–93	3.7	−.34	2.14	1.71	42.60
Outside the U.S.	1960–93	3.0	−.23	2.43	.76	68.37
Wheat						
Wheat, U.S.	1955–93	7.7	.61	4.15	4.56	10.22
	1955–57 } 1959–93	6.7	−.07	2.65	.22	89.54
Major Exporting Nations	1960–93	10.5	−.37	2.69	.90	63.84
European Union	1960–93	6.7	1.19	5.51	16.95	.02
	1960–83 } 1985–93	5.3	.12	2.08	1.25	53.59
Rest of the World	1960–93	6.4	−.52	3.02	1.52	46.82
Outside the U.S.	1960–93	5.2	−.11	2.19	1.00	60.55
Oilseeds						
Soybeans, U.S.	1955–93	7.0	−.44	2.71	1.42	49.24
European Union	1964–93	11.9	.20	2.14	1.11	57.31
Soybeans, Brazil and Argentina	1964–93	9.6	−.19	2.88	.21	90.24
EU, Brazil, and Argentina	1964–93	6.8	−.66	3.35	2.36	30.79

[a]Variability of yields is measured by percentage deviations from trend as established by double exponential smoothing.
[b]Jarque-Bera Normality test statistic.

Bera (Bera and Jarque, 1980). A normal distribution has a skewness value of 0. The skewness coefficient on corn was −1.20 as shown in Table 10-1.

Most distributions of yield variability are skewed to the low side; that is, the coefficient is negative, as is apparent in Table 10-1. This was the case with all the coarse grain yields tested. On U.S. wheat, the skewness was positive, but the elimination of the very favorable year of 1958 turned the positive sign to slightly negative. On wheat yields in the EU, the skewness was reduced from strongly positive to slightly positive by eliminating 1984, a year of extremely high yields. On oilseeds, the skewness was negative on U.S. and South American soybeans, but positive on EU oilseeds.

Another measure of normality is kurtosis which applies to the thickness of tails in the distribution. A normal distribution has a kurtosis coefficient of three. Values above three indicate thicker-than-normal tails; values below three indicate thinner-than-normal tails. The yield variabilities on the crops listed in Table 10-1 exhibit no strong tendency toward high or low kurtosis. High absolute values for skewness are associated with high values for kurtosis. The elimination of single outlier years for wheat in the U.S. and EU brought kurtosis levels closer to three. As a general statement, this particular study suggests that skewness is a more prevalent characteristic of variability in crop yields than is kurtosis, at least at the level of aggregation given in Table 10-1.

Combining measures of skewness and kurtosis, Jarque and Bera devised a statistic that follows a Chi-square distribution. From that, they calculate the probability that a distribution is normal. This probability is shown in the last column of Table 10-1. The variability around trend of U.S. corn yields has clearly not been normal. Based on the entire 1955–1993 period, one would conclude that variability in U.S. wheat yields was not normal either. But the sensitivity of the Jarque-Bera statistic is illustrated on U.S. wheat for which the probability of a normal distribution increased from 10.22 percent to 89.54 percent just by dropping the favorable year of 1958 out of the 39-year span from 1955 to 1993. The probability of a normal distribution on EU wheat yield variability went from practically nil to 53.59 percent by dropping the very favorable year of 1984 from the 1960–1993 period.

This crop yield study suggests that normalcy can be assumed in a number of cases, but not all. To properly conduct stochastic modeling, analysts may need to devise ways to generate non-normal distributions. One way is to randomly draw from a data set of the actual deviations from trend in an historical period.

AGGREGATION OF COUNTRIES OR REGIONS

Another procedure that may be warranted is to aggregate countries or regions. If the major concern was the yield variability outside of the U.S. in a crop year, then trying to establish appropriate yield probability distributions for each of the major foreign nations producing that crop may not be necessary. The analyst should concentrate on the aggregate of foreign nations.

In Table 10-1, the three regions outside the U.S. on coarse grain and also on wheat were combined into "Outside the U.S." The EU, Brazil, and Argentina were combined on oilseeds. This step can be taken only if the analyst does not require information from a specific region. Obviously, if the size of the South American soybean crop is important, aggregation is not appropriate. As indicated in Table 10-1, the probability of a normal yield distribution outside the U.S. on coarse grain is about 68 percent, substantially higher than the probabilities for the separate regions of the major exporting nations, EU and other. On wheat outside the U.S., the probability of a normal distribution on yield variability is just over 60 percent, somewhat below major exporting nations, but above the EU and other. On oilseeds, however, the analyst might well keep the EU and South America separate.

Another reason to aggregate nations and regions, if separate analysis is not necessary to the problem, is that the variability in yields is usually reduced. Note in Table 10-1 that the standard deviation in coarse grain yields outside the U.S. was only 3.0 percentage points compared to the separate estimates of 5.7 percentage points in major exporting nations, 5.4 percent in EU, and 3.7 percent in the rest of the world. The reason is obvious. The broader the geographic area involved, the more likely that weather patterns will be offsetting. The smaller the geographic area, the more extreme will be the weather effects.

By aggregating nations and regions, yield variability was also reduced on wheat and oilseeds (Table 10-1). The standard deviation in percentage points on wheat outside the U.S. was 5.2 percent in 1960–1993 and on oilseeds in the EU and South America combined was 6.8 percent. In both cases, these standard deviations were less than in the separate regions.

DISTRIBUTIONS AND CORRELATIONS

After searching for the appropriate level of aggregation, the next step is to select the appropriate distribution. Several alternatives to a normal distribution are available such as the Poisson, log normal, gamma, F, t and Chi-squared. These distributions are discussed in a number of books on statistics and econometrics (see Stapleton, 1995). Another question is whether a software program can generate the appropriate distribution. MicroTSP includes random number generators that return normal and rectangular distributions. Special versions would have to be created for other distributions.

So far in this chapter, several questions have been posed for the analyst delving into stochastic modeling:

1 How should variability be measured?
2 Has the variability increased over time?
3 How many years are required for a reasonable estimate of the parameters of the distribution?
4 Should you eliminate outlier years?
5 What is the appropriate level of aggregation, geographically?
6 If the distribution is not normal, what is the appropriate distribution to incorporate and does your software program facilitate use of the appropriate distribution?

An additional question for large econometric models in agriculture incorporating stochastic crop yields is:

7 Are the variabilities of yields on the crops included in the model correlated?

This question is particularly important for crops grown in the same general area with parallel growing seasons, such as corn and soybeans in the U.S. In models focusing on particular states or regions as compared with those nationwide, the need to treat these relationships is compelling as these smaller areas are more likely to receive similar impacts from the weather.

Correlations in yield variability among nations may also require attention. For example, stochastic models of U.S. spring wheat would need to account for the yield correlation with Canada's spring wheat crop.

Unfortunately, the complexity of stochastic models is such that the analyst may be quite limited in how many correlations can be specified. In Table 10-1 are four crops in the U.S.—corn, other coarse grain, wheat, and soybeans. Outside the U.S. are three regions for coarse grain, three regions for wheat, and two regions for oilseeds. In total, this represents 12 different yield series and 66 pairs of correlations. The analyst could proceed along two directions: (1) sort out only the pairs with the strongest correlation, and/or (2) further combine the regions as was done in Table 10-1.

TABLE 10-2 CORRELATIONS IN YIELD VARIABILITY ON SELECTED CROPS IN THE U.S. AND OUTSIDE THE U.S., PERIODS WITHIN 1955–1993[a]

	U.S.[b]				Outside the U.S.[c]		
Crop	Corn	Other Coarse Grain	Soybeans	Wheat	Coarse Grain	Wheat	Oilseeds
U.S.							
Corn		.79	.72	.22	–.11	.01	–.19
Other Coarse Grains			.69	.48	–.14	.01	–.26
Soybeans				.23	–.18	–.07	–.27
Wheat					.15	.20	–.15
Outside U.S.							
Coarse Grain						.72	–.01
Wheat							[d]
Oilseeds							

[a]Variability of yields is measured by percentage deviations from trend as established by double exponential smoothing.
[b]Inter-U.S. correlations were based on 1955–1993 crop years.
[c]Correlation with crops outside the U.S. were based on 1960–1993 crop years for coarse grain and wheat and 1964–1993 for oilseeds. Oilseed data were restricted to EU and soybeans in Argentina and Brazil.
[d]Less than .01.

An example of a manageable set of yield correlations is presented in Table 10-2 under the presumption that information loss from aggregation is not a problem. For the U.S. crops, attention would need to be given to the ties between yield variability on: (1) corn and other coarse grain, (2) corn and soybeans, (3) other coarse grain and soybeans, and (4) other coarse grain and wheat. The analyst might ignore the relatively low correlation between: (1) corn and wheat and (2) soybeans and wheat. No strong relationships are apparent between yields on U.S. crops and the aggregation of crops outside the U.S. However, the correlation between coarse grain and wheat yields outside the U.S. must be taken into account. These relationships suggest that five pairs of correlations should be incorporated in such a world model.

The cut-off between significant and insignificant correlations is a matter of judgment, as is true with all statistical measurements. Again, considering the complexity of the problem and inherent errors in econometric analysis, correlations below some level, say .30, could be ignored. Also, negative correlations might be regarded as spurious, although rationalized in some situations.

AN EXAMPLE WITH MICROTSP

To provide analysts with some perspectives on how to incorporate stochastic yields into their models, a fairly simplified example is presented (Ferris, "Generation of . . . ," 1989). In this case, normality is assumed on percentage deviation of corn yields from trend as established by double exponential smoothing over the period of 1955–1993 (see Figure 10-1). As indicated in Table 10-1, the standard deviation of corn yields from trend in this period was 9.9 percent.

Converting the percent designations in Table 10-1 to decimals, stochastic corn yields could be incorporated in a model with the following two lines in the program:

(1) RYCNP = 1.000 + .099 * NRND

(2) YCN = YCNP * RYCNP

where: RYCNP = ratio of actual corn yields to trend

NRND = random numbers that are normally distributed with a mean of 0 and a variance or standard deviation of 1

YCNP = projected trend yield on corn in bushels per acre

YCN = yield of corn in bushels per acre

The model would have to be solved a large number of times in order to approximate a normal distribution on the deviation of corn yields from trend. Clearly, a more accurate representation of this dispersion can be generated with the appropriate non-normal distribution, when such possibilities are available. For a year or two into the future, the model should be run at least 200 times to provide reasonable estimates of the probability distributions on yields and other variables of interest that are affected by yields. For projections 10 years or more into the future, analysts will have to explore by trial and error how many iterations will provide reasonable distributions.

The second step in the illustration relates to handling correlations. As indicated in Table 10-2, deviations from trend on corn and soybean yields have a correlation coefficient of .72. Considering that corn is the dominant crop of the two in terms of acreage and production, deviation in soybean yields were assumed to be a function of the deviation in corn yields and trend as indicated in the following OLS equation:

(3) DYSBP =– 376 + .551* DYCNP + .191 * TIME
(7.39) (2.95)

$R^2 = .62$

where: DYSBP = deviation from trend yield in percent for soybeans

DYCNP = deviation from trend yield in percent for corn

TIME = serial time, i.e., 1955 = 1955, 1956 = 1956, etc.

Numbers in parentheses are *t* values.

This equation indicates that soybean yields have been significantly associated with corn yields, which is to be expected, a priori, since corn and soybean production is heavily concentrated in the U.S. Corn Belt and share the same growing season. The equation also indicates that the percentage variability of soybean yields has been increasing relative to corn.

FIGURE 10-5 Deviation of soybean yields from a regression on deviation of corn yields*.

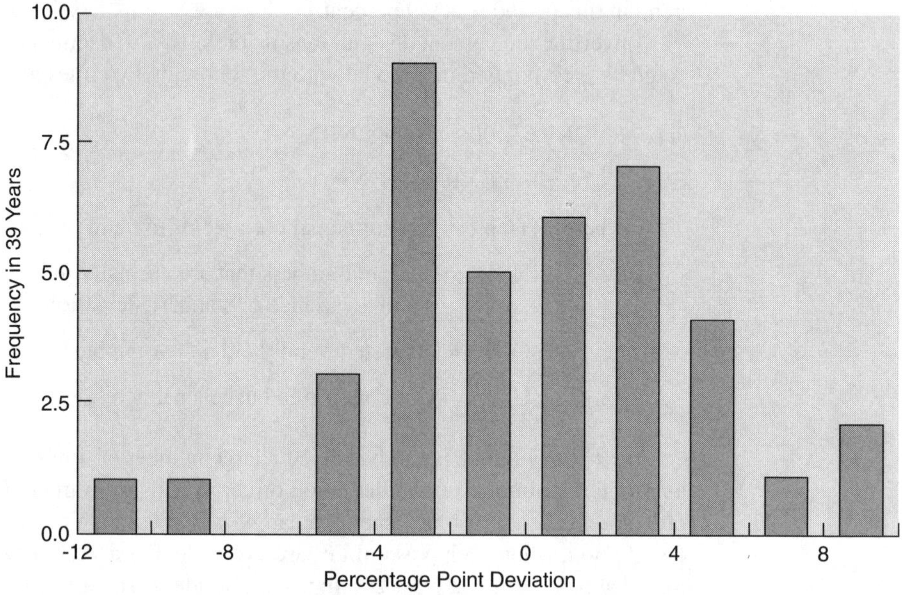

*Variables are percent deviation of yields from DES trend, 1955–1993.

The stochastic representation of soybean yields (rather than the distribution illustrated in Figure 10-2, noticeably skewed to the low side like corn) can be incorporated as the residual for equation (3), illustrated in Figure 10-5. The skewness coefficient for the residual in equation (3) is −.12 compared with −.44 for Figure 10-2. The probability of a normal distribution is 82 percent for Figure 10-5 versus 49 percent for Figure 10-2. The standard deviation of the residuals in equation (3) is 7.04 percentage points. Converting percentages to ratios, the equation set for soybean yields in a model would be:

(4) RYSBCN = 1.000 − 3.76 + .551 * DYCNP + .00191 * TIME + DYSBCN

(5) DYSBCN = .0704 * NRND

(6) YSB = YSBP * RYSBCN

where: RYSBCN = ratio of soybean yields to corn yields

DYCNP = deviation from trend yield for corn (percent/100)

TIME = serial time

DYSBCN = normal distribution of deviation of soybean yields relative to deviation in corn yields with a standard deviation of .0704

NRND = generator of normal distribution

FIGURE 10-6 Stochastic Projections of the Yield (YPTF) and Farm Price (FPPTFF) of fall potatoes in the United States for 1994, with 1,000 runs of an econometric potato model.

SMPL range: 1 – 1000
Number of observations: 1000

Variable	Mean	S.D.	Maximum	Minimum
YPTF	339.08592	11.782857	378.60680	299.82680

INTERVAL	COUNT	HISTOGRAM
297.0 >= YPTF < 301.5	1	
301.5 >= YPTF < 306.0	2	
306.0 >= YPTF < 310.5	3	
310.5 >= YPTF < 315.0	10	
315.0 >= YPTF < 319.5	35	
319.5 >= YPTF < 324.0	47	
324.0 >= YPTF < 328.5	91	
328.5 >= YPTF < 333.0	129	
333.0 >= YPTF < 337.5	146	
337.5 >= YPTF < 342.0	135	
342.0 >= YPTF < 346.5	122	
346.5 >= YPTF < 351.0	122	
351.0 >= YPTF < 355.5	80	
355.5 >= YPTF < 360.0	40	
360.0 >= YPTF < 364.5	24	
364.5 >= YPTF < 369.0	9	
369.0 >= YPTF < 373.5	1	
373.5 >= YPTF < 378.0	2	
378.0 >= YPTF < 382.5	1	

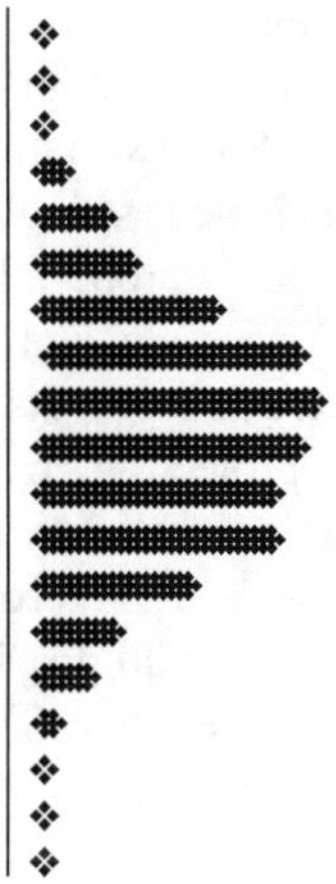

Skewness 0.016778 Kurtosis 2.913625
Jarque-Bera normality test stat. 0.357781 Probability 0.836197

SMPL range: 1 – 1000
Number of observations: 1000

Variable	Mean	S.D.	Maximum	Minimum
FPPTFF	5.3559078	0.7085654	8.0028380	3.3910190

INTERVAL	COUNT	HISTOGRAM
3.3 >= FPPTFF < 3.6	3	
3.6 >= FPPTFF < 3.9	13	
3.9 >= FPPTFF < 4.2	40	
4.2 >= FPPTFF < 4.5	51	
4.5 >= FPPTFF < 4.8	104	
4.8 >= FPPTFF < 5.1	157	
5.1 >= FPPTFF < 5.4	156	
5.4 >= FPPTFF < 5.7	167	
5.7 >= FPPTFF < 6.0	128	
6.0 >= FPPTFF < 6.3	89	
6.3 >= FPPTFF < 6.6	49	
6.6 >= FPPTFF < 6.9	26	
6.9 >= FPPTFF < 7.2	9	
7.2 >= FPPTFF < 7.5	4	
7.5 >= FPPTFF < 7.8	2	
7.8 >= FPPTFF < 8.1	2	

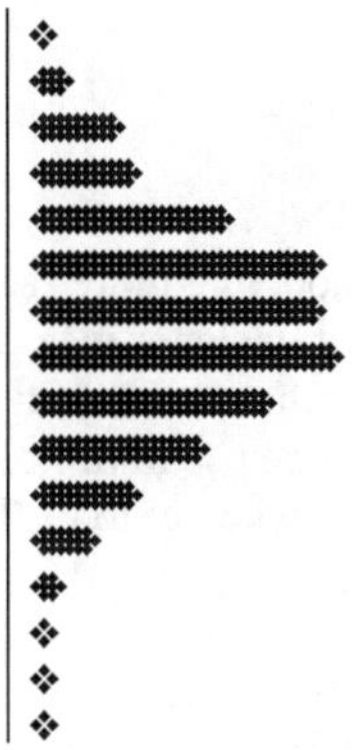

Skewness 0.159440 Kurtosis 3.142049
Jarque-Bera normality test stat. 5.077595 Probability 0.078961

YSBP = projected trend yield on soybeans in bushels per acre

YSB = yield of soybeans in bushels per acre

Programs can be written to solve models with these stochastic elements, saving each iteration, and after a prescribed number of runs, end the process and produce histograms of the variables of interest. Some variables may be relatively unaffected by those entered stochastically and can be viewed as single-valued projections. Of most interest, of course, would be how distributions of crop yields affect distributions of crop production, crop exports, and crop prices over time, and subsequent impacts on the livestock sectors.

As an example of MicroTSP outputs for stochastic projections, Figure 10-6 displays histograms of stochastic projections from a model of U.S. fall potatoes for 1994. The yield of fall potatoes was generated by a combination of trend and 1,000 draws from a normal distribution with a mean of zero and a standard deviation of 3.57 percent of the trend yield. This produced a yield distribution with about an 84-percent probability of normalcy under the Jarque-Bera test. The price distribution was not normal, but this is to be expected if prices or any other variables are not linear functions of yields.

SUMMARY

Stochastic procedures are available to assist analysts in defining important error terms in their models. In agriculture, such possibilities are particularly important in forecasting crop yields. A major requirement is that the models can be solved rapidly.

Special attention must be given to the form of the error term distribution (normal, other), geographic aggregation, and correlation of yield variability among crops. The greater the number of years into the projection period, the greater the number of iterations required to establish meaningful distributions on the endogenous variables.

QUESTIONS FOR STUDY

1 Why is stochastic modeling more relevant for agriculture than for other industries?
2 What might be the rationale for measuring deviations of crop yields from trends in *percentage* terms rather than the deviations in bushels per acre or MT per hectare?
3 What criteria might one use in deciding on the length of time for measuring variability in crop yields and whether to exclude "outlier" years?
4 Define skewness.
5 Define kurtosis.
6 Crop yields tend to be skewed to the low side. Explain and indicate possible ways to simulate such a pattern.
7 Explain why aggregations of states, regions, or nations might be preferable in stochastic crop yield analysis to modeling yields in the separate geographic units.
8 Why should one check correlations of yield variabilities among crops included in a model?

9 Conceptualize how a stochastic-type model of agriculture might be linked to stochastic-type models of individual farms.

10 Select a crop with which you are familiar and plot its yield per acre (hectare) for the past 20 years. Draw in a trend line. Estimate the deviation from trend and plot the deviations in a histogram. By inspection, does the distribution appear normal? (Alternatively, do the same exercise with a statistical software package, using linear regression or double exponential smoothing to trace the trend in yield.)

SECTION THREE

LONG-TERM PROJECTIONS AND APPLICATIONS

11

GENERATING LONG-TERM PROJECTIONS AND FORECASTS

POINTS:

1 Projections as distinguished from forecasts and predictions.
2 Simple projection technology.
3 Measuring and applying alternative functional forms to income-consumption relationships.
4 Eliciting expert opinion about future social, political, economic, and technological developments.
5 Organizing long-range outlook projects.

Previous chapters have focused on models designed to generate forecasts for the coming year and possibly four or five years into the future. In a five-year time frame, generally assumptions about the socioeconomic, political, and technological structure can be assumed to be relatively stable. In the U.S., presidential elections are held every four years. Farm programs have typically been designed for about five years. Changes in consumer tastes and preferences and in public attitudes toward social justice and other issues do change, but the change is usually gradual. Technological breakthroughs can be abrupt, but the impact is phased in over time. Other structural changes of these types can be cited.

Beyond five years into the future, analysts must deal somehow with this changing underlying structure. The easiest and most often-used approach is to assume no changes or assume that change will follow some path definable by past trends. For developments that could be crucial to forecasts, but unpredictable, analysts might choose to postulate alternative scenarios built around plausible developments. Typical examples of the latter technique are projections assuming high, medium, or low economic growth or high, medium, or low population growth. Projection procedures discussed in this chapter are particularly relevant for extrapolating exogenous variables for econometric/simulation models.

The terms "projections," "forecasts," and "predictions" are used interchangeably in mapping future developments and events. Some clarification might be achieved if projections could be separated from forecasts and predictions. Projections could be defined as "What will happen if . . ." and forecasts and predictions could be defined as "What will happen." The latter is a much greater challenge to the analyst who must assess the future course of events normally relegated to assumptions. This involves answering questions like "Who will win the next election?" "What will be the next new fad?" "When will biological scientists develop a durable, tasteful tomato?" or "What is the probability that a comet like the one hitting Jupiter would collide with Earth in the next century?" How to address these questions will be discussed in the second section of this chapter. First to be covered is the evolution of quantitative projections.

QUANTITATIVE APPROACH

Projections can be simplistic extrapolations of past trends. Commonly, linear extrapolations are generated from equations of the form,

$$X = \alpha + \beta * T$$

where α and β are estimated by OLS over some past period with X regressed on T which is denominated in some measure of time, i.e., years, quarters, months, etc. Plugging into the equation a value for T that represents the projection year that is the target, the analyst can quickly generate a value for X.

A critical choice is the past period to use in the OLS measurement. If projecting 10 years into the future, the analyst would usually require at least 10 years of observations, ideally even more. On the other hand, because of structural changes, the most recent years are more relevant to the future than years of the distant past. Techniques are available to give more weight to recent years such as double exponential smoothing as discussed in Chapter 10.

If, over the period of observations, the analyst discerns non-linearity, other functional forms could be applied such as a quadratic,

$$X = \alpha + \beta T + \gamma T^2$$

or a semi-log function,

$$X = \alpha + \beta \log T$$

Demand

Obviously, such projection techniques, while simple and easily accomplished, are devoid of any economic theory. They might be useful as naive-type models to evaluate structural models, but would be unfulfilling to an economist. But as economists know, researchers have limited time and financial resources and must choose tools that fit the task at hand. This was apparent to modelers of the Food and Agriculture Organization of the United Nations when they were asked to generate projections of the demand for major foods of numerous nations back in the early 1960s. They were also hampered by limited time series data.

The FAO analysts improved upon the simplistic projection techniques by introducing structural parameters. Their basic formula was,

$$d = \beta + \mu y + z$$

where: d = annual rate of change in consumption

β = annual rate of change in population

μ = income elasticity

y = annual rate of change in income per capita

z = annual trend factor

The income elasticity may have been derived from a time series analysis or cross-section analysis in the nation in question, but in many cases, because of insufficient data, the parameter may have been based on assumptions. Also, the projected population and income growth rates may have been derived from simplistic projections combined with judgment. The trend factor addressed the collection of influences not captured by population and income changes.

The next step was to apply this formula to aggregate consumption in a base year as follows:

$$D_t = D_0 (1 + d)^t$$

where: D_t = total consumption in year *t*

D_0 = total consumption in the base year

t = number of years after the base year

An example of the application of these formulas relates to some nation with the following values on wheat assumed for a 10-year projection period.

Population growth rate = 1.8 percent

Per capita income growth rate = 2.0 percent

Trend factor = 0

Income elasticity = +.4

Quantity of wheat consumed in base year = 5 million MT

$d = 1.8 + .4 * 2.0 + 0$

$d = 2.6$ percent

Projection of consumption 10 years into the future

$D_{10} = 5\ (1 + .026)^{10}$

$D_{10} = 5\ (1.293) = 6.46$ million MT

This technique to project total consumption of a food product for a nation was still crude, but at least incorporated some elements of the economics of demand. An obvious weakness is the assumption that the income elasticity is constant. In the short-run, such an assumption is appropriate, but over the course of a number of years as per-capita incomes increase significantly, income elasticities would be expected to change on many food items, and typically would decline.

A refinement to the equation set for projecting demand was to formulate income elasticity as a function of income, i.e.,

$$\mu = f(y)$$

By 1967, FAO analysts were able to explore alternative formulas (United Nations, FAO, 1967). The choice of the functional form depended on the type of food. If the food item was a luxury good and consumption was well below saturation, a constant income elasticity might be appropriate. If the food item was between a luxury good and a staple, income elasticity might decline over the projection period, but not reach zero—i.e., saturation would not be reached. For a staple food item, income elasticity might approach zero in the projection period. Some food items might have a positive income elasticity at present levels of consumer income, but would be regarded as "inferior" goods at income levels likely to be attained in the projection period. On these food items, income elasticities will not only approach zero, but actually turn negative in the projection period. Of course, for some populations, analysts might postulate negative income elasticities for an "inferior" good over the entire projection period.[1]

Rather than formulas related to rate of change of total consumption of a food product, consider equations that have per-capita consumption as the dependent variable with per-capita income as the only independent variable,

$$DC_t = f\ (YC_t)$$

To capture four different income elasticity scenarios, the functional forms presented in Table 11-1 could be applied. For food items that are expected to be "inferior" throughout

[1]"Inferior" in this context is a term used by economists to define those consumer goods that experience declining demand with rising incomes. The term does not denote lack of nutritional value.

TABLE 11-1 ALTERNATIVE FUNCTIONS RELATED TO PER-CAPITA CONSUMER INCOME FOR PROJECTING PER-CAPITA CONSUMPTION OF FOOD PRODUCTS

Function	*Description*	*Food Examples*
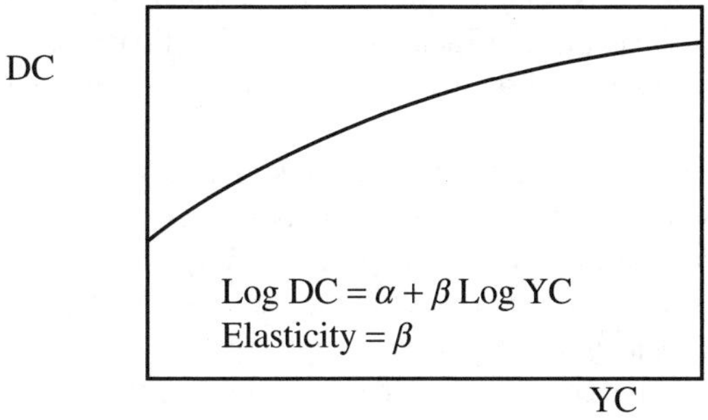 DC; $\text{Log DC} = \alpha + \beta \text{ Log YC}$; Elasticity $= \beta$; YC	Log-log function; constant elasticity; for luxury foods below saturation	Meats, selected meats; food consumed in "tablecloth" restaurants
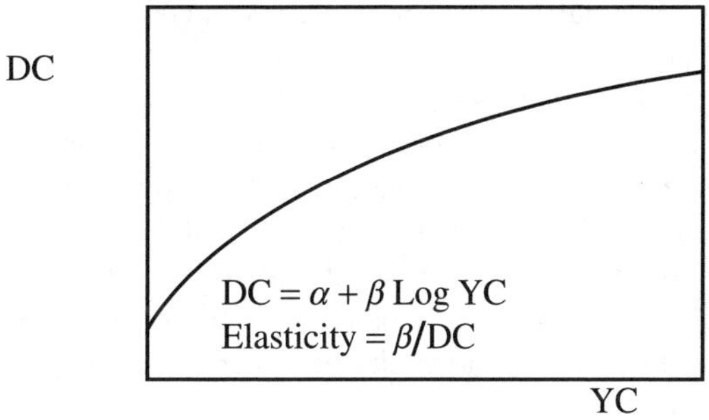 DC; $\text{DC} = \alpha + \beta \text{ Log YC}$; Elasticity $= \beta/\text{DC}$; YC	Semi-log function; elasticity declines, but not asymptotic to zero; for foods between luxuries and staples	Whole milk; cheese
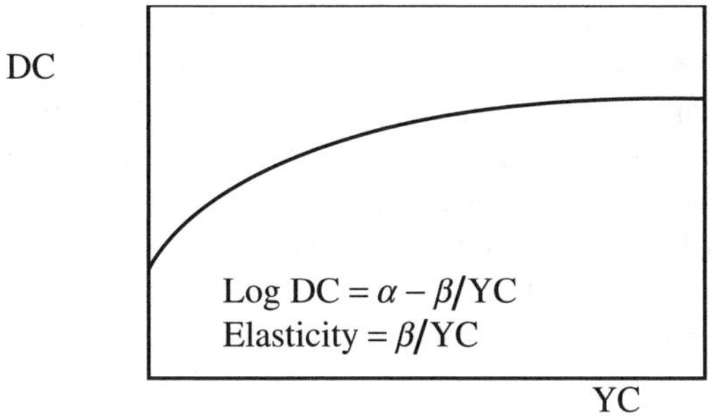 DC; $\text{Log DC} = \alpha - \beta/\text{YC}$; Elasticity $= \beta/\text{YC}$; YC	Log inverse function; elasticity declines and is asymptotic to zero; for staples	Sweeteners
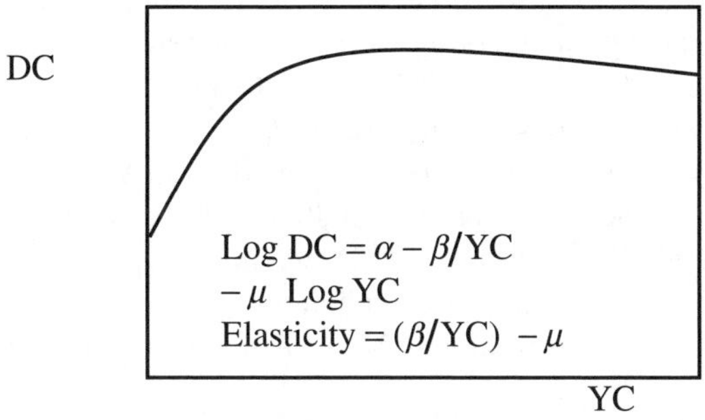 DC; $\text{Log DC} = \alpha - \beta/\text{YC} - \mu \text{ Log YC}$; Elasticity $= (\beta/\text{YC}) - \mu$; YC	Log-log inverse function; elasticity declines and then turns negative; for potentially "inferior" foods	Cereal grains; dry beans

the projection period, the same functional forms could be applied except that the signs on the coefficients of YC would be the opposite to those in Table 11-1. Other functional forms could be investigated. Those presented in Table 11-1 serve as examples of commonly used formulations.

In addition to choosing the appropriate functional form, the analyst must also provide estimates of the parameters. For many nations, time series data may not provide much of a clue as to future changes in income elasticities. For this reason, analysts may turn to cross-section data such as household consumption surveys in the nation in question or from patterns of consumption in nations at a higher stage of development. In all these approaches, the presumption is that low-income consumers will emulate high-income consumers as their (low-income consumers) incomes rise. However, analysts must make allowances for inherent differences between populations related to tastes and preferences, food prices, and certain trend factors.

To test the functional forms applied to the examples listed in Table 11-1, the most recent consumption data for 75 nations, compiled by the Food and Agriculture Organization of the United Nations, were compared with the respective Gross Domestic Products per capita denominated in 1987 U.S. dollars. The observations and the fitted values are presented in Figures 11-1 through 11-4. In some cases, certain nations were omitted. For example, high prices on meat and dairy products rendered Japan an outlier with low consumption of animal protein and milk and high on cereals, relative to per-capita GNP—a situation not duplicated in nearly all the other nations.

Perhaps other functional forms would have produced closer fits. Also, a division between low- and high-income nations would have provided more definitive relationships. The purpose, however, is to illustrate the procedure, which has the advantage that a long time series is not required. If substantial time series data are available, that information could be incorporated in the analysis either as a separate approach or in combination with a cross-sectional analysis with demand data from other nations.

Use of strictly time series data for testing alternative functional forms is certainly warranted. For a given nation or combination of nations, choice of functional forms is critical for projections into the intermediate term—five years or maybe ten years into the future. For the longer-term projections, extrapolation from these functions may be suspect.

As an illustration, annual data for 1960–1995 were used to test for the appropriate functional form to relate per-capita consumption to consumer income on selected agricultural products. The results are presented in Table 11-2. Based on t values on the income coefficients, the case for the log-log functions was the strongest on fish and caloric sweeteners in the U.S. and eggs and wheat for food in the rest of the world (ROW). However, the R^2s for caloric sweeteners and wheat for food were higher with the semi-log function. The log-inverse function provided the best fit for U.S. fluid milk (positive sign on log-inverse signified a negative relationship) and, based on t values, grains for livestock feed in ROW. The R^2 on feed grains was only slightly below that for the semi-log function.

While choosing the best-fitting functional form from time series analysis would be appropriate for intermediate-term projections, one might question the results—especially on grains for livestock feed outside the U.S.—for the long-term.

FIGURE 11-1 Per-capita consumption of animal protein related to per-capita GDP in 73 nations*.

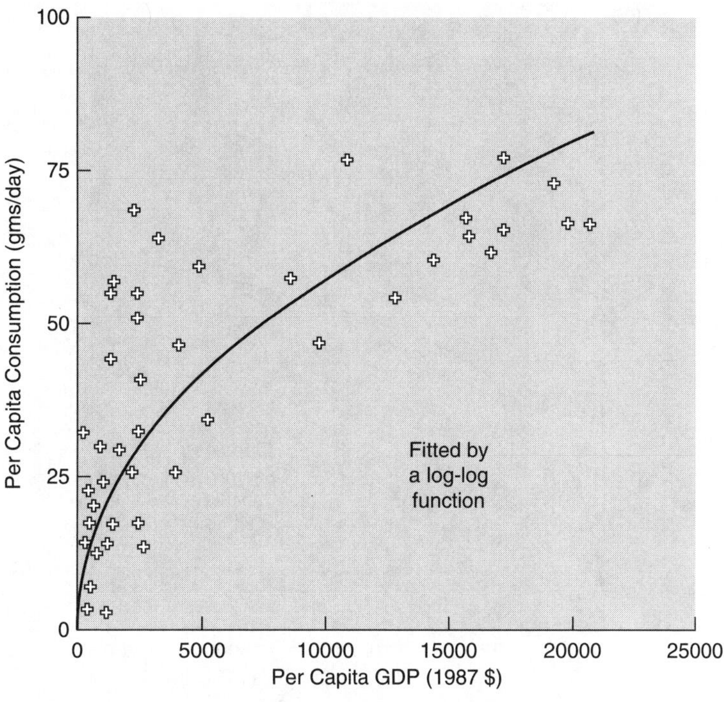

*Source: FAO, UN. Average consumption in 1986–88; GDP in 1990.

Application of these functional forms to individual foods or food groups for the purpose of generating long-term projections should be performed in the context of the total diet of the population. Constraints would need to be imposed to ensure that total per-capita intake of quantities, calories, protein, and fat are within reason. The analyst would often be compelled also to project these broad categories of the diet. In fact, projections of total calories, for example, should be more accurate than projections of an individual food or food classification; similarly, protein and fat content of diets change more gradually than the individual food items.

Allowances also need to be made for variety in the diet, nutrition, and total expenditures on food relative to consumer incomes. For these and other reasons, a demand systems approach to long-term projections of food demand has considerable merit. At the minimum, projections of individual foods should be subjected to the consistency checks noted here.

Cross-sectional analysis can also address the impact of price on consumption. For example, relatively high retail prices on meat and dairy products in Japan partially explain why consumption of those products is low relative to consumer incomes. Each nation also has its own sets of tastes and preferences that will likely be maintained over a period of time. Analysts drawing on data from other nations would appropriately give most

FIGURE 11-2 Per-capita consumption of milk related to per-capita GDP in 71 nations*.

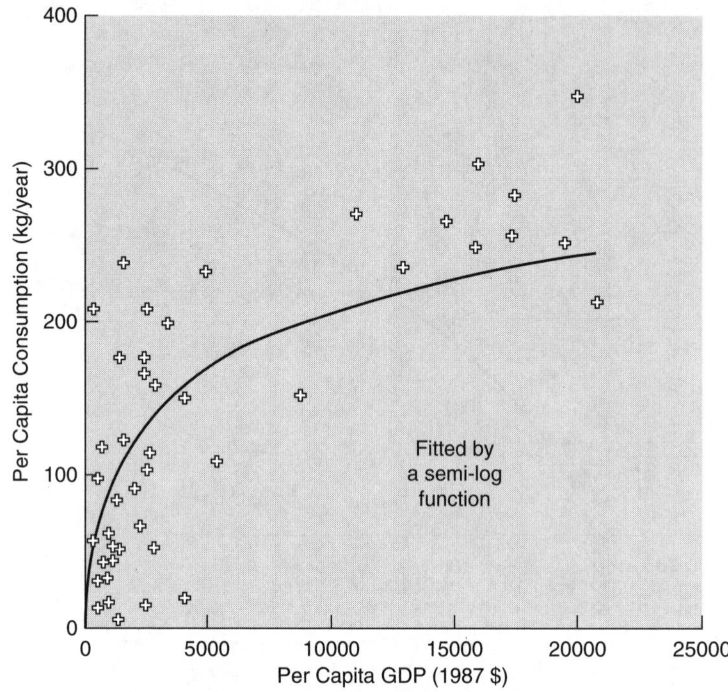

*Source: FAO, UN. Average consumption in 1988–90; GDP in 1990.

attention to those countries with similar demographic, ethnic, and cultural characteristics.

As indicated in Chapter 3, time series analysis has been the major analytical tool to forecast food consumption in the short-run, say up to about five years. For long-term projections, however, cross-sectional analysis may hold more promise. This may be especially true in projecting the influence of such trend factors as tastes, living patterns, nutrition concerns, etc. Consider, for example, what was clearly apparent back in 1970 and even earlier about the potential for expansion of American fast-food restaurant chains in other developed nations and eventually into the developing world. California has often been cited as the harbinger for the other states, setting the pace for shifts to ethnic foods—tofu, sushi, Chinese, Mexican, etc.

With rapid globalization and trade liberalization, the pace at which nations draw upon the success stories of other nations may quicken. This is not entirely a matter of less-developed nations emulating the developed nations, but a sharing of cuisine and other cultural practices. This is already happening.

Supply

Attempts to project food supplies far into the future have evolved in a manner similar to demand. Simple models of past trends, combined with judgment, were applied by FAO

FIGURE 11-3 Per-capita consumption of sweeteners related to per-capita GDP in 75 nations*.

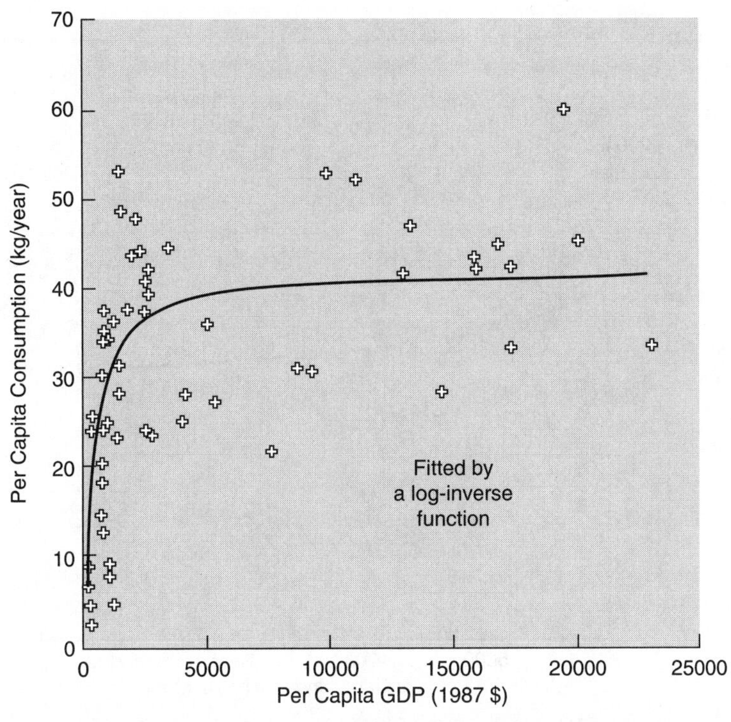

*Source: FAO, UN. Average consumption in 1988–90; GDP in 1990.

(United Nations, FAO, 1971). The focus was on crops and ruminant livestock (which depended heavily on pasture and forage crops). Projections of non-ruminant livestock were projected to match demand, presuming that few physical or economic restrictions would stand in the way.

More recent endeavors by FAO have employed more sophisticated methodology, including input from a world model used primarily for medium-term commodity projections (United Nations, FAO, 1995). However, even this "FAO World Food Model" was only one part of the process. Considerable effort went into evaluating the quantity and quality of the land base available and yield potential. The judgment of specialists from various disciplines was still paramount.

An early study at Iowa State University on world food supplies employed 3,000 data sets and a collection of alternative functional forms to project area, yield, and production (Blakeslee et al., 1973). Most frequently used were simple extrapolations from: (1) linear functions of time and (2) the square root of time. Also used were a linear function of the log of time, mean values, and mean values from the most recent years. Cropland available was established with the judgment of a crop scientist.

Later, the USDA introduced more structural components into projections with their Grain-Oilseed-Livestock (GOL) model (Rojko et al., 1978). One step was to project the

FIGURE 11-4 Per-capita consumption of cereals related to per-capita income in 75 nations*.

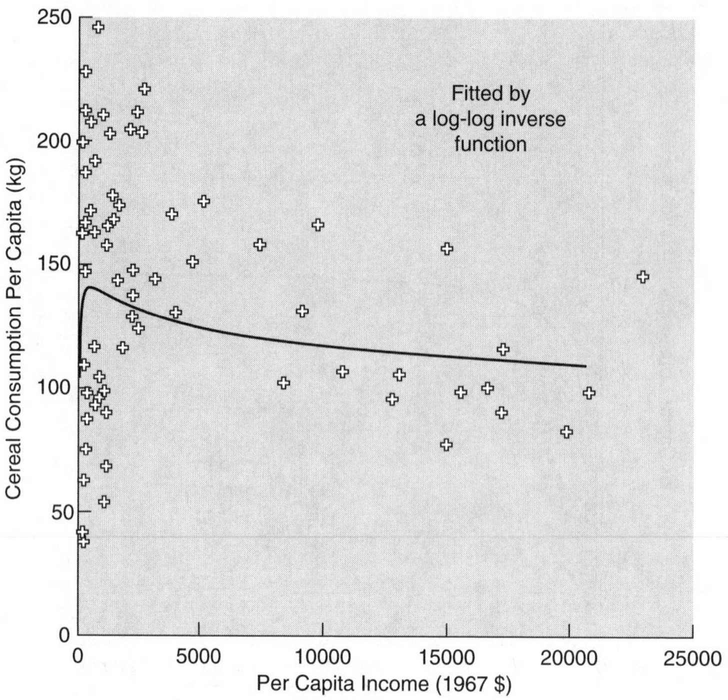

*Source: FAO, UN. Average consumption in 1988–90; GDP in 1990.

total area available to crops. Second, the projected area for each of the major crops was based on relative prices and long-term shifts in acreages. Then, yields were projected with account taken for trends, relative prices, and shift variables for different levels of inputs. Livestock supply projections were based on direct and cross-price elasticities on products and feed and also shift variables reflecting long-term growth factors. The GOL modeling activity eventually merged into SWOPSIM described in Chapter 8.

Projections of technical coefficients can be based on time series analysis or cross-sectional analysis. Typically, technical coefficients can be represented as functions of time with very occasional quantum leaps (as with the development of hybrid corn). The analyst would do well to compare how the best producers are performing relative to the average—basically a cross-section approach. How much higher are crop yields or milk production per cow on the more progressive farms than the state average? As a greater share of a state's production is taken over by these farmers, their production records become a useful guide to the future course of the state averages—and these top farmers will improve their own performance also.

Linear programming-type models could serve analysts very well in this task. These models can implement known or projected technology in farm systems and establish optimum combinations of inputs and outputs to maximize an objective function—normally net profit. Constraints can also be imposed to account for other considerations than some

TABLE 11-2 STATISTICAL PROPERTIES FROM OLS REGRESSION OF PER-CAPITA CONSUMPTION ON PER-CAPITA INCOME FOR SELECTED ITEMS, USING ALTERNATIVE FUNCTIONAL FORMS; ANNUAL DATA FOR 1960–1995

		Functional Form		
Region and Item	Statistical Property[a]	Log-Log[b]	Semi-Log	Log-Inverse[b]
United States				
Fish	*t*	17.7	15.8	–14.3
	R^2	.885	.880	.822
Caloric sweetener	*t*	9.6	9.2	–8.9
	R^2	.670	.750	.604
Milk fluid	*t*	–14.6	–14.4	15.3
	R^2	.872	.881	.885
Rest of World				
Eggs	*t*	11.3	9.3	–10.4
	R^2	.658	.722	.577
Wheat for food	*t*	12.7	12.2	–11.0
	R^2	.793	.820	.771
Grains for livestock feed	*t*	17.7	17.7	–20.7
	R^2	.877	.905	.903

[a]*t* values of the coefficient on the per-capita income variable.
[b]R^2s were calculated after converting the dependent variables (in logs) to actual values.

discounted net profit stream. Since adjustments farmers make from their current position to the optimum require several years, the analyst can also establish the time path.

A discourse on linear programming (LP) is beyond the scope of this book. However, this technique should be regarded as an alternative to simple time series or even more sophisticated econometric/simulation models for generating long-term supply projections. LP allows the analyst to pursue much more detail about representative firms in an industry and to treat many questions other models cannot address directly. However, data demands for LP are enormous, solution procedures can be cumbersome, and rapid technological change can render the vast number of underlying coefficients as inappropriate for looking many years into the future. As is often the case, the economic analyst must choose the appropriate tools to fit the assignment and for long-range projections, LP is frequently out of the question.

Prices

At this point in this chapter, little attention has been given to projecting prices on products or their substitutes. Typically, past efforts to project consumption and production for the long-run have involved the assumption that real prices will remain constant. This omission has been due to lack of accurate price data in many nations and the admission that such a refinement cannot be easily handled anyway in an extended projection period.

If projections could be made based on assumptions that farmers would respond to profit incentives as in the past, an analyst could explore what would happen to production under various price scenarios in the long-run employing models such as described in Chapter 6, i.e.,

$$Q_t = \alpha + [\beta\ \lambda/(1-\lambda)]\ P_{t-1}$$

where: Q_t = the equilibrium output in the long run

P_{t-1} = the set value for price or a profit variable for the entire projection period

Linked with a demand sector, the supply equation described above could trace the pattern of output over time and generate the long-term equilibrium price where the amount produced equalled the amount consumed (in a closed economy). While models such as this would be appropriate for a 5-year or even 10-year projection period, looking 20 to 25 years ahead or beyond would severely test this methodology.

Even those studies in which constant, real prices were assumed, the results can at least establish the probable direction of future prices. For example, if the projected output fell short of projected demand for a nation, the consequences would be either mass starvation, higher real prices, or both. Conversely, if projected output exceeded projected consumption, the government would have to accumulate and dispose of surpluses, real prices would fall, or both.

The FAO did attempt to quantify the price implications (United Nations, FAO, 1968). Simply, if current supply-and-demand parameters could be extended into the long-term future, the price effects could be estimated as illustrated in Figure 11-5. How prices adjust to the new equilibrium position is unspecified, but in the long-run, such detail may be unimportant anyway. Most suspect is the assumption that current supply-and-demand parameters will not change.

COMBINING SUBJECTIVE WITH QUANTITATIVE METHODS

Even the most competent quantitative economists need to reach far beyond their own discipline when generating long-term projections and forecasts. Such assistance is required even to establish a realistic set of scenarios, let alone determine which scenario is the most probable. For want of a better definition, inputs into the projection process outside of the quantitative tools of econometricians will be labeled as "subjective." This recognizes that, indeed, judgment and subjectivity also underlie highly quantitative projection procedures.

Interdisciplinary subjective methods are needed to discern societal goals and national objectives and forecast changes in the political, social, and cultural structure. Such tools are also required for technological forecasting. These perspectives are all basic to establishing a manageable set of assumptions for long-term economic projections.

The challenge then is how to pull out expert opinion from social and physical scientists, philosophers, and others who have insights on the wave of the future. The process to accomplish this is still in a somewhat formative stage, but can be broadly classified as: (1) individual insights and (2) group efforts. The individual approach, as described by E.I. Green, involves "systematic thinking" and "intuitive thinking" (Green, 1954). Systematic thinking is the deliberate act of the conscious mind. Intuitive thinking is the gracious gift of the subconscious in return for the previous labors of the conscious mind.

FIGURE 11-5 Price implications of long-term projections of amount supplied and amount demanded if current supply-and-demand parameters prevail.

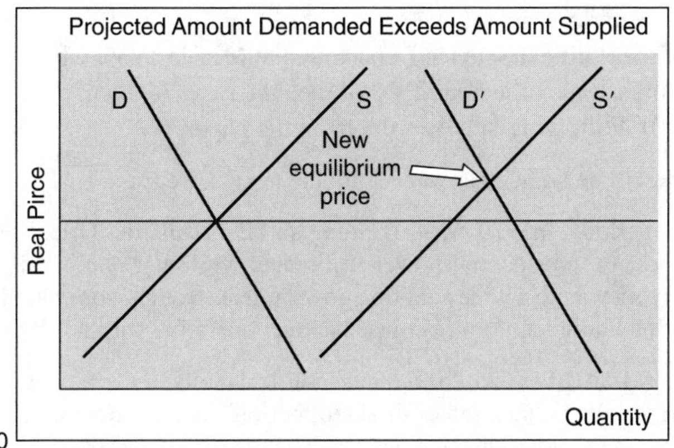

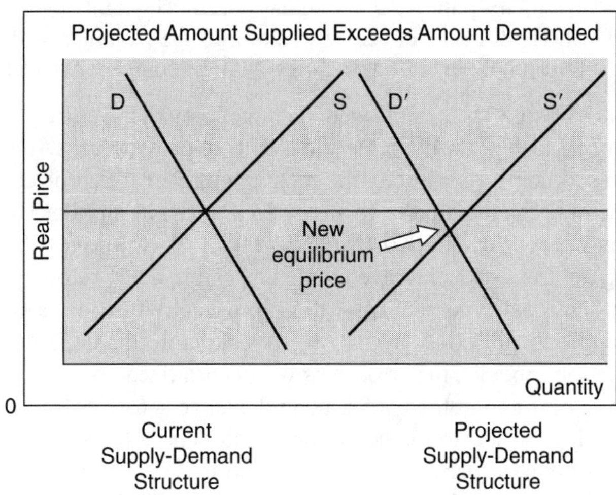

Applied to subjective forecasting, this suggests that individuals deeply involved in assessing the future course of events in their specialty or dealing with needed new technology can conjure up ideas about plausible new directions in their respective fields.

Scenario Writing

Individuals may engage in "scenario writing." Jantsch defines scenario writing as "A technique which attempts to set up a logical sequence of events in order to show how, starting from the present (or any other given) situation, a future state might evolve step-by-step" (Jantsch, 1967). The scenario is particularly suited to dealing with several aspects of a problem more or less simultaneously. By use of a relatively extensive scenario, the analysts may be able to get a "feel" for events and branching points dependent upon critical choices.

Few scenario writers have been as bold and as specific as was Ithiel De Sola Pool, Chair of the Political Science Department at MIT in 1965, when he made predictions for the Commission on the Year 2000 of the American Academy of Arts and Sciences (Bell, ed., 1970). Following are excerpts from his paper:

> There will be no nuclear war within the next 50 years.
>
> In the period 1965–70, Mao-Tse-tung and De Gaulle will die. Within two years after De Gaulle's death, presidential power in France, while not abolished, will largely have atrophied, giving way to a wide coalition government strongly committed to European economic cooperation and integration, but just as noncooperative with NATO as De Gaulle was.
>
> Around 1980, there will be a major political crisis in the Soviet Union, marked by large-scale strikes, the publication of dissident periodicals, a temporary disruption of central control over some regions, and an open clash between the major sectors of the bureaucracy over questions of military policy and consumer goods. This will stop just short of revolution, though it will result in the effectual abolition of the Communist Party. . . . During these events, the Soviet hold over Eastern Europe will be completely broken.

Not all of Pool's predictions were on target or with the correct timing, but he did have enough of a grasp of unfolding world events to provide very useful baselines for long-term projection efforts. Among the most comprehensive projects to monitor and forecast structural change are the works of John Naisbitt and Patricia Aburdene in *Megatrends* and *Megatrends 2000* (Naisbitt, 1982; Naisbitt and Aburdene, 1990). While checking out trends was involved in this research, many of the conclusions were based on cross-sectional-type analysis—describing activities in various parts of the world that could be identified as progressive. While more than one individual was involved in writing these books, the effort was very centralized.

Because of the complexity of structural change across the economic, social, political, and technological spectrum, the logical question for a futurist is, "How can we elicit the judgment of experts across all these areas so that their total contribution can add up to more than the sum of their individual perspectives?" This has been employed in many informal ways—committees, review panels, "think tanks," conferences, etc. The communication discipline has provided guidelines on how to bring out thoughts and ideas through "brainstorming" techniques and "buzz groups," generally in small groups.

Delphi

Early efforts to obtain expert opinion in a formal way were conducted by the Rand Corporation in the early 1960s (Gordon and Helmer, 1964). They introduced the so-called "Delphi" technique, a systematic elicitation of futuristic ideas from select authorities. The Delphi approach has had several forms. Typically, a group of experts respond in writing to a survey containing questions about future events. The results of the first survey are sent back to the panel who are asked to reconsider their first response. Anonymity of the responses is preserved. There could be several rounds in this process with the presumption that some consensus would emerge.

Delphi has been applied in a number of ways. In 1971, the entire faculty of the College of Agriculture and Natural Resources (plus other departments with Agricultural Experiment Station and Cooperative Extension Service appointments) of Michigan State University were surveyed and asked to list specific events or developments that would have an impact on rural Michigan (Ferris, 1973). They were asked to concentrate on their fields of expertise, but were not limited to those areas. In any case, their statements were to be concise enough that, by the year 2000, it would be possible to evaluate whether that event or development had occurred—whether it be a technological breakthrough, an adoption rate, a structural change, a new institution, etc.

The responses from the first round were classified and organized into a second questionnaire that was also distributed to the entire faculty. For each item, they were asked to (1) evaluate their own expertise in the subject and (2) evaluate the likelihood of the event or development occurring by the year 2000. This activity was part of a much broader project to look ahead at rural Michigan and served to stimulate broad participation in the effort. The final step in the Delphi approach is scheduled for the year 2000 when not only the foresight of the faculty can be evaluated, but also whether degree of expertise is positively and significantly related to making correct predictions.

A Delphi process was employed in a study mandated by Congress in 1985 and reported in a publication entitled *Embargoes, Surplus Disposal and U.S. Agriculture* (USDA, 1986). The problem was how to determine behavioral parameters for an international trade model—by direct econometric estimation or by synthesis of functions from knowledge based on existing econometric evidence and expert judgments. Because of problems inherent in direct estimation and the complexities involved, Delphi was chosen as a major approach and explained as follows:

> We used the Delphi process by compiling existing econometric estimates of demand, stocks adjustment and international transmission elasticities for each of the major grain-trading regions or countries included in the spatial equilibrium model. The compilation results were shared among the study participants. They developed a consensus on a set of assumptions related to parameters and elasticities. Though these elasticities were not always the result of direct econometric estimation, they are based on considerable experience and prior research. In most cases, values for individual countries are well within the range of econometric estimates published in the literature.

While not identified as a Delphi process, the global study of food supply and demand projected to 2010 by FAO employed expert opinion as a major input (United Nations, FAO, 1995). A formal model was also a part of the methodology. Considering that the study encompassed 100 or so countries, over 35 commodities and up to six sets of production conditions per crop, the coordinators had little choice, but to draw heavily on the opinions of multidisciplinary specialists. FAO concluded that future efforts of this kind might well follow the procedure of the aforementioned 1986 USDA project and direct the expert opinion toward estimating and evaluating model parameters. In that way, results could be replicated and alternative scenarios developed in a consistent manner.

The advantage of Delphi is that rather concise written statements of areas of consensus and descensus can be produced. With anonymity, the possible bias from strong personalities, chain of authority, taking an unpopular stand, modifying previously stated positions, and "bandwagon" effects are minimized. However, a Delphi conference "often compromises the desirable features of a conventional conference such as speed, ability to perform a large number of iterations, and intellectual stimulation" (Enzer, 1970).

Nominal Group Technique

A procedure that addresses some of the weaknesses of Delphi is called Nominal Group Technique (NGT) (Delbecq et al., 1975). According to NGT, each group should be no larger than 12. There are five steps. Phase I, the nominal stage, includes: (1) the silent listing of ideas (or response to specific questions) in writing by each individual in the group and (2) sharing and recording in round-robin fashion of all ideas until all members of the group have no further ideas to share. The ideas are to be listed quickly, *without discussion.*

Phase II is a "discussion" stage that is not free-wheeling: (3) Instead, each idea is given attention with the authors provided the opportunity to clarify or explain his or her position. Others can add support or question the position. The round-robin discussion of ideas ensures input from all members without domination by any one.

Phase III is: (4) the voting stage in which each individual privately and in writing ranks or rates items numerically. (5) The collective group decision is based on the pooled outcome of individual votes.

NGT provides the stimulation of interpersonal exchanges and minimizes, but does not eliminate, the dominance of some individuals. This procedure has merit, but will require refining to fit the needs of futurists.

Example of Long-range Outlook Projects

The author has been involved in a number of projection studies in the College of Agriculture and Natural Resources at Michigan State University (Ferris, 1966; Ferris, 1973; Ferris, 1993; Keisling and Bralts, 1995). The purpose of these studies has generally been to look ahead 10 to 15 years at likely developments in rural Michigan and determine the potential for agriculture and natural resources. Each project has been structured somewhat differently, but the main format has been as follows:

1. The entire College or major segments were involved with strong support from the Dean, Associate Deans, and Department Chairs.
2. In the first phase, background papers were prepared on the expected demographic, macro-economic, social, and political scene for the projection period.
3. Also in the first phase, where possible, quantitative projections were generated econometrically for the various enterprises in agriculture and natural resources.
4. In the second phase, faculty committees organized around commodities or services prepared drafts of papers that contained specific projections and identified opportunities and impending problems. While furnished with econometrically derived projections from Phase I, the committees were responsible for the final set. The committees were interdepartmental in composition.

5 Rural leaders, organizational representatives, agribusinesses, legislators, and others outside the College were invited to review the papers and interact with faculty at a conference.
6 Final drafts of the papers were prepared and published.
7 Organizations were encouraged to take action steps based on the final reports.

Similar projects have been conducted at other universities, which attest to their value and popularity. Much of the value is the experience gained from participating, the cross-discipline interaction, and goodwill established between the University and clientele groups. The outlook theme also draws participation.

Key to the success of such projects is to provide a structured environment without stifling input from a broad base of authorities and those very close to the respective scenes. This means furnishing the committees with relevant background information, historical data and projections, if possible, and a set of guidelines for each to follow. Discussion leaders at the conference may well use NGT as a means to stimulate interaction among the participants. Participants can also be enlivened if they know important action steps will be taken as a result of the conference.

A major purpose of such programs is to identify opportunities and gain a jump on possible problems. In some cases, the future course of events cannot be easily changed. In other instances, action can alter the future—and, of course, invalidate the projections. Even so, the projections will have served the intended purpose.

Soliciting subjective input for long-run projections and forecasts remains something of an art. The procedure must be geared to the scale of the project. The professional forecaster with the quantitative tools will at least need to identify those persons who can complement his or her skills with a feel for what is happening to the industry being modeled and society in general.

SUMMARY

Generating projections beyond about five years into the future poses some special considerations due to structural change. This structural change includes supply-and-demand elasticities, technical coefficients, and the political, social and cultural environment. While quantitative tools are available to help account for such changes, interdisciplinary expert opinion may also be required. More formal techniques are being developed to elicit that input. The combination of quantitative and subjective procedures is especially valuable for projecting exogenous variables for econometric-simulation models.

The broad involvement of experts, leaders, and other authoritative individuals in long-range projection programs can provide important outputs, both the projections and the process. Decision makers as "part owners" of the outcome are more apt to act on the project's implications.

QUESTIONS FOR STUDY

1 Why is the challenge of generating projections 10 to 15 years into the future so different from projecting five years ahead?
2 In essence, what is the major difference between projections and forecasts?

3 What function relating income to per-capita consumption would be most appropriate for sweeteners (caloric plus non-caloric)?

4 What is meant by "cross-sectional analysis" versus time series analysis as related to measurement of demand for food items?

5 Why have long-range projections of supply for non-ruminant livestock been essentially matched with the projections of demand?

6 How can "cross-sectional" analysis be applied to long-range projections of supply?

7 While constant real prices are often assumed in long-range projections for agriculture and food, discuss how some indication of changes in equilibrium prices might be extracted from such procedures.

8 Develop a scenario to the year 2010 describing what you, personally, expect to happen to the balance between world food demand and world food supplies, articulating the pattern over the intervening years. Alternatively, select another subject with which you are very familiar and project the supply-demand balance to the year 2010.

9 Compare Delphi with Nominal Group Technique to elicit expert opinion.

10 Assemble 10 to 15 people and show them a chart with annual changes in world population over the last 50 years (or whatever period your database covers). Ask them to write on a piece of paper (without discussion) when (if ever) the world will experience zero population growth. Their answers should be anonymous. Collect their answers and display them visually for all to see, indicating dates (*never* is also acceptable). You may want to calculate the mean of the specific dates (excluding *never*). In the second round, repeat the procedure and display the results. After three or more rounds, determine whether the group was moving toward a consensus with less dispersion in the answers.

12

SPATIAL COMMODITY ANALYSIS AND TRADE

POINTS:

1 Selecting representative prices for a region or nation.
2 Spatial price surfaces under competitive conditions.
3 Simple trade model and refinements.
4 Location of agricultural production and interregional competition—economic and non-economic influences.
5 Application of shift-share analysis.
6 Locating a food processing plant.

In the long-run, we observe significant shifts in the location of agricultural production, within nations and between nations. This chapter addresses analytical procedures to project these changes.

A treatise on commodity analysis would not be complete without introducing spatial considerations, even though such treatment must be truncated. This subject embraces interregional competition, international trade, plant location analysis, the complexities of transportation costs, and institutional realities such as regulations on trade and transportation. This chapter will touch only on some of the bare essentials.

REPRESENTATIVE PRICES

Analysts of U.S. agriculture have a large number of choices when selecting prices to incorporate in their models. For products readily transportable, one particular price series may suffice as representative for the U.S. as a whole. One way to decide on what price series might best represent the industry is to note what series the U.S. Department of Agriculture is highlighting.

The USDA's World Agriculture Outlook Board features the average crop year prices received by U.S. farmers on major crops and wholesale prices at Decatur, IL, on soybean meal and soybean oil (USDA, WAOB, 1995). On livestock, their quotes have been as follows:

Choice steers	Nebraska, Direct, 1100–1300 lbs.
Barrows and gilts	Iowa and southern Minnesota, No. 1–3
Broilers	Wholesale, 12-city average
Turkeys	8–16 lbs., hens, Eastern region
Eggs	Grade A, large, New York, volume buyers
Milk	Price received by farmers for all milk

Looking at this list, a logical question might be, "How representative are the specific market prices for the nation as a whole?" The prices on Grade A large eggs in New York, for example, have averaged 10 cents per dozen above the average prices received by U.S. farmers for all eggs. However, the correlation between these prices, based on annual data for 1977–1993, was over 99 percent. A regression of the U.S. farm egg prices on the New York series explained over 98 percent of the variation and produced a standard error of less than one cent per dozen.

Obviously, prices on these products differ from one part of the nation to another, but they tend to follow parallel patterns. By knowing the normal relationship between the price quoted and prices at other locations, one can easily interpret the quoted forecasts for other markets.

A competitive process called arbitrage tends to keep price differences in line with transportation costs. Simply put, if price differences exceed transfer costs (including the economist's "normal" profit), resources will be attracted to that activity until price differences narrow to a point where abnormal profits are eliminated.

PRICE SURFACES

In the context of a competitive transportation industry dealing with a homogeneous product, a price surface can be mapped as shown in Figure 12-1. A central consumption point is identified around which production is dispersed.

A slice down a section of the map would establish the graph on the right side of Figure 12-1. Price would be a linear function with the price at the consumption center as the constant, the transportation cost per mile as the coefficient on distance; in this case, .10 units per mile. More realistically, transportation costs per mile decline

FIGURE 12-1 Contour map and graph of a market area with dispersed production and a central consumption point*.

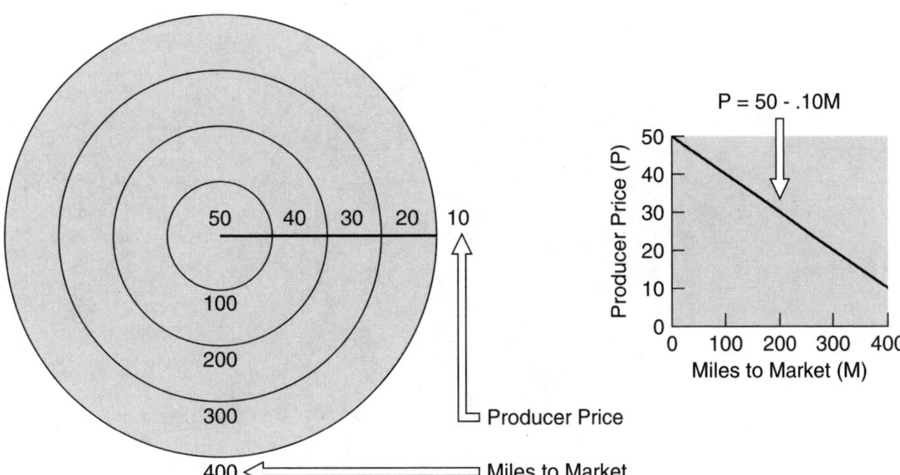

*Transfer (transportation) costs = .10 per mile.

as the distance from market increases and the price line is convex to the origin (Bressler and King, 1970). For exposition purposes, linear relationships are assumed in the illustration.

Alternatively, a situation with a central production point with dispersed consumption is depicted in Figure 12-2. This would be characteristic of a region around a food processor. Prices for the product to consumers are progressively and linearly higher in the ring around the production point as described by transportation costs and distance. Such diagrams seem trivial, but provide a base needed to explain spatial differences in prices.

MARKET DIVISION

Somewhat more complex is the delineation between two markets, i.e., central consumption points as illustrated in Figure 12-3. If prices were the same at $50 at point A and point B, and transportation costs to the two markets were the same per mile (as postulated by the values for the isoquants labeled above the center points), the dividing line would be a straight vertical line bisecting the two markets.

This means that production to the left of this line would realize the higher return moving to Consumption Point A, and production to the right of this line would be shipped to Consumption Point B to realize the higher return. For the direct line between A and B, the graph at the bottom of Figure 12-3 illustrates the same conclusion by the height of the heavy solid lines that directs the product to the most profitable market.

A second situation is posed in which prices at Consumption Point A are $10 per unit higher than at Consumption Point B. The isoquants are re-labeled below Consumption

FIGURE 12-2 Contour map and graph of a market area with a central production point and dispersed consumption*.

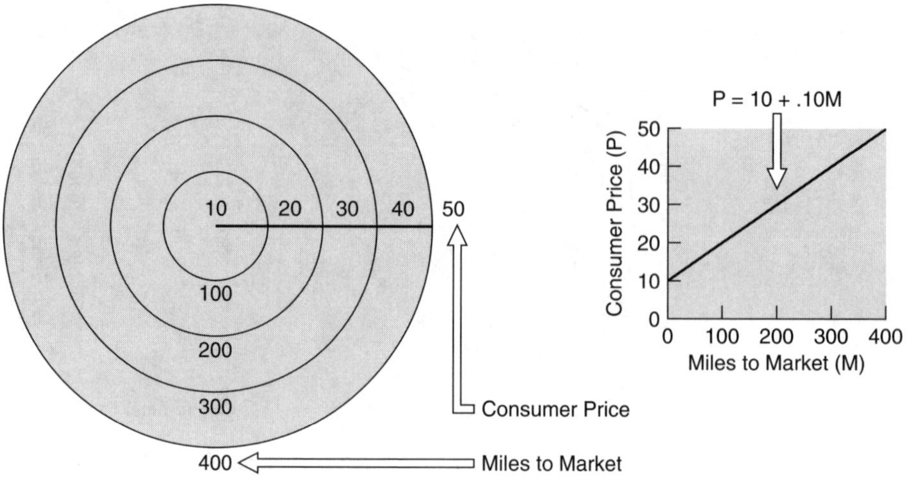

*Transfer (transportation) costs = .10 per mile.

Point A and a curved line is introduced to delineate the two markets. What may be counter-intuitive is that the dividing line between A and B is not a straight line that shifts toward B, but is a hyperbola. (See Bressler and King, 1970). The curved line is drawn at the intersection of the same isoquants of Markets A and B. The graph at the bottom of Figure 12-3 with the upward shift in demand in Market A (light line) illustrates the new point of market separation on the line between the two markets. (See Tomek and Robinson, 1990.)

Such examples are devoid of complications related to natural barriers to transportation, effects from economies of scale in transportation, "back haul" opportunities, and other factors that interrupt the concentric circles of an isoquant map. Also, production costs are not stipulated. Differential cost structures would modify the location of production relative to consumption centers in the long-run.

SIMPLE TRADE MODEL

The next example is one in which two separately defined regions, each with specified supply-and-demand relationships, potentially trade with each other. If the price difference between the two regions is greater than the transportation costs, arbitrage in a competitive environment will bring price differences down equal to transportation costs. Simply put, arbitrage brings resources into balancing supplies with consumption so that price differences just equal the economic costs of moving the product into the deficit area.

The first example is illustrated in Figure 12-4. (See Tomek and Robinson, 1990; Baker, 1961.) At a price of 40 per unit, the excess supply in Region A is equal to the excess demand in Region B, which is 20 units. If there were no transportation costs,

FIGURE 12-3 Dividing line between two central consumption points, A and B, each with dispersed production*.

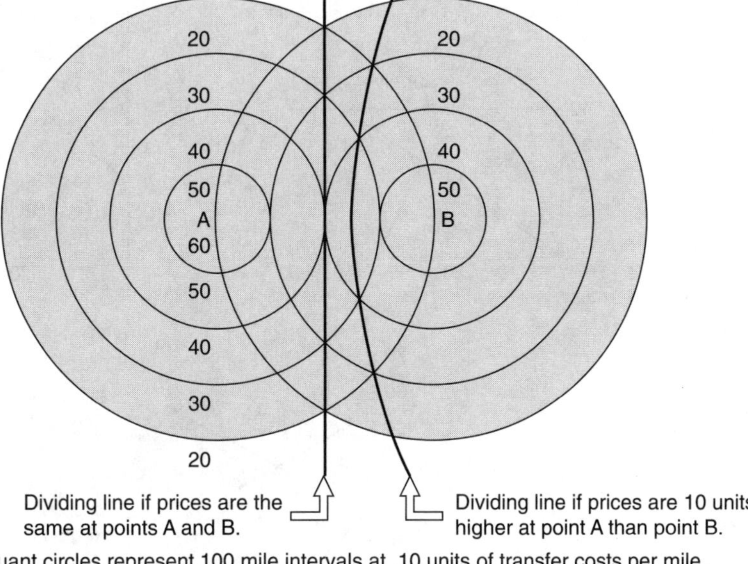

*Iso-quant circles represent 100 mile intervals at .10 units of transfer costs per mile.

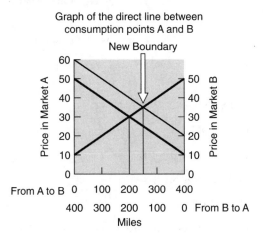

Region A would sell 20 units to Region B. At equilibrium in Region A, without exports, the price would be 25 per unit and at equilibrium in Region B, without imports, the price would be 55 per unit, a difference of 30 per unit at the equilibrium in Region A versus Region B. If the transportation cost was 30 per unit or above, no product would be shipped from A to B. If less than 30 per unit, the volume of trade line in Figure 12-4 describes the amount of trade and the difference in price between regions A and B at equilibrium.

The same concepts can be represented algebraically. Assume the following supply-and-demand equations for a given product in regions A and B:

FIGURE 12-4 Illustration of trade on a given commodity between two regions.

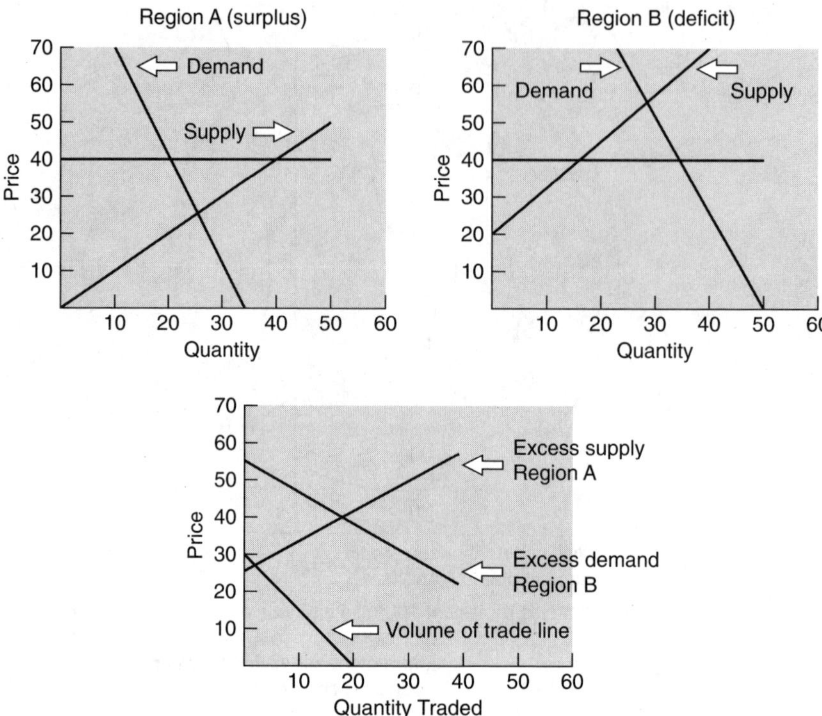

QDA = 60 – 1.2 PA

QSA = .8 PA

QDB = 160 – 1.5 PB

QSB = 20 + .5 PB

T = 10

where: QDA = quantity demanded in Region A

PA = price in Region A

QSA = quantity supplied in Region A

QDB = quantity demanded in Region B

PB = price in Region B

QSB = quantity supplied in Region B

T = transportation costs

Given these market structures, what will be the equilibrium prices and quantities produced in each region and how much will be traded? The amount of trade is defined as QT.

The solution to this problem proceeds as follows:

At equilibrium:

$$PB = PA + T$$

$$ESA = EDB = QT$$

where: ESA = excess supply in Region A

EDB = excess demand in Region B

$$ESA = QSA - QDA$$

$$= .8\ PA - (60 - 1.2\ PA) = -60 + 2\ PA$$

$$EDB = QDB - QSB$$

$$= (160 - 1.5\ PB) - (20 + .5\ PB)$$

$$= 140 - 2\ PB$$

Therefore:

$$-60 + 2\ PA = 140 - 2\ (PA + T)$$

$$2\ PA = 200 - 2\ PA - 2\ T$$

$$4\ PA = 200 - 2\ T$$

$$PA = 50 - .5\ T$$

If: T = 10	ESA = 30	QDA = 6
PA = 45	EDB = 30	QSA = 36
PB = 55	QT = 30	QDB = 77.5
		QSB = 47.5

The maximum price differential is equal to the difference between the price in Region B when EDB = 0 and the price in Region A when ESA = 0, i.e.:

$0 = -60 + 2\ PA$	$0 = 140 - 2\ PB$
$60 = 2\ PA$	$-140 = -2\ PB$
$30 = PA$	$70 = PB$

The maximum price differential would be 40 (70 – 30).

If T = 0 and ESA = ESB, the equilibrium would be PA = 50, PB = 50, ESA = 40 and EDB = 40. By this process, one could easily derive the equation,

$$QT = 40 - T$$

This procedure could be followed to derive solutions for more than two regions. What is required is the supply-and-demand relationships for each region and the transportation costs. Solutions can be obtained for the prices in each region that will equate aggregate demand and supply. Excess supply and demand is estimated for each region.

In reality, such equilibrium solutions are not observed for several reasons. Among the reasons is the absence of perfect competition—monopolistic influences, lack of knowledge, lack of homogeneity of product, and price discrimination. In the spatial price patterns, imperfections arise from institutional distortions such as quotas, export subsidies, health and safety regulations, etc.

The competitive model is a useful standard for analysts in studying trade patterns just the same. Such a starting point enables one to identify possible barriers such as lack of port facilities, uncertain exchange rates, credit problems with buyers, inappropriate packaging or form of the product, etc. For a more complete treatment of international trade, theory, and institutions, read Luther Tweeten's *Agricultural Trade, Principles and Policies,* and particularly the overview of agricultural trade models in Chapter 12 (Tweeten, 1992).

For a comprehensive empirical analysis of international trade flows, refer to *Embargoes, Surplus Disposal and U.S. Agriculture* (U.S. Department of Agriculture, 1986). In an evaluation of the impact on U.S. agriculture of the 1980 embargo of grain shipments to the U.S.S.R., three models were employed. One was a spatial equilibrium model, mostly an extension of the two-country example presented above. In addition, stock adjustment equations were included as were elasticities of price transmission (relationships between domestic and international prices).

The second alternative was the "Armington Model" (Armington, 1969). The major difference from the spatial equilibrium model is that the country of origin for a given product becomes a differentiating factor. The importing nation can discriminate between sources based on quality, consistency, political and cultural reasons, etc. The spatial equilibrium model treats a given product as homogeneous regardless of origin.

The Armington Model involves a two-step procedure. The first step is to measure the excess demand for each of the importing nations or regions, much like discussed in Chapter 4 in the "Demand for Exports" section. The second stage allocates the import demand for a given commodity from each exporter to each importer. Because of the complexity of such a procedure, certain assumptions apply to make the model operational.

A third approach, called the "price discrimination model," was designed to measure whether other exporting nations may have exploited the U.S. action through taxes or subsidies. Large countries with market power can initiate policies that capture rents from other nations.

INTERREGIONAL ANALYSIS

Linear programming has been a traditional tool for spatial studies, particularly to gain perspectives on interregional adjustments and least-cost routing systems for transportation. Programming techniques were most popular in the 1960s, with a number of studies completed by Judge, Havlicek, Rizek, Brokken, Heady and others (Judge, Havlicek and Rizek, 1964; Brokken and Heady, 1968).

A discussion of linear programming studies using this technique is beyond the scope of this book. This omission is not intended to diminish the importance of linear programming as a tool for spatial analysis, but it is limited in explaining some of the shifts in location of production over time. Comparative advantage as a concept is alive and well, but has to be viewed in a broader context than in the typical economic principles textbook. (See Chapter 9 in Seitz, 1994.)

In addition to and in combination with comparative advantage, what agricultural products are produced where in the U.S. could be attributed to:

1 Physical conditions
Example: The soils and climate of the Midwest favor corn production; the semi-tropical climate of Florida and southern California accommodates citrus.

2 Costs of production
Example: Hog production is concentrated in the Midwest because of lower feed prices.

3 Transportation costs
Example: New York produces milk primarily for fluid use and Wisconsin for manufacturing use. Wisconsin, being some distance from major population centers, has a comparative advantage in converting milk to butter, cheese, and non-fat dry milk—forms that involve much lower transportation cost per hundredweight of the fluid form.

4 Scale economies
Example: Large, specialized dairy farms in California, where input prices are generally higher, can convert those inputs into cheaper milk than Wisconsin. As a result, California has become the number one dairy state.

5 Institutional
Example: A combination of the initiative of "integrators," receptive farmers, the Tennessee Valley Authority, and perhaps other conditions vaulted Georgia into a leading broiler state, more than offsetting an apparent cost advantage of the Midwest.

6 Nuisance factors
Example: Large-scale cattle-feeding operations tend to be concentrated in isolated areas such as in Kansas.

7 Public policy
Example: Some states have laws against the establishment of large livestock operations.

8 Leadership
Example: Michigan is the center of the breakfast food and pizza industries because the founders happened to be located in this state.

The solution to a linear programming analysis in *Interregional Adjustments in Crop and Livestock Production,* completed in 1968, keeps hogs in the Corn Belt and leaves California deficit in milk (Brokken and Heady, 1968). The results seemed reasonable, and few agricultural economists would have expected that California would become a surplus dairy state or North Carolina would surpass Indiana and Illinois in hog production. The growth of hog production in North Carolina has apparently been due to leadership in integrating production and processing, a declining tobacco industry, and an accommodating state government.

INTERREGIONAL ANALYSIS EXPANDED

Considering the complexities of interregional competition in agriculture and the surprises that have emerged since the 1960s, commodity analysts may need to acquire new tools. At least, researchers should recognize that traditional techniques are necessary, but not sufficient, to forecast future shifts in geographic production patterns. These points were emphasized in a comprehensive study on international competition (Porter, 1990).

To assist farmers in a given state or region to assess their future absolute and competitive positions in their respective industries, a score card of relevant considerations was developed around the paradigm in Figure 12-5. This can also provide analysts with a checklist of points they need to cover in appraising the potential for specific areas

FIGURE 12-5 Schematic on agricultural competition.

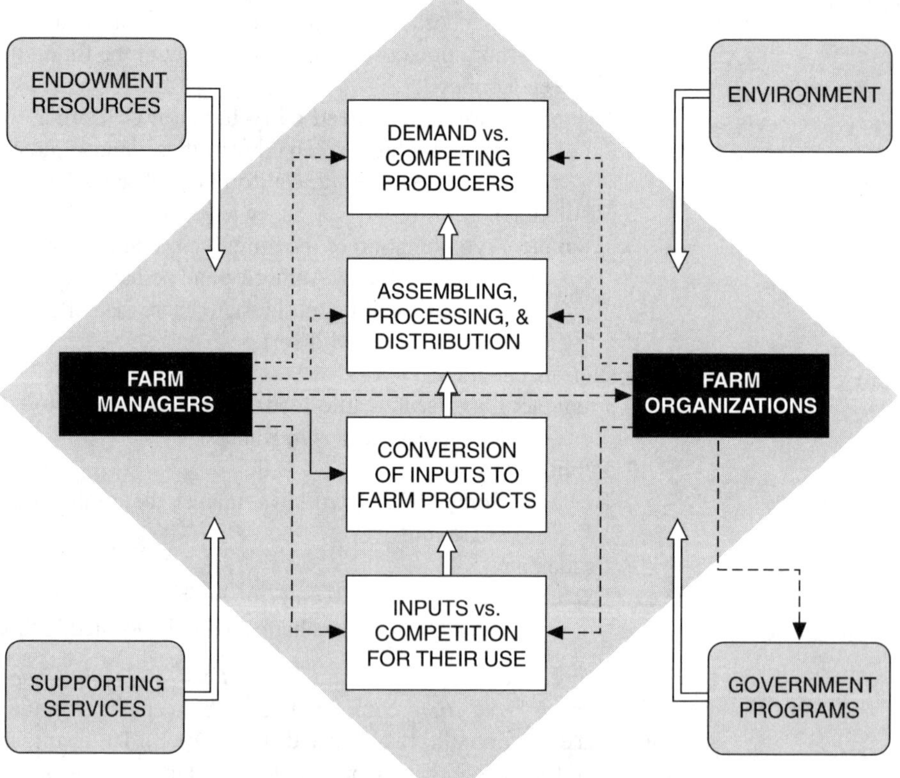

within an interregional competition matrix. Following are some relevant questions to ask whether addressing farmers and their organizations, agribusinesses, processors, public policy makers, or others.

Figure 12-5 on a "Schematic on Agricultural Competition" is simply a framework for decision makers to think about the total system in which they operate. Within the trapezoid, farm managers have major control over conversion of inputs into farm products. They also influence farm organizations who have other decision makers with an important role from input supply through assembly, processing, distribution, and, in some cases, the final stages before consumer purchases. At each of these stages, entrepreneurs are very dominant in determining the strength of that industry.

Within the trapezoid, the economist would appropriately concentrate on the following questions:

I Demand, Marketing Facilities, and Processing
- **A** Domestic and export demand
  - **1** Has demand been increasing and will it likely continue to increase?
  - **2** What is the location of the market relative to producers and processors?
  - **3** What is the potential competition from other producers and processors?
  - **4** Are there possibilities to fulfill market niches?
- **B** Marketing and processing facilities
  - **1** What is the capacity, efficiency, and state of the arts of the current facilities?
  - **2** How progressive and forward looking is the management?

II Producers or Farm Managers
- **A** Structure and management ability
  - **1** What size of farm is economically viable and what percent of total output is on these farms in comparison with competing areas?
  - **2** What quotient would you assign to the ability and progressiveness of farm managers?
- **B** Inputs
  - **1** Prices: How do prices compare with major competing areas?
  - **2** Quality: What is your assessment of the quality of hired labor, replacement stock, forage, and other inputs, particularly those with a wide range of quality imbedded?
  - **3** Availability: Do farmers have ready access to land, labor, capital, and other inputs, and what is the competition for that access?

III Farm Organizations, General and Commodity
- **A** What services are provided?
- **B** What is the strength of their leadership and how progressive are they?
- **C** Do they have political power and how much?

Outside the trapezoid are elements sometimes overlooked by analysts, but quite important in the total assessment for growth or feasibility of major new investments. To a degree, they are outside the control of the industry itself.

IV Endowment Resources: These are basically what Mother Nature provides and explain, in a major way, what is being produced where; included are such basic elements as soils, topography, climate, water, and related natural resources. These are usually taken as given and fairly permanent.

V Environment: These external influences may borrow from Mother Nature, but are more the product of human endeavor—land, air, and water transportation facilities; communication systems; recreational facilities; general amenities; quality of living in terms of a healthy climate, educational and cultural facilities, etc. (Do people like to settle here?) This is a very broad aspect including such characteristics as the extent of the rural–urban interface, availability of off-farm employment, the diversity of the state's agriculture, and the existence of complementary industries that contribute to the profitability of agriculture (such as food processors furnishing byproducts to agriculture as animal feed). In addition, overall societal concerns, such as environmental quality and regulations, food safety, and animal welfare must be factored in.

VI Supporting Services: A true analysis of a region's comparative advantage must evaluate the infrastructure of educational and research institutions. Public-supported programs that are quality can provide a competitive edge to local industries.

VII Government Programs: This is a very broad area that includes agricultural adjustment and support programs under the watchful eye of GATT and its successor, the World Trade Organization. But also important are many other government-sponsored programs, including crop and livestock estimates, market news, inspections, grades and standards, zoning, right-to-farm legislation, and taxation, which may be particularly important in either evaluating interregional or international competition.

Numerous state programs have been devised to attract and retain industries. Conway Data, Inc. has tabulated 18 ways states provide financial assistance to industry, 15 tax incentives for industry, 18 special services for industrial development, 19 forms of industrial revenue bond financing and 10 incentive programs for pollution control (Conway Data, Inc., 1986).

This presentation on interregional competition may appear a bit imprecise. While some quantitative tools are available as earlier described, this area of research is still in a formative stage. Regardless, many efforts are underway to get a handle on economic development prospects in local areas not only in agriculture, but in the overall rural and urban scene as well. While this book is directed toward a quantitative methodology, the purpose of the foregoing material is to divert analysts from the naive presumptions that quantitative tools are readily available to answer questions related to regional development and the feasibility of major capital investments.

SHIFT-SHARE ANALYSIS

One quantitative tool, easily applied, but devoid of much substance in the explanatory power of economic theory, is "shift-share analysis." Simply stated, this is a tracking of the production in a given state or region relative to the national total on some sub-region relative to a larger geographic body—or, internationally, a comparison of the production in a given country relative to the world total. Similarly, researching international trade often focuses on "market share," i.e., the exports of a given country relative to total exports.

Shift-share analysis is more of a monitoring activity. If a state or region has been consistently increasing its share of the national product, one might conclude that it owns a comparative advantage; if losing, a comparative disadvantage is earmarked. Conveniently, OLS application to these percentage terms can establish the signs, positive or negative, over the relevant past period as a linear (or non-linear) function of a time variable. Also, *t* values will verify whether the negative or positive coefficients are significantly positive or negative at whatever level the analyst requires.

Of course, such an analysis will not provide the investigator an answer of why a given state or region is gaining on or losing out to the nation or a relevant sub-region; but it still is a fairly powerful tool in getting to the bottom line—"Are we gaining/losing market share and by what level of significance?" Second, but not irrelevant, shift-share analysis is relatively straight-forward and easily understood, not only by professional decision-makers, but the general public as well.

Shift-share analysis is not, by any means, an isolated methodological tool. It has been extensively used by U.S. government economists. Kalbacher claims that it was first applied in 1942 in a study of manufacturing industries (Kalbacher, 1979). More recently, the Bureau of Economic Analysis of the U.S. Department of Commerce described how they projected employment by state to the year 2010 as follows:

> Basic industries are those that produce products that are generally exportable out of a state. Because of the potentially broad market for such products, it was assumed that each state competes for a share of the national market of each basic industry. Accordingly, in each state, employment in each basic industry was projected according to the historical trend in the state's share of employment in that industry nationally. The projections of basic-industry employment reflected the assumption that the factors affecting the state's employment share in the past (for example, relative wage rates, access to inputs and markets, etc.) will continue to affect it in the future, but less strongly, so that in all cases the rate of change in employment share slows. In other words, each state's share of each basic industry was assumed to change at a decelerating rate toward a long-term equilibrium. This assumption ensured that no industry in a state would have an unreasonably large or small share of national employment in the industry at the end of the projection period. (U.S. Department of Commerce, B.E.A., 1990.)

Because shift-share analysis lacks the underlying economic explanatory powers, rigor is absent in applying this methodology to forecasting. However, practicality may dictate that this methodology be put into service as a predictor, at least as a baseline data set. A validation for this procedure is that once a shift-share direction is established, it tends to continue several years into the future. Econometric purists will label such projection methodology as "naive empiricism," but in absence of practical alternatives, such an approach can be defended.

This is accomplished with the following set of equations:

$$\text{SHQSUB}_t = \text{QSUB}_t/\text{QNAT}_t$$

$$\text{SHQSUBP}_t = \text{f (TIME) as estimated by OLS}$$

$$QSUBP_t = SHQSUBP_t * QNATP_t$$

where: $QSUB_t$ = total production of a given commodity in sub-region in year t

$QNAT_t$ = total national production of a given commodity in year t

$SHQSUB_t$ = share in a sub-region of total national production of a given commodity in year t

$SHQSUBP_t$ = estimated share in a sub-region of total national production of a given product over some past period as established by OLS; projection is established by setting the value of TIME to the projection year

$QNATP_t$ = value of national production in projection year t

$QSUBP_t$ = value of product in a sub-region in projection year t

TIME = serial time, i.e., 1990=1990, 1991=1991, etc., or 1, 2, 3, etc., beginning with the first year of the data set

The analyst will need to explore alternative functional forms, or as is routinely applied by the USDC, use functions that diminish trends in share, positive or negative. The signs and *t*-values for the coefficients of TIME provide insights on the direction and significance of past shifts in a sub-region's share of the national output. This information itself provides clues to the strength of the comparative advantage of that sub-region. Estimating values in the projection year is a simple matter of setting the TIME variable at the value of the projection year.

Of course, the analyst may need to intercede with some judgment about the future course of output in the sub-region relative to the past. When applied to the major field crops, will the implied acreage be within feasible limits? Will local forage supplies support the numbers of ruminant animals being projected? Accompanying such a program would be analyses of technical coefficients such as yields per acre, conversion rates of feed input to livestock production, etc.

PLANT LOCATION

An excellent reference for empirical analysis of spatial markets is Bressler and King's *Markets, Prices and Interregional Trade* (Bressler and King, 1970). This brief discussion on plant location was abstracted from their book to provide readers with an intuitive idea of this methodology.

The economical organization of a system of processing plants involves the simultaneous consideration of: (1) costs of collection, (2) costs of plant operation, including scale economies, and (3) costs of plant-to-market transportation. From the data set, fairly obvious generalizations emerge. If transportation costs of raw materials are greater than on finished products, processing plants tend to be production oriented. The optimum location for processing will usually be at the raw material site or market site and not at an intermediate location.

Formal models are available that can determine, at equilibrium, the location, size, and number of plants as well as the allocation of territory among them. The following mathematical model on plant location was described by Stollsteimer (Stollsteimer, 1963):

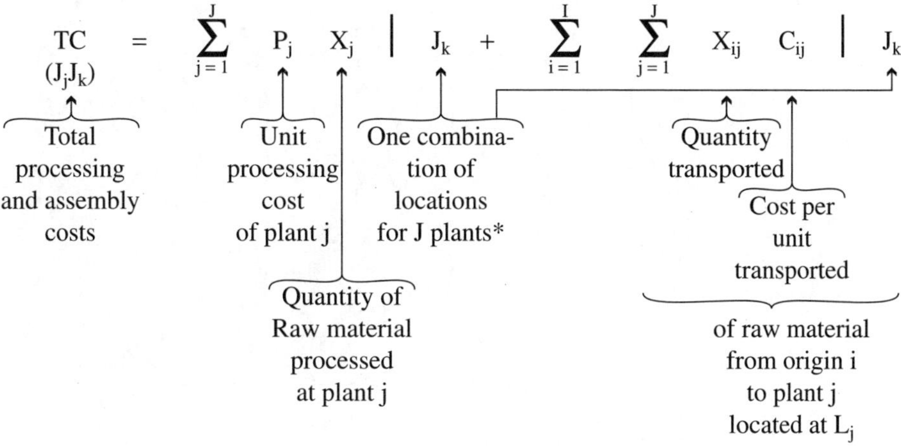

Problem: Minimize TC with respect to plant numbers J, $(J \le L)$, and locations J_k, $[k = 1, \ldots \binom{L}{J}]$ subject to:

$$\sum_{j=1}^{J} X_{ij} = X_i$$

$$\sum_{i=1}^{I} X_{ij} = X_j$$

$$\sum_{i=1}^{I} X_i = \sum_{j=1}^{J} X_j = X = \text{Total quantity of raw material produced in the supply area} \qquad X_{ij} \ge 0 \quad X_j \ge 0$$

The solution process is as follows:

1. Compute a transfer cost function that is minimized with respect to plant locations L for varying values of J.
2. Derive the relationship between the cost of processing a fixed quantity of raw material and varying numbers of plants. (Total cost function for an individual plant is assumed to be linear and positively sloping with a positive intercept. Plants at each location are identical.)
3. Derive a *total combined* cost function by adding the total assembly cost function and the total processing cost function for varying numbers of plants.

*Among the $\binom{L}{J}$ possible combinations of locations for J plants, given L potential plant locations.

FIGURE 12-6 Example of a supply area and alternative sites for processing plants.

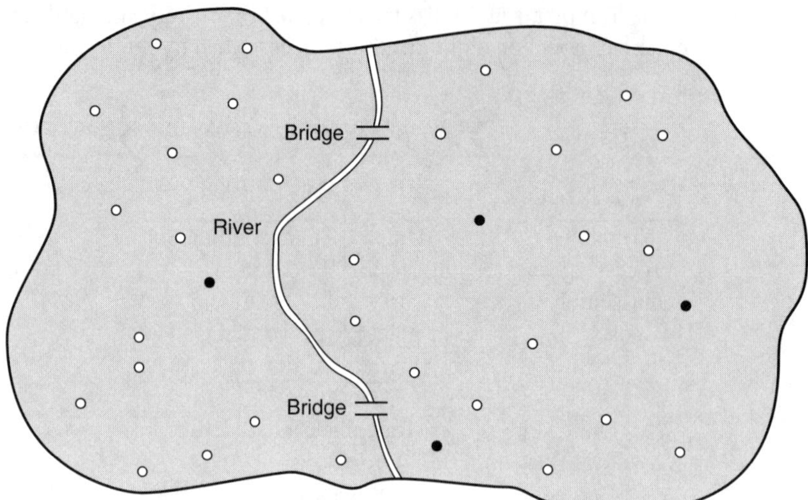

○ = Origin of raw materials, i.e., farms.
● = Potential plant sites, i.e., L.

To visualize the problem, look at Figure 12-6, which is a map of a hypothetical supply area with designated points of origin of the raw material (farms) and potential plant sites. Simply stated, the problem is to determine how many plants and in which locations would minimize the total cost of assembly and processing. In this particular example, costs of shipping the processed product to consumers are excluded from the problem.

Assume that of the L potential locations, 4 (or J = 4) were identified as plausible or possible. Perhaps the communities and local Chambers of Commerce were quite supportive. The problem then becomes: (1) How many plants should be constructed? and (2) Where should they be located? Erecting plants at each of the four sites would minimize assembly costs, but would maximize processing cost.

The solution to the problem is illustrated in Figure 12-7. There are four alternative sites for one plant. The location combination with the lowest assembly costs is identified, as shown in the left section of Figure 12-7. For two plants, there are six combinations for where those plants could be located and the combination with the lowest assembly cost is identified. Similarly, there are four combinations for locating three plants and one combination for locating four plants. The combinations for one, two, three, or four plants, which have the lowest assembly costs, are joined by the "least assembly cost line."

Since the plants are assumed to be identical with no economies to scale, total processing cost increases linearly with the number of plants as indicated in the right section of Figure 12-7. Adding the total assembly cost (from the least assembly cost line) to the processing cost establishes the total cost line. The solution, then, is to erect two plants at the sites providing the least assembly costs.

FIGURE 12-7 Illustration of methodology for determining the optimum number and location of processing plants in a supply area.

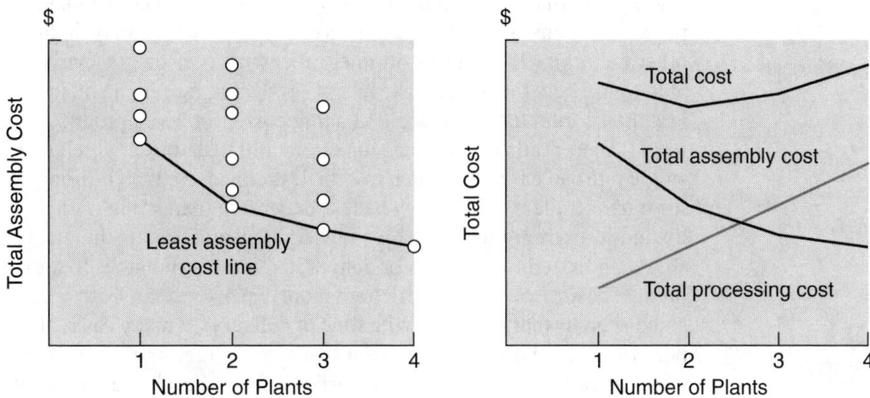

This problem could be expanded to include economies of scale, costs of distribution of the processed product, and other refinements. If distribution costs were added to the problem, the solution might be somewhat different. Possibly, the least cost for assembly, processing, and distribution might be achieved with more than two plants.

Still, this is nothing more than a "bare bones" treatment of the subject. Those who may be advising food processors on where to locate need a much broader base of information. An extensive quote from Dr. Smith Greig who had a long experience working with food processors provides some of the needed perspective (Greig, 1984).

Procurement Costs

In the case of agricultural commodities for processing, the cost of raw product delivered to a processing plant may be affected by soils, climate, availability of water for irrigation, terrain, density of production, size of farms, on-farm technologies, land costs, labor availability and costs, alternatives to produce other crops, alternative market outlets, producer bargaining power (including legal monopolistic bargaining power of producers of some crops in some states), perishability, availability of storage facilities, and a myriad of other factors. If the processing is a multiproduct processing plant, the objective would be to minimize all costs of all inputs including not only raw agricultural inputs, but also such items as cans, bottles, other packaging materials, chemicals, and other supplies.

Processing Costs

Processing costs may vary depending on (1) the total volume of raw product, i.e., the total supply and elasticity of supply; (2) quality factors including quality of the raw and finished products; (3) economics of scale in size of plant; (4) labor wage rates and labor fringe benefits, which may depend on a variety of factors; (5) length of the processing season; (6) the product mix; (7) fuel costs; (8) electrical costs; (9) costs and availability of water; (10) state and local taxes; (11) by-product utilization; and (12) waste disposal costs, and many other costs.

Distribution Costs

These costs may vary depending on (1) relative distances to market (which may depend on population densities and per capita consumption, which may, in turn, depend on income and other factors); (2) locations of other processors; (3) size of markets (a large market may be able to use several railroad car lots of product at a time; a smaller market may only require less than a truckload); (4) scale of shipments—for some products there are 1 million lb. rail rates (several railroad carloads under one bill of lading), which may be less expensive than single railroad car rates, which may be less expensive than railroad flat car "piggyback" rates for tractor trailers, which may be less expensive than straight truck shipment; (5) perishability and form of product, i.e., on a raw equivalent basis, fresh potatoes are more expensive to ship than frozen french fries or dehydrated mashed potatoes, but on a per pound of finished product basis, frozen french fries are more expensive than fresh potatoes; (6) costs, premiums, and discounts that may vary with time of delivery: in many cases, the minimum cost for transportation may be by rail shipments, but other factors such as timeliness of delivery may make truck transportation more feasible; (7) availability of back hauls; (8) availability of a product mix (for buyers wanting mixed loads of several products).

Traditional commodity market analysis must be an integral part of feasibility studies related to capital investments in processing plants for agricultural inputs or products. So, much of this book is relevant to that effort. A complete feasibility study, however, requires the input of engineers and others with a strong technical understanding of the industry. Not to be overlooked in such an analysis are two fundamental questions:

1 Does the plan have budget to hire competent managers and staff?
2 Has the response of competitors in imperfect market situations been properly evaluated?

SUMMARY

Spatial aspects of economic analysis are particularly important for agriculture and food because production is widely dispersed geographically, and consumption is in more concentrated areas, typically at some distance from production. Competitive structures that influence location of production are continually changing, forcing analysts to monitor such dynamics. Also, the political subdivisions of nations, states, and regions, each very sensitive to the shifts in their share of markets, place additional pressure on economists to understand and forecast future directions.

Some quantitative tools are available to analyze interregional and international competition, such as linear programming, trade models, and shift-share monitoring. However, the task transcends economics and must encompass a broad range of political, social, and environmental considerations.

QUESTIONS FOR STUDY

1 What is meant by "arbitrage"?
2 Without looking at the solution to the simple trade model represented algebraically in Chapter 12, derive the equilibrium solution.
3 What is the major feature of the "Armington Model" relative to other trade models?

4 Why is Wisconsin the number one cheese state and California the number one milk production state?

5 Enumerate the advantages and disadvantages of "shift-share" analysis.

6 Select a commodity of interest to you. Determine what key price series on this commodity is featured in USDA publications. See, for example, *Agricultural Outlook,* a monthly publication of the USDA. Select another price series on this commodity at some distance from the market the USDA quotes. Calculate the correlation between the two series. Is the correlation high?

7 Find a set of weekly or monthly prices at two markets linked by the fact that the product moves from one market to the other. Determine:

a How closely are the prices correlated?

b Are prices in the destination market consistently above the origin market by transportation costs?

8 Note where the production of a commodity of interest to you is concentrated. Explain the reasons for the concentration you observe.

9 Locate state and national production figures over about a 20-year period for a commodity of interest to you. Calculate the share the state has of national production over time. Regress with OLS that share on a time variable. Try alternative functional forms, linear, time squared, log of time, square root of time, etc. Is the share positively or negatively related to time? Is the relationship significant? What functional form performs the best?

10 Interview the manager of an agribusiness plant. What factors were considered originally about where a plant(s) was(were) located. Is the current location the most appropriate today?

13

APPLICATION OF MODELS TO LONG-RANGE PLANNING AND POLICY ANALYSIS

POINTS:

1 Applying econometric models to decision support systems for farmers.
2 Introducing stochastics into decision support systems and policy analysis.
3 Modeling program parameters and decision makers in agricultural legislation.
4 Applying net present value estimates in policy analysis.
5 Use of models in evaluating public policy impacts on various sectors in the economy.
6 Use of models in technology assessment.

As stated by the French futurist, Bertrand de Jouvenel, "I would willingly say that forecasting would be an absurd enterprise were it not inevitable. We have to make wagers about the future; we have no choice in the matter." Many decisions require basic assumptions—explicit or implicit—about a distant time horizon. Farmers and agribusinesses appropriately develop long-term budgets when deciding on enterprise combinations, capital outlays, plant location, market development, etc. Agricultural policy makers need similar insights to effectively develop farm programs, allocate research and education funds, assist developing nations, etc.

The econometric/simulation models discussed in Chapter 8, enlarged upon in Chapters 10 and 11 on stochastic modeling and long-term projections, and extended to regional effects in Chapter 12, need to be tailored to fit particular decision-making frameworks.

This may require expanding the core model or developing satellite models that furnish the needed information to the decision maker. Satellite models draw selected variables from the core model, but are not part of the core model solution. The general modeler would do well to interact closely with those in the particular industry involved to gain necessary understanding.

While various types of econometric/simulation models might be relevant, this chapter focuses on the value of models that provide dynamic (year-by-year) projections for a 5-, 10-, or 15-year period. Capability for generating stochastic projections is also considered.

FARMERS AND AGRIBUSINESSES

Farmers and agribusinesses have available a number of comprehensive decision support systems, particularly accounting models that provide income statements, balance sheets, discounting formulas, and other aids for long-range financial planning. FINPACK, a software program developed at the University of Minnesota, has been a popular farm accounting system with a special section on long-range planning (Center for Farm Financial Management). Useful as FINPACK and other decision aids have been, minimal attention has been given to the derivation of the underlying price and cost projections.

FINPACK encourages farmers to "consider your average yields and prices received for the past several years with what you think the outlook will be for the next several years." Farm management texts suggest consulting extension specialists and other authorities (Harsh, Connor and Schwab, 1981; Boehlje and Eidmann, 1984). In any case, there is little evidence that formal econometric models are very prominent in long-term farm budgeting. A reason is that price and cost projections, carefully monitored to reflect current conditions, have not been widely available in the past.

Decision aids such as FINPACK do allow farmers to examine alternative scenarios quickly and therefore provide some ways to measure risk in the planning process. Still, the analysis is imprecise.

In assessing the state of the arts in long-range budgeting, more formalized procedures for inputting prices and costs into the decision support systems would seem appropriate. Such inputs could be year-by-year projections over the planning horizon or even variations from the baseline generated by stochastic processes. The farm model itself could be stochastic.

Michigan State University has developed such a decision aid called the Strategic Financial Planning Model (SFPM) (Harsh et al., 1995). AGMOD provides stochastic price and cost projections related to Michigan and SFPM simulates types of farms in a risk environment. Harsh cites the following advantages of SFPM over more traditional planning models:

1 Present market value under risk is estimated.
2 Probability of insolvency is provided.
3 Liquidation values are approximated.
4 Capital requirements may be internally determined.
5 Statistical measures of uncertainty may be applied to the final condition of the firm and to key financial accounts for all periods.

A joint project between the Food and Agricultural Policy Research Institute (FAPRI) at the University of Missouri and Iowa State University and the Agriculture and Food Policy Center (AFPC) at Texas A&M University has tied baseline forecasts (FAPRI) to representative farm models (AFPC) (Smith et al., 1996). The farm level simulation model incorporates both price and yield risks.

In a simulation for 1996–2002, yield variability for crops and livestock experienced in the previous ten years was assumed to prevail for some 71 representative crop and livestock operations in major U.S. production regions. Market prices for crops and livestock were tied to FAPRI's baseline projections and were assumed to be approximately 20 percent more variable than over the previous ten years due to the provisions of the new farm program, the Federal Agricultural Improvement and Reform Act of 1996. The FAPRI/AFPC project, along with SFPM, points to the possibilities for more comprehensive long-range budgeting for farms incorporating both baselines and risk (Richardson, 1996).

Similar opportunities exist for agribusinesses. As with representative farms, econometric/simulation models would have to be tailored to the decision support system relevant to particular firms.

POLICY ANALYSIS

Some modelers may claim that the accuracy of the baseline forecasts is not so critical for policy analysis because the same conclusions could be reached even if the baseline turned out to depart from reality. To a degree, this may be true in that production and investment decisions require some precision in forecasts and probability statements not so crucial to policy decisions. Policy decisions may be based on direction of change from a baseline and this direction may be the same under a number of alternative baselines. However, emphasis still should be placed on careful development of baseline projections for policy analysis because an errant baseline can lead to wrong policy decisions.

Policy Instruments

Therefore, the first step in policy analysis is to generate baseline projections over the relevant time period. The model itself should contain key policy tools in the core sector. Such tools can be classified as:

1 Provisions established by law.
2 Provisions with administrative flexibility.

In Chapter 6 on "Measuring Farm Supply," an example was given on how to incorporate provisions of the U.S. Feed Grain Program, in effect prior to 1996, in an equation representing the expected gross margin for a farmer participant. Four policy variables were included—the target price (TPCN), the non-recourse loan rate (LRCN), the percent of base that must be set aside (DRCN), and the program yields assigned to farmers (PYCN) in terms of a national average.

In the Food, Agriculture, Conservation and Trade Act of 1990 (FACTA), TPCN was frozen at $2.75 per bushel for 1991–1995 and LRCN was set by a complex formula involving the moving average price received by farmers for corn in the past five years, excluding the highest and lowest prices, with some latitude on the part of the Secretary of Agriculture in response to the corn stocks/use ratio. DRCN also involved a combination of a formula and some administrative flexibility of the Secretary of Agriculture. On PYCN, the policy has been to hold this figure at some historical level for each farmer so as not to encourage farmers to increase yields just to earn higher government payments.

Under the Federal Agricultural Improvement and Reform Act (FAIR) of 1996, TPCN and DRCN were eliminated. Participants received fixed payments over the 1996–2002 period regardless of price levels and regardless of how many acres of corn they planted — a feature defined as "decoupling".

LRCN was retained in FAIR as a "non-recourse marketing assistance loan." The major difference between a marketing loan and the traditional non-recourse loan is that the government does not take over the grain as a repayment. Instead, if producers elect to pay off the loan when market prices are below the loan rate, they repay the loan at the market price and retain the difference between the loan rate and the market price. In essence, they are still guaranteed a minimum return related to the loan rate.

With the traditional non-recourse loan, delivering grain to the government propped up market prices, benefiting non-participants and foreign producers. However, the non-recourse government assistance loan does expose the Federal Treasury to outlays when market prices are severely depressed.

Government farm programs on other feed grain and wheat have been very similar to the above example on corn. With the implementation of the 2002 Farm Bill, soybeans and other oilseeds are treated in the same way as the grains.

The 2002 Farm Bill did modify the program on major crops. Target prices were reinstated. Replacing the fixed payment scheme of FAIR, a combination of fixed and counter-cyclical payments was introduced. This addressed a fault of FAIR in which farmers received substantial fixed payments even in years of high market prices. The counter-cyclical payments in the 2002 Farm Bill converge to zero as prices rise to the target level. The rates for the non-recourse marketing assistance loans were fixed rather than based on a formula.

A national dairy market loss payment program was established in the 2002 Farm Bill. The payment rate was set at 45 percent of the difference between the Class I price of milk in the Boston Federal Marketing Order and $16.94/cwt.

Not only are government farm programs complex but, as indicated above, they are subject to major changes. Beginning with FAIR, farmers had the flexibility of shifting acres since the direct payments were decoupled from the acres actually planted. Farmers' decisions on how many acres of each crop to plant shifted from their expectations about prices *in combination with direct payments* to expected prices alone. Econometric models of farm supply based on time series data had to accommodate both the period before FAIR and the period beginning with FAIR. The gross margin type variable discussed in Chapter 6 are suited to incorporate such changes.

Modeling Decision Makers and Modifying Policy Assumptions

The Secretary of Agriculture has some authority to reduce the loan rates if the ratio of ending stocks to use in any given year is expected to exceed specified levels. A modeler could easily incorporate the minimums and maximums as defined by the law. Some judgment would be required, however, to establish whether and how much (within the legislated limits) the Secretary would lower the loan rates. If the Secretary has been in office for some time, an analyst might review actions taken in the past under legislated authority or statements made on the political philosophy of the current administration. Sometimes, an appropriate dummy variable to include is one which has the value of one in an election year and zero in other years.

Other examples of how policy variables can be incorporated into models could be cited. The Meat Import Law had a fairly specific formula for counter cyclical quotas directed primarily at manufacturing (frozen, boneless) beef from Oceana. This law has been replaced by tariffs and a tariff rate quota as mandated by GATT. The European Union (EU) has set-aside programs. Both the U.S. and the EU have subsidized exports. The North American Free Trade Agreement, as well as the negotiated changes in international trade restrictions under GATT and WTO, have established schedules for lowering trade barriers.

While models can incorporate policy instruments for purposes of generating forecasts, the forecasts themselves may provide insights into future policy. For example, if the eventual effect of an existing program were to result in an untenable situation for some sector of the economy, the modeler may be persuaded to modify the policy assumptions.

In addition to generating forecasts, given some assurance about the prospective agricultural legislation, econometric models can be very useful in evaluating alternative programs before they become a fixture. This has been a major function of the FAPRI model at the University of Missouri/Iowa State University (Food and Agricultural Policy Research Institute, 1995).

While the examples in this chapter focus on federal agricultural policy, decisions at the state and local levels may also benefit from econometric analysis. Policy tools available for states would include taxing, regulatory activities, grants for economic development, funding Land Grant universities, improvement of the infrastructure, etc. While the states have a somewhat different set of tools and objectives, the econometric analysis needed to support decision making at this level is similar to that at the national level.

NEW CHALLENGES

Modelers will be challenged in the future as the world moves toward international trade liberalization and domestic farm programs are dismantled. Eventually, however, the task may be easier as market forces replace complex farm programs.

Nevertheless, public policy will retain an important role in agriculture, shifting from price support and income enhancement to rural development and environmental issues. Econometric modeling activity in production agriculture has benefited from a fairly extensive database. Turning to rural development and the environment, econometricians will face some frustrations until statistical measurements are more firmly established.

As a critique on the application of econometric models for agricultural policy analysis, consider what has been, is, and could be. In the past, models have focused on the impact of alternative government programs on farm prices, production, incomes, domestic consumption, exports, carryover, and governmental costs. In some cases, such impacts were measured in terms of some target year, like five years into the future, or in terms of a year-by-year compilation. Certainly the latter format is preferred in that the path from the present to some target year is crucial—economically, socially, and politically.

Dynamic vs. Static

As an example of the limitations of certain static models that focus on some target year in the future, consider the conclusions of applying SWOPSIM to unilateral trade liberalization by the U.S. in 1986–1987. The conclusion was that world wheat and coarse grain prices would be about 11 to 12 percent higher and prices on oilseed and products would be slightly lower than in the baseline (Roningen and Dixit, 1989). The target year was unspecified, but considered to be about three to five years into the future. A similar conclusion was reached by the application of AGMOD to the same scenario, although seven to eight years elapsed before corn and wheat prices moved above the baseline (Ferris, 1990).

The point is that the near-term effect was negative for corn and wheat prices and net cash farm income, even though the eventual effect was positive. Such results are so common in policy analysis. The longer-term impacts, because of farmers' response, can be completely opposite the short-run impacts. This is why models generating year-to-year forecasts provide much more insight into the impacts of alternative farm policies than static models.

Having forecasts for each year into the future, the analyst can apply net present value (NPV) estimates for alternative farm program proposals. For example, the farm program initiated in 1996 (FAIR) was compared with a scenario of continuing the previous farm program (FACTA) for the period of 1996–2002. AGMOD generated net cash farm income projections for the U.S. under the two alternatives with the following NPV formula:

$$\sum_{t=1996}^{2002} NCSIN_t * (1 + IRFM/100)^{-N}$$

where: $NCSIN_t$ = projected net cash farm income in year t

IRFM = projected average interest rates paid by farmers

N = years, with 1996=0, 1997=1, 1998=2, etc.

Using the NPV estimates, net cash farm income was projected to be 3.8 percent higher under FAIR than FACTA. Without discounting, net cash farm income would be 3.3 percent higher under FAIR. The difference can be attributed to the scheduled reduction in government payments in the latter part of the 1996–2002 period.

A similar calculation was applied to gross margins per acre over variable cash costs on corn (for participants). The NPV returns from FAIR were 11.0 percent higher than from FACTA. Without discounting, returns from FAIR were 9.7 percent higher.

While the results in these cases were not dramatically different under the two methods, discounting an income stream is a refinement that should routinely be applied to policy analysis just as it is to investment analysis. In addition to evaluating the effects on farm income, NPV could also be applied to program costs, consumer expenditures, export earnings, processor sales, foreign producers' incomes, etc. Static models do not easily provide this opportunity.

In defense of static models such as SWOPSIM, their structural parameters are fairly transparent and provide insights into how policies affect a nation's agriculture. Their design stems from the need to include many individual nations in a world model, precluding the complexity dynamic models introduce.

Stochastic Impacts

But even models that do generate year-by-year projections under alternative policy assumptions, the forecasts have been primarily single valued with little or no attention to stochastic elements. A Secretary of Agriculture should have a strong conception of the probable variability patterns in U.S. and international crop yields over several future years when making farm program decisions for a given year. In addition to measuring the average effects over a period of years on the variables of interest, policy analysis should identify the risks involved and provide empirical values. Projections of year-by-year impacts of alternative government programs in terms of departures from a baseline should be accompanied with some indication of whether such policies will increase or reduce variability in such items as farm prices, costs, incomes, production, exports, etc.

Implications to Producers, Consumers, and Taxpayers

Agricultural policy analysis has centered on effects on producers. In some cases, how farm programs affect consumers and taxpayers has also been addressed. Efforts of the Organization for Economic Cooperation and Development (OECD) and the USDA to measure "Producer Subsidy Equivalents" (PSE) and "Consumer Subsidy Equivalents" (CSE) by commodities have provided econometricians with much more usable data for international policy analysis (OECD, 1991; Webb et al., 1990; Roberts and Johnson, 1994). By classifying producer subsidies into "market price support," "direct payments," "reduction in input costs," and "other," the differential impacts on producers, consumers, and taxpayers can be more carefully delineated. The extent of the subsidies on given commodities can be compared among nations.

A PSE "estimates the amount of subsidy that would be needed to compensate producers for eliminating government programs such as price supports, import quotas or tariffs" (Mabbs-Zeno and Dommen, 1989). Subsidy equivalents are either the sum of costs to a government for direct payments to its producers or a calculation of a price wedge. A price wedge is the difference between the domestic price and the international price of a commodity.

A CSE "estimates the amount of subsidy consumers would need to maintain their economic well being if all agricultural programs were removed" (Mabbs-Zeno and Dommen, 1989). Nations that have supported producers usually have taxed consumers. Therefore, CSE's are usually the mirror images of PSE's.

Impacts on Types of Farms by Regions

A fine-tuned farm policy analysis would relate impacts on particular commodities to types of farms and regions of the nation. Such a comprehensive study would be demanding of data, but is feasible considering information available from the USDA and Land Grant universities.

Farm policies do have differential impacts on regions of the nation and even districts of individual states. Often programs that benefit certain types of farms or regions negatively impact other types of farms and regions. Much interest is expressed in Washington to have farm program impacts delineated even by Congressional districts.

Implications to Total Food System and Economy

Probably a major void in farm policy analysis has been the neglect of the non-farm sector of the food and fiber system. Out of gross cash income over $200 billion, U.S. farmers spent $155 billion for cash inputs in 1995. Part of this was for inputs of farm origin (feed, livestock, seed) amounting to $43 billion, but the balance was for inputs from non-farm sources and for taxes. On the processing, marketing, and distribution side of the food system, farm policies can also have important implications, particularly at the first-handler and processor level.

Farm program evaluation could benefit from greater application of input–output analysis. Models such as REMI and MicroIMPLAN are now available to extend the traditional farm program studies beyond the farm gate (Fulton and Grimes, 1988; Minnesota IMPLAN Group, Inc., 1996). MicroIMPLAN generates several types of multipliers that measure direct, indirect, and induced effects on several indicators, including value of production, personal income, total income, value added, and employment. These multipliers are specified for states as well as for the U.S. as a whole and even for counties.

Evaluation of Research and Education

As with commodity programs, econometric models can incorporate new technology in generating forecasts—either to provide an appropriate scenario given the technology that is available or to assist research administrators in allocating funds most effectively given certain objectives. Possibly, such models have been underutilized in the latter role.

To illustrate how new technology can be incorporated into models, AGMOD was modified to accommodate the impact of bST, the growth hormone introduced into milk production in the early 1990s. The modification was based on research at Cornell University which indicated the potential for increased milk production per cow and reduced feed requirements per cwt. of milk (Kalter and Milligan, 1986). Second, the rate of adoption by the industry over an extended period was derived from interacting with those close to the dairy industry.

SUMMARY

The weak link in decision support systems for farmers is the lack of comprehensive long-range projections of prices and costs and the risks inherent with those projections. The current state of the arts in econometric modeling is capable of filling this void.

Similarly, procedures are available to model the provisions of farm programs and their implementation. Opportunities for more precise evaluation of farm programs include the application of net present value criteria, stochastic impacts, implication to consumers and taxpayers as well as producers, regional impacts, and effects on agribusiness. In addition, econometric models can be used more effectively in evaluating allocation of funds to research and education in agriculture and natural resources.

QUESTIONS FOR STUDY

1 What is meant by a "decision support system"?
2 Discuss the weaknesses in the traditional ways long-term farm budgeting has been conducted.
3 Why has risk increased for farmer participants under FAIR versus FACTA?
4 How would you "model" the decisions the Secretary of Agriculture might make on those program areas left to administrative discretion?
5 What is the difference between the traditional non-recourse loan and the non-recourse marketing assistance loan?
6 Write out a supply equation based on the past 25 years of annual data for a commodity with farm program parameters—a commodity with which you are familiar.
7 Why should agricultural policy analysis incorporate net present value?
8 Can you think of farm programs that benefit one type of farm to the detriment of another type of farm? Give an example.
9 In general terms, how might you apply an econometric model of production agriculture to an agribusiness supplying inputs to that sector?
10 Write out a supply equation for a commodity with which you are familiar, detailing how you would formulate it in forecasting the impact of new technology.

SECTION FOUR

SHORT-TERM FORECASTING, FUTURES MARKETS, AND SOURCES OF MARKET INFORMATION

14

SEASONALS

POINTS:

1. Removing trends and cycles from a database.
2. Calculating a monthly seasonal index.
3. Calculating a standard deviation for each month.
4. Measuring shifts in the seasonal pattern.
5. Interpreting seasonal patterns for storage decisions on crops.

Previous chapters have dealt extensively with the identification and measurement of trends and cycles in agricultural commodities. Trends relate to unidirectional tendencies of prices or other variables over a period of years. In an extended period of time, a commodity could display more than one trend, but the change in direction would not occur with regularity that could be described as a cycle.

Cycles are regularly occurring upward and downward movements that span more than a year, generally a minimum of two. No maximum number of years are specified, but at one time in the past, a "17-year cattle cycle" was observed. Not all commodities have definable cycles, and those that do seldom follow consistent patterns that can be easily forecast.

Seasonals are regular movements of prices or other variables within a year. Many agricultural commodities trace out fairly definable and consistent seasonal patterns. This is primarily due to the seasonal nature of agricultural production, but may also relate to seasonal demand factors.

Because seasonals are so important to agricultural commodities, special treatment of this subject is warranted in this chapter. The focus is on seasonal *price* patterns, but similar techniques could be applied to non-price variables as well. Also, the examples will be monthly average prices. The methods described could be modified for weekly, two-week, quarterly, or other time frames within a year that are of particular interest.

GENERATING A SEASONAL PRICE PATTERN

The first step in seasonal price analysis is to generate a "pure" representation of the underlying seasonal pattern and the variability around it. Think of a monthly price series as having the following components:

$$P = T + C + S + I$$

where: P = monthly price series

T = trend component

C = cycle component

S = seasonal component

I = irregular component

To prepare the price series for programs that estimate S and I, the analyst may want to remove T and C.

Several alternatives are available to deal with T. If the historical period is one of general inflation, the price series could be deflated, that is, divided by an appropriate deflator such as the Consumer Price Index or the Gross Domestic Product Deflator. Alternatively or in addition to deflating, linear trend or trends could be removed from the series, as follows:

$$\hat{P}_i = a + b\ \text{TIME}$$

where: $\hat{P}_i$ = the predicted values of undeflated or deflated prices, P_i, regressed on TIME

TIME = serial time

a, b = estimates from an OLS equation

The analyst could construct a de-trended series as follows:

$$DTP_i = P_i - \hat{P}_i + \bar{P}_i$$

where: $\bar{P}_i$ is the mean of prices over the period

The seasonal program would then be applied to the de-trended series, DTP_i.

Another alternative is to apply the seasonal program to the original nominal or deflated series. The rationale for this would be: (1) T is minor, (2) T will continue into the future about as it has in the past; therefore in applying seasonals in the future, the adjustment to T is built into the projected seasonal pattern, or (3) adjusting for T is more bother than it is worth, given the importance of I.

If C is an important component of P_i or DTP_i, the easiest way to remove it from the data series is simply to make sure that the historical period for the analysis embraces full cycles. Other procedures are available to remove cycles, but generally are not needed.

The seasonal program described in this chapter was developed by programmers in the Department of Agricultural Economics at Michigan State University following the methods described in a number of publications (Croxton and Cowden, 1960; Foote and Fox, 1952; U.S. Department of Commerce, 1960; Hannan, 1963). Other programs are available, but this one provides not only useful seasonal characteristics, but an intuitive idea of the rationale.

The steps and formulas are as follows:

1 Calculate a "centered" 12-month moving average for each month for a data series, P_m (P_m represents the analyst's choice from P_i or DTP_i):

$$CMA_m = 1/12\,[\sum_{m-5}^{m+5} P_m + .5P_{m-6} + .5P_{m+6}]$$

For the center month, m=0. Since the number of months in a year is an even number, 12, there is no convenient way to construct a moving average centered on a given month, so the P_m six months earlier and six months later are brought into the formula by giving each a weight of .5.

2 Calculate a ratio for each month for P_m to CMA_m and express this as a percent:

$$RCMA_m = (P_m/CMA_m) * 100$$

3 Calculate a mean of $RCMA_m$ for each month for the years in the database:

$$MRCMA_{jan} = 1/n \sum_{i=1}^{n} RCMA_{jan}$$

$$MRCMA_{feb} = 1/n \sum_{i=1}^{n} RCMA_{feb}$$

etc.

where: $MRCMA_{jan}$ = mean of the ratio of P_m to its CMA_m for each January

$MRCMA_{feb}$ = mean of the ratio of P_m to its CMA_m for each February

n = number of years tabulated for P_m

4 Calculate the standard deviation for $RCMA_m$ for each month.

$$SDRCMA_{jan} = \sqrt{\sum_{i=1}^{n}(RCMA_{jan} - MRCMA_{jan})^2/n - 1}$$

$$SDRCMA_{feb} = \sqrt{\sum_{i=1}^{n}(RCMA_{feb} - MRCMA_{feb})^2/n - 1}$$

etc.

5 Apply the OLS regression analysis to $RCMA_m$ for each month with TIME as the independent variable.

$$RCMA_{jan} = a_{jan} + b_{jan}\ TIME$$

$$RCMA_{feb} = a_{feb} + b_{feb}\ TIME$$

where: TIME = serial time

a, b = coefficients on the linear regression for each month

6 Record the b values for each month and their *t* values and project the predicted values for RCMA for each month into the future, i.e., beyond the historical database. These projections are usually not needed more than a year or two beyond the present. This simply involves setting the value for TIME for the projected years.

The procedure through Step 4 is fairly routine and covered by a number of seasonal programs. The additional steps that involve a regression analysis of the ratios are a recognition that seasonal patterns may not be stable and may shift in a predictable way. This usually is due to changes in the structure of the industry, such as the increase in year-round farrowing on hogs, expansion in cattle feeding, increased importance of South America in soybean production, expansion in on-farm grain storage, etc. The regression analysis tests whether shifts in seasonal price patterns are significant and, if so, provides a straight-forward way to project the seasonal patterns into the future taking those shifts into account.

EXAMPLE ON HOGS

A price series on barrows and gilts at six or seven major markets in the Midwest was collected and graphed as shown in Figure 14-1. By visual inspection, the period since 1972 portrays a structural shift in the hog industry. Primary factors were higher corn prices and accelerated general inflation. What is not apparent is that a shift to multiple around-the-year farrowing and use of combined farrowing and finishing facilities had proceeded through much of the period from 1950 to the early 1970s and then stabilized to some extent afterward. While other structural changes occurred after 1972, particularly the consolidation of production into fewer operations, the period of 1973–1993 was selected as appropriate for a seasonal analysis.

How many years are required to obtain reasonable measurements of seasonal patterns is subject to judgment and an understanding of the industry. One would prefer at least 20 years to estimate not only the mean, but also trends and other characteristics.

The first step is to calculate the centered 12-month moving average (CMA) of monthly hog prices. The actual and CMA of monthly hog prices are plotted in Figure 14-2 for

FIGURE 14-1 Hog prices at six to seven major midwest markets, by months, 1950 to 1993.

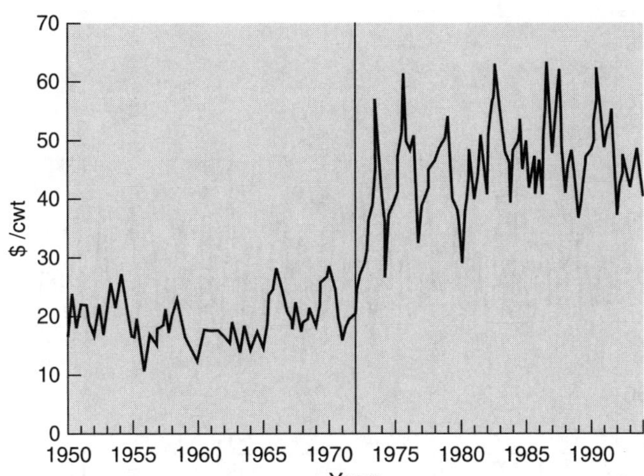

FIGURE 14-2 Actual and centered 12-month moving average of monthly hog prices at major midwest markets.

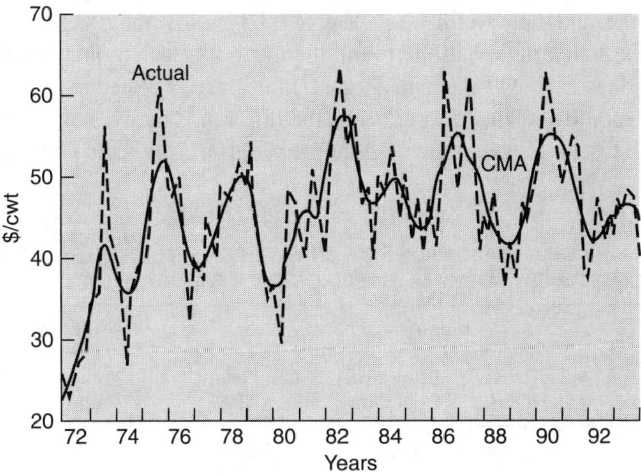

1972–1993. The ratio of the actual to the CMA is graphed in Figure 14-3. Note that while some trends can be discerned in the actual and centered moving average prices, the ratio between the two in terms of percent fluctuates around 100.

Steps 3 and 4 involve calculating the means and standard deviations for each month. Step 5 checks for shifts in the seasonal pattern. Finally, linear extensions of trends should be explored, especially if the trends are significant. The results are presented in Table 14-1.

The mean price index reached a minor peak in February at 100.5, i.e., about the average for the year, and then dropped to a low in April at 93.6, or about 6.4 below average.

FIGURE 14-3 The ratio of hog prices to the centered moving average expressed in percent, by months, 1972–1993.

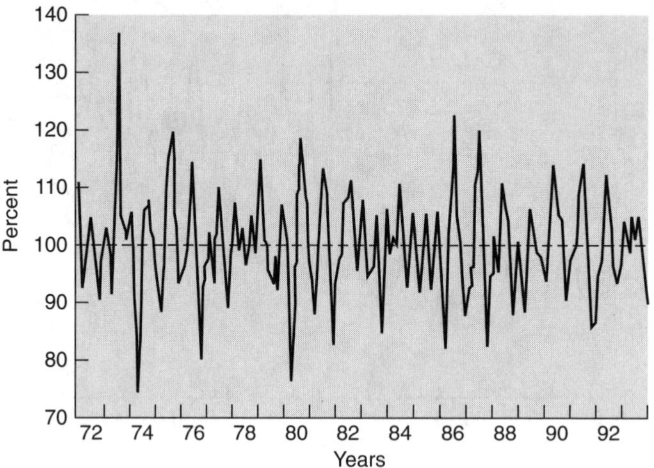

The mean index rose steadily to a peak in August at 108.5, or 8.5 percent above the yearly average, and then declined to a low of 93.5 in November.

The standard deviation around the mean for each month is tabulated. Most variable are prices in May, June, and August. It also can be noted that the standard deviation for each month, except July, exceeds the difference between the index for that month and 100. This, of course, indicates that the pattern is subject to considerable variability from

TABLE 14-1 SUMMARY OF A SEASONAL PRICE ANALYSIS ON PRICES OF BARROWS AND GILTS AT MAJOR MIDWEST MARKETS, BASED ON DATA FOR 1972–1993

	Mean		Trend Analysis[a]			
Month	Value	Standard Deviation	Coefficient on TIME	"t" Value	Projection to 1995	Standard Deviation
	Index	*Index*	*Index*		*Index*	*Index*
January	98.7	6.8	−.44	−2.06	93.3	6.3
February	100.5	6.6	−.37	−1.77	95.9	6.3
March	95.8	5.6	−.07	−.35	95.0	5.7
April	93.6	7.0	.30	1.29	97.3	6.9
May	99.0	10.2	.73	2.36	108.1	9.2
June	103.6	9.3	.70	2.52	112.4	8.3
July	107.7	7.3	.09	.36	108.9	7.5
August	108.5	9.4	−.28	−.89	105.0	9.5
September	102.7	7.3	−.19	−.75	100.4	7.4
October	98.7	8.2	−.07	−.23	97.9	8.3
November	93.5	7.5	−.22	−.86	90.8	7.6
December	96.6	6.8	−.38	−1.71	91.9	6.5

[a]Based on linear regression of the ratio of price to the centered 12-month moving average as the dependent variable and years (TIME) as the independent variable.

year-to-year with at least one chance in three that the price for a given month will be on the opposite side of 100.

Measurement of trends in individual months are absent from many software programs related to seasonal analysis. As can be seen in Table 14-1, a substantially different seasonal pattern emerges if trends in the ratio of prices to CMA in individual months are taken into account.

The coefficient on TIME indicates the direction and extent of linear trends per year for each month. For example, the index for January was trending down at the rate of .44 index points per year. This was significant at the 95-percent confidence level as shown by the *t* value of –2.06. The results of the trend analysis point to an upward shift in prices in April to July and declines in August to March.

To apply seasonals with significant trends to a future year, the forecaster would have to look a year beyond the database underlying the measurements. In this case, the database started in July 1971 and ended in June 1994, even though the price ratios to CMA were for January 1972 to December 1993. Obviously, the CMA requires data six months back and six months forward. For this reason, trends should be extended beyond the last year of the data, or in this example, to 1995.

Note in Table 14-1 the difference between the mean values for the indices and the projected values to 1995. The projected indices were lower and relatively flat through the first quarter compared with the means, moved up to an earlier and higher peak, and then declined to a somewhat lower low in November than for the mean values. This change reflected a shift in the timing of movement of hogs to slaughter to a smaller share of annual marketings in the second quarter and an increased share in the third.

As with the means, the standard deviation for each month for the 1995 projections are presented in the last column of Table 14-1. These are the standard errors of the regression for the months. Care should be taken in projecting these seasonal indices much beyond a year or two forward of the database. This suggests the need for a regular update of the entire seasonal analysis.

To amplify the importance of adjusting seasonals for structural shifts in the industry, Figure 14-4 contains plots of the price ratios to CMA for each month for 1972–1993. The dash lines are the fitted values using linear OLS equations extended to the projection year of 1995. This set of charts emphasizes why trend projections of the ratios and not the mean of ratios should be used in constructing seasonal price indices for agricultural commodities.

The product of trend analysis can be presented in the same way as the means and their respective standard deviations. An example of how this could be accomplished is shown in Figure 14-5 with the average (AVE) and the average plus and minus the standard deviations (SD). The average refers to the projected values for 1995.

FITTING SEASONALS TO DECISION MAKING

While the example on hogs was constructed with monthly averages, two-week averages might be more helpful for short-run decisions related to timing of marketings. Hog producers have a greater window of opportunity in timing sales over a two-week period than holding hogs off the market for an entire month.

FIGURE 14-4 Hog prices as a percent of a centered moving average, 1972–1993, with fitted values for 1972–1993 and projections to 1995.

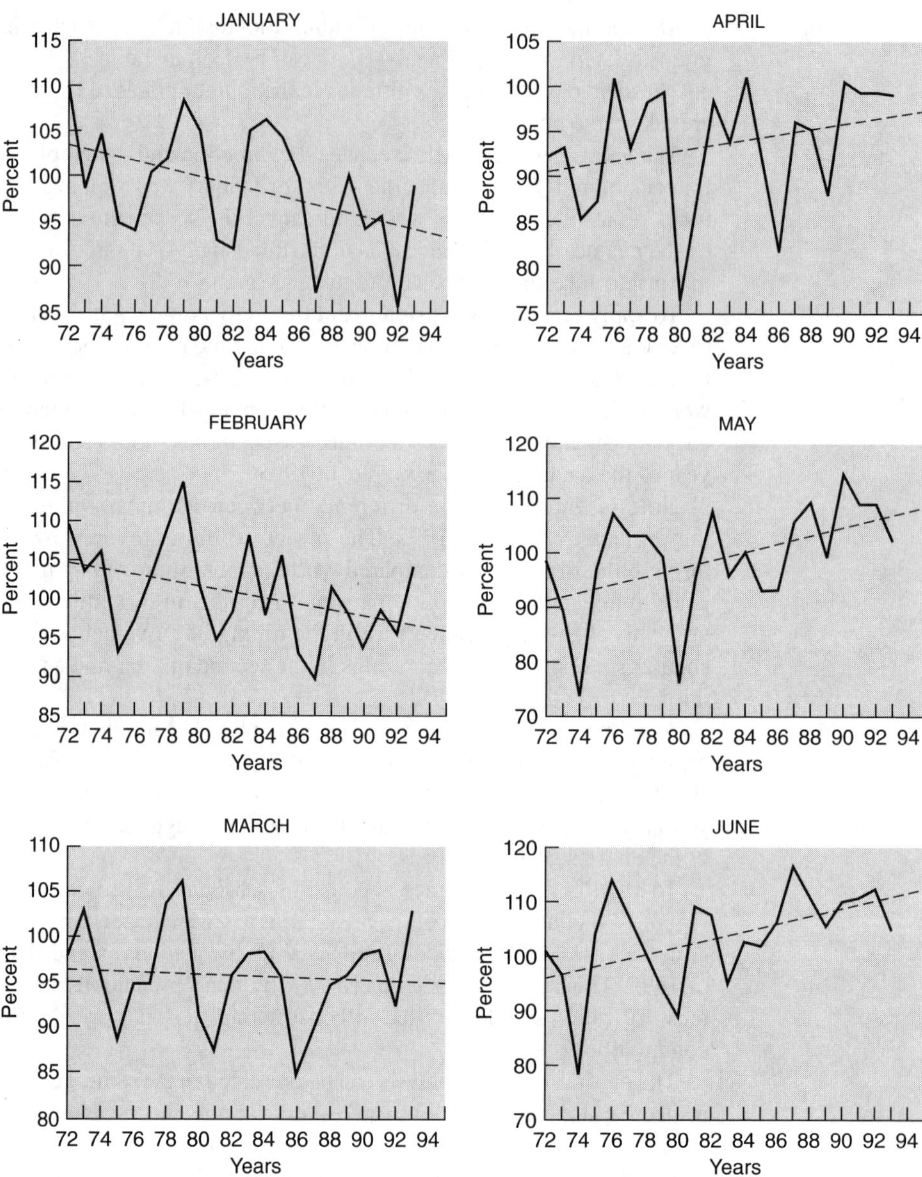

FIGURE 14-4 (continued)

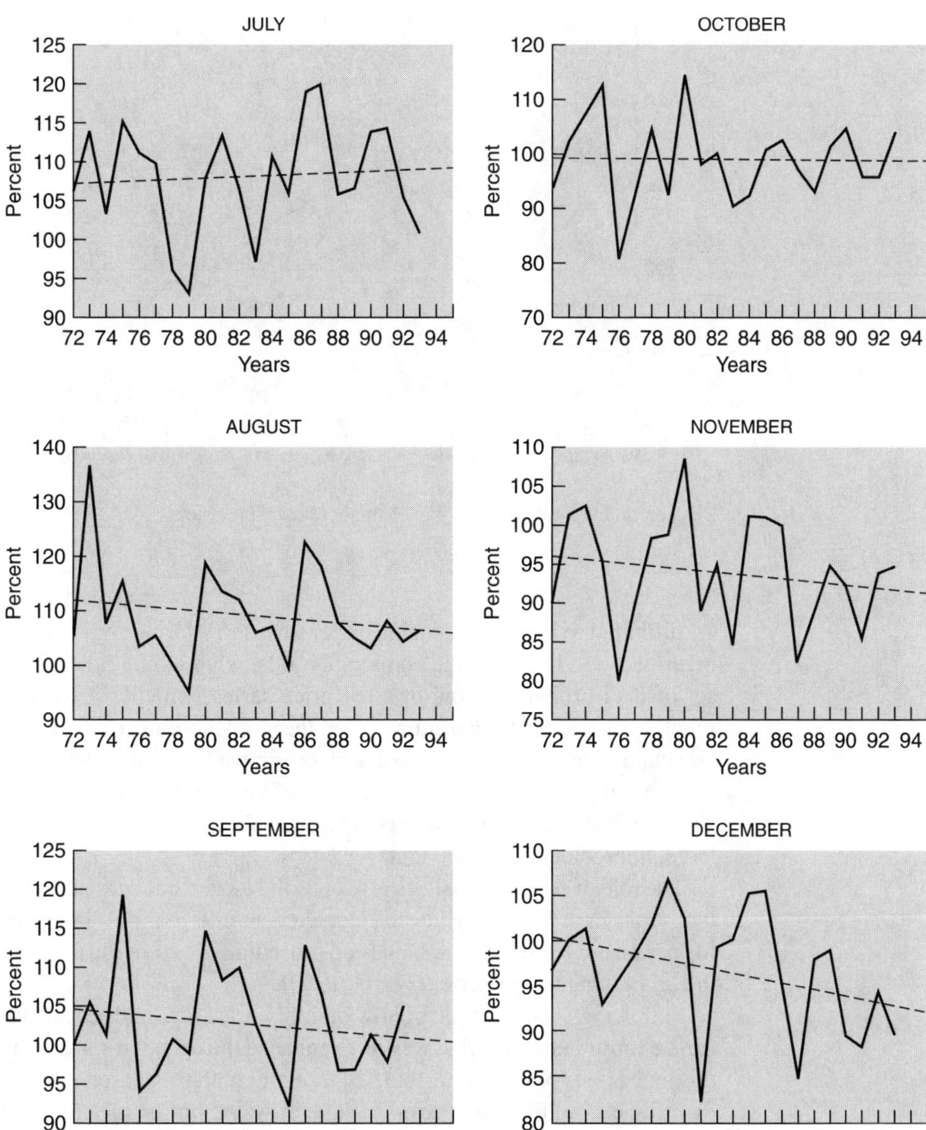

FIGURE 14-5 Seasonal price pattern on hogs with standard deviation as projected to 1995 from data for 1972–1993*.

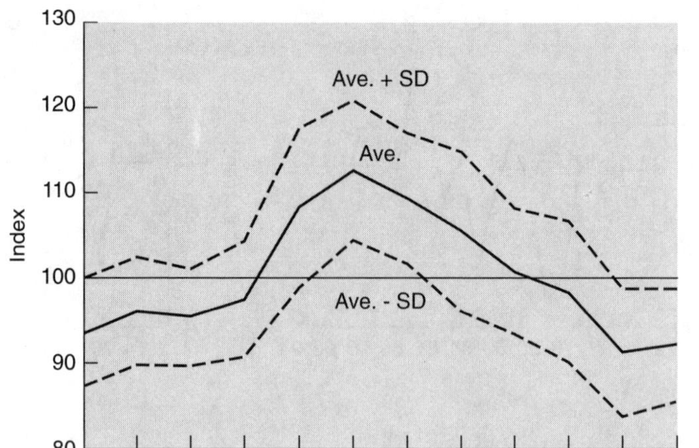

*Prices on barrows and gilts at 6–7 major Midwest markets.

If limited to handing one table on seasonals to a farmer, an agribusiness person or any other decision maker in the commodity area, what would it be? The most useful single set of data probably is the original price series, whether it be weekly, two-week, or monthly averages. With a trained eye, the decision maker could discern which alternative courses of action would have been profitable in the past. This, of course, requires additional information relative to the costs of targeting sales in one period versus another. This particular decision maker could also evaluate risks, as the commodity market has a large, unpredictable component.

The role of seasonal analysis is to consolidate and condense information from the original series in order to assist decision makers in interpreting a large database—sorting information out from noise. A suggested procedure is to provide the original data series *and* the processing of this series (Ferris, 1996).

Following is an example of how monthly price data and seasonal analysis of this data can be formulated in such a way as to enhance the decision-making process on corn. The original data is presented in Table 14-2, along with the seasonal computations. The original prices could be interpreted in several ways, but mainly for storage decisions. If a farmer or commercial operator could reconstruct what storage costs were in the past, they could determine the probability of profitable storage between any two months. Looking at the index at the bottom of the table (mean values for 1960–1992 crop years), they could convert percentage changes between any two months to profits if they knew normal storage costs.

The bottom section, which includes standard deviations around the mean values, may also help decision makers evaluate risks. The trend coefficients provide additional information on whether analysts should adjust their seasonal forecasts above or below the mean values and by how much.

TABLE 14-2 SEASONALITY OF CASH CORN PRICES AT CHICAGO ($/BU.)

	Oct	Nov	Dec	Jan	Feb	Mar	Apr	May	Jun	Jul	Aug	Sep
1960	1.06	0.96	1.02	1.10	1.13	1.11	1.08	1.13	1.12	1.14	1.12	1.10
1961	1.09	1.10	1.08	1.08	1.07	1.11	1.12	1.15	1.14	1.12	1.10	1.11
1962	1.10	1.07	1.12	1.18	1.19	1.22	1.20	1.23	1.29	1.32	1.32	1.35
1963	1.18	1.15	1.19	1.22	1.19	1.21	1.24	1.28	1.26	1.22	1.25	1.26
1964	1.21	1.17	1.24	1.26	1.29	1.31	1.33	1.36	1.34	1.33	1.28	1.28
1965	1.19	1.14	1.22	1.29	1.29	1.25	1.28	1.28	1.32	1.39	1.48	1.44
1966	1.37	1.31	1.42	1.40	1.38	1.38	1.36	1.37	1.35	1.28	1.22	1.19
1967	1.15	1.06	1.11	1.10	1.12	1.14	1.13	1.17	1.13	1.10	1.06	1.06
1968	1.06	1.13	1.14	1.18	1.16	1.15	1.20	1.30	1.30	1.27	1.28	1.19
1969	1.16	1.15	1.15	1.22	1.23	1.22	1.26	1.30	1.34	1.38	1.47	1.50
1970	1.43	1.43	1.56	1.59	1.58	1.55	1.52	1.52	1.57	1.49	1.30	1.16
1971	1.11	1.08	1.22	1.22	1.21	1.23	1.26	1.29	1.25	1.29	1.30	1.40
1972	1.33	1.33	1.58	1.58	1.60	1.59	1.65	2.02	2.44	2.52	2.92	2.48
1973	2.38	2.50	2.69	2.91	3.13	2.99	2.69	2.70	2.93	3.34	3.63	3.56
1974	3.74	3.51	3.52	3.20	2.97	2.92	2.99	2.86	2.91	2.98	3.17	3.02
1975	2.74	2.60	2.60	2.63	2.70	2.71	2.70	2.86	2.97	2.98	2.86	2.79
1976	2.51	2.35	2.48	2.56	2.57	2.54	2.53	2.43	2.29	2.07	1.81	1.84
1977	1.89	2.19	2.22	2.21	2.23	2.39	2.54	2.61	2.53	2.30	2.18	2.16
1978	2.25	2.31	2.30	2.31	2.39	2.46	2.56	2.66	2.83	3.00	2.82	2.78
1979	2.73	2.59	2.69	2.53	2.65	2.60	2.61	2.70	2.70	3.08	3.36	3.44
1980	3.43	3.43	3.54	3.56	3.49	3.48	3.53	3.47	3.36	3.28	3.06	2.72
1981	2.60	2.61	2.52	2.63	2.63	2.68	2.78	2.79	2.77	2.68	2.43	2.36
1982	2.16	2.37	2.44	2.54	2.78	3.01	3.24	3.24	3.29	3.38	3.68	3.63
1983	3.00	3.50	3.38	3.30	3.29	3.52	3.61	3.61	3.62	3.45	3.23	2.95
1984	2.81	2.79	2.72	2.79	2.79	2.84	2.90	2.85	2.83	2.76	2.50	2.31
1985	2.26	2.46	2.50	2.51	2.49	2.45	2.46	2.55	2.52	1.98	1.68	1.49
1986	1.51	1.68	1.66	1.57	1.50	1.60	1.68	1.89	1.88	1.68	1.53	1.62
1987	1.73	1.86	1.89	1.95	2.01	2.03	2.03	2.09	2.74	2.93	2.79	2.79
1988	2.81	2.65	2.69	2.74	2.72	2.78	2.72	2.77	2.60	2.50	2.30	2.32
1989	2.36	2.37	2.34	2.36	2.41	2.50	2.72	2.83	2.84	2.73	2.52	2.33
1990	2.24	2.33	2.33	2.39	2.44	2.52	2.59	2.50	2.43	2.41	2.52	2.48
1991	2.49	2.46	2.49	2.59	2.67	2.72	2.57	2.60	2.59	2.37	2.24	2.29
1992	2.09	2.13	2.17	2.18	2.14	2.23	2.31	2.29	2.20	2.38	2.37	2.34

Index of Seasonality

	Oct	Nov	Dec	Jan	Feb	Mar	Apr	May	Jun	Jul	Aug	Sep
INDEX	94.6	94.9	97.6	98.7	99.1	100.2	101.4	103.6	104.6	103.3	100.9	98.2
STD DEV	6.5	4.9	3.9	3.3	4.1	4.8	6.2	6.6	6.5	5.3	8.4	7.6
TREND	–0.1	0.1	0.0	–0.1	0.0	0.1	0.2	0.1	0.1	0.0	–0.2	–0.3

TABLE 14-3 TABULATION OF ON-FARM STORAGE MARGINS ON CHICAGO CORN, CROP YEARS BEGINNING IN 1960 TO 1992 IN 1992 DOLLARS*

Item	Unit or Years	Months										
		Nov	Dec	Jan	Feb	Mar	Apr	May	Jun	Jul	Aug	Sep
Average Margin												
1960–92	$/bu.	–.05	.06	.08	.08	.08	.08	.16	.20	.16	.08	–.08
1975–92	$/bu.	.04	.03	.02	.03	.08	.13	.15	.13	.01	–.20	–.34
1983–92	$/bu.	.09	.05	.04	.02	.08	.10	.12	.12	–.04	–.25	–.38
Standard Deviation												
1975–92	$/bu.	.30	.27	.27	.29	.40	.49	.52	.62	.73	.90	.96
Percent of Total	1960–92	12	9	9	3	6	3	21	3	9	12	12
Years with	1975–92	17	11	11	0	11	6	11	6	17	6	6
Highest Margin	1983–92	20	10	10	0	20	10	10	0	20	0	0
Percent of Total	1960–92	30	3	6	0	0	0	3	3	0	9	45
Years with	1975–92	11	0	11	0	0	0	0	6	0	11	61
Lowest Margin	1983–92	10	0	0	0	0	0	0	10	0	10	70
Percent of Total	1960–92	61	42	33	42	36	39	42	33	42	52	56
Years that	1975–92	50	44	44	50	39	44	44	44	44	61	67
Storage Losses	1983–92	40	40	30	40	20	30	30	40	50	70	80
Occurred												
Percent of Total	1960–92	36	67	55	48	58	61	64	33	39	33	24
Years that	1975–92	50	56	50	50	72	61	56	22	28	17	17
Storing from	1983–92	60	50	50	40	90	60	60	10	20	10	10
Previous Month												
Paid												

*From the change in prices after October were deducted direct on-farm storage costs composed mostly of foregone interest on stored grain. This storage cost was about equal to .6 cent to 1 cent per bushel per month in 1960–1972; about 2 cents per bushel in 1973–1978; 3 to 4 cents in 1979–1984; and 2 to 3 cents in 1985–1992. The storage margins were then divided by the CPI (1992 = 100 percent).

The next level of processing of the monthly price data is outlined in Table 14-3. In this table, assumed on-farm storage costs were deducted from price changes after harvest. As stated, this was mostly foregone interest costs on the stored grain since the fixed costs of the facility were already committed and not a part of the year-to-year storage decision. (For more detail on storage costs, see reference to "Uhrig, Cost of Grain Storage.") To compare storage returns over a period ranging up to 33 years, nominal profits were divided by the Consumer Price Index, converting the returns into 1992 dollars.

To account for structural change in storage profits, the results were tabulated for the entire period of 1960–1992 crop years, 1975–1992 crop years, and the recent 10-year period of 1983–1992. Apparently, the expansion of on-farm storage facilities has tended to cut back on profits from storing corn after January.

Several lines in the table provide indicators of the rewards and risks from storing corn on the farm, i.e., "Standard Deviation," "Percent of Years with Highest Margin," "Percent of Years with Lowest Margin," and "Percent of Total Years that Storage Losses Occurred." The conclusion is that risks increase as the prospects for the new crop become known late in the storage season.

Finally, the last line in the table computes the probability of a profit from storing one more month. The probabilities for profit are mostly 50 percent or better for month-to-month storage in the first part of the season (but not much), improve for the March-to-May period, and then drop well below 50 percent. This means that if you are holding corn in May, you are taking a long shot to store into June.

Rather than an analysis related to specific months, storage strategies over a series of months could be examined. For example, regular sales out of on-farm storage from January to June in 1960–1992 would have netted farmers a profit of 11 cents per bushel in 1992 dollars, with positive returns in two-thirds of the years. Higher and more assured profits were noted in years the size of the corn crop was average or above.

These are some examples of how seasonal price data can be transformed into more useful information for decision makers. But as mentioned earlier, the raw data also can be interpreted in a straightforward manner in combination with records on storage costs. This suggests that the raw data *and* the transformations should be a part of the kit of tools for marketing decisions.

SUMMARY

Agricultural commodities trace out fairly definable and consistent seasonal price patterns due primarily to the seasonal nature of agricultural production and secondarily due to demand. Quantitative techniques are available to identify these seasonal price patterns, through ratios to a centered moving average, and to establish the reliability of the pattern and its shifts over time.

To be more useful for decision making, costs of production or storage relevant to sales at specific times of the year can be introduced. With this added information, insights can be gained about timing sales considering potential profit and risk.

QUESTIONS FOR STUDY

1 Why are seasonal price patterns useful in forecasting farm prices?
2 Why "de-trend" a price series before applying a program to generate a seasonal index? Why might you *not* "de-trend" the series?
3 How would you select a database for a seasonal analysis on a product exhibiting strong cyclical patterns?
4 What is meant by a "centered" 12-month average of prices?
5 Describe the application of trends in seasonal indexes in projecting the seasonals a year or two beyond the historical database.
6 How would you interpret the standard deviation of the index for a given month to a lay audience?
7 Why were the on-farm storage margins deflated by the CPI in Table 14-3?
8 On a seasonal analysis of monthly corn prices, shown in Table 14-3, evaluate alternative storage strategies taking both returns and risks into account.
9 Tabulate ten years of monthly prices on a product of interest to you. If you do not have a software package to estimate seasonals, calculate a 12-month centered moving average and ratio of each month to that average. Multiply by 100 and average the indexes for each month. Plot the means on a graph. Looking at individual years, are the seasonal indexes representative?
10 In question 9, are monthly averages the appropriate frequency for decisions to be made based on seasonals? If not, what frequency would be most useful?

15

COMMODITY FUTURES AND OPTIONS MARKETS

POINTS:

1. Definitions and roles of commodity futures and options.
2. Scope of the markets.
3. Who trades.
4. Margin accounts.
5. Offset versus delivery.
6. Differences in speculating with futures and options.
7. Factors affecting option premiums and formulas for evaluating premiums.

Futures markets are and have been very important institutions in commodity pricing. These markets, prominent in the U.S. for more than a century, are being extended globally. Precursors of futures can be traced back several centuries in many points around the world (Chicago Board of Trade, 1985). Activity in futures trading has expanded over time with accelerated growth recently in non-agricultural entities—common stock indices, interest rates, and exchange rates among others. Called "derivatives" because their pricing is based on the underlying financial instruments, volume of trading on these instruments has exceeded that on commodities.

The focus of Chapter 15 is on a description of commodity futures and options, and Chapter 16 will elaborate on how they are used in forward pricing. Many of the same principles apply to derivatives, but for a more complete discussion of this subject, see *An*

Introduction to Options and Futures (Chance, 1991) and *Futures and Options, Theory and Practice* (Stoll and Whaley, 1993).

WHAT ARE FUTURES MARKETS?

One can think of futures markets as very similar to large organized cash markets with many buyers and sellers. Instead of the product being exchanged on the spot, the asking and bidding is over contracts for future delivery. Cash markets dealing in forward contracts do exist, but would not be considered futures markets.

Description

A unique characteristic of futures is that the sellers are not linked with specific buyers, as would be the case in forward contracts. The intermediary between buyer and seller is a "clearing house" that makes certain that contracts held to delivery are fulfilled. In a forward contract market, both buyers and sellers are at some risk relative to "non-performance" of the other party. One party may default, go bankrupt, etc. The system of futures markets does not allow this to happen. Buyers and sellers are guaranteed performance.

If you buy a futures contract, you have a right to take delivery on the cash commodity at a given price in a specified future period and are defined as "long" in that contract. If you sell a futures contract, you have a right to deliver the cash commodity at a given price in a specified future period and are defined as "short" in that contract. Typically, an array of contracts are available that relate to specified months up to two years into the future.

Another feature of futures is that only a small fraction of the volume of trades results in fulfillment of the contract (normally less than three percent). Nearly all trades are "offset" (sellers buy back their contract to deliver, and buyers sell the contract to take delivery before the delivery date).

Actually, futures markets do not want to become cash markets. At the same time, as will be discussed in Chapter 16, it is very important that *some* deliveries are made. This keeps futures and cash markets in line. For this reason, futures markets provide delivery opportunities, but for most buyers and sellers who deal in the cash commodity, offset is more profitable than delivery.

The market facility is normally provided by a muncipality that charges the participants a fee. For example, the City of Chicago owns the Chicago Board of Trade (CBT) and the Chicago Mercantile Exchange (CME). Rules and regulations emanate from several sources, including members of the exchanges, a government agency known as the Commodity Futures Trading Commission (CFTC), and an organization of the brokerage industry itself known as the National Futures Association.

To be more specific, a futures contract has been defined as:

> A legally binding commitment to deliver or take delivery of a given quantity and quality of a commodity, at a price agreed upon when the contract is made, with delivery at the seller's prerogative sometime during the specified future delivery month.

To clarify what may seem to be rather technical in this definition relative to a delivery, a typical system to facilitate the delivery process is as follows: At the beginning of the delivery month, sellers still holding a contract may declare their intentions to deliver. The clearing house matches up the first sellers to make such declaration with the earliest buyers still holding their contracts into the delivery month.

In a futures contract, the basic grade is specified which is the focal point for the price quotations. Delivery of a certain amount of product not meeting that grade is allowed, with set discounts or premiums established. Delivery points are listed along with times deliveries can be made. In a couple of cases, a "cash settlement" alternative is provided, but this is the exception. (See Glossary at end of this chapter.)

Futures markets set which months are to be traded. Commercial needs do not require contracts for every month. The markets establish the trading unit, such as the CBT's 5,000 bushels on corn and the CME's 40,000 pounds on live cattle. Minimum price fluctuations in the bidding-and-asking process are set, such as one-quarter cent per bushel on corn and 2.5 cents per hundredweight on live cattle.

To avoid unwarranted swings in prices, the markets establish maximum daily price fluctuations. In Chicago, this is 12 cents per bushel on corn and $1.50 per hundredweight on cattle. The limit refers to price changes, up or down, during a trading day relative to the closing or settle price of the previous trading day. The rationale is to allow re-assessment of market fundamentals overnight and avoid unfounded panic on a given market day. If the market moves the limit in the same direction in following days, the limit is removed on the logic that the fundamentals justify the market seeking its new level.

Position limits are set for individual traders. This means that upper bounds are established on how many contracts a participant can hold as a buyer or seller. The purpose is to prevent a trader from affecting the market to his or her advantage. This is called "cornering" the market. Other terms are "squeezing" or "pinching." The critical period is usually toward the delivery date when few positions remain open in the market.

How Futures Prices Are Quoted

Futures prices are quoted widely in printed and electronic media. Up-to-the-minute quotes are available through electronic media. An example of the type of information published daily is shown in Table 15-1. The contract months for corn at the CBT are March, May, July, September, and December. On April 24, 1996, trading was taking place on contracts through 1997. For each contract, the CBT reports the open (beginning of the market day), the high, the low, and the settle (closing) price. The change in the settle price on that day relative to the settle on the previous market day is recorded. The open interest is shown for each contract and, at the bottom of Table 15-1, totals are given for volume and open interest.

Open interest refers to the number of contracts that must be either offset or delivered. Since longs must equal shorts, open interest equals the number of contracts long or short, not the sum of the two. Volume refers to the number of contracts traded in a given day. Most of the activity had been registered in the July 1996 and December 1996 contracts with only limited trading in 1997 futures.

TABLE 15-1 QUOTATIONS ON CORN FUTURES AT THE CHICAGO BOARD OF TRADE, 5,000 BUSHEL CONTRACTS IN CENTS PER BUSHEL, APRIL 24, 1996[a]

Contract Month	Open	High	Low	Settle	Change	Open Interest
1996						
May	479	488	471	487	+8	55,087
July	461	471	451	470	+10	168,699
September	374	374	366	372	−2	56,545
December	335	335	327	333	−1	129,056
1997						
March	336	339	332	338	−1	13,239
May	336	341	336	329	−2	1,294
July	336	341	336	339	−2	3,447
December	291	294	291	292	0	3,802
Volume	120,978 contracts					
Total open interest	341,169 contracts					

[a]Prices are rounded to nearest whole number.

Who Participates?

Traders in futures contracts can roughly be classified as: (1) speculators and (2) hedgers. Speculators are in the game to profit from a move up or down in the market. They may also speculate on "spreads" in which they buy one futures contract and sell another hoping the difference will change in their favor. Hedgers use the futures primarily to reduce their price risks in dealing with the cash commodity. They may speculate to some extent on the relationship between futures prices and cash prices, but their goal is to avoid the substantial declines or rises in prices often encountered in the commodity market. They accomplish this by taking an opposite position in the futures market to their position in the cash market, which is the essence of hedging.

Anyone can participate in these markets. Standing in the pits at the CBT or active in other exchanges are floor traders who may be trading in their own account and/or executing buy-and-sell orders for others. Members on these exchanges must pay a fee to participate, but through brokerage houses (members or connected to members), any person wanting to speculate or hedge can participate if they meet certain financial requirements.

To trade through a broker, an individual must set up a "margin account." A broker will require verification that a speculator has substantial liquidity and be able to handle the risk. Brokers will require that hedgers be legitimate commercial operators in the cash market. Both will have to establish a margin in terms of a cash (or highly liquid) good faith deposit. The amount of the deposit, however, will be only a fraction of the value of the contracts being traded, normally about 5 to 15 percent.

What Commodities Are Traded, Where, and Why?

A wide variety of commodities and instruments are actively traded in futures markets. Among agricultural products are grains and oilseeds, livestock and meat, milk, dairy products, tropical products such as sugar, coffee and cocoa, frozen orange juice, and cotton. Other commodities include metals and petroleum, lumber, and fertilizer. Also, a recent addition of state crop yields to futures contracts indicates that non-price variables are candidates for trading. The most active markets in recent years have been the financials—U.S. Treasury bills and bonds, common stock indices, and exchange rates on currencies.

Futures markets are worldwide. In addition to 13 exchanges in the U.S., 12 other nations have futures markets. They include Australia, Brazil, Canada (four), France (three), Hong Kong, Japan (four), Malaysia, The Netherlands, New Zealand, Singapore, Sweden, and the United Kingdom (nine).

In reviewing the list of commodities traded in futures markets, certain common characteristics are apparent:

1 Prices are volatile.
2 Products are standardized. Grading is established.
3 Products are broadly produced and marketed.
4 Most products are storable.

Volatility attracts both speculative and hedger interest. Speculators can profit (or lose) in a volatile market, but have little opportunity for profit in a stable market. Hedgers need protection in a volatile market, but have no need for such protection in a stable market.

Because trading in futures markets focuses on a base grade, with the possibility of delivery, the product must have grades and standards acceptable to the industry. This is particularly important with agricultural commodities that are not easily produced to a particular standard. The distribution of commodity output across the quality spectrum can vary greatly from year-to-year due to weather and pests.

Products broadly produced and marketed have a better chance of success as actively traded commodities than those with concentrated production areas with few marketing channels. For example, live cattle futures succeeded, but beef carcasses did not, ostensibly because live cattle had a broad production base while beef carcass production was much more concentrated. Navy beans are a candidate for trading, but production and marketing are in relatively few hands. Many speculators who could participate in these markets would feel disadvantaged in the crucial process of gaining market information and would shy away.

At one time, storability was felt to be a prime consideration. Reasons for this related to the delivery process. However, the continuance of live cattle, feeder cattle, and hog futures is testimony that storability is not a necessary condition. However, very perishable products such as fresh fruits and vegetables are not viable candidates.

Economic Functions

On the surface, one might wonder whether futures markets were nothing more than gambling casinos—huge lotteries in commodities and financial instruments. In the sense that the futures market provides speculators the opportunity to leverage capital in a risky game, there is a grain of truth in this assertion. However, futures markets provide a number of very useful economic functions. They can be enumerated in terms of their role in:

1 Enabling hedgers to transfer price risk to speculators.
2 Facilitating price discovery.
3 Enhancing information collection and dissemination.
4 Assisting in the coordination of economic activity.
5 Stabilizing markets and providing liquidity.
6 Providing flexibility in forward pricing.

Probably the most important function is in risk transfer, which will be covered in some detail in Chapter 16.

Futures markets provide central facilities for buyers and sellers to interact and bring all the forces impinging on price formation together. In many cases, this is a face-to-face confrontation of buyers and sellers in octagonal pits or similar sites. Typically, the trading is by open outcry in a very transparent process. The floor brokers involved are mainly representing the real buyers and sellers, who may be from all parts of the world. Also active are "scalpers," speculators who seek profits on small price movements and provide liquidity in the markets. These may be "day traders" who cancel all positions by the end of the day as compared to "position traders" who remain long or short over several days, weeks, or months.

Information needed for effective use of futures markets is so valuable that many resources are devoted to collection and dissemination. This involves both public and private organizations. Within the U.S. Department of Agriculture, the National Agricultural Statistics Service (NASS), and the Market News Branch of the Agricultural Marketing Service (AMS), along with cooperating state counterparts, play a major role in providing comprehensive, unbiased crop and livestock estimates, and market information. Private consulting firms and specialized market news services are also prominent. Futures markets themselves collect and make available an extensive amount of data on prices, volume, and open interest. Open position data on hedgers, small traders, and large traders are also generated and distributed.

Another economic function of futures markets is to help coordinate economic activity. So prevalent is futures price information that commercial houses simply refer to cash prices in terms of relationships to futures (so many cents or dollars per unit over or under futures). This facilitates day-to-day operations in moving products through the system. With prices on products and/or inputs locked in, a firm can devote more energy into the production line operation and increasing efficiency.

Without futures, the process would be more risky and inefficient. The importance of futures in this regard can be observed when, for whatever reason, futures are not operating. This might be due to severe weather at the location of the exchange, limit moves in the contract price, etc. At those times in the grain trade, the comment is often heard that, "elevators are taking protection." This means that being unable to hedge, they widen their margins as they face increased price risks.

The traditional view is that the existence of futures markets helps stabilize prices. Active futures markets are liquid (many buyers and sellers are ever present either on the trading floor or linked to brokerage offices). At times, cash markets can be a bit clumsy allowing gluts in supplies to unduly depress prices. At other times, shortages can move markets above levels warranted by supply-demand conditions.

Some do question whether futures help stabilize prices and cite examples of high volatility in futures at times. Research on commodities that have been on and off of futures trading supports the contention that futures stabilize markets. However, in the very short time context, futures may be less stable because market information can quickly be reflected in price moves as compared to more dispersed and less coordinated cash markets.

Related to the transfer of risk, futures markets provide commercial operators considerable flexibility in forward pricing both products and inputs. They can choose to use futures or not and can decide what proportion of their products and inputs to hedge, determining how much risk they are willing to assume.

Concepts About Futures Not Easily Understood

The first exposure to explanations of futures markets can be bewildering. Because so few futures contracts end up with delivery of the physical product, some novices may see futures as merely "paper trading." This may be amplified to the skeptics if told that the total bushels of corn traded on the CBT in a year often exceeds the total U.S. corn crop! Be that as it may, these contracts are real and performance is required if held to the delivery period.

But what if buyers hold more contracts into the delivery month than there is cash product available? While technically this could be true, the price on these futures would likely have risen enough to entice most of these buyers to sell long before the delivery month. A related question is, "What if many want to sell, but there are few buyers?" The answer is that the price will take care of it. Price will drop to the point where the number of contracts offered for sale will be exactly matched by the number that will be purchased. Price is the equilibrating mechanism.

What happens to contracts purchased that are sold before delivery? Nothing, really. They just vanish. The buyer may have profited or lost in the action, but the contract sold (offset) becomes extinct.

Suppose you bet $100 that a certain major league team would win the World Series. Your team loses the first three games. You go to the other party and offer $60 to cancel the bet. If the other party accepts, the bet is off—just like offset.

When you buy a futures contract, not having sold before, you are "long" on a contract. You are said to be a "long." If you sell a futures contract, not having purchased before, you are "short." You are referred to as a "short," having made a "short sale."

Some have a hard time grasping that you can sell something you don't have, and in the case of futures, don't expect to have in terms of the physical commodities. Short sales, actually, are quite common even in forward contract markets. When you order a new car from a dealer, the car may not even be manufactured. You sign a contract to take delivery at a future date, and the dealer signs the contract to furnish the new car. The dealer has made a short sale. You are long. If you contracted to buy a car that was "hot" on the market and deliveries were slow, you might find someone willing to buy your contract and pay you a premium. This is quite similar to the action on futures markets.

Futures markets are easily accessed and are very liquid. Orders can be called in over the phone to the broker involved and executed within minutes on the appropriate exchange. If you buy, say, two soybean futures contracts on the CBT and hold them until you get a delivery notice, they won't dump 10,000 bushels in your front yard. You will simply start paying storage costs at a warehouse somewhere in the rail switching district of Chicago, or as an alternative delivery point, Toledo.[1] You will have to decide when to sell 10,000 bushels of cash soybeans.

If soybean futures are trading at $6.00 per bushel, 10,000 bushels would be valued at $60,000. How much money would you have to deposit in a margin account to buy (or sell) $60,000 worth of soybean futures? Margins vary, but in this case, could be as low as $3,000—only five percent of the value of the contract. Can you name any other investment where you could leverage your money twenty-fold?

If soybean prices were to increase by 30 cents per bushel, your purchase would show a $3,000 profit—double your money. If soybean futures dropped 30 cents, you would lose all your margin.

But, before this 30-cent drop would happen, you would receive a "margin call" from your broker. You would be called the day after the equity in your account dropped to about 75 percent of the initial level and be required to bring your margin back to the initial level. In other words, if soybean prices dropped by more than about 8 cents a bushel after you bought the contracts, you would have to add the difference between your current equity and $3,000. On the other hand, if soybean futures were to rise, you would be able to draw off any amount in your margin account over $3,000.

At the close of each business day, the clearing houses in futures "mark to the market." This means that they bring records up to date with all of the member brokerages. Because both buying and selling are involved, each brokerage has a *net* long or short position with the clearing house. To protect themselves, each brokerage makes certain that its clients have maintained the required margin, or if not, can do so the following day. If clients cannot bring their margins up to the initial level, they are "closed out" (their position in the market is quickly liquidated). They are denied the opportunity to recoup their losses in the market, or, mercifully, kept from losing more.

In this example, the assumption was made that you bought soybean futures, or established a *long* position. This you would do if you expected prices to rise, that is, you were "bullish." On the other hand, if you had expected prices to fall, that is, you were "bearish," you would have sold short.

OPTIONS ON FUTURES

"Options" are another marketing tool in agriculture and are not really new to the scene. Stock options have been trading for a number of years in the U.S., as have certain agricultural options outside the U.S. Irregularities in trading in options on U.S. agricultural commodities in the 1930s resulted in their being banned. They were reintroduced in 1984 on a pilot basis in several futures exchanges and now have become an established adjunct to futures. To understand options, a number of definitions are needed. The glossary at the end of this chapter provides clarification for both futures and options.

Essentially, commodity options provide the "opportunity," but not the "obligation" to

[1]Delivery locations may change as the marketing structure shifts.

sell or buy a commodity at a certain price. In the markets to be described, the underlying commodity is a *futures contract* and not the physical commodity.

There are two types of options: "puts" and "calls." A put is a contract that gives the holder the right to *sell* at a specific price—"to put it on them." A call is a contract that gives the holder the right to *buy* at a specified price—"to call from them." (See McKissick, Shumaker, and Williams, 1984).

The options buyer (holder) is the person who obtains the rights conveyed by the option. The option seller (grantor or writer) is the person who grants the rights contained in it. In the options markets, there are: (1) buyers and sellers of puts, and (2) buyers and sellers of calls (two different markets).

The specified price is called the exercise or strike price. The bidding is manifested in the option premium, which is the market value of the option. A buyer pays the premium for the right to sell or buy futures at the indicated strike price. In a sense, the option premium is the cost of price insurance.

The "intrinsic value" of an option is the positive difference between the strike price and the underlying futures price. For a put, the intrinsic value is the amount that the strike price *exceeds* the futures price. For a call, the intrinsic value is the amount that the strike price is below the futures price. If the strike price for a put is below the futures, the intrinsic value is zero, not negative. Similarly, a call with a strike price above the futures has no intrinsic value, but is not considered negative.

Options are said to be "in-the-money" if they have intrinsic value and "out-of-the-money" if they have no intrinsic value. If the strike price equals the futures price, puts and calls are "at-the-money."

Factors Affecting Premiums

Premiums, of course, are affected by the intrinsic value, and also the length of time to expiration of the option. This latter element is called "time value." Time value originates from the fact that the longer the time until expiration, the more opportunity for buyers and sellers to profit—therefore, the premium will reflect more than just the intrinsic value. Time value decreases with the length of time until expiration.

The more volatile the market, the more opportunity for profit. Therefore, option premiums are positively correlated with the amplitude of futures price swings. To a minor extent, interest rates are negatively related to option premiums. This is because option buyers must deposit the premiums and sellers must maintain margin accounts.

The maximum loss for option buyers is the premium plus brokerage costs. The potential loss for an option seller is unlimited except that a seller of puts has a lower bound on losses at a futures price of zero.

The expiration date for options is usually about one month ahead of the expiration on the underlying futures. If buyers (holders) of options elect to exercise those options, they are assigned a position in the futures market. A buyer of a put would be assigned a short position in the respective futures. A buyer of a call would be assigned a long position.[2] As with futures, most holders of options elect to offset (sell their options before expiration).

[2]At the CBT, sellers of options are drawn at random to take the opposite position in futures to the buyer when the buyer decides to exercise.

For farmers and commercial operators in the commodity business, looking for a way to reduce price risks, options offer a means to establish a minimum price on a product for sale or a maximum price on an input to be bought—plus some other more exotic pricing possibilities. This forward pricing mechanism will be discussed in Chapter 16.

How Options Prices Are Quoted

Like futures, options premiums are quoted widely in the media. Only the settle or closing premiums are quoted because space limitations preclude much more detail. As an example, Table 15-2 presents the quotes for July 1996 and December 1996 corn options on April 24, 1996. Options are traded for the other futures months as well—March and May and September.

The strike prices on July options ranged from 370 cents ($3.70) to 480 cents ($4.80) per bushel in 10-cent increments. On December 1996 corn options, strike prices ranged from 290 to 400 cents per bushel. Total volume in number of contracts daily for all corn options and total open interest for puts and calls were also listed.

Following is an illustration of how the intrinsic and time values are determined. On the same day, December corn futures closed at 333 cents per bushel (Table 15-1). The intrinsic value of a December corn put with a strike price of 350 cents at that time was 17 cents (350-333). The premium was 43 cents. The difference between the 43 and

TABLE 15-2 CLOSING QUOTATIONS ON SELECTED CORN OPTIONS AT THE CHICAGO BOARD OF TRADE, 5,000-BUSHEL CONTRACTS IN CENTS PER BUSHEL, APRIL 24, 1996[a]

Contract Month					
July 1996[b]			December 1996[c]		
Strike Price	Puts	Calls	Strike Price	Puts	Calls
370	1	100	290	12	54
380	1	90	300	16	48
390	2	81	310	20	42
400	3	72	320	26	38
410	4	64	330	32	34
420	6	55	340	37	30
430	9	48	350	43	27
440	13	43	360	50	24
450	16	36	370	58	22
460	22	31	380	65	20
470	26	26	390	73	17
480	—	22	400	81	16
Total for all corn options:		Volume = 22,564 calls; 24,094 puts Open interest = 221,695 calls; 234,961 puts			

[a]Option premiums are rounded to nearest whole number.
[b]Settle price on July 1996 futures was 470 cents.
[c]Settle price on December 1996 futures was 333 cents.

17 cents represents the time value of 26 cents. This contract would be considered "in the money."

The December corn put with a strike price of 300 settled at a premium of 16 cents on that day. This put option, which carries the right to sell December corn futures at 300, is "out-of-the-money" with the market price at 333. All of the 16 cents premium is time value.

On the other hand, the December call with a strike of 300 cents is "in-the-money" because it conveys the right to buy at a price below the market. The intrinsic value is 33 cents (333–300). The time value is 15 cents calculated by subtracting the 33 cents from the 48-cent premium. The 350 strike December call is "out-of-the-money" with the entire 27-cent premium as time value.

PROFIT PATTERNS DIAGRAMMED

To gain a clearer understanding of the option market, a comparison with the futures market may be helpful. The top section of Figure 15-1 is a simple diagram on how a change in prices affects profits of long and short speculators in futures. Profits of longs are directly related to changes in futures prices; profits of shorts are inversely related. The charts on options in Figure 15-1 plot the relationship between a change in futures after a position has been taken in the option market and subsequent profits at expiration.

How changes in prices of the underlying futures affect buyers and sellers of puts is shown in the two charts in the center section of Figure 15-1. The buyer of a put has purchased the opportunity (but not the obligation) to *sell* the underlying futures at a given strike price. If prices on the underlying futures decline, the right to sell at a given strike price becomes more valuable. If the additional value at expiration exceeds the time value paid by the buyer for that right (plus commissions), a profit is realized.

On the other hand, if prices on the underlying futures increase, the intrinsic value declines, eventually to zero. Also, the time value converges to zero as the expiration date approaches. This establishes the maximum loss for a buyer of puts—the entire premium (plus commissions). In a sense, a buyer of puts has no upper bound on profits, but a lower bound on losses.

In contrast, a seller of puts has an upper bound on profits with losses virtually unlimited except in the unlikely event that the price on the underlying futures drops to zero. If the prices on the underlying futures rise, the seller pockets the premium—the maximum return (less commissions and interest on a margin account).

Note in Figure 15-1 that if prices on the underlying futures do not change, the seller of puts gains and the buyer loses. Essentially, the buyer pays the seller the time value of the option, since the intrinsic value does not change.

For buyers (longs) of put options in the money, a decline in futures immediately increases the intrinsic value. By expiration, if the increase in intrinsic value exceeds the original time value, the buyer profits. If futures increase, intrinsic value immediately declines. When futures rise to and above the strike price, the intrinsic value becomes zero and at expiration, the buyer of the put would incur losses equal to the original premium (intrinsic value, plus time value, plus commissions). However, no matter how much futures increase, the maximum loss is the original premium, plus commissions.

FIGURE 15-1 Effects of changes in futures prices on profits of speculators in futures and options (by expiration)[a].

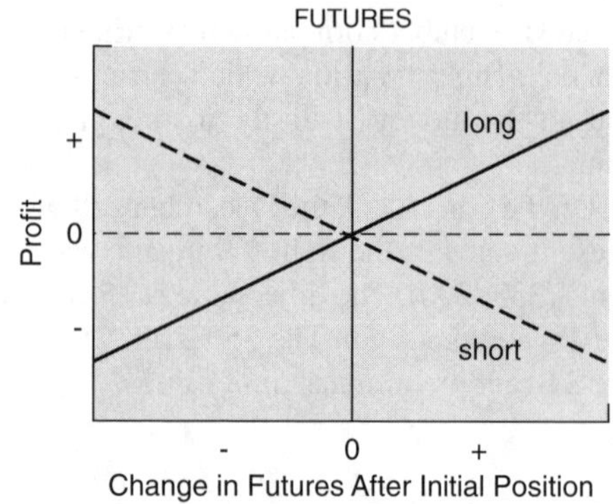

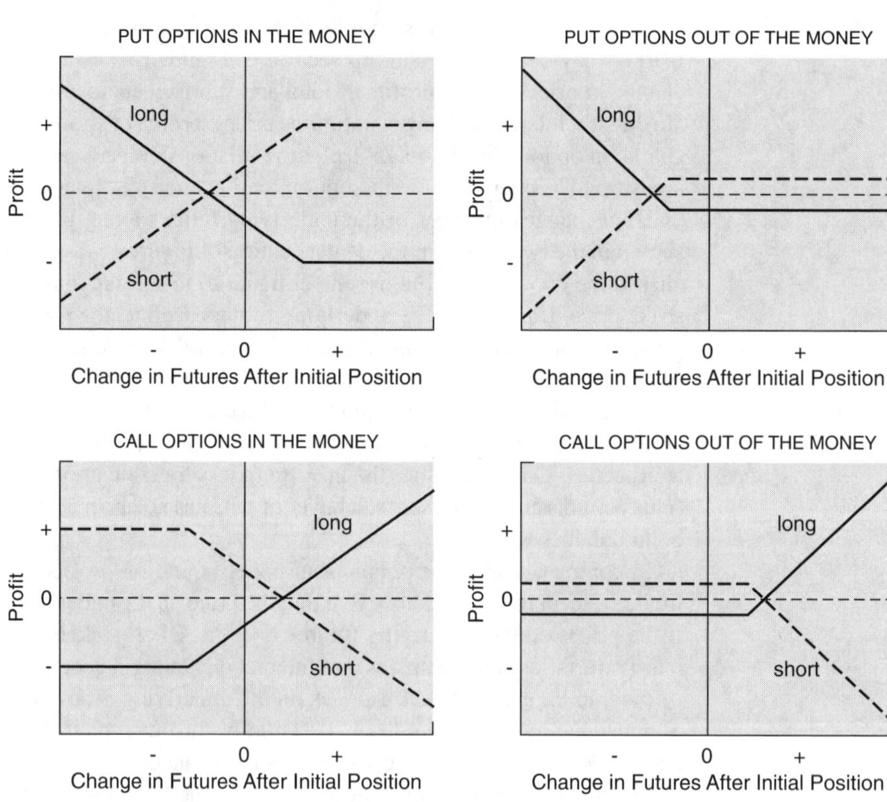

[a]Excluding commissions and interest on margin account.

The sellers (shorts) of puts in the money would incur losses if futures decline more than the time value on the option. As can be noted in Figure 15-1, the losses are unbounded and the profits have an upper bound equal to the original premium on the option (less commissions and interest on the margin account).

Similar relationships are evident in the chart on puts out of the money. The buyer of an out-of-the-money put is risking less on the premium than with in-the-money puts, but usually must count on a greater drop in price before the put has intrinsic value and the premium on the put begins to increase. The seller of the put has a wide range of prices that will provide a profit. Even with some decline in futures, the seller's maximum profit remains intact.

In the bottom section of Figure 15-1 is diagrammed the effects of changes in the price of the underlying futures on profits of buyers and sellers of calls. The buyer of a call purchases the right to *buy* the underlying futures at a specific strike price. When the price of the underlying futures rises, this right becomes more valuable. By expiration, if the intrinsic value has increased enough to exceed the original time value paid by the buyer, a profit is realized. A decline in the price of the underlying futures reduces the value of that right and eventually renders it worthless as time value evaporates. The maximum loss is the original premium (plus commissions).

The seller of the call faces the opposite pattern. A rise in price eventually results in declines in the premium that exceeds the original premium received by the seller for underwriting the call, and losses accumulate with further increases in futures prices. A drop in futures to or below the strike price renders the call worthless at expiration, providing the seller with a profit equal to the original premium. This premium is the maximum profit for the seller of calls (less commission and interest on margins).

As with puts, the buyer of a call faces no upper bound on profits, but has lower bound on losses. The seller has an upper limit on profits, but no bound on losses. With no or little price change on the underlying futures, the seller profits and the buyer loses.

The futures-profit relationships on calls, shown in the two charts at the bottom of Figure 15-1, are essentially mirror images of the puts. With in-the-money calls, the intrinsic value (and premium) would be directly related to futures over a range of prices. At expiration, if futures had declined to the strike price or lower, the buyer's losses would be capped at the premium paid and the seller's gains would be at their upper limit.

For call options out-of-the-money, risks for buyers and profit opportunities for sellers would be less than for in-the-money calls. Buyers would have to count on futures reaching and exceeding the strike price before profits would be realized.

PRICING OPTIONS

As mentioned earlier, the premium on an option is directly related to: (1) the intrinsic value, (2) time to expiration, and (3) volatility of the market, and inversely related to (4) interest rates. Given this information, formulas have been developed to determine the value of options at given points in time, indicative of what the premiums should be. If the premium differs from the calculated value, arbitrage should bring the premium into line, unless, of course, traders perceive that the expected volatility differs from that measured by the formula.

Black/Scholes Model

Best known among these formulas is the Black/Scholes option pricing model (Chance, 1991). This model applies to European options on non-dividend-paying stocks. A difference between European and American options is that European options cannot be exercised before expiration.

In 1976, Black developed a variant of the option pricing formula to specifically value options on futures contracts (Chicago Board of Trade, 1987). This model is defined as follows:

$$VLCL = e^{-IT} * [FTP * N(d_1) - STP * N(d_2)]$$

$$VLPT = -e^{-IT} * [FTP * N(-d_1) - STP * N(-d_2)]$$

where: $d_1 = [\ln (FTP/STP) + SD^2 * T * .5]/(SD * \sqrt{T})$

$d_2 = d_1 - (SD * \sqrt{T})$

VLCL = value of the call

VLPT = value of the put

FTP = price of the underlying futures

STP = strike price

T = time to expiration in terms of proportion of a year

I = short-term annual interest rate on low-risk securities

SD = historical annualized standard deviation of the daily percentage change in the price of the underlying futures

$N(d_1)$, $N(d_2)$ = cumulative normal probability values of d_1 and d_2, respectively

The application of the formula may be clearer in the following example with value for December 1993 corn futures and options on February 17, 1993:

FTP = \$2.40 per bushel

STP = \$2.50 per bushel

T = .75 (from February 17 to expiration in November is three-fourths of a year)

I = .031 (U.S. Treasury Bill's rate of 3.1 percent)

Assume that:

SD = .20 (historical annualized standard deviation of the daily percent change in FTP = 20 percent)

Calculations:

$d_1 = [\ln (2.40/2.50) + (.20)^2 * .75 * .5]/(.20 * \sqrt{.75})$

$$= [-.040822 + .04 * .75 * .5]/(.20 * .866025)$$

$$= [-.040822 + .015]/.1732$$

$$=- .025822/.17325 =- .149$$

$$d_2 =- .14909 - .20 * \sqrt{.75}$$

$$=- .14909 - .17325 =- .322$$

$$N(d_1) = N(-.149) = .441$$

$$N(d_2) = N(-.322) = .374$$

$$VLCL = e^{-.031 * .75} * [2.40 * .441 - 2.50 * .374]$$

$$= .977 * [1.0584 - .9350]$$

$$= .977 * .1234 = .12058 \sim 12¢ \text{ per bushel}$$

$$VLPT =- .977 * [2.40 * .559 - 2.50 * .626]$$

$$=- .977 * [1.3416 - 1.565]$$

$$=- .977 * [-.2234] = .21826 \sim 22¢ \text{ per bushel}$$

On the call:

Intrinsic value = 0¢ per bushel

Time value = 12¢ per bushel

On the put:

Intrinsic value = 10¢ per bushel

Time value = 12¢ per bushel

These values were very close to the actual premiums on February 17, indicating that the assumed SD of .20 was in line with expectations for volatility at that time.

In his evaluation of pre-harvest corn futures and marketing strategies in Iowa and Nebraska, Robert Wisner applied the Black Model and historical volatility in calculating premiums for years in which actual options trading did not exist (Wisner, 1991). He concluded that, based on the correlation between synthetic and actual premiums for the years, 1985–1988, the application of synthetically derived premiums for 1979–1984 was warranted for evaluating forward pricing schemes over that period. That is, "synthetic premiums for the 1979–1984 crop years are a good representation of market premiums that would have occurred if actual trading had existed. . . ."

The most difficult estimate to enter into the Black formulas is expected volatility. As was incorporated by Wisner, volatility is based on historical evidence. Yet, on commodities like corn and soybeans, rather than converting daily price changes in recent weeks to a computation of expected volatility for the growing season, more relevant would be the patterns for this season in recent years. This is because volatility generally increases as weather becomes more of a factor in May to October. Myers and Hanson have demonstrated that a GARCH option pricing model can address the problem of time-varying volatility and out-perform the standard Black Model (Myers and Hanson, 1993).

As can be discerned in the example on December corn options, another application of the Black formulas is to calculate the expected volatility implied by the current actual premiums. This, in a sense, works the formulas backwards. Rather than incorporating an estimate of expected volatility to determine whether the market is over- or underestimating what the premium should be, the supposition is that the market is correct and the premium can be used to estimate the impending volatility. If the market is correct, such information has implications to commercial operators about forthcoming price variability and their need for price protection.

Delta Formulas

The Black formulas provide the means to calculate a relationship called "delta." Delta relates the change in the option premium to the change in the price of the underlying futures contract. The delta formulas are as follows:

$$DLTCL = e^{-IT} * N(d_1)$$

$$DLTPT = - e^{-IT} * N(d_1)$$

where: $DLTCL$ = delta for a call

$DLTPT$ = delta for a put

In the example for calculating the premiums for calls and puts on December corn futures and options on February 17:

$$DLTCL = e^{-.031 * .75} * .441$$
$$= .977 * .441 = .431$$
$$DLTPT = - e^{-.031 * .75} * .559$$
$$= - .977 * .559 = - .546$$

These delta figures also indicate "hedge ratios" for options. Both being relatively close to $|.5|$, approximately two calls or puts are necessary to offset one futures contract. If either the call or put are "deep in the money," the intrinsic value will be highly correlated to changes in the price of the underlying futures and will provide closer to one-to-one coverage in hedging. Also, for speculators, buying or selling "deep-in-the-money" options is more risky than trading cheaper options. Premiums for the expensive options will be more sensitive to rises and falls in prices of the underlying futures—providing more opportunity for profits, but also subjecting the trader to more exposure for losses.

SUMMARY

Futures markets are important global institutions for establishing prices on commodities. Trading in these highly organized establishments is over contracts to deliver or take delivery on specified product grades at some point in the future. A clearing house acts as an intermediary between buyers and sellers and guarantees performance on the contracts. In reality, only small amounts of the product are delivered as the contracts are offset by appropriate sales or purchases before the delivery period.

Speculators and hedgers participate in these markets; speculators to profit from correctly forecasting price moves, hedgers to protect themselves from adverse price moves. The major functions of these markets are to allow hedgers to transfer price risks to speculators and to facilitate price discovery.

Options were introduced into futures markets in the mid 1980s which provide the opportunity, but not the obligation, to buy or sell a futures contract at a certain price. Buyers of options face limited losses and unlimited profits. Sellers face limited profits and unlimited losses and are paid "time value" by the buyers for assuming this risk. Formulas have been developed to determine what the premiums on options should be, given their intrinsic value, time to expiration, expected price volatility in the futures market, and interest rates.

QUESTIONS FOR STUDY

1. The "clearing house" represents a significant difference between futures and forward contract (cash) markets. Explain.
2. How can the number of units traded on the futures market exceed the number of units produced?
3. What is the rationale for limits placed on the daily ranges in futures prices relative to the close of the previous business day? Why are these limits removed if limits are reached in the same direction on successive business days?
4. You can speculate by being a short. What does this mean?
5. If you were speculating with a 10-percent margin, what would happen to your return on investment if prices increased 10 percent? Declined 10 percent?
6. Bananas are widely traded, but not on futures markets. Why?
7. If June cattle futures are trading at $60 per cwt., would a cattle put with a strike price of $66 be in or out of the money? Explain why.
8. If you buy a corn call and pay 20 cents per bushel, what is the maximum you could lose? If you would sell (not having purchased) that same call, what is the maximum you could lose?
9. If a futures market became more volatile, what would you expect to happen to premiums on the associated options? Why?
10. If an option is "deep in the money," the delta will be relatively high. Explain.

GLOSSARY

at the money Situation where the relevant futures price is equal to the strike price.

basis The difference between the price for a given *futures* contract and the *cash* price for a commodity at a given location, i.e., the difference between futures and cash prices. This may be expressed as "futures minus cash" or "cash minus futures," but preferably "cash minus futures."

basis contract Cash contract in which the buyer (elevator) agrees to pay the seller some fixed amount below a designated futures contract. The seller determines when to accept the futures price, at which time the "basis contract" becomes a "forward contract."

basis risk The deviation of basis at the conclusion of a hedge from what was expected at the beginning of a hedge.

bearish (bear) Attitude or market condition pointing to lower prices. A person who expects prices to decline is a "bear."

Black or Black/Scholes Formula Formulas used to calculate the value of options, given the price of the underlying futures, the strike price, time to expiration, volatility, and interest rates on safe securities.

brokerage cost Commission charges for trading futures plus interest paid or foregone for maintaining margins at a brokerage establishment.

bullish (bull) Attitude or market condition pointing to higher prices. A person who expects prices to increase is a "bull."

calls Options that confer the right, but not the obligation, to buy a futures contract at a stated price (strike) during a specified time period.

cash market price The current (or forward contract) price relating to a physical commodity at a specified location and time and with specified terms of sale. This could be net at the farm or at an elevator, local livestock market, a terminal market, etc.

cash settlement On feeder cattle futures at the Chicago Mercantile Exchange and on milk futures at the Coffee, Sugar and Cocoa Exchange, an alternative to delivery is a settlement procedure with prices based on representative cash prices rather than futures.

commercial house, commercials, commercial operators Firms with title to the cash product such as storage operators, processors, exporters, wholesalers, retailers, etc. Farmers would be considered as commercials.

cross hedging Hedging a product that is dissimilar to the base commodity on the futures market.

day traders Speculators whose positions taken during a day are cancelled by the end of the day.

delivery month Month in which the physical commodity could be delivered at specified locations to fulfill the relevant futures contract. The period is usually the first three weeks of the month.

delayed pricing (price later agreements) Arrangements in which the farmer relinquishes title on a crop to the buyer (elevator) which, in turn, may store or sell the crop. The farmer decides on when to accept a subsequent cash price for the product. The buyer (elevator) charges the farmer for storage and service costs.

delta The ratio of change in an option premium relative to a change in the price of the underlying futures.

elevator A term generally applied to the first receiver (buyer) of a farmer's grain, oilseeds, or similar crops.

exercising an option Making use of the right conveyed by an option. Buyer of a put would be assigned a short (sell) position in the relevant futures. Buyer of a call would be assigned a long (buy) position.

exercise price Same as strike price.

expected basis The basis anticipated at the time a hedge is placed *for the time the hedge is concluded.* Historical patterns are normally reviewed in order to make this forecast.

expiration of an option The date at which the option buyer loses the right to exercise the option. This is about one month prior to the final delivery date of the respective futures.

fence Position for a long in the cash commodity achieved by buying put options "near the money" and selling calls one strike price above the current futures. This places both a lower bound and an upper bound on the net price received.

forward contract An agreement between buyers and sellers of the physical (cash) commodity for the delivery of the product at some future period at a specific price with considerations on quality and other terms of sale.

forward pricing The process of establishing price levels or certain price assurances in advance of cash sales (or purchases). This may involve forward contracting, hedging, use of options, or combinations of these and other tools.

futures contracts Legally binding commitments to deliver or take delivery of a given quantity and quality of a commodity, at a price agreed upon when the contract is made, with delivery at the seller's prerogative sometime during the specified future delivery month.

futures markets Facilities for trading futures regulated in the U.S. by a government agency, the Commodity Futures Trading Commission. Both futures and options are traded in these markets. Best known among these markets are the Chicago Board of Trade and the Chicago Mercantile Exchange, both operations of the City of Chicago.

government loan Guarantees that allow participants in government programs to establish floors on their prices. Loans are available at specified prices that farmers would elect to repay if market prices exceed the loan rate or deliver to the government if market prices do not rise enough above the loan rate to pay interest. (Interest is forgiven if farmers deliver.) For wheat, feed grains, and oilseeds, "nonrecourse marketing assistance loans" have been available which allow farmers to repay loans at market prices below the loan rate rather than delivering.

hedge-to-arrive contracts Cash contracts in which the buyer (elevator) hedges for the farmers. Basis is not established until the farmer so elects. At that time, hedge-to-arrive contracts become forward contracts if the decision is made before harvest.

hedging (hedgers) The process of establishing and maintaining a position in the futures market opposite to the position taken in the cash market. Those following this procedure are called hedgers. A hog producer who must buy corn could establish profit margins in advance by selling hog futures and buying corn futures. As cash corn is purchased, the corn futures would be sold. When the hogs are ready for sale, the hog futures would be purchased.

in the money Situation where on a put, the relevant futures price is *below* the strike price. On a call, the relevant futures price is *above* the strike price.

intrinsic value On a put, the difference between the relevant futures price and the strike price when the futures price is *below* the strike; otherwise, the intrinsic value is zero. On a call, the difference between the relevant futures price and the strike price when the futures price is *above* the strike; otherwise, the intrinsic value is zero.

long A position in a cash or futures market involving a commitment to later sell. A farmer planting soybeans is taking a long position in the cash soybean market. A speculator who buys soybean futures (excluding the situation where a speculator is offsetting a previously established short position) is taking a long position in soybean futures. This speculator must later sell soybean futures (or take delivery on soybeans that would put him/her in a long position in cash soybeans).

margin "Good faith" money that must be deposited with brokers in order to buy or sell futures. (Margin is also required of option sellers.) The requirements are generally less than 10 percent of the market value of the futures traded. Additional margin will be required if the equity in the account declines. Margin money may be withdrawn if the equity increases. Margin requirements for hedgers are less than for speculators.

margin call Communications from brokers indicating that additional margin money is required to maintain the established position in the futures markets. Such margin must be furnished quickly or the position will be closed out.

maximum buying price The expected maximum price the buyer of a cash input could establish by buying calls. The actual maximum is determined by what basis turns out to be. Alternatively, basis risk could be eliminated by simultaneously forward contracting the input and buying puts.

minimum price contracts Cash contracts offered by buyers (elevators) that establish a price floor for a seller of the cash product. The buyer (elevator) uses options in order to provide farmers this type of forward pricing.

minimum price hedge-to-arrive contracts Cash contracts in which the buyer (elevator) buys puts for the farmer, establishing an approximate minimum price, but not locking in the basis.

minimum selling price The expected minimum price the seller of a cash product could establish by buying puts. The actual minimum is determined by what basis turns out to be. Alternatively, basis risk could be eliminated by simultaneously forward contracting the product and buying calls.

offset Liquidation of a position in the futures or option markets prior to expiration. In futures, this means buying having previously sold or selling having previously bought. In options, buyers of puts or calls would sell prior to expiration and would not exercise.

open interest Number of contracts that must be either offset or deliveries made and taken, measured as the number of contracts long or short, not the sum of the two.

option buyer A person who obtains the rights conveyed by the option.

option contract Rights to buy or sell futures contracts at a stated price (strike) during a specified time period.

option premium The price of an option contract.

option seller (writer) A person who sells the rights conveyed by the option.

out of the money Situation where, on a put, the relevant futures price is *above* the strike price. On a call, the relevant futures price is *below* the strike price.

position traders Speculators who remain long or short over several days, weeks, or months.

puts Options that confer the right, but not the obligation, to sell a futures contract at a stated price (strike) during a specified time period.

scalpers Speculators who seek profits from small changes in futures prices.

short A position in a cash or futures market involving a commitment to later buy. A hog producer who has not purchased needed soybean meal is short in the soybean meal cash market. A speculator who sells soybean meal futures (excluding the situation where a speculator is offsetting a previously established long position) is taking a short position in soybean meal futures. This speculator must later buy soybean meal futures (or deliver soybean meal which means he/she must buy cash soybean meal to fulfill the futures contract).

speculating (speculators) The process of establishing positions in the cash, futures, or options markets in order to profit from a favorable change in prices (premiums). Those engaged in this activity are called speculators. Speculators are traditionally viewed as individuals trading futures or options with no connection to the cash commodity. However, the largest group of speculators in agricultural commodities are farmers—speculating in the cash market. Most farmers have substantial commitments in product and input markets not covered by forward pricing.

strike price The price at which the option can be exercised and a position established in the futures market. Strike prices are set by the administration of the futures markets.

synthetic put The combination of selling futures and buying calls with a strike price closest to the underlying futures.

time value The amount by which an option's premium exceeds its intrinsic value. The time value is directly related to the amount of time remaining until expiration. The longer the time until expiration, the greater the probability of a profitable move for the buyer. If an option has no intrinsic value, its premium is entirely time value.

volatility Variance in prices. For option pricing, volatility has been defined as the annualized standard deviation of the daily percentage change in the price of the underlying futures.

volume in futures and options Number of contracts traded in a given business day.

16

FORWARD PRICING WITH FUTURES AND OPTIONS

POINTS:

1 How futures and options provide risk-reducing forward pricing for commercial operators, including farmers.
2 Different results from forward pricing a cash commodity with futures and options.
3 Alternative cash forward contracts based on futures and options and their evaluation.
4 "Basis" as the key to effective forward pricing.
5 Use of hedge ratios for risk reduction and multiple-year pricing.

Commodity futures and options provide commercial operators, farmers included, with a wide array of forward pricing alternatives. Positions (long or short) in the cash market can be combined with positions in futures and options to allow decision makers to establish forward price possibilities in line with their financial ability and inclination to handle risk. These alternatives will be discussed in terms of both selling a cash product and buying a cash product or raw material. First to be covered is selling a cash product.

SELLING A CASH PRODUCT

The term *hedging* applies to action in the futures market appropriate for forward pricing the cash product. The essence of hedging is to have an opposite position in the futures market as in the cash market. If you have a long position in the cash product, you need to have an equal and opposite (or short) position in the futures market to be fully hedged.

Since prices on a given product in a cash market tend to move in parallel fashion with the futures on that product, a loss in the cash market means a gain in futures and vice versa. As a textbook example, a farmer harvesting corn in October essentially has a long position in the corn market. To hedge, this farmer would sell futures, which means going short in the futures market. Later, when the farmer decided to sell the corn, if cash prices had dropped 20 cents per bushel, this loss would tend to be offset by a similar profit in futures. The farmer could buy back the futures about 20 cents less than the selling price. This example, of course, excludes storage and brokerage costs.

On the other hand, if the cash market had increased 20 cents per bushel, this profit would tend to be offset by a similar rise in futures. The farmer would have to buy back the futures sold at a price about 20 cents higher than the price at which the futures had been sold—again ignoring storage and brokerage costs. The point is that hedging allows the farmer to set an approximate forward price, with protection from potential loss in the cash market, but also with negation of the potential profits from a rise in cash prices.

While this example would appear to be a rather sterile "no-loss, no-gain" forward pricing action, profits are to be made in hedging. The key to effective hedging is being able to predict the "basis." As defined in the Glossary to Chapter 15, "basis" is the difference between the price for a given *futures* contract and the *cash* price for a commodity at a given location. The preferred formula for basis is:

Basis = Cash Price – Futures Price[1]

Simple Storage Hedge

To illustrate a fairly simple hedge and introduce basis considerations, along with storage and brokerage costs, Table 16-1 outlines how forward pricing decisions might have been made under two situations. The storage operator buys cash soybeans on January 15 at $5.60 per bushel. To hedge, this individual selects July as the appropriate contract to use in a storage hedge. Presumably, July futures prices were enough above the interim contracts (March and May) to pay for storage into July. The action taken was to sell July soybean futures at $6.20.

Assume that on June 15, the storage operator elected to sell the cash soybeans at the local market price of $5.00. To "lift" the hedge on that day, this individual called a broker and initiated a buy order on July soybeans which was $5.18 per bushel.

Looking at the cash side of Table 16-1, it is apparent that the operator lost 60 cents in the market drop from $5.60 to $5.00. In addition, the cost of storage of 30 cents per bushel brought the total loss to 90 cents per bushel. On the futures side, buying back the July contract at $1.02 less than the sale price netted $1.00 after a brokerage cost of 2 cents was deducted.

The gain from futures more than offset the loss in the cash market, and the storage operator posted a 10-cent profit. Adding 10 cents to the initial buying price of $5.60 meant the final net price for the soybeans amounted to $5.70 per bushel.

[1]Alternatively the formula could be: Basis = Futures Price – Cash Price. While somewhat arbitrary, reasons can be given for adopting the preferred formulation.

TABLE 16-1 RESULTS FROM HEDGING SOYBEANS IN STORAGE

Prices Decline				
	Cash		July Futures	
Date/Item	Action	$/bu.	Action	$/bu.
1/15	Buy	5.60	Sell	6.20
6/15	Sell	5.00	Buy	5.18
Difference		−.60		+1.02
Brokerage				−.02
Storage costs		−.30		
Cash net		−.90		
Futures net		+1.00		+1.00
Hedge net		+.10		
Net price received		5.70		

Prices Rise				
	Cash		July Futures	
Date/Item	Action	$/bu.	Action	$/bu.
1/15	Buy	5.60	Sell	6.20
6/15	Sell	7.00	Buy	7.18
Difference		+1.40		−.98
Brokerage				−.02
Storage costs		−.30		
Cash net		+1.10		
Futures net		−1.00		−1.00
Hedge net		+.10		
Net price received		5.70		

Alternatively, assume that prices rose between January and June as illustrated in the bottom section of Table 16-1. On June 15, the storage operator sold cash soybeans for $7.00 for a nice gain of $1.40 which left $1.10 after storage costs were deducted. On the futures side of the ledger, buying July futures at a much higher price left a loss of $1.00 after brokerage costs were deducted. A $1.10 net gain from the cash side less the $1.00 loss on futures left the storage operator in the same position as when prices fell. The net from the hedge was +10 cents per bushel, resulting in an identical net price received of $5.70 per bushel.

Note that in both examples the basis on June 15 was −18 cents ($5.00 – 5.18 and $7.00 – 7.18). That is a special case and not often observed, but assumed here for purposes of exposition.

Similar examples are presented in Table 16-2. The only difference is that a set of two columns is added on basis, and basis risk is introduced. In these cases, the storage operator evaluates his or her opportunities for profit on January 15 by a careful inspection of basis.

TABLE 16-2 EXPECTATIONS AND RESULTS FROM HEDGING SOYBEANS IN STORAGE

Prices Decline

	Cash		July Futures		Basis	
Date/Item	Action	$/bu.	Action	$/bu.	Expected[a] $/bu.	Actual $/bu.
1/15	Buy	***5.60***	*Sell*	***6.20***	×	***−.60***
6/15	Sell	5.00	Buy	5.18	***−.20***	−.18
Difference		−.60		+1.02	***+.40***[b]	+.42[c]
Brokerage				−.02	***−.02***	−.02
Storage costs		−.30			***−.30***	−.30
Cash net		−.90				
Futures net		+1.00		+1.00		
Hedge net		+.10			***+.08***	+.10
Net price:						
Expected		***5.68***				
Received		5.70				+.02

Prices Rise

	Cash		July Futures		Basis	
Date/Item	Action	$/bu.	Action	$/bu.	Expected[a] $/bu.	Actual $/bu.
1/15	Buy	***5.60***	*Sell*	***6.20***	×	***−.60***
6/15	Sell	7.00	Buy	7.23	***−.20***	−.23
Difference		+1.40		−1.03	***+.40***[b]	+.37[c]
Brokerage				−.02	***−.02***	−.02
Storage costs		−.30			***−.30***	−.30
Cash net		+1.10				
Futures net		−1.05		−1.05		
Hedge net		+.05			***+.08***	+.05
Net price:						
Expected		***5.68***				
Received		5.65				−.03

[a]This column to be filled out in advance of the hedge to determine likely profitability. Likely profitability (hedge net in expected basis column), in combination with buy price (cash column), determines net price expected (cash column).
[b]Expected basis for the end of the hedge minus actual basis at the beginning of the hedge.
[c]Actual basis at the end of the hedge minus actual basis at the beginning of the hedge.

The numbers in boldface italics are generally known or expected at the time the decision is made. The current cash and futures prices are easily obtained. Storage and brokerage costs are reasonably predictable. A major exception might be the interest on margin money required if prices rise—but this is not a major cost item over a five-month period. The expected basis of –20 cents per bushel in June is derived from records of past years and some judgment about possible departures from the past. Because basis does vary from year-to-year, this is only an estimate, but it does convey very important information to the storage operator.

The expected basis column of Table 16-2 can be filled out in advance of making the storage decision. The storage operator looks at the current (January 15) basis of –60 cents per bushel and compares this with his or her best estimate of what basis will be in mid June, which is –20 cents. The difference is +40 cents (–20 cents – (–60 cents) =+ 40 cents). In the terminology of the trade, the basis is expected to strengthen by 40 cents per bushel. The next question is, "Will the strengthening of basis of +40 cents be enough to cover storage costs of 30 cents and pay the broker 2 cents?" The answer is "yes" and this would also point to a net return of 8 cents from the hedge.

In the case of a price decline, the net from the hedge of 10 cents turned out to be 2 cents more than expected. This can quickly be confirmed by the fact that basis was –18 cents on June 15, 2 cents stronger than expected.

The case of a price rise was slightly modified from Table 16-1. In this case, the basis turned out to be 3 cents weaker than expected, with the cash market 23 cents per bushel under July futures on June 15. This resulted in a net from the hedge of 5 cents, 3 cents less than projected.

The important consideration is that the net returns from the two cases ranged from 10 cents to 5 cents, compared to an unhedged position in which the net would have ranged from a $.90 loss to a $1.10 per bushel gain. The storage operator avoided possible bankruptcy if prices had declined, but of course, was deprived of a large windfall in the cash market had prices risen. Not knowing which way the prices might go after January 15, the operator made the correct decision by hedging.

Another major point is, that once fully hedged, the storage operator does not care whether the cash and futures markets go up or down. The only concern is what happens to the difference, i.e., the basis. The entire story is told in the final two columns of Table 16-2—what was expected in advance and what finally materialized. Commercial houses focus on the basis and bet their skills on forecasting that relationship rather than movements in the level of price.

In Table 16-2, if the projected change in basis was +25 cents per bushel rather than +40 cents per bushel, the change would not have covered the cost of storage and brokerage. The message to the storage operator would have been not to buy cash soybeans. Or if a farmer happened to own cash soybeans on January 15, the message would have been: (1) sell the soybeans or (2) continue to store and take a chance on a price rise (if the risk can be handled). But, in any case, don't hedge. If you did hedge, chances are you would lock in a loss relative to selling on January 15.

Storing Soybeans and Buying Puts

Extending this example to one where the storage operator was considering buying soybeans and covering that position with long puts, the expectations and results are shown in Table 16-3. The beginning situation is the same as in Table 16-2 with the cash price of $5.60 and July futures at $6.20. Assume that on January 15, July soybean puts, with a strike price of $6.50, were trading at a 55-cent premium. By inspection, this means that the time value is 25 cents since the intrinsic value is 30 cents per bushel.

The downside risk can be calculated in advance as shown in the right-hand column. The put provides the right to sell July futures at $6.50. Subtracting: (1) the premium which could be as low as zero at expiration, (2) the expected basis since the storage operator will sell cash soybeans locally, (3) brokerage costs, and (4) storage costs, gives an

TABLE 16.3 EXPECTATIONS AND RESULTS FROM STORING SOYBEANS AND BUYING JULY SOYBEAN PUTS WITH A $6.50 STRIKE PRICE

Prices Decline

	Cash		July Futures	July $6.50 Puts		Net Minimum Price Expected[a]
Date/Item	Action	$/bu.	$/bu.	Action	Premium	$/bu.
Strike Price						**6.50**
1/15	Buy	**5.60**	**6.20**	*Buy*	**.55**	**−.55**
6/15	Sell	5.00	5.18	Sell	1.33[b]	**0**[c]
Difference		−.60	−1.02		+.78	**−.55**
Expected Basis						**−.20**
Brokerage					−.02	**−.02**
Storage Costs		−.30				**−.30**
Cash Net		−.90				
Options Net		+.76			+.76	
Combination Net		−.14				
Net price						
Minimum Expected		**5.43**				**5.43**[d]
Received		5.46				

Prices Rise

	Cash		July Futures	July $6.50 Puts		Net Minimum Price Expected[a]
Date/Item	Action	$/bu.	$/bu.	Action	Premium	$/bu.
Strike Price						**6.50**
1/15	Buy	**5.60**	**6.20**	*Buy*	**.55**	**−.55**
6/15	Sell	7.00	7.23	Sell	.01[b]	**0**[c]
Difference		+1.40	+1.03		−.54	**−.55**
Expected Basis						**−.20**
Brokerage					−.02	**−.02**
Storage Costs		−.30				**−.30**
Cash Net		+1.10				
Options Net		−.56			−.56	
Combination Net		+.54				
Net price:						
Minimum Expected		**5.43**				**5.43**[d]
Received		6.14				

[a]This column to be filled out in advance of the hedge to determine net minimum price expected.
[b]Actual premium assuming time value = $.01.
[c]Expected premium assuming no intrinsic value and time value = $0.
[d]Strike price less the total of: (1) original option premium less time value when sold, i.e., line marked "Difference" above; (2) expected basis; (3) brokerage; and (4) storage.

expected *minimum* cash price of $5.43. This is well below the current price and the expected net price from hedging of $5.68 as given in Table 16-2. The storer could rationalize buying puts over hedging if he or she: (1) could handle the risk of a possible 17-cent per bushel loss (relative to *not* buying soybeans on January 15), emotionally and financially, (2) did need some downside price protection, and (3) had strong convictions that market prices would increase substantially.

If cash prices did drop sharply as in the top section of Table 16-3, the put would become more valuable and could be sold at a profit in mid June. However, the storer had to pay the seller of the puts 24 cents in time value and the 76-cent profit on the puts was not enough to offset the 90-cent loss in the cash side of the ledger. The net loss from the combination of storing soybeans and buying puts was 14 cents per bushel, leaving the net price received to be $5.46. However, the storer accepted the risk. Due to the basis being 2 cents stronger than anticipated and the put carrying a slight 1 cent time value in mid June, the net price received was 3 cents per bushel above the expected minimum.

On the other hand, if prices increased substantially as shown in the bottom section of Table 16-3, the advantage of buying puts over hedging is apparent. The option was nearly worthless on June 15 because July futures were well above the $6.50 strike price. The total loss on the puts amounted to 56 cents per bushel. However, the sharp rise in the cash price of $1.10 provided a net return of +54 cents for a net price received of $6.14 per bushel. This was 49 cents greater than the net price from the hedge depicted in Table 16-2.

Forward Pricing Alternatives for a New Crop

To illustrate the array of forward pricing opportunities available to farmers and to commercial operators who also have title to commodities, Tables 16-4 through 16-8 display five different situations and results in forward pricing new crop corn. With some modifications, very similar opportunities are available for covering stored crops and also for forward pricing livestock.

The initial situation is as follows. On May 1, the farmer calculated his or her variable or direct cost of production at $1.75 per bushel for the current crop year. In a sense, this represents the farmer's "long" position in the cash market even though the product will not be harvested for five to six months. But the farmer is long in the resources to produce the product—in land, labor, and capital. The $1.75, of course, understates the total commitment since important fixed costs are omitted. But the decision to plant corn in any given year is determined by the relationship between expected prices and variable costs.

Weak Basis

Tables 16-4 through 16-6 portray a situation labeled as "weak basis." Usual first receivers of grain from farms, called country elevators, can offer farmers cash forward contracts because these elevators can, in turn, hedge their positions in futures. Their offerings relative to futures vary from time to time, sending signals to farmers about how anxious they might be to obtain the cash product. A "weak basis" means that this offering is low relative to futures. This may have implications to farmers on which forward pricing scheme to use.

TABLE 16-4 FORWARD PRICING ALTERNATIVES FOR NEW CROP CORN, ASSUMING A WEAK BASIS AND A DECLINE IN PRICE

Date	Cash Market			Futures		Put Options			Forward Contract and Buy Calls	
5/1	Production Cost (variable)		$1.75	December (Futures Month)	2.40 (Sell)	December (Futures Month)			December (Futures Month)	
	Forward Contract Price	(1)	2.02							
				Less:		Strike Price	2.40	2.60	Strike Price	2.30
	Basis Contract Relative to December (Futures Month)		–.38	Expected Basis[b]	–.30					
				Brokerage Costs[c]	–.02	Less: Option Premium	–.18 (Buy)	–.30 (Buy)	Forward Contract Price	2.02
	Net Government Loan Rate	(2)[a]	1.46	Equals Net Price Expected From Hedge	2.08				Less:	
						Expected Basis[b]	-.30	–.30	Option Premium	–.22
						Brokerage Costs[c]	–.02	–.02	Brokerage Costs[c]	–.02
	Expected Harvest Price									
	Optimistic		2.50							
	Average		2.00							
	Pessimistic		1.50			Equals Minimum Selling Price Expected	1.90	1.98	Equals Minimum Selling Price	1.78
11/1	Harvest Price	(3)	1.40	December (Futures Month)	1.73 (Buy)	December (Futures Month)				
	Net Price From Basis Contract = Futures + Basis Contract	(4)	1.35	Actual Basis[d]	-.33	Optimum Premium[e]	.67 (Sell)	.87 (Sell)		0 (Sell)
Net Price Received From Hedge and Options									Forward Contract	
Cash Price at Harvest					1.40		1.40	1.40	Price	2.02
Plus Net Returns From Futures and Options										
Sell and Buy (Futures) or Buy and Sell (Options)				+.67		+.49		+.57	-.22	
Less Brokerage Costs[c]				–.02		–.02		–.02	-.02	
Equals Net Returns					+.65		+.47	+.55		–.24
Equals Net Price Received				(5)	2.05		1.87 (6)	1.95 (7)	(8)	1.78

[a]Government loan rate less storage costs to maturity.
[b]The expected value, at harvest, of the cash price less the given futures.
[c]Commissions and interest on margins or premiums.
[d]The actual value, at harvest, of the cash price less the given futures.
[e]Assumes no time value.

TABLE 16-5 FORWARD PRICING ALTERNATIVES FOR NEW CROP CORN, ASSUMING A WEAK BASIS AND A RISE IN PRICE

Date	Cash Market		Futures		Put Options			Forward Contract and Buy Calls	
5/1	Production Cost (variable)	$1.75	December (Futures Month)	2.40 (Sell)	December (Futures Month)			December (Futures Month)	
	Forward Contract Price (1)	2.02							
	Basis Contract Relative to December (Futures Month)	-.38	Less: Expected Basis[b]	-.30	Strike Price	2.40	2.60	Strike Price	2.30
			Brokerage Costs[c]	-.02	Less: Option Premium	-.18 (Buy)	-.30 (Buy)	Forward Contract Price	2.02
	Net Government Loan Rate (2)[a]	1.46	Equals Net Price Expected From Hedge	2.08				Less:	
	Expected Harvest Price				Expected Basis[b]	-.30	-.30	Option Premium	-.22
					Brokerage Costs[c]	-.02	-.02	Brokerage Costs[c]	-.02
	Optimistic	2.50							
	Average	2.00							
	Pessimistic	1.50			Equals Minimum Selling Price Expected	1.90	1.98	Equals Minimum Selling Price	1.78
11/1	Harvest Price (3)	3.00	December (Futures Month)	3.28 (Buy)	December (Futures Month)				
	Net Price From Basis Contract = Futures + Basis Contract (4)	2.90	Actual Basis[d]	-.28	Optimum Premium[e]	0 (Sell)	0 (Sell)		.98 (Sell)
Net Price Received From Hedge and Options									
	Cash Price at Harvest			3.00		3.00	3.00	Forward Contract Price	2.02
Plus Net Returns From Futures and Options									
	Sell and Buy (Futures) or Buy and Sell (Options)		-.88		-.18		-.30	+.76	
	Less Brokerage Costs[c]		-.02		-.02		-.02	-.02	
	Equals Net Returns			-.90		-.20	-.32		+.74
Equals Net Price Received			(5)	2.10		2.80 (6)	2.68 (7)	(8)	2.76

[a]Government loan rate less storage costs to maturity.
[b]The expected value, at harvest, of the cash price less the given futures.
[c]Commissions and interest on margins or premiums.
[d]The actual value, at harvest, of the cash price less the given futures.
[e]Assumes no time value.

TABLE 16-6 FORWARD PRICING ALTERNATIVES FOR NEW CROP CORN, ASSUMING A WEAK BASIS AND STABLE PRICES

Date	Cash Market		Futures		Put Options			Forward Contract and Buy Calls	
5/1	Production Cost (variable)	$1.75	December (Futures Month)	2.40 (Sell)	December (Futures Month)			December (Futures Month)	
	Forward Contract Price (1)	2.02							
			Less:		Strike Price	2.40	2.60	Strike Price	2.30
	Basis Contract Relative to December (Futures Month)	–.38	Expected Basis[b]	–.30					
			Brokerage Costs[c]	–.02	Less: Option Premium	–.18 (Buy)	–.30 (Buy)	Forward Contract Price	2.02
	Net Government Loan Rate (2)[a]	1.46	Equals Net Price Expected From Hedge	2.08				Less:	
					Expected Basis[b]	-.30	–.30	Option Premium	–.22
					Brokerage Costs[c]	–.02	–.02	Brokerage Costs[c]	–.02
	Expected Harvest Price								
	Optimistic	2.50							
	Average	2.00			Equals Minimum Selling Price			Equals Minimum Selling Price	1.78
	Pessimistic	1.50			Expected	1.90	1.98		
11/1	Harvest Price (3)	2.10	December (Futures Month)	2.40 (Buy)	December (Futures Month)				
	Net Price From Basis Contract = Futures + Basis Contract (4)	2.02	Actual Basis[d]	-.30	Optimum Premium[e]	0 (Sell)	.20 (Sell)		.10 (Sell)
Net Price Received From Hedge and Options								Forward Contract	
Cash Price at Harvest				2.10		2.10	2.10	Price	2.02
Plus Net Returns From Futures and Options									
Sell and Buy (Futures) or Buy and Sell (Options)			0		-.18		-.10	-.12	
Less Brokerage Costs[c]			–.02		–.02		–.02	-.02	
Equals Net Returns				-.02		-.20	-.12		–.14
Equals Net Price Received			(5)	2.08		1.90 (6)	1.98 (7)	(8)	1.88

[a]Government loan rate less storage costs to maturity.
[b]The expected value, at harvest, of the cash price less the given futures.
[c]Commissions and interest on margins or premiums.
[d]The actual value, at harvest, of the cash price less the given futures.
[e]Assumes no time value.

TABLE 16-7 FORWARD PRICING ALTERNATIVES FOR NEW CROP CORN, ASSUMING A STRONG BASIS AND A DECLINE IN PRICE

Date	Cash Market			Futures		Put Options			Forward Contract and Buy Calls	
5/1	Production Cost (variable)		$1.75	December (Futures Month)	2.40 (Sell)	December (Futures Month)			December (Futures Month)	
	Forward Contract Price	(1)	2.20	Less:		Strike Price	2.40	2.60	Strike Price	2.30
	Basis Contract Relative to December (Futures Month)		−.20	Expected Basis[b]	−.30	Less:			Forward Contract Price	2.20
				Brokerage Costs[c]	−.02	Option Premium	−.18 (Buy)	−.30 (Buy)		
	Net Government Loan Rate	(2)[a]	1.46	Equals Net Price Expected From Hedge	2.08				Less:	
						Expected Basis[b]	-.30	-.30	Option Premium	−.22
						Brokerage Costs[c]	−.02	−.02	Brokerage Costs[c]	−.02
	Expected Harvest Price									
	Optimistic		2.50							
	Average		2.00							
	Pessimistic		1.50			Equals Minimum Selling Price Expected	1.90	1.98	Equals Minimum Selling Price	1.96
11/1	Harvest Price	(3)	1.40	December (Futures Month)	1.65 (Buy)	December (Futures Month)				
	Net Price From Basis Contract = Futures + Basis Contract	(4)	1.45	Actual Basis[d]	-.25	Optimum Premium[e]	.75 (Sell)	.95 (Sell)		.0 (Sell)
Net Price Received From Hedge and Options										
Cash Price at Harvest					1.40		1.40	1.40	Forward Contract Price	2.20
Plus Net Returns From Futures and Options										
Sell and Buy (Futures) or Buy and Sell (Options)				+.75		+.57		+.65	-.22	
Less Brokerage Costs[c]				−.02		−.02		−.02	-.02	
Equals Net Returns					+.73		+.55	+.63		-.24
Equals Net Price Received				(5)	2.13		1.95 (6)	2.03 (7)	(8)	1.96

[a]Government loan rate less storage costs to maturity.
[b]The expected value, at harvest, of the cash price less the given futures.
[c]Commissions and interest on margins or premiums.
[d]The actual value, at harvest, of the cash price less the given futures.
[e]Assumes no time value.

TABLE 16-8 FORWARD PRICING ALTERNATIVES FOR NEW CROP CORN, ASSUMING A STRONG BASIS AND A RISE IN PRICE

Date	Cash Market		Futures		Put Options			Forward Contract and Buy Calls	
5/1	Production Cost (variable)	$1.75	December (Futures Month)	2.40 (Sell)	December (Futures Month)			December (Futures Month)	
	Forward Contract Price (1)	2.20	Less:		Strike Price	2.40	2.60	Strike Price	2.30
	Basis Contract Relative to December (Futures Month)	-.20	Expected Basis[b]	-.30	Less:			Forward Contract Price	2.20
			Brokerage Costs[c]	-.02	Option Premium	-.18 (Buy)	-.30 (Buy)	Less:	
	Net Government Loan Rate (2)[a]	1.46	Equals Net Price Expected From Hedge	2.08	Expected Basis[b]	-.30	-.30	Option Premium	-.22
	Expected Harvest Price				Brokerage Costs[c]	-.02	-.02	Brokerage Costs[c]	-.02
	Optimistic	2.50							
	Average	2.00			Equals Minimum Selling Price			Equals Minimum Selling Price	1.96
	Pessimistic	1.50			Expected	1.90	1.98		
11/1	Harvest Price (3)	3.00	December (Futures Month)	3.25 (Buy)	December (Futures Month)				
	Net Price From Basis Contract = Futures + Basis Contract (4)	3.05	Actual Basis[d]	-.25	Optimum Premium[e]	0 (Sell)	0 (Sell)		.95 (Sell)
Net Price Received From Hedge and Options									
	Cash Price at Harvest			3.00		3.00	3.00	Forward Contract Price	2.20
	Plus Net Returns From Futures and Options Sell and Buy (Futures) or Buy and Sell (Options)		-.85		-.18		-.30	+.73	
	Less Brokerage Costs[c]		-.02		-.02		-.02	-.02	
	Equals Net Returns			-.87		-.20	-.32		+.71
Equals Net Price Received			(5)	2.13		2.80 (6)	2.68 (7)	(8)	2.91

[a]Government loan rate less storage costs to maturity.
[b]The expected value, at harvest, of the cash price less the given futures.
[c]Commissions and interest on margins or premiums.
[d]The actual value, at harvest, of the cash price less the given futures.
[e]Assumes no time value.

The initial situations in Tables 16-4 through 16-6 are the same. On May 1, the farmer could forward contract with the elevator for $2.02 per bushel. This means that the elevator is obligated to pay the farmer $2.02 on a specified amount at harvest in October or November. On May 1, December futures (nearest futures after harvest) traded at $2.40. The forward contract, then, was 38 cents under December futures (a basis of –38 cents per bushel).

In addition to the cash forward contract of $2.02, elevators also offer "basis contracts." A basis contract is simply an agreement that the elevator will write a forward contract with the farmer at a specified amount relative to futures. The farmer determines the timing. In Tables 16-4 through 16-6, the basis contract was 38 cents below December futures on May 1. From historical information, the expected basis at harvest is –30 cents per bushel. This is why this example is labeled "weak basis."

Deducting expected basis and brokerage costs from December futures provides the net price expected from hedging of $2.08 per bushel. This figure is 6 cents above the forward contract and might persuade the farmer to hedge rather than enter a forward contract.

The alternative forward pricing schemes are to forward contract at $2.02, enter a basis contract at –38 cents relative to December futures, hedge with an expected net price of $2.08, or do nothing. Another consideration is the government support price or net government loan rate of $1.46 which would tend to put a lower bound on market returns. Also, the fundamental outlook might weigh on the farmer's decision, assumed here to range between $1.50 and $2.50 per bushel, with the average at $2.00. A pessimistic forecast would make farmers more inclined to take price protection.

Three other forward pricing alternatives are presented in Tables 16-4 through 16-6, two with put options and one with call options. The examples with purchasing December put options compare the results with two different strike prices, $2.40 and $2.60. Obviously the right to sell at $2.60 is more costly (30 cents) than the right to sell at $2.40 (18 cents). Deducting premiums, expected basis and brokerage costs from the strike prices, the $2.40 put sets an expected minimum price at $1.90 and the $2.60 put sets an expected minimum at $1.98.

At first glance, one might ask why buy the cheaper put which sets a lower minimum. The answer will be clearer when the results between a price fall and a price rise are examined.

Finally, one example is presented under the title "Forward Contract and Buy Calls." As the title indicates, this is a combination of a cash forward contract entered on May 1 and the purchase of a December call. Subtracting the option premium and brokerage costs from the *forward contract price* equals the minimum selling price of $1.78. There is no basis risk; that is, the forward contract of $2.02 is guaranteed regardless of what happens to futures. The most the farmer can lose from the call is 24 cents, which would be the case with a significant price decline.

In other words, added to the forward pricing alternatives on May 1 discussed earlier which set approximate or fixed prices, the farmer also can set lower bounds on prices without incurring an upper limit. While the forward contract and hedging point to higher established prices than turning to puts and calls, farmers who are optimistic about prices rising, but who require some price protection, have the tools to fit their risk preferences.

The weak basis, however, does convey information about which tools to use. Farmers would want to avoid locking in the basis which would happen with: (1) forward contracts, (2) basis contracts, and (3) forward contracts and long calls. Choices among the other alternatives would depend upon the farmer's financial situation, aversion to risk, and price expectations.

Table 16-4 portrays what might happen if prices decline significantly between May 1 and November 1. The numbers in the boxes represent the final results from eight forward pricing alternatives.

In Box 1 is the forward cash contract of $2.02 established on May 1. Taking out a government loan (Box 2) would have netted $1.46 for complying farmers, slightly better than the $1.40 from doing nothing (Box 3). The return from the basis contract was $1.35 (Box 4), assuming the farmer held the contract until November 1. The calculations of the return is simply December futures on November 1 of $1.73 plus the basis contract of –38 cents which equals $1.35. On doing nothing, taking out a government loan, and entering the basis contract, the farmer would have failed to cover variable costs.

Note in the futures column that basis turned out to be –33 cents on November 1, 3 cents weaker than expected. Buying back the December futures netted 67 cents less 2 cents brokerage for a profit of 65 cents to add to the cash price of $1.40 to give a net price received of $2.05 (Box 5). The weaker-than-expected basis resulted in a net price 3 cents less than anticipated on May 1, but still above the forward contract price.

With the sharp drop in futures prices, the puts became more valuable and protected the farmer from major downside losses in the cash market. (Assumed in these cases is that time value is nil and the final premium is equal to the intrinsic value.) The net price received under the two schemes at $1.87 (Box 6) and $1.95 (Box 7) were 3 cents less than expected minimums because basis was 3 cents weaker than expected.

The basis having been locked in, the minimum selling price realized with the forward contracting and purchase of calls was $1.78 (Box 8), below the net prices from the puts. As can be noted, the calls expired worthless leaving the net price at the minimum calculated on May 1.

The worst alternative was the basis contract (Box 4) followed by doing nothing (Box 3). Again, the basis contract locked in a weak basis; it is better to take chances on a favorable move in futures with no basis contracts. Among the options, the puts outperformed the forward contract and purchase of calls—again because the latter locked in a weak basis. Between the $2.40 and $2.60 puts, the advantage went to the more expensive option which set the higher expected minimum.

The top return was with the hedge at $2.05 (Box 5). Under the circumstances, hedging was a logical choice over a forward contract for reasons similar to buying puts—the weak basis on May 1 was not locked in.

In Table 16-5, the only differences from Table 16-4 is that: (1) prices rise substantially between May 1 and November 1, and (2) the basis turned out to be slightly stronger than expected on November 1. With the basis 2 cents stronger than expected, the net price received from the hedge (Box 5) was 2 cents above the expected level and 8 cents above the forward contract (Box 1).

The most profitable alternative was to do nothing (Box 3) and second best was the basis contract (Box 4). Farmers with government non-recourse loans (Box 2) would have eventually sold corn on the market and repaid the loan. As could be anticipated, pricing tools that set minimums resulted in higher nets than forward contracting and hedging, but because of premiums and brokerage costs, did not match doing nothing or basis contracts.

The puts expired worthless, but the $2.40 put lost only 18 cents in the premium versus the 30 cents loss for the $2.60 put. For this reason, the net price received from the $2.40 put was 12 cents above the $2.60 put; that is, $2.80 (Box 6) compared with $2.68 (Box 7). Therein is the reason a farmer might logically choose a put that sets a lower minimum than a more expensive put. In the event of a price rise, the cheaper put will net a higher price.

The net price received from the forward contract and purchase of a $2.30 December call was $2.76 (Box 8), above the net from the $2.60 put, but still below the net from the $2.40 put. The $2.40 put was clearly the preferred alternative to the combination of a forward contract and purchase of the $2.30 call—netting higher returns in both eventual price declines and increases. The $2.40 put not only provided a higher minimum expected price, but also carried a lower premium than the $2.30 call.

For purposes of exposition, no time value was assumed on the options as of November 1. Since the expiration date on December options is late in November, some time value might remain on November 1, but would be small. Therefore, the option premiums on November 1 reflect intrinsic value, zero for the puts in Table 16-5 and 98 cents for the call.

In Table 16-6, the only differences from the previous two tables were: (1) futures prices did not change between May 1 and November 1, and (2) basis happened to turn out exactly as expected, –30 cents.

Because basis was as expected, the net prices from the hedge and purchases of puts were as expected. Also, the advantages were with these same alternatives that did not lock in the weak basis. The advantage of doing nothing over entering a basis contract can be noted.

The main point to be made in Table 16-6 is that *stable prices discriminate against options* as forward pricing tools. As stated in Chapter 15, in a stable market, the buyer of options pays the seller time value. So, as can be seen in Table 16-6, the net prices received from options were the lowest among all the alternatives (except the government loan that would not be relevant with market prices well above it).

In a sharply rising market, purchasers of put options gain from increases in the cash prices, and those locked into a forward contract with a long position in calls gain from increased premiums in calls. This beats forward contracting and hedging, but falls behind doing nothing or entering basis contracts.

In a sharply falling market, puts become more valuable and forward contractors who are long in calls are sustained by the forward contract. This position beats doing nothing or basis contracts, but loses out to forward contracting alone or hedging.

In other words, the forward pricing alternatives involving options are second best to other alternatives in case of sharply falling or rising prices and the least profitable with stable prices. This is not an argument against use of options, but emphasizes that they are most appropriate in situations of volatile prices in which farmers and other commercial operators perceive reasonable chances of a substantial rise (or fall) in prices, but need some downside (or upside) protection. (See section on "Buying a Cash Product.")

Strong Basis

Forward pricing situations covered in Tables 16-7 and 16-8 differ from Tables 16-4 through 16-6 in that, on May 1, cash contracting opportunities reflected a strong basis.

The basis offered was 20 cents under December futures compared to the expected 30 cents under. Second, the actual basis on November 1 also turned out to be stronger than expected at 25 cents under.

In this case, the preferred alternatives on May 1 differed from those when the basis was weak. Forward contracting was clearly superior to a hedge. In essence, a forward contract locks in both futures and basis. Hedging only locks in futures. Hedgers face basis risk. For this reason, a guaranteed price of $2.20 is preferred over an expected price of $2.08 from a hedge. Only if basis turned out to be stronger than −18 cents on November 1 would hedging have netted higher returns than forward contracting.

For risk takers who do not require downside price protection and who expect prices to rise, a basis contract is preferable over doing nothing. These individuals are simply wagering that futures will increase more than their cash market—a reasonable bet considering historical basis data.

Those who need some downside price protection, but also believe prices will rise, would be advised to forward contract (locking in the favorable basis) and buy calls. This combination would tend to net higher prices than the alternatives of buying puts which lock in strike prices, but not basis.

You can follow the effects of significant price drops and rises in Tables 16-7 and 16-8. The results were as anticipated with the stronger performance by forward pricing techniques that had locked in the basis. One exception was the net price received from a $2.60 put in Table 16-7 (in the event of a price drop) exceeded that from forward contracting and buying calls. This can be traced to the potential to establish a somewhat higher minimum price ($1.98 versus $1.96) and the fact that basis turned out to be 5 cents stronger on November 1 than anticipated on May 1—although 5 cents weaker than could be locked in on May 1. With the price rise in Table 16-8, the advantage of forward contracting and buying calls is apparent.

Tables 16-4 through 16-8 apply to two specific points in time, May 1 (planting) and November 1 (harvest). Realistically, forward pricing decisions can be made well before May 1, between May 1 and November 1 and after November 1—whenever attractive opportunities are available. For example, a farmer might hedge corn in January well before planting, see forward contract prices decline to near the government loan rate by mid summer and lift the hedge, deciding downside risks on returns were minimal. At harvest, this farmer might see forward pricing opportunities on this same crop—indications that storage promised more profit than selling at harvest.

As can be discerned, forward pricing using futures and options offers many choices, some clear and some not so clear. Are there any rules of thumb that may provide assistance to decision makers?

EMERGING RULES

From the examples presented so far in this chapter, certain forward pricing guidelines emerge. These rules apply to the various alternatives included in the examples and some additional tools available to farmers and other commercial operators. The diagram in Figure 16-1 is an attempt to capture the essence of these rules on one page.

This figure introduces some new pricing instruments that are defined in the glossary of terms in Chapter 15. Delayed pricing is a variation on "storing or waiting to price" except

FIGURE 16-1 Pricing decision chart for cash product sellers.

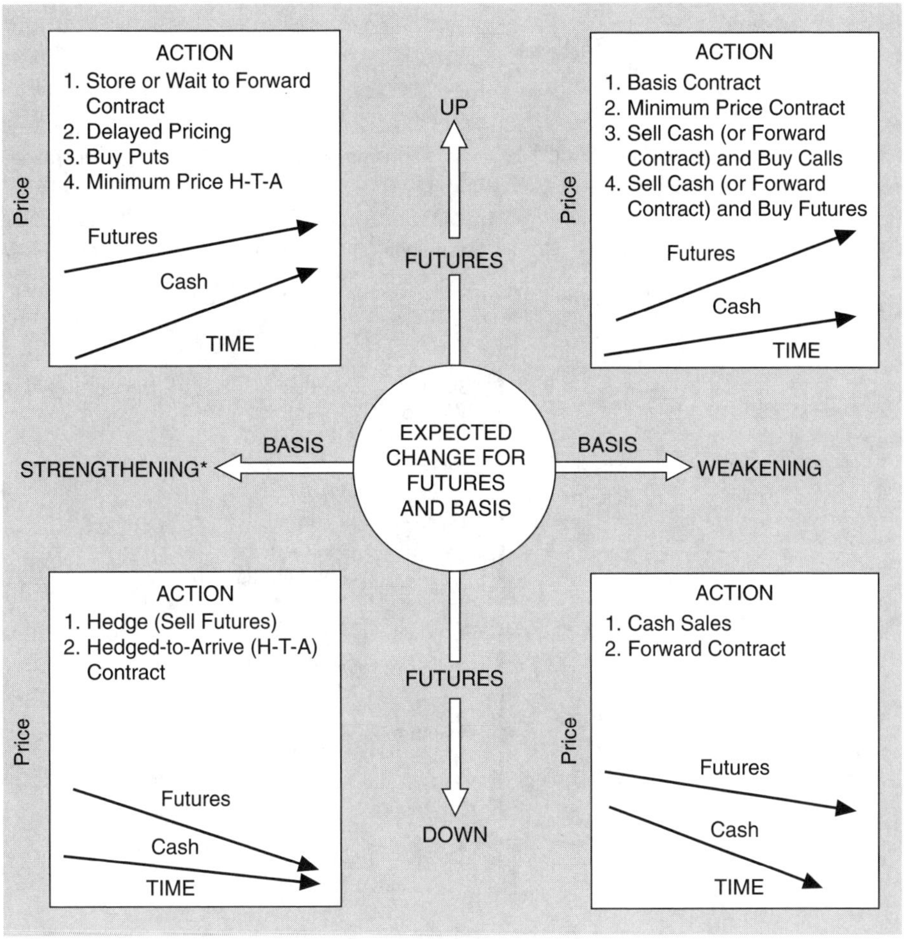

ACTION
1. Store or Wait to Forward Contract
2. Delayed Pricing
3. Buy Puts
4. Minimum Price H-T-A
Price
Futures
Cash
TIME

UP
FUTURES

ACTION
1. Basis Contract
2. Minimum Price Contract
3. Sell Cash (or Forward Contract) and Buy Calls
4. Sell Cash (or Forward Contract) and Buy Futures
Price
Futures
Cash
TIME

STRENGTHENING* BASIS
EXPECTED CHANGE FOR FUTURES AND BASIS
BASIS WEAKENING

ACTION
1. Hedge (Sell Futures)
2. Hedged-to-Arrive (H-T-A) Contract
Price
Futures
Cash
TIME

FUTURES
DOWN

ACTION
1. Cash Sales
2. Forward Contract
Price
Futures
Cash
TIME

*Basis should strengthen enough to exceed storage costs.

Source:
Derived from *Developing Marketing Strategies and Keeping Records on Corn, Soybeans and Wheat,* NCR Extension Publication No. 217, Producer Marketing Management - Fact Sheet #4, December 1985.

the product moves on in the marketing system rather than remaining on the farm. The minimum price contract is with an elevator that guarantees a minimum price to the farmer in a way similar to the farmer's forward contracting and buying calls. The hedged-to-arrive (H-T-A) contract is like hedging and the minimum price hedged-to-arrive contract is like buying puts, except these actions are handled by the elevator—and, of course, basis is not locked in.

The four quadrants enumerate which tools are appropriate depending upon expectations about: (1) the direction of futures and (2) whether basis will strengthen or weaken.

FIGURE 16-2 Decision tree on selling crops.

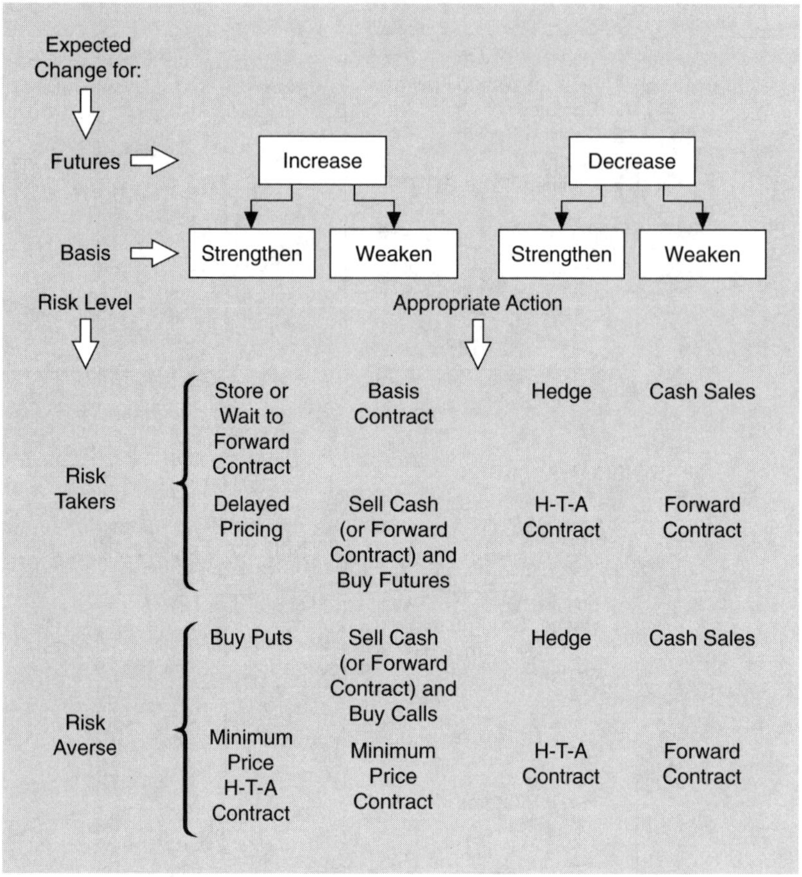

Expected Change for:

Futures	Increase		Decrease	
Basis	Strengthen	Weaken	Strengthen	Weaken
Risk Level	Appropriate Action			
Risk Takers	Store or Wait to Forward Contract	Basis Contract	Hedge	Cash Sales
	Delayed Pricing	Sell Cash (or Forward Contract) and Buy Futures	H-T-A Contract	Forward Contract
Risk Averse	Buy Puts	Sell Cash (or Forward Contract) and Buy Calls	Hedge	Cash Sales
	Minimum Price H-T-A Contract	Minimum Price Contract	H-T-A Contract	Forward Contract

These combinations are also illustrated by the arrows labeled "Futures" and "Cash" diagrammed against "Time."

Figure 16-2 provides another perspective on choosing the appropriate forward pricing action, delineated by level of risk aversion. The rationale for the designations in this figure should be fairly obvious with a couple of comments to be added. The risk of an unfavorable move in futures is much greater than an unfavorable move in basis. Also, basis is more predictable than futures. For this reason, all of the instruments appropriate for the risk averse have futures locked in directly or indirectly (a forward contract implies that both futures and basis are locked in).

For risk takers expecting futures to rise, the four alternatives listed do not lock in futures. The alternative to "Sell Cash (or Forward Contract) and Buy Futures" is very much like a "Basis Contract," taking advantage of a favorable basis when the level of futures may not be attractive. Those bullish risk takers storing cash grain when basis is strong might better sell the grain and buy the equivalent in futures.

As can be noted, both the risk takers and risk averse should consider the same techniques if a decline in futures is expected. Of course, risk takers could ride the market down by selling more futures than needed to cover their cash position, but such action is not traditional for commercial operators. However, one could argue that such action is no more speculative than carrying inventory unhedged.

Figures 16-1 and 16-2 could apply to selling livestock and other commodities with futures and options markets. Some of the contracts based on futures and options may not be available at this time, but similar contracts could be established by the industry.

MORE EXOTIC FORWARD PRICING SCHEMES

A number of other combinations could be explored in forward pricing. One is called a "synthetic put." This involves hedging (selling futures) and buying a call with a strike price closest to the underlying futures. This is similar to forward contracting and buying a call except that basis is not locked in—which also makes this procedure much like simply buying puts.

Another is called a "fence" that Robert Wisner describes as purchasing put options with strike prices near current futures prices and selling calls one strike price above the futures (Wisner, 1991). Selling calls helps pay for the purchases of the puts. The fence places both a lower bound *and an upper bound* on net prices received.

Other forward pricing schemes suggest selling calls. A bullish commercial operator could sell calls at a strike price above the current market, but considered to be attainable. If futures reach that strike price *and* the call is exercised (by a buyer), the seller would be assigned a short position in futures at that strike price. The seller would also pocket the premium. A disadvantage is that the call might not be exercised by a buyer.

Also, a bearish commercial operator could forward contract and sell a call with a strike price above the market. If futures drop, the value of the forward contract is enhanced by the premium less service charges. If futures rise and the call is exercised (by a buyer), the seller would be assigned a short position on another lot (5,000 bushels), which would be priced above the first contract. There is no guarantee, however, that the call will be exercised.

Other combinations of cash contracts, futures, and options could be employed. A popular one is to sell out-of-the-money calls when long in the cash product. If futures remain about the same, this action enhances profits. If futures fall, the individual loses in the cash market, but pockets the premium on the call. If futures rise, increases in cash prices offset the losses on the call. In total, all the combinations discussed in this chapter represent an array that allows farmers and other commercial operators a great deal of flexibility in forward pricing to achieve profit objectives in line with risk preference.

BUYING A CASH PRODUCT

Many of the same forward pricing techniques available for selling a cash product can also be used for buying a cash product. Processors who have established a selling price for their product may need to be assured that the cost of raw material still to be purchased will fit into the budget. A hog farmer may have forward contracted or hedged the sale of hogs, but still has soybean meal to buy. An exporter may have negotiated a sale of wheat still to be purchased.

Such commercial operators need protection from an unexpected rise in the cash price of the item to be purchased. To establish an approximate price on the input, they would buy futures. Just as product sellers can establish *minimum* prices with options, buyers can establish *maximum* prices with options. This could be accomplished by buying calls.

Rather than a lengthy discourse on forward pricing a purchase, a brief reference to the parallel (in a mirror image sense) relationship to forward pricing a sale may be sufficient. Figure 16-3 is a guide similar to Figure 16-1 except that it is directed toward establishing prices on purchases.

If futures are expected to increase and basis to strengthen (upper left quadrant), the safest recommendation would be to buy the cash product now or forward contract it. If futures are expected to rise and basis to weaken (upper right quadrant), a purchase of fu-

FIGURE 16-3 Pricing decision chart for cash product buyers.

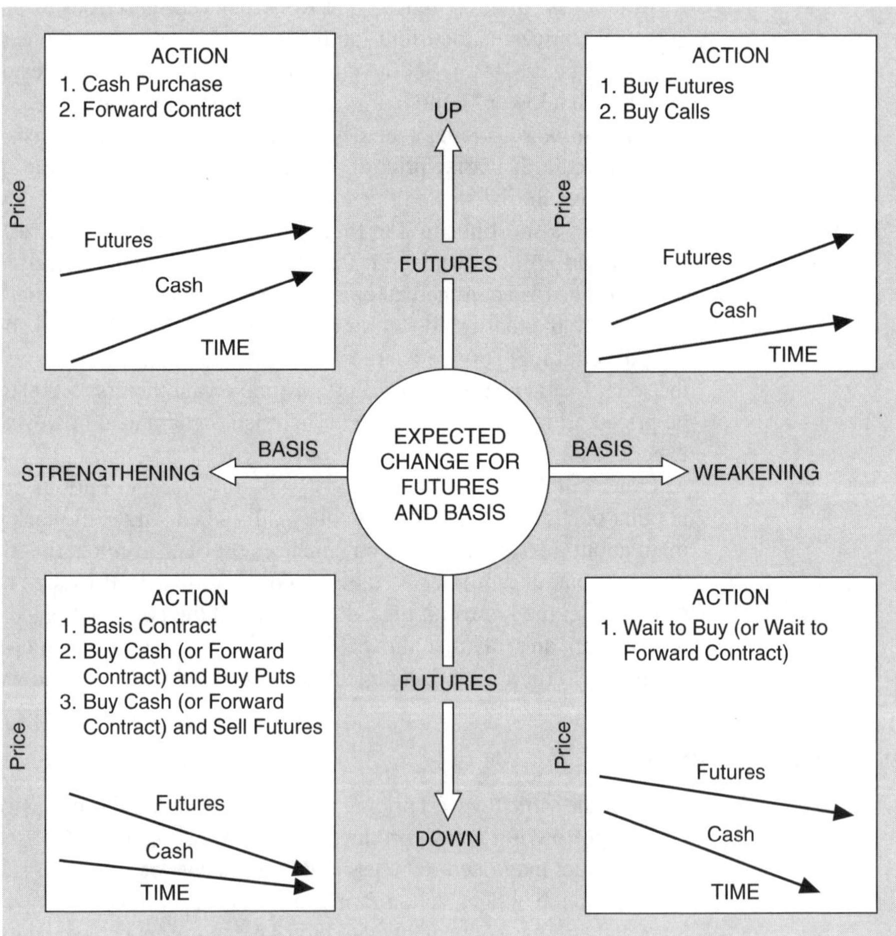

tures would provide protection from rising cash prices, but allow cost savings from a weaker basis later on. A purchase of a call would lock in the right to buy at a price, setting the maximum by adding the premium and brokerage to the strike price adjusted for basis. Rising futures prices would be offset by higher premiums, and hopefully, cash prices would increase less. Alternatively, the buyer could take advantage of an unexpected drop in cash prices even as the calls become worthless.

If futures are expected to decline and basis to strengthen (lower left quadrant), the purchaser should enter a basis contract, if available. Alternatively, the purchaser should buy the cash product now or forward contract it (locking in the weak basis) and buy puts. The puts would cheapen the purchase with the decline in futures. If, unexpectedly, futures should rise, the buyer has established a maximum purchase price—the cash or forward purchase price plus the premium and brokerage on the put. In a similar action, the purchaser could sell futures rather than buy puts. Should futures decline as expected, the cost would be cheapened more than with buying puts, but with a futures rise, the net cost would not have an upper limit.

If futures are expected to decline and basis to weaken (lower right-hand quadrant), a risk taker wanting to buy a product would be advised to wait.

As indicated, which alternative buyers should pursue depends on their inclination and ability to handle risk, just as with those choices of sellers. Those commercial operators in volatile product and input markets should carefully consider protecting themselves on both sides. For example, soybean processors typically watch for opportunities to lock in favorable crushing margins by selling soybean meal and oil futures and buying soybean futures.

BASIS—A KEY TO EFFECTIVE FORWARD PRICING

As stated in Chapter 15, some deliveries are made on futures contracts that tend to keep cash prices and futures prices in line. Any buyer or seller of futures has delivery as an alternative. But few deliveries materialize simply because it is more profitable to buy or sell on local cash markets than to incur the transportation costs and other costs and the inconvenience of making or taking delivery. At the same time, if the cash and futures markets become far out of line, arbitrage will quickly bring them back in a competitive market.

Basis does vary over time due to localized supply-demand situations, transportation difficulties, structural change in the marketing system, etc. Also, grades and qualities of products that differ from the deliverable grade will experience more basis variability than for the deliverable grade. (See section on "Price Spreads Related to Quality Differences" in Chapter 5.) For effective hedging, variability in basis should be small relative to variability in the futures contract.

Basis can be forecast in several ways. A simple procedure would be to calculate a moving average of the past five or so years. Alternatively, to cancel out unusual years, an Olympic average has merit. A five-year Olympic average is constructed by omitting the high and low extremes and averaging the remaining three years. Econometric models could also be incorporated to forecast basis. Independent variables could include production in the region surrounding the cash market, dummies to represent structural changes in the transportation system, etc.

Basis can be measured in three ways. One is what is called "continuation basis" or basis relative to the nearby futures (Figure 16-4). This is simply the specific cash price less the futures price of the nearest contract month ahead. Basis defined in this way has the advantage that one can, on one table or chart, calculate the normal basis for any futures contract within two or three months of the expiration of that contract. The disadvantage is that the basis table or chart will exhibit discontinuities in the transition from one futures month to another.

Another type of basis relative to crops is termed a "new crop basis" table or chart. This is the cash forward contract less the futures price nearest to and after harvest. This also could be applied to livestock—the forward contract price from a marketing agency less the futures price nearest to and following the contract time specification.

A third type of basis table or chart is termed "storage basis" and applies to crops. This basis is the current cash price less the futures price for some month during the storage season. Such a table or chart enables a commercial operator to determine the potential profit from storing and when to buy and sell from storage. A set of such tables or charts also indicates which futures month to use in a storage hedge. This is determined by the month that provides the most "carry" in the market; that is, "basis less storage costs."

Whether following a new crop basis table or a storage basis table, the most important information is the basis within a couple of months of the delivery date. This allows the

FIGURE 16-4 A continuation basis chart on corn, with cash prices at the Gulf and in Central Illinois compared with nearby futures on the Chicago Board of Trade, 1995–1996.

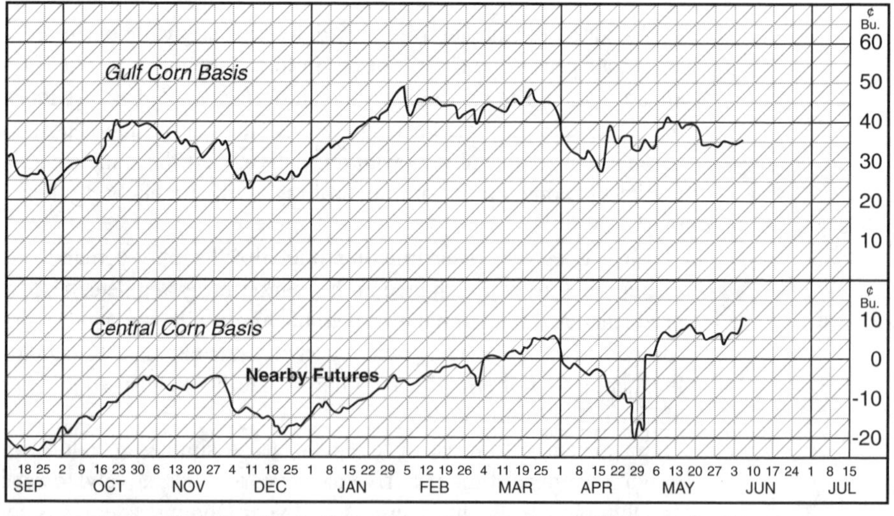

Source: *Commodity Price Charts*, Oster Communications, Inc., 219 Parkade, P.O. Box 6, Ceder Falls, IA 50613. Reprinted by permission from Commodity Price Charts, a weekly publication.

hedger to evaluate whether the current basis is strong or weak and which of the many alternative forward pricing schemes promises the greatest profit. This is why continuation basis tables or charts are popular and instructive.

New Crop Basis

As an example, Figure 16-5 charts what can be called the "harvest or new crop basis" on corn sold at the Saginaw, Michigan terminal of Countrymark Cooperative, Inc., for 1982–1993. The close parallel relationship between December futures on corn at the CBT and the Saginaw cash price from mid October to mid November can be observed in the top section of the figure. The bottom section is simply the difference in terms of the cash price minus the futures.

The mean value of basis was –23 cents with a range from –16 cents to –37 cents and a standard deviation of 5.7 cents per bushel. In contrast, the standard deviation on December futures over this period was 45.5 cents per bushel. These are measures of basis risk in comparison with futures risk and can be calculated as a percentage—12.5 percent (5.7/45.5). On white wheat, which is not deliverable at the CBT, the harvest basis at Saginaw relative to September wheat at the CBT had a standard deviation of 10.4 cents versus a standard deviation for September futures of 48.3 cents, or a percentage of 21.5 percent. The lower the percentage, the more effective hedging can be in reducing price risk.

Storage Basis

The parallel movement of cash and futures prices on corn *during* a crop year is illustrated in Figure 16-6 for Saginaw in 1993–1994. By close inspection, one can not only detect

FIGURE 16-5 Harvest prices on corn at Saginaw, MI, December futures at harvest and basis*.

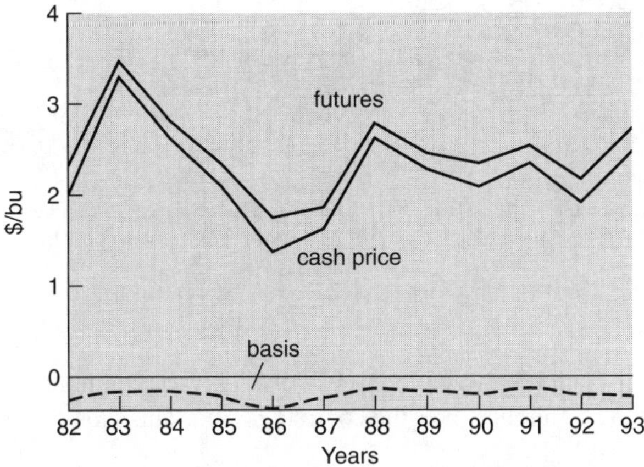

*Basis = cash price - futures. Harvest is from mid October to mid November.

FIGURE 16-6 Cash corn prices at Saginaw, MI, and July futures at the CBT, 1993–1994.

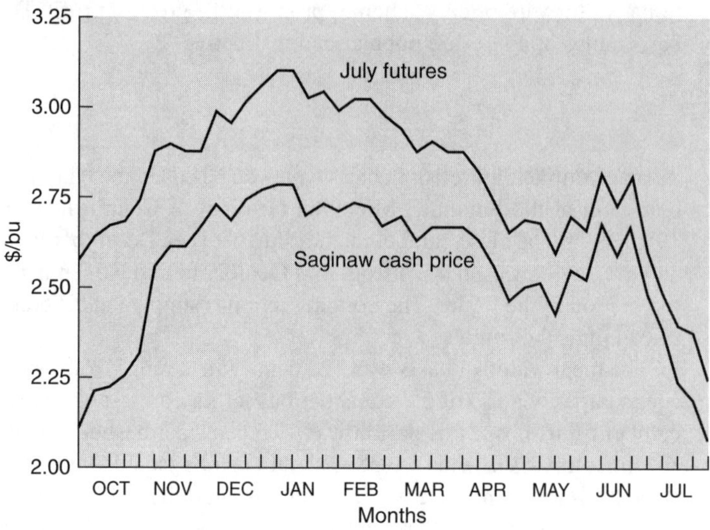

FIGURE 16-7 Basis chart for corn in storage, 1993–1994, cash prices at Saginaw, MI, vs. July futures.

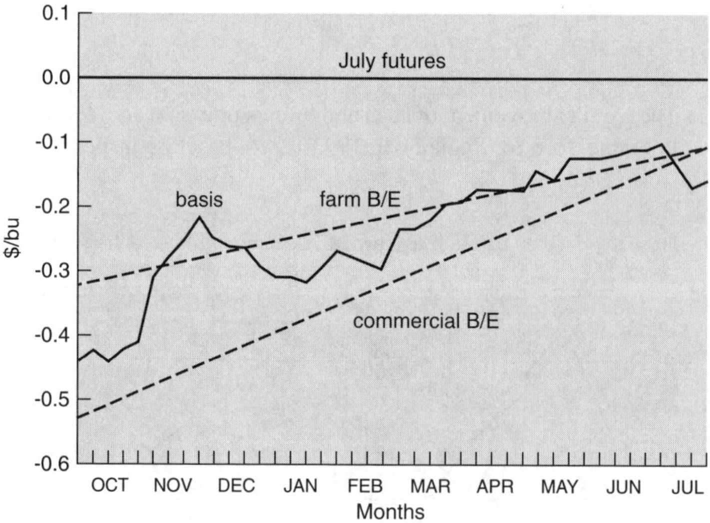

the high correlation between the week-to-week variation in the two series, but also the closing of the difference over the contract period. This closing represents a strengthening of the basis.

The basis pattern can be more clearly seen in Figure 16-7. This storage basis chart is calculated simply by orienting the cash price around July futures represented as a baseline of zero. As discussed earlier in this chapter, basis must strengthen over the storage period enough to cover storage (and brokerage) costs to make hedging a break-even proposition, and even more to make it profitable.

A farmer at harvest, in order to judge whether basis might strengthen enough to cover storage costs, has to evaluate the current basis in terms of what that basis might be toward the end of the storage period. To do this, records of past basis are invaluable. In this case, with respect to July corn futures, the Saginaw basis from mid June to mid July averaged –13 cents per bushel in 1982–1992. The Olympic average for the 1988–1992 crop years was –12 cents and was plotted at the right edge of Figure 16-7.

In order to evaluate, at any time between harvest and the end of the storage season, whether storage under a hedge will pay, a "break-even" line with an upward slope representing storage costs can be drawn with the expected basis at the end of the season as the fulcrum.

For a farmer or other commercial storage operator with existing facilities, the decision of whether a storage hedge would be profitable depends on direct costs and not the combination of direct and fixed costs. Fixed costs will be incurred regardless of whether a crop is stored. This direct cost can be calculated by multiplying the price of the crop at harvest by annual interest rates times the proportion of a year that the crop will be stored. What interest rate the commercial operator uses depends on whether the crop is stored on borrowed capital or whether the capital tied up in the crop represents foregone returns on investments of comparable risk. Some small additional direct costs relate to maintaining quality of the grain, insurance on the grain, etc.

In Figure 16-7, storage costs were calculated for two alternatives. One was using direct costs of storage on the farm multiplying short-term interest rates in the Midwest by the price of corn at Saginaw at harvest times two-thirds of a year. This, plus the small additional costs, amounted to about 20 cents per bushel. Deducting 20 cents from –12 cents resulted in –32 cents which is plotted on the left edge of Figure 16-7. Connecting that point to –12 cents on the right edge provided the construction of a break-even basis line at the farm, assuming existing facilities.

The commercial break-even line includes the interest cost on stored grain plus an elevator charge of 3 cents per bushel per month. These two lines in Figure 16-7 represent the range between minimal storage costs and toward the upper range of storage costs.

For a farmer with existing storage, the actual basis at harvest at Saginaw was well below the break-even line, suggesting storage under a hedge would pay. In practice, the farmer faces some "in" or "up-front" costs and might not be inclined to hedge unless basis was 5 to 10 cents per bushel below the break-even line at harvest.

Assuming this farmer did hedge, the break-even basis line provides a guideline on when to lift the hedge. The rise in basis above the farm break-even line in late November and early December was a signal to the farmer to lift the hedge; that is, buy back the July futures sold at harvest and sell cash corn. If the farmer remained bullish about the prospects for increases in the general level of corn prices at that time, he or she could establish a long position in futures. With basis that strong, prospects for profit were greater with futures than with cash or, on the downside, possible losses would be less with futures than with cash if prices declined.

A farmer who continued to store into June would still profit equal to the negative difference between basis and break-even basis at harvest, plus the positive difference between basis and break-even basis when the hedge is lifted. The unexpected weakening of the basis in July underscores a rule of thumb to lift hedges before the contract month at which time basis frequently becomes somewhat erratic.

A storage operator, with the break-even basis line similar to the farmer, would buy corn and hedge at harvest, lift the hedge in late November and early December; then buy corn in January and then lift the hedge in May or June. Basis trading will not generate large profits, but will provide more assured income than betting on the movement of futures. Between January and June, a hedged inventory in 1994 would have collected a profit of about 10 cents per bushel in this example. An unhedged inventory would have lost 10 cents or so in the market, plus storage costs of another 10 cents per bushel.

Farmers or others storing commercially facing both foregone interest on the grain, plus a 3-cent per bushel per month charge, would not have tended to hedge at harvest because basis was above the "commercial" break-even line (Figure 16-7). Only in those periods when the slope of the basis line was greater than the slope of the commercial break-even line would hedging have paid, but those periods are difficult to predict.

Commercial storage costs are close to total costs for on-farm storage which include fixed costs. The expansion in storage facilities on and off the farm has resulted in ample capacity and a competitive industry. As a result, the "carry" in the market has not been highly attractive in recent years to encourage the construction of new facilities. The picture in Figure 16-7 for 1993–1994 is fairly typical of the previous 10 to 15 years. Erecting on-farm storage still may be economical due to convenience and to the broader marketing alternatives available such as in trucking in larger lots and over greater distances.

HEDGE RATIOS

As mentioned earlier, farmers and others relying on forward pricing crops or livestock have an array of tools to fit their inclination and ability to handle risk. Another choice they can make is to determine the proportion of their cash position to hedge. The percentage of cash position that is hedged or priced with options is known as the "hedge ratio."

Farmers covering new crop sales in advance of harvest are dealing with *anticipated* production. The proportion of the expected crop to be forward priced depends on the variability of yield. If yields fall below 90 percent of trend frequently, but seldom below 80 percent, perhaps no more than 80 to 85 percent of the anticipated crop should be forward contracted or hedged—as a rule of thumb. The uncertain portion of the new crop could be priced with other tools such as options or not forward priced at all. Also, a farmer could purchase crop insurance and hedge up to the level of protection that insurance would provide.

A farmer fully hedged in the event of a short crop might have to buy futures back at a higher price than when the hedge was placed without having a similar amount of the cash product to offset losses in futures. This, of course, depends on whether the farmer's yields are positively correlated with national yields that tend to be negatively related to prices. This farmer would gain if over-hedged and futures fell.

If the amount of the cash product to be forward priced is clearly known, then 100 percent hedging could be considered. In fact, over the years, many elevator managers who did not fully protect their inventory, electing to speculate on some portion, lost their jobs in the process as the markets turned against them.

In "cross hedging," that is, hedging a product substantially different than the futures contract, or in situations in which there is substantial basis risk, the commercial operator may want to calculate an "optimal hedge ratio." If the price variability between the cash product and futures is highly correlated, but the cash price is less variable, effective hedging could be accomplished with less than a 100 percent relationship between the amount hedged and the amount of cash product in inventory. If the cash price is more variable, effective hedging will require greater than 100 percent coverage.

Following procedures outlined by Myers and Thompson, and Stoll and Whaley, an OLS analysis was applied to week-to-week changes in cash prices on corn at Saginaw as a function of week-to-week changes in July futures at the CBT over the storage period from the first of October to the delivery period in the following July (Myers and Thompson, 1989; Stoll and Whaley, 1993).[2] The crop years from 1982–1983 to 1993–1994 were examined. Since the cash price at Saginaw is for No. 2 corn, the grade standard is close to the CBT delivery standard. Each crop year was analyzed separately.

For the 1993–1994 crop year, the OLS results were as follows:

$$DPCN93 = .0071 + 1.063 * DFTJL93$$
$$(20.41)$$

$\bar{R}^2 = .912$ DW = 1.86 *t* value is in parenthesis

where: DPCN93 = change in the week-to-week price of corn at Saginaw, MI, in \$/bu.

DFTJL93 = change in the week-to-week price of July corn futures at the CBT, in \$/bu.

The constant reflects the weekly strengthening of basis of .71 cents, slightly above the estimated .50 cents for on-farm direct storage costs. The coefficient on DFTJL93 of 1.063 indicates the optimum hedge ratio; that is, selling 6.3 percent more futures than the long cash position in the corn inventory. However, the average coefficient for the 12 storage seasons for 1982–1983 to 1993–1994 was .915 with a range from .600 to 1.091. The conclusion in this case is that full hedging of the inventory is probably the best policy unless you have a technique to forecast the coefficient each year.

A similar conclusion was reached on hedging soft white wheat at Saginaw. Wheat is subject to more basis risk than corn because white wheat is not deliverable at Chicago. Over the 12 storage seasons (July to mid November) from 1982 to 1993, the coefficient on the week-to-week change in December wheat futures, as these changes affected cash prices on white wheat at Saginaw, averaged .969, ranging from .762 to 1.207.

The only practical application of the optimal hedge ratio is with commodities that are: (1) quite dissimilar to the base grade of the futures contract or (2) far out of position to be delivered and for which transportation costs are a major element. If the coefficient on

[2]Myers and Thompson developed a more generalized model with conditions imposed but found the results very close to a simple regression using price changes.

the first difference of futures turned out to be, say, around .5, then the cash product would require only half the volume of futures for effective hedging.

Relevant to the optimal hedge ratio for an individual farmer, who wants to protect gross income of a crop in advance of harvest, is the correlation between the yields of that farmer and national yields. If national yields impact prices in an inverse relationship, an unhedged farmer whose yields are closely correlated with national yields will be compensated by higher market prices, if prevailing yields are low. If highly hedged, this farmer might find gross income more variable than if he or she were not hedged. For this reason, such farmers would find their optimal hedge ratio less than farmers whose yields are not highly correlated with the national picture.

One advantage of using options to set lower bounds on prices received is that farmers whose yields correlate with the national average can receive compensating higher prices in the event of an unfavorable growing season. If prevailing yields are above average, such farmers also have sizeable crops to offset the lower prices bounded by the protection of the options.

In some situations, farmers may want to use hedge ratios well above 1.000. If futures are at unusually high levels and not likely to average higher the next several years, farmers could apply a hedge ratio of, say, 3.000, and forward price 75 percent of their *total* expected production over the next four crop years. This "multiple crop year pricing" would be accomplished by "rolling ahead" the remaining hedges as futures expire, i.e., buying back short positions and taking short positions in more distant futures.

Appropriate use of futures and options to enhance profits and manage risks is clearly a very complex process for an individual farmer or any commercial operator. While their understanding of the principles is essential, professional guidance may also be required. Timing in placing and lifting hedges, for example, is especially difficult for those not closely in tune with everyday market action.

SUMMARY

Farmers and other commercial operators have many forward pricing choices with futures and options or cash contracts based on these instruments. They can establish approximate prices in advance on products or inputs. Combinations with options allow them to set lower bounds on product prices and upper bounds on input prices. Appropriate application of futures and options can substantially reduce price risks in very volatile markets. Careful attention to basis can reward farmers and agribusinesses with profits under controlled risk situations.

QUESTIONS FOR STUDY

1 The essence of hedging is to take the opposite position (short or long) in the futures market as in the cash market (long or short). Explain.
2 For effective hedging, why should basis variability be small in proportion to variability in the level of prices?
3 Explain how a farmer could use option markets to place a minimum on net returns from sales of a product.

4 Why is the use of options in forward pricing a commodity generally the least profitable among alternatives if prices don't change very much?

5 Why would a farmer accept a lower minimum return using options than a higher and fairly assured return by forward contracting or hedging?

6 What is the difference between hedging on your own and entering hedge-to-arrive contracts with a local elevator?

7 Under what circumstances would you, as a farmer, forward contract and buy calls rather than buy puts to establish lower bounds on returns?

8 As a risk averse farmer, how would you forward price a commodity if you expected:

a Prices to rise and basis to strengthen?

b Prices to fall and basis to weaken?

9 If you were considering storing a crop and needing price protection, you would sell futures only if you expected basis to strengthen more than storage costs. If not, you might as well sell on the current cash market. Explain.

10 Under what circumstance might you sell the equivalent in wheat futures three times more than you expect to produce? How would you proceed with that marketing strategy?

17

TECHNICAL ANALYSIS

POINTS

1 Difference between technical and fundamental analysis.
2 The process of price discovery related to market efficiency.
3 Rationale for technical analysis.
4 Technical tools and how to use them.
5 Evaluation of historical performance of technical analysis.

The previous chapters have dealt almost exclusively with what is termed "fundamental analysis." This is essentially measurement of the parameters of supply-and-demand relationships and their application to forecasting. In contrast, a very sizeable group of market forecasters subscribe to a methodology known as technical analysis. While fundamentalists draw heavily from economic theory, technicians (also called chartists) do not. Technical analysts base their price predictions on historical patterns and may, in a way, be drawing on human psychology and some vaguely defined theories on how prices are established as buyers and sellers interact in the marketplace.

PRICE DISCOVERY AND MARKET EFFICIENCY

In the short-run, we might identify a process called "price discovery." The market is searching for a price that will equate supply and demand and not result in excessive or deficient inventories. Futures markets, livestock auctions, computer systems, and other institutions provide the means for buyers and sellers to communicate in establishing market clearing prices. Such prices may function well for a given day but may not reflect true supply-and-demand conditions in a longer-run context. What might be established on a daily basis is a price too high that results in unacceptably burdensome stocks or a price too low that depletes stocks to uncomfortably minimal levels. When stocks become known to the market, prices respond in a way to adjudicate the extremes, converging toward an equilibrium. The technician wants to uncover this process.

Technicians may agree that supply and demand are important in price formation over time, but in the very short-run, these forces are unknown or difficult to measure. In the intra-day movement in prices and the day-to-day, week-to-week, and even month-to-month price changes, fundamental analysis is quite limited or non-existent. Yet, this time frame is very important to commercial operators and to speculators. Volatility in commodity markets is often such that timing of purchases and sales within the context of days or weeks is crucial.

For this reason, substantial resources are devoted to discern underlying patterns in prices that have value for short-run forecasting. Many periodicals and books are written on technical analysis and the associated approach known as charting. Regular services are available to update this information and provide interpretation. Computer programs are extensively applied to this task. An excellent guide on how to do technical analysis is in NCR Extension Publication No. 217, *Producer Marketing Management Fact Sheet #20* (Uhrig, Technical Analysis).

While fundamental analysis is involved in forecasting supplies, demands, exports, stocks, etc., in addition to price, technical analysis focuses exclusively on price. Although technical analysis has been used extensively in forecasting stock prices and could be applied to cash commodity markets, the activity has been almost entirely directed at futures markets.

Some devoted technicians also use their tools for long-range price forecasts, applying such instruments as cycles and past highs and lows. The theory behind this application is quite weak and will not be treated in this book.

In arguments over the validity of technical analysis, several questions can be raised:

1 Do commodity futures prices follow a "random walk"?[1]

2 If commodity futures prices follow a "random walk," can technicians extract profits from the market?

3 If these prices are not a "random walk," that is, patterns do exist, can these patterns last very long if they are arbitraged by technicians?

A "random walk" relates to the following price equation:

$$\text{Price}_t = \text{Price}_{t-1} + e_t$$

where: e_t is a random number with some defined variance and a mean of zero.

[1]The term "random walk" is defined with more precision in Chapter 18.

The interpretation is that price at any given point in time is related to the price in the most recent period, but the direction from the previous period cannot be predicted.

If prices truly do follow a random walk, and markets are efficient, how does one explain the prevalence of technical analysis in commodity markets? Even many who espouse to be basically fundamentalists pay attention to the "technical position of the market" in day-to-day trading. In any case, technical analysis is difficult to ignore, and deserves attention even though questions raised above may not be answered in this chapter. The following examples apply to daily statistics from futures markets, although other frequencies are sometimes used by technicians such as weekly, monthly, or even intra-day.

VERTICAL BAR CHARTS

A basic tool of technicians is the vertical bar chart, such as plotted in Figure 17-1. The bar embraces the high and low of trading on a futures contract during a particular day with a horizontal line that denotes the closing or settlement price. Some charts also designate the opening price. Vertical bar charts are also drawn for weeks and months.

Formations

The patterns these vertical bars generate over time are of critical importance to chartists. A classic formation is the head and shoulders top as depicted in Figure 17-2. Such a formation could not be identified until the market had clearly fallen below the neckline. At that point, a technical trader would have sold short with a plan to buy at a point or points

FIGURE 17-1 October live cattle futures, June 1994.

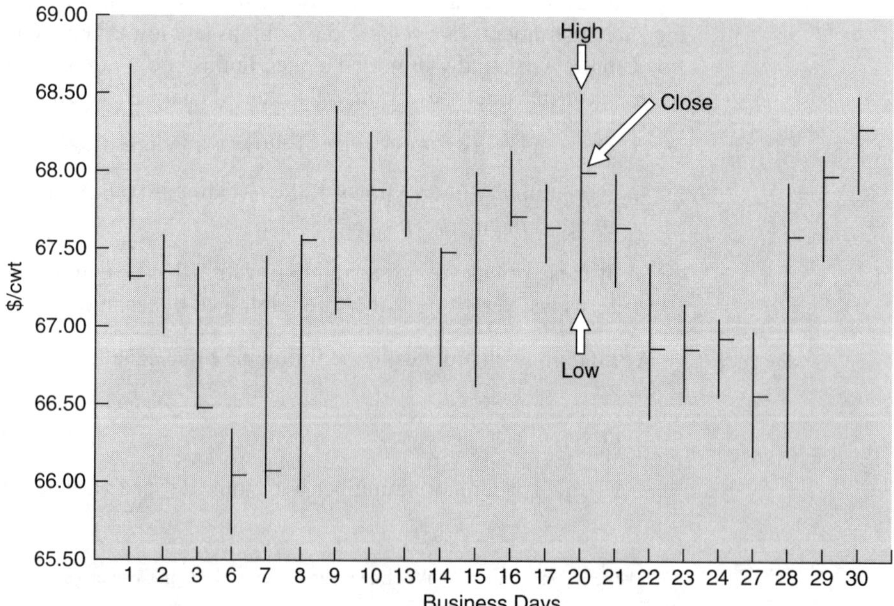

FIGURE 17-2 Head and shoulders top vertical bar chart.

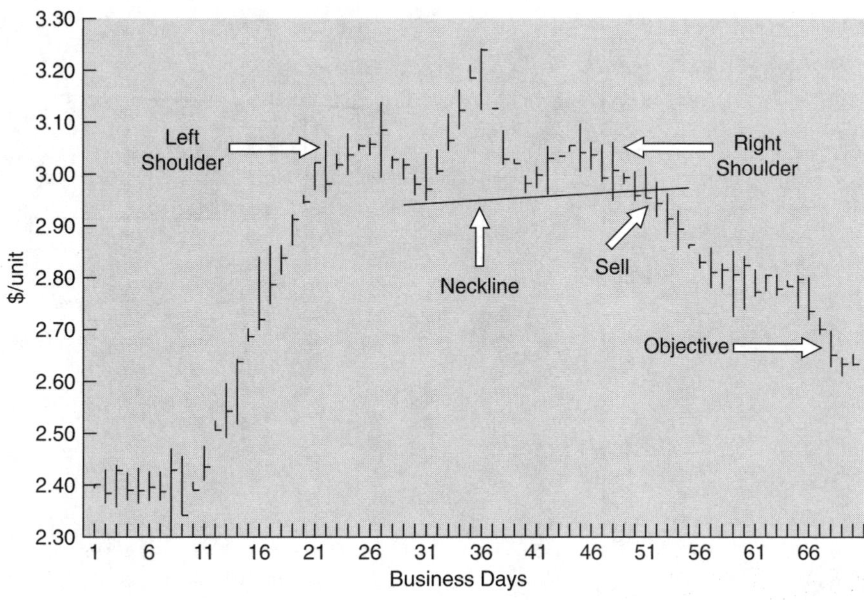

indicated by the formation. One point would have been the distance below the neckline equal to the distance from the neckline to the top of the head, labeled in Figure 17-2 as "objective."

Just as there are "head and shoulders top" formations to signal when to sell futures, buy signs are indicated by the inverse—"head and shoulder bottom" formations. More common are formations with fairly obvious titles of "double tops" and "double bottoms."

In the double top formation shown in Figure 17-3, rising prices meet resistance, fall back, and then test that resistance again. Chartists are very sensitive to this action in the market. If prices fail to penetrate the previous high, this signals that, for some unknown reason, the market is revealing its hand and is pointing to a down turn. A bear market is confirmed if prices drop below the middle of the "M" formation and a sell signal is flashed. Alternatively, if prices move back up to the highs and are repulsed again, a triple top is formed that gives more credence to taking a short position when prices reach where the sell signal is positioned in Figure 17-3.

The first objective for a buy would be at a point below the lower bound of the top formation that equals the vertical range of the formation. This is indicated by the arrow labeled "Objective" in Figure 17-3.

A "double bottom" formation, as pictured in Figure 17-4, can be interpreted in a similar way to the double top. In the terminology of the trade, declining prices reach a support level, rise, and then fall back to that level. Should prices penetrate that support, the market would be regarded as technically weak and chartists would search for a new lower support level. If the market rebounds from the support level shown in Figure 17-4 and moves above the middle of the "W," a buy is signaled with a sale objective above

FIGURE 17-3 Double top vertical bar chart.

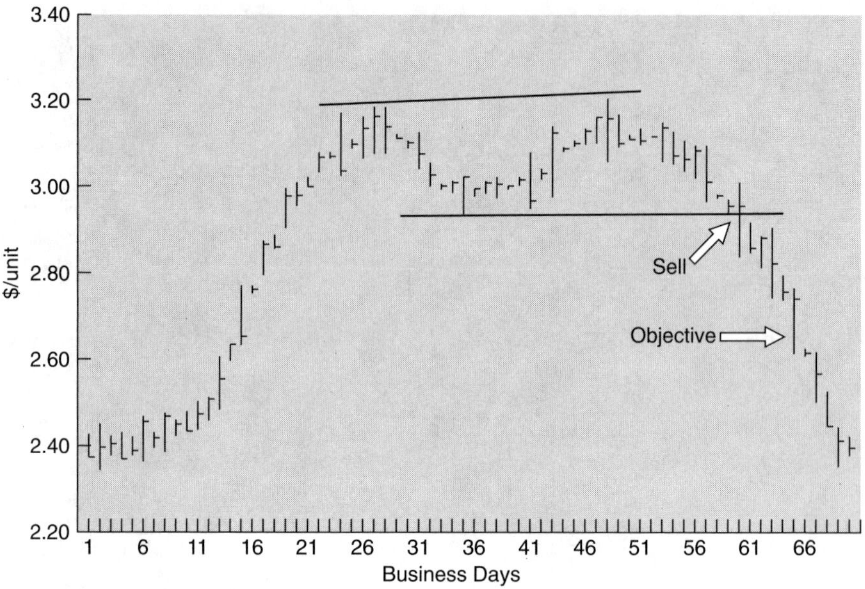

FIGURE 17-4 Double bottom vertical bar chart.

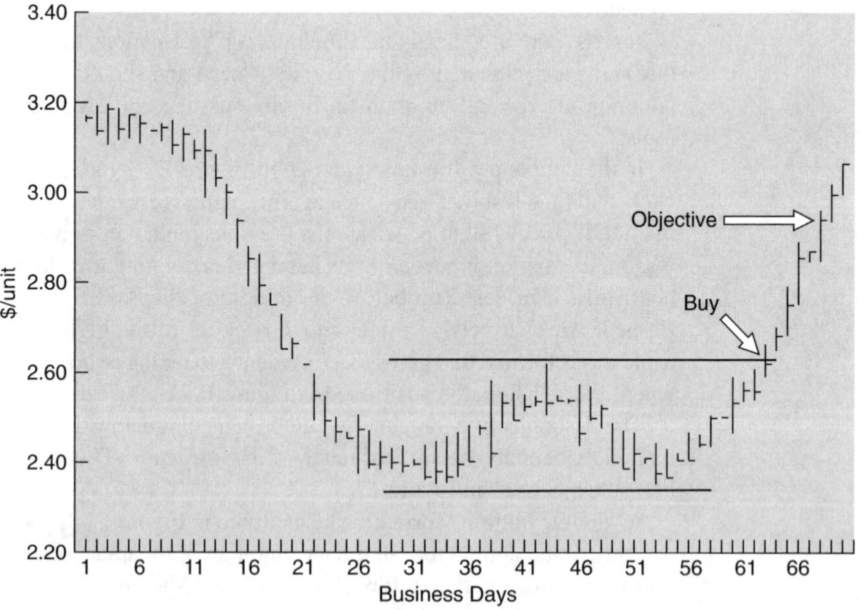

the buy at distance equal to the difference between the low and the top of the middle of the "W."

The arsenal of chartists contains many more formations than illustrated here. These examples, however, are among the more common tools and show how they are used in establishing long or short positions in the market and in exiting the market.

Trend Lines

Futures prices tend to be trendy. Traders want to be on the right side of these basic movements. As a common saying goes in this industry, "The trend is your friend." Once a trader discerns a trend, the appropriate position is taken. Once that is accomplished, the chartists will be attentive to evidence that the trend is being reversed. This, of course, takes some skill in deciphering the price patterns.

An up-trend that is later reversed is pictured in Figure 17-5. An alert chartist would probably buy into this market sometime between business days 16 and 21. Following the point of entry, a chartist would draw trend lines daily across the bottom of the formations in order to make a judgment about a clear-cut reversal. Between business days 26 and 31, a short trend line could have been drawn at a much steeper angle than the long-term trend line, but a trained chartist knows that steep trend lines are less reliable than ones with a more gradual incline (or decline).

In any case, the patient chartist would wait for a clear sell signal that would appear with a close noticeably below the up-trend line. While this point is easily detected in

FIGURE 17-5 Charting an up-trend vertical bar chart.

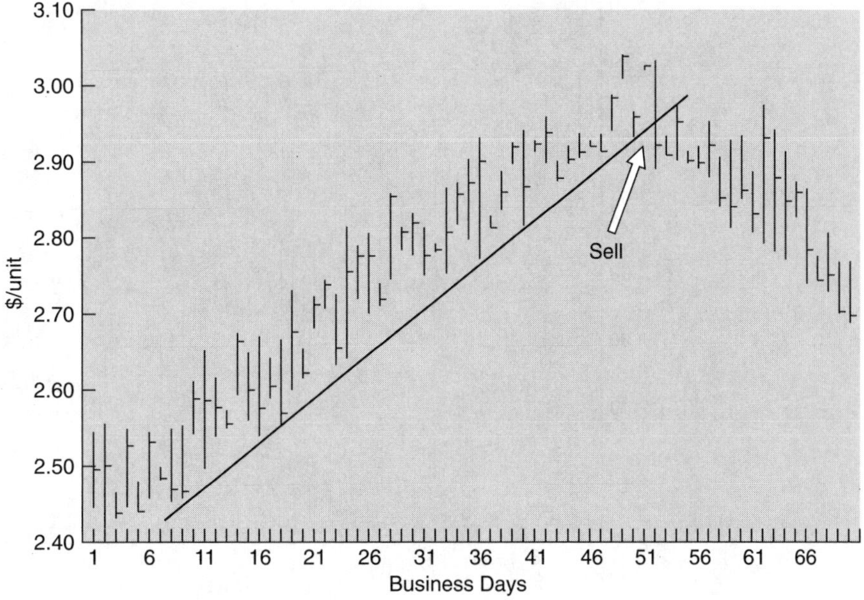

Figure 17-5, many wrong signals may be flashed in similar bull markets. In major market moves, as indicated in Figure 17-5, the chartist's objective after acting on the reversal is half of the range. In other words, the rise in the market was from around $2.50/unit to about $2.90. The chartist would remain short until prices reached about $2.70.

To be a bit more specific, how a speculator who is also a chartist might play the market is illustrated in Figure 17-5; the entry would occur only after an up-trend was detected, say at about $2.60 on or about day 19. The chartist gave up 10 cents of the move because an uptrend was not evident before at least a 10-cent move had happened.

Say the speculator bought 10 contracts at $2.60. By selling these 10 contracts at $2.90 on day 52, a profit of 30 cents was realized, less brokerage costs. However, an aggressive trader might have sold *20* contracts on day 52 to take a profit on 10 contracts and go short on 10. If prices reached the downside objective of $2.70, the speculator would either exit the market by buying 10 contracts or could find reason to switch to a long position and buy, say, 20 contracts instead. In any case, chart readers may maintain positions on either side of the market, or if the signs are indeterminant, stay on the sidelines.

In a down-trending market, as shown in Figure 17-6, the chartist, having taken a short position, will be drawing straight lines over the top of the formation in order to detect a reversal to the up-side. In the first day or two after this happens, with closes above the down-trend line, the speculator will buy either to exit the market or to exchange a short position for a long position.

The process of entering and exiting markets can be illustrated by a consolidation formation pictured in Figure 17-7. In a sense, a consolidation can be regarded as a trend,

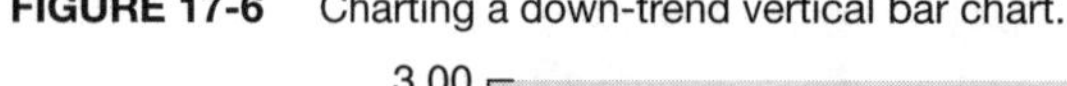

FIGURE 17-6 Charting a down-trend vertical bar chart.

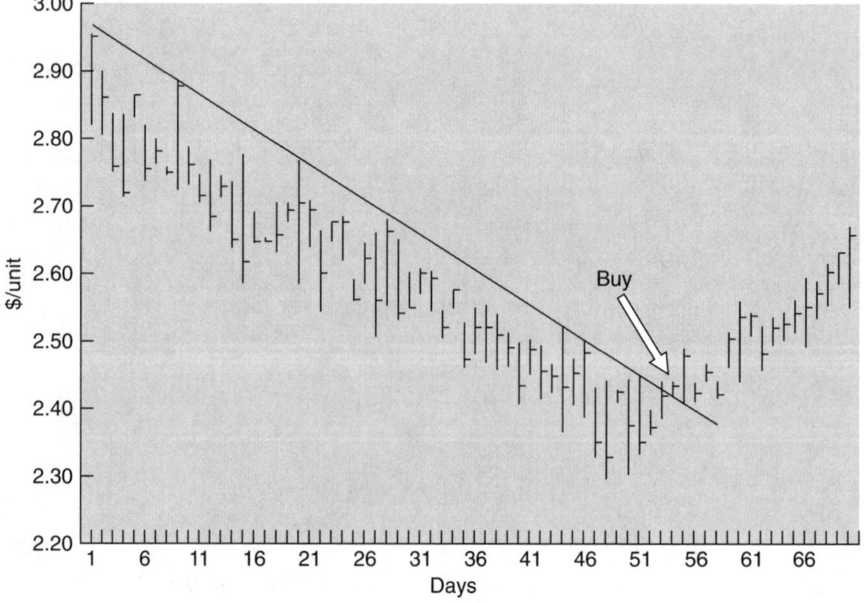

FIGURE 17-7 Consolidation vertical bar chart.

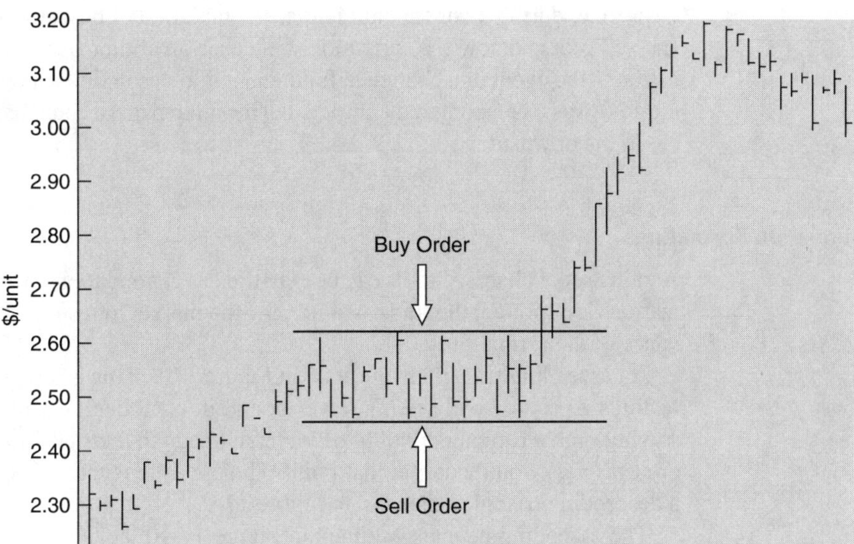

zero trend, that is. In this case, the chartist will draw straight horizontal lines both above and below the formation. Should the market penetrate the line on top of the formation, a buy signal would be flashed; or conversely, a price drop below the line beneath the formation would trigger a sell signal.

A rule of chartists is that, "The longer the market is in a consolidation, the greater the breakout on either side, up or down." Such a rule does have logic if one considers how speculators use orders in entering and exiting markets.

During the period that the market is in a consolidation, three types of traders can be identified:

1 Longs with "stop loss" orders to sell below the consolidation.
2 Shorts with "stop loss" orders to buy above the consolidation.
3 Sideliners with buy orders above the consolidation and sell orders below the consolidation.

The trick is to know how much above the known consolidation to place buy orders and how much below to place sell orders. In Figure 17-7, such margins would be on the order of a few cents per unit. The longer the time the market is in a consolidation, the more pronounced this formation becomes, attracting more and more traders who either want to protect themselves from losses if they have taken a position or those who have no opinion on the likely direction of the market (the sideliners), but want to be on the right side in the event of a breakout.

For this reason, the rule of thumb of the chartists becomes a self-fulfilling prophesy. Over time, during a consolidation, the accumulation of buy orders above the formation and sell orders below the formation will cause an abrupt rise or fall out of the consolidation in the event of a change in fundamental forces in the market. The example in Figure 17-7 was a breakout to the upside, but a similar pattern could be illustrated on a breakout to the downside.

Continuation Formations

Another set of chartists' tools can be classified as continuation formations. Once such formations are spotted, the trader would play the market to resume the trend evident in advance of the formation.

An ascending triangle is outlined in Figure 17-8. This is a type of consolidation that features a progressively rising lower bound in combination with a flat top. Longs observing such a formation would be inclined to add to their position above the formation or new longs would enter at that point. The opposite is the case for shorts who observe a descending triangle as shown in Figure 17-9.

The ascending pennant outlined in Figure 17-10 looks the same as in a chart of declining prices except for the direction of price trends. Such a consolidation simply is a pause on a long-term rise (ascending pennant) or fall (descending pennant) in prices. Chartists would take appropriate action in these events.

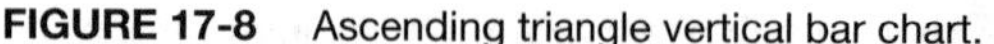

FIGURE 17-8 Ascending triangle vertical bar chart.

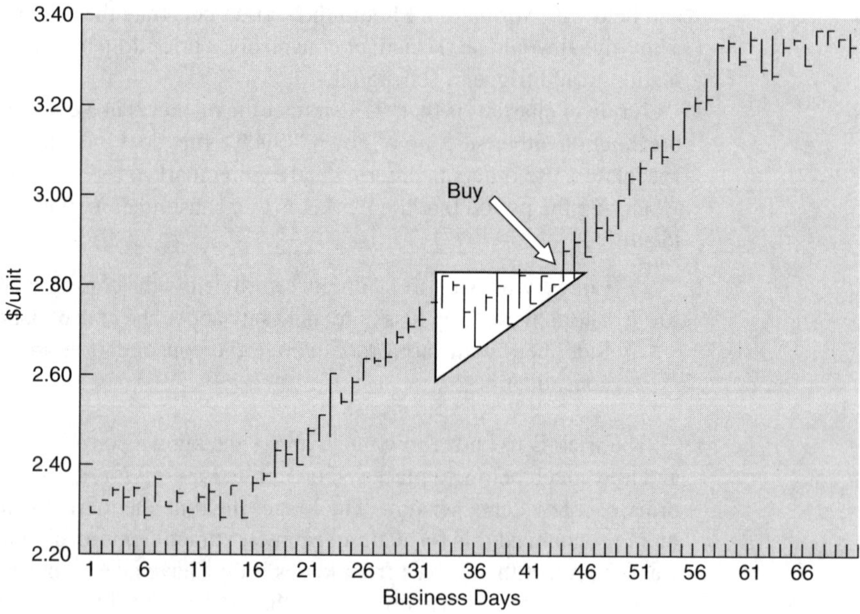

FIGURE 17-9 Descending triangle vertical bar chart.

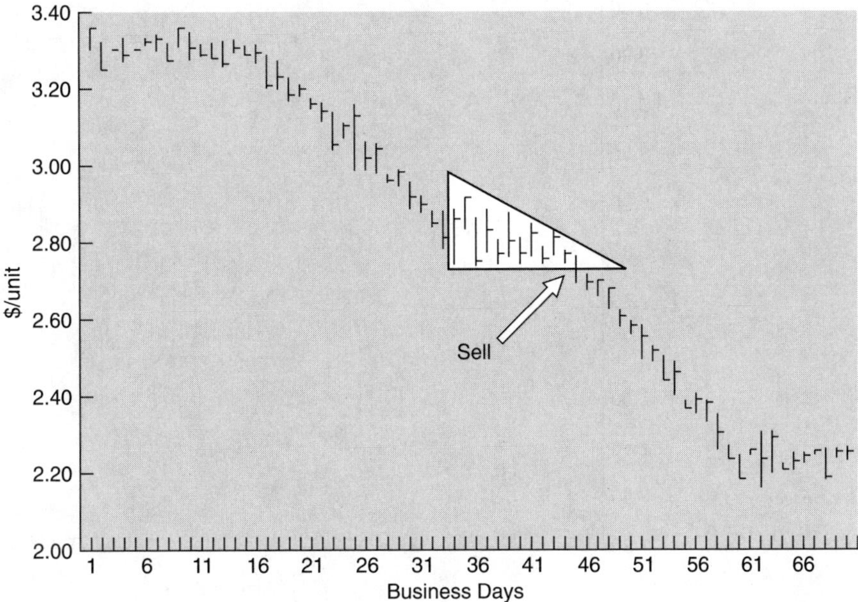

FIGURE 17-10 Ascending pennant vertical bar chart.

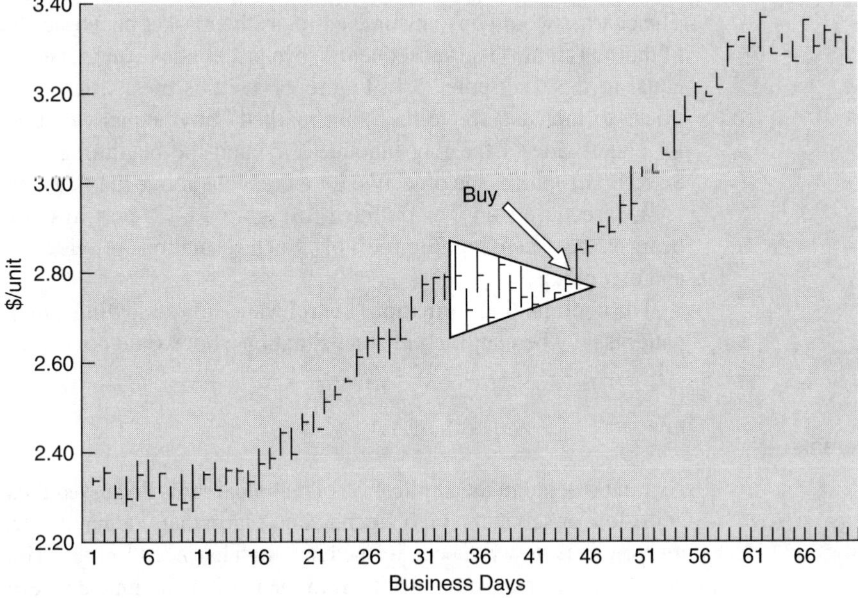

FIGURE 17-11 Ascending flag vertical bar chart.

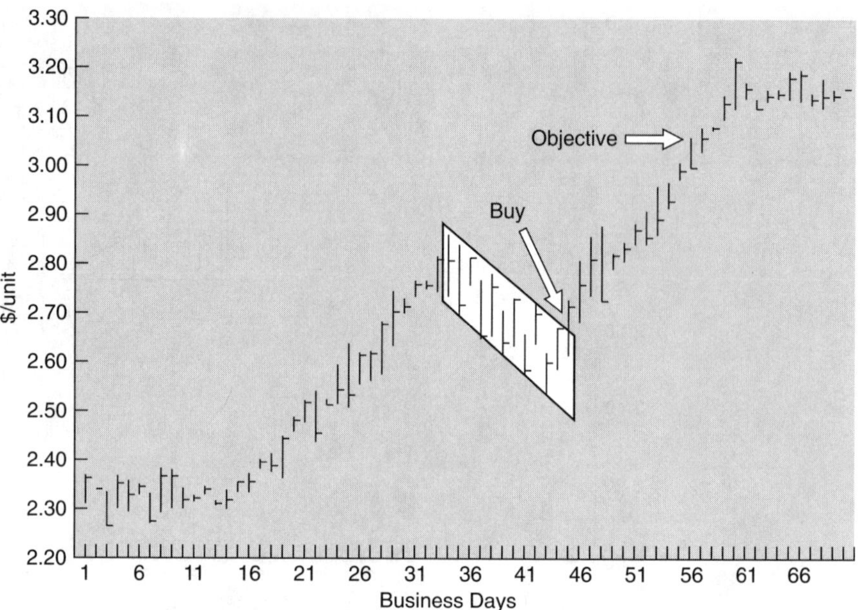

Another set of continuation formations is known as "flags." An ascending flag (Figure 17-11) captures progressively lower highs and lows following a distinct rise in prices. The chartist would buy, at some point, as the market penetrates the upper bound. A rule of thumb is that, "The subsequent rise in prices above an ascending (bullish) flag will be equal to the 'flag pole.' " In Figure 17-11, this means that the chartist would expect prices to increase above the point marked "buy" equal to the difference between the lower left side of the flag (about $2.75) and the beginning of the bull market (about $2.35). This places the objective for a breakout above the flag at about 3.08 (2.68 + .40).

A descending flag, as outlined in Figure 17-12, portrays similar opportunities for bears as the ascending flag for bulls. Such formations provide guidelines for both entry and exit points.

The continuation formations are relevant only following a major market move. Such patterns may be identified in other situations, but would not carry the same implications.

Reversals

As can be noted in the application of technical tools discussed thus far, none signal a buy at the low or sell at the high. Technicians claim that you have to let the price movements tell you that a low has been formed or a high has been formed. This is possible only after you have given up some profits from the market. Technical forecasting procedures confirm the direction of the market only after some delay.

FIGURE 17-12 Descending flag vertical bar chart.

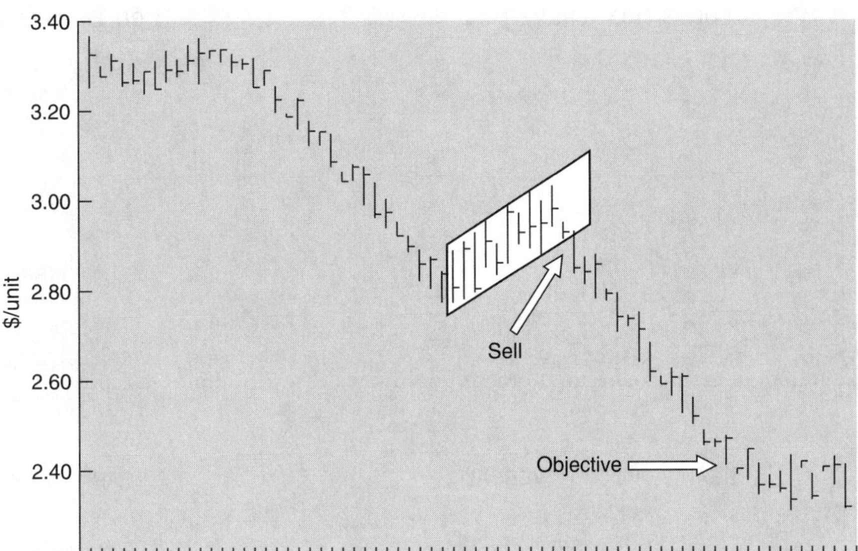

Among the "quickest" of the technical tools to identify a change of direction in the market are chart developments called "reversals." Reversals name *the day* that the market has turned.

Four types of reversals are illustrated in Figure 17-13. A *bullish hook* reversal is identified in a down-trending market if, on a given day, the low is below the previous day's low and high is below the previous day's high and the close is above the previous day's close. A *bullish key* reversal is similar to a *bullish hook* reversal except that the given day's high is *above* the previous day's high.

On the opposite side, a *bearish hook* reversal occurs in a rising market when the high of a given day is above the previous day's high, the low is above the previous day's low, and the close is below the previous day's close. A bearish key reversal is like the bearish hook reversal except that the low on the given day is below the previous day's low.

Two points need to be emphasized. These reversals are relevant only after a major move up or down and not in a fairly stable or choppy market. Second, the hook reversals are seen more often than key reversals, but the key reversals are more reliable indicators of turns in the market.

Gaps

Among the more puzzling harbingers of market moves are "gaps." Gaps are simply occurrences in which the price range in a given day does not intersect with the price range of the previous day. As a chartist might say, "The market hates gaps and wants to close

FIGURE 17-13 Reversals in vertical bar charts.

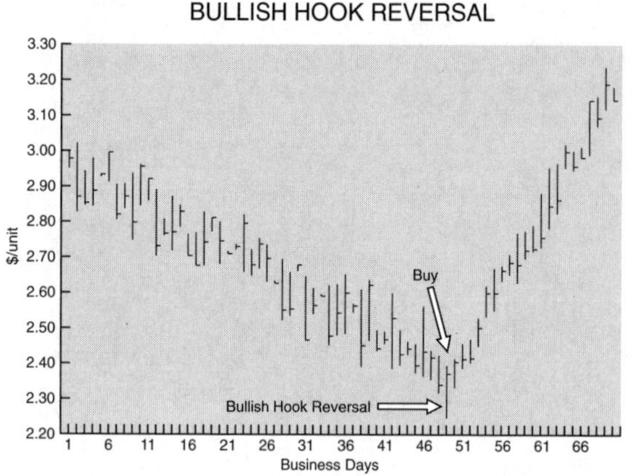

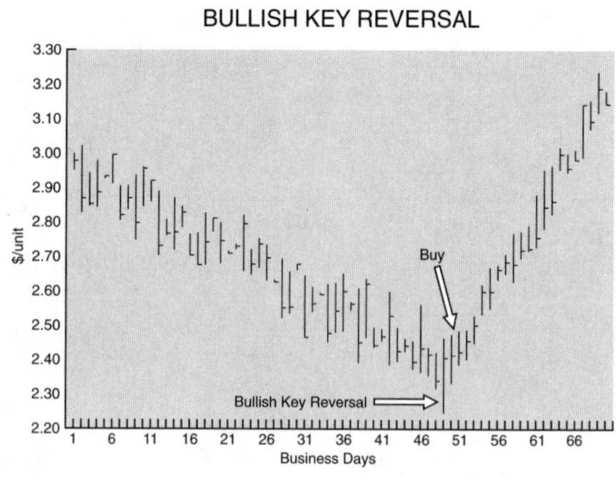

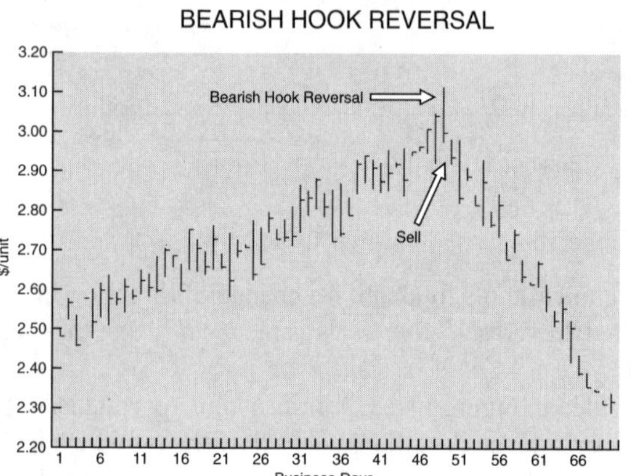

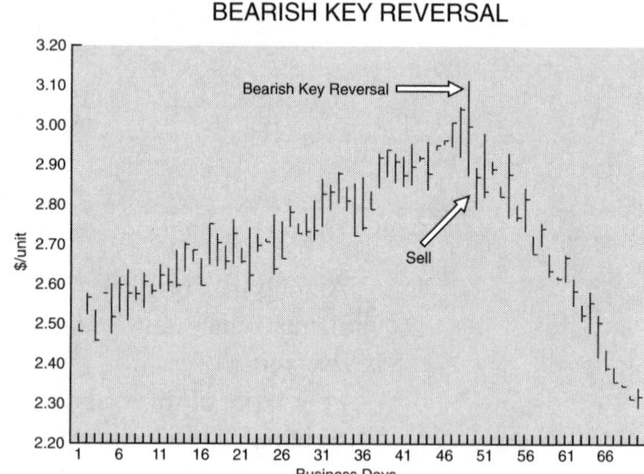

them quickly." For this rather obscure reason, the most usual phenomenon after a gap appears is that the market moves back within a few days to "close" the gap. If this doesn't happen, the gap may take on new meaning.

Types of gaps are illustrated in Figure 17-14. The normal consequence of a gap is subsequent closures, a pattern labeled "common gap." However, a gap that is not closed within a few days may signal a major move in the market is underway. This usually occurs following a fairly stable market and is often triggered by a major change in supply or demand fundamentals.

As shown in Figure 17-14, such a separation is labeled a "breakaway gap," in this case signalling a possible major bull market. When such becomes evident, the chartist would look for another gap called a "measuring gap" that indicates about a half-way point in the market move. As the bull market continues to gain momentum following a measuring gap, the news spreads, emotion overtakes good judgment, and another gap appears

FIGURE 17-14 Types of gaps in vertical bar charts.

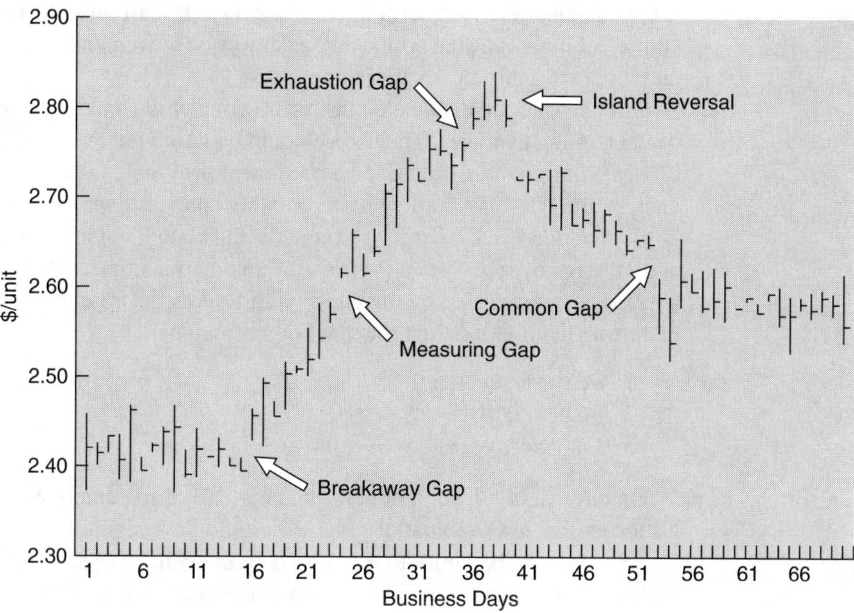

near the end of the move labeled the "exhaustion gap." This gap is also named after the late buyers into the market—"the sucker surge!"

The turn-around that follows is often dramatic and another gap is formed early in the decline. This creates a market top called "island reversal" that points to a major bear market.

MOVING AVERAGES AND STOCHASTICS

Interpretation of vertical bar chart formations, reversals, and gaps requires keen and experienced eyes and is quite subjective. These approaches are difficult to quantify. There are technical approaches that can be quantified and are amenable to computer programming. Once an analyst selects the parameters to such a system, no further judgment is required as the method automatically flashes buy and sell signals.

Moving Averages

One of the more popular tools is called moving averages. Such a procedure may be as simple as calculating only two series, one being an average of market closes over the most recent few days; and the other, an average over the recent few days plus some number of preceding days. As an example, the short-term moving average might be over the past three days and the long-term moving average over the past ten days. The trader might devise the rule that he or she would go long if the short-term moving average went above the long-term moving average and go short if the short-term moving average dropped below the long-term moving average. Use of moving averages screens out the "noise" of the somewhat erratic day-to-day price movements and provides very clear, unambiguous signals on whether to buy or sell.

Critical, of course, is the choice of how many days to incorporate in the calculation of the moving averages. The choice could be based on a very extensive empirical study of what combinations would have been most profitable in the past. As a challenge to the analyst, the optimum combination probably changes over time.

Commodity Price Charts has routinely calculated moving averages of 4-days, 9-days, and 18-days over the years (Oster Communications, Inc., 1994). A simulation of these averages, accompanied by the underlying futures, is presented in Figure 17-15. A speculator might choose one of the three combinations:

1 4-day versus 9-day.
2 4-day versus 18-day.
3 9-day versus 18-day.

On day 18, at the beginning of the chart, all of the combinations would recommend a short position. Combinations 1 and 2 would have signalled twice to buy and then sell in the choppy market prior to day 40—both likely to be unprofitable after brokerage costs were deducted. However, when the major bear market turned into a bull market around day 55, combination 1 first flashed a buy, followed by combination 2 and only after about 10 days had passed did combination 3 indicate a buy. On the other hand, combination 3 avoided the buys and sells in the choppy market prior to day 40.

FIGURE 17-15 Comparison of moving averages with current price changes.

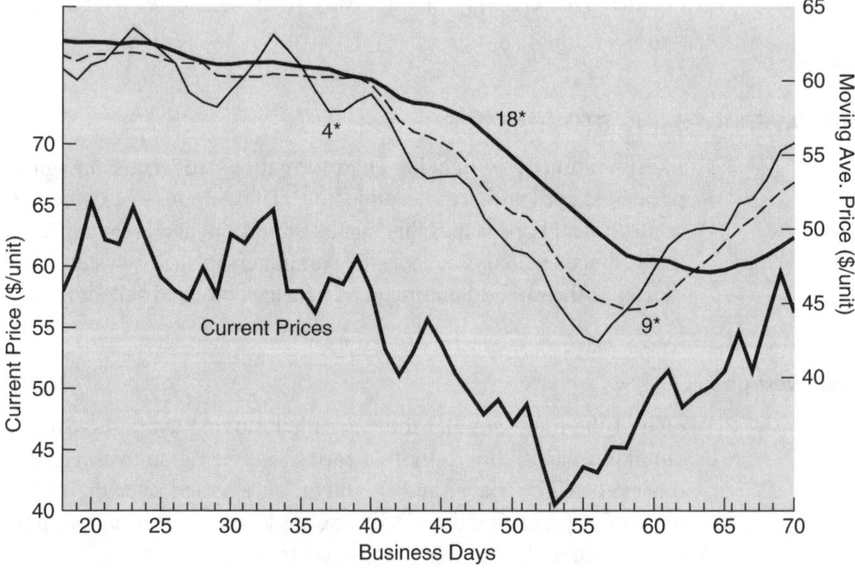

*Moving averages of the indicated number of days including the current day.

The point is that the shorter-term moving averages will put a trader on the right side of a major price move the quickest, but also may generate more wrong signals in a volatile, but directionless market.

Stochastics

Stochastics as applied in technical analysis refers to a relationship between recent prices and a range in prices over some past period. A standard approach is published and described in *Commodity Price Charts* (Oster Communications, Inc.). Three series are calculated: labeled "raw value," "% K" and "% D." These series are plotted on a scale from 0 to 100. The formula for the raw value is:

$$\text{Raw value} = 100 * (\text{previous close} - \text{20-day low}) / (\text{20-day high} - \text{20-day low})$$

The % K is a 3-day moving average of the raw value and the % D is a 3-day moving average of the % K. A conservative trader would buy when % K crosses the % D from below *after* the two series climb out of the "oversold" zone between 0 and 25 percent. They would sell when the % K crosses to % D from above as they drop below the "overbought" zone of 75 to 100 percent. More aggressive traders would buy or sell when the two lines cross as long as the two lines have gone into the oversold or overbought zones.

An example of the application of 20-day stochastics is presented in Figure 17-16. On day 25, both % K and % D are in the oversold zone. An aggressive trader might buy on

FIGURE 17-16 Illustration of 20-day stochastics.

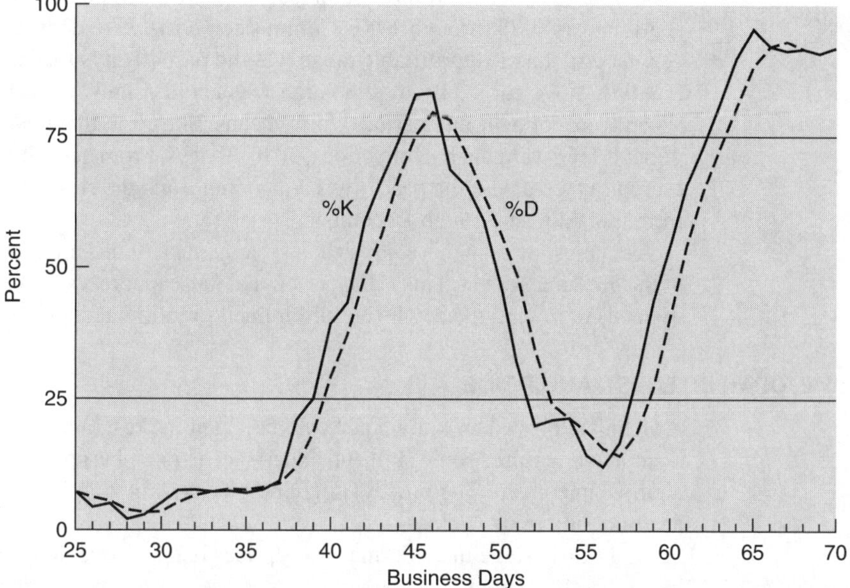

day 30 or day 37 or 38 when the % K moved above % D. The conservative trader would wait until day 40 when both lines emerged from the oversold zone. These positions would be held until sell signals were flashed as % K dropped below % D on day 47. Converting long to short positions would then allow the speculators to profit from the following bear market and they would again reverse their position on days 58, 59, or 60.

In this particular example, the aggressive trader taking positions earlier than the more conservative trader would have likely reaped extra profits by doing so. However, such traders might be subjected to choppy markets and the early positions in the oversold and overbought zones could be losers. For example, a trader who had bought on day 30 might be holding this long position in a down-trending market. Current price declines *in combination* with a declining 20-day low could leave the % K and % D flat or even rising.

The selection of a 20-day period to establish the range for a stochastic system is, of course, arbitrary. Other time periods are examined, such as a five-day time span.

Somewhat of a variation on the stochastics approach has been applied to corn and soybean futures by Stevens at the University of Minnesota (Stevens, 1988). He examined various lag periods in establishing a price range; from the past two, three and on up to ten days, and in five-day intervals up to the past 40 days. The decision rule was that if futures on any given day exceeded the high of the past X days by "one tick" (1/4 cent), a buy signal would be flashed. If futures dropped below the low of the past X days by one tick, a sell sign would emerge.

If a long position is held, it is retained until a sell signal is given; a short position is retained until a buy signal is flashed. The trader would have either a long or short position at all times after the first buy or sell is indicated by the system.

Stevens applied the system to March corn futures from December 1 to February 28 and December corn futures from March 1 through November 30. On soybeans, January futures were used for November 1 through December 31, March contracts for January 1 to February 28, and November futures from March 1 through October 31. The period of analysis was 1973 through 1983. Commission costs were deducted.

On corn, the most profitable range was the past 40 days for January to early July and 6 to 9 days for early July to mid August. For mid August to early December, the least *losses* were for a 40-day period. On soybeans, like corn, the greatest profits for January through June were the longer periods, 20 to 40 days. From early July to mid August, highest returns were with the past 7- to 10-day range, and the shorter periods performed best from mid August through December.

A conclusion from this study is that systems such as this are most effective in the heart of the growing season. This is the period that these markets are the most volatile. Volatility tends to reward those who are disciplined to follow technical systems.

VOLUME, OPEN INTEREST, AND PRICE

A technical procedure known as "volume, open interest, and price" is a momentum indicator and requires some skill and experience in deciphering. The technician must view all three in concert. The process might best be explained in Figure 17-17 in terms of the anatomy of a price cycle.

At an early stage in a bull market as prices begin to rise, longs are drawn to the market and both open interest and volume increase. This indicates a building of momentum

FIGURE 17-17 Anatomy of a price cycle.

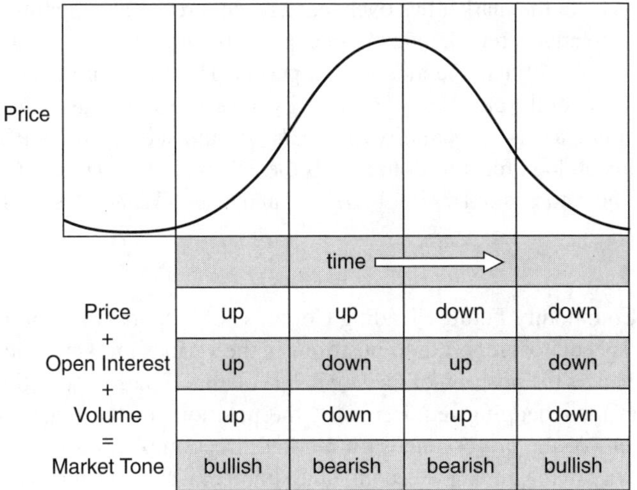

is likely to carry prices even higher—and the market reflects a "bullish tone." Later, as the bulls take profits and bears lick their wounds (i.e., what is known as "short covering"), open interest declines, volume drops off and, even though prices continue to rise, the bloom is off the market. The bull market has matured and a "bearish tone" sets in.

As prices begin to fall in the third stage of the cycle, bears are attracted to the market, both open interest and volume increase, signalling growing momentum to the downside—a definite bearish tone. Like the bull market, the bearish market matures as evidenced by declining open interest and volume—and a bullish tone emerges, signalling an impending reversal.

While changes in volume, open interest, and price are watched closely, the patterns are seldom so neatly traced as in Figure 17-17. Richard Brock points out that open interest has a seasonal pattern and that this variable has to be evaluated in terms of positive or negative departures from that seasonal (Brock, 1981). Open interest on corn futures, for example, normally increases during harvest as country elevators sell futures to offset cash purchases.

Brock also points out that a rapidly accelerating volume following a substantial upward movement in price often signals a major top and a possible price reversal. This pattern, which counters the description of "the anatomy of a price cycle," would appear more likely in a wild bull market as emotions prevail and late longs are convinced that "the sky is the limit."

RELATIVE STRENGTH INDEX

Another technical tool highlighted by *Commodity Price Charts* is the "relative strength index" (RSI). The logical basis for this tool is the aberrant behavior of commodity prices to rise or fall consistently. In the event of such an occurrence, the appropriate interpretation is that the market has over-reacted and a reversal is imminent.

The relative strength index is an exponential moving average and the earlier data carries less weight than the most recent period. The basic formula is a ratio of the average increase over the past X days divided by the average increase, plus the average decrease in absolute terms. *Commodity Price Charts* publishes a 14-day RSI. If the RSI is below 30 percent, look for futures to rise. If the RSI is above 70 percent, look for declining futures. For more details, refer to Wilder and Oster (Wilder, Oster; 1978).

NET TRADER POSITIONS

The Commodity Futures Trading Commission requires that commercial operators and large speculators report their positions in the various markets twice monthly. The residual, then, is the position of the small speculators. Since the position of the commercials reflect their hedging requirements, the positions of the large speculators reflect the opinions of the professionals on market direction. A prudent small speculator, whose longevity in the market is usually quite limited, wants to be on the side of the large speculator who has strong staying power. Data on net trader position also help analysts track the activity of commodity funds that have become more important players in the market.

Knowing that your position in the market is allied with the large speculators should fortify your predictions. The difficulty often is that the lag in reporting the net long or short position of the large speculators is too late for you to take the appropriate action.

OTHER TECHNICAL TOOLS

Many other systems could be described, some of which are subjects of entire books. This chapter is intended to only present major procedures and not a complete enumeration.

Point and Figure Charting

One common technical tool is called "point and figure" charting. The time dimension is not included on the horizontal axis, only cases of reversals. Once a price interval is selected, the chartist begins filling in chart paper in the form of boxes. Price is on the vertical scale. The decision rule relates to the correct box size and what constitutes a reversal.

On soybeans, *Commodity Price Charts* incorporates a 2-cent per bushel box and an eight-box reversal. This means that a box can be filled for a 2-cent movement in price. The direction of price will not be reversed until eight boxes can be filled (16 cents) in the opposite direction. An example is presented in Figure 17-18.

Beginning on April 22, 1994, boxes could be filled with X's as long as prices were increasing and reversals less than 16 cents (eight boxes) did not occur. When this did happen, a column to the right was filled with O's down until a reversal of at least eight boxes emerged to occupy the next column to the right with X's. This procedure continued through mid September 1994.

The buy–sell rule was that if an X occupied a cell above the most recent column of X's, buy; if an O occupied a cell below the most recent column of O's, sell. Obviously,

FIGURE 17-18 Point and figure chart on 1994 November soybean futures*.

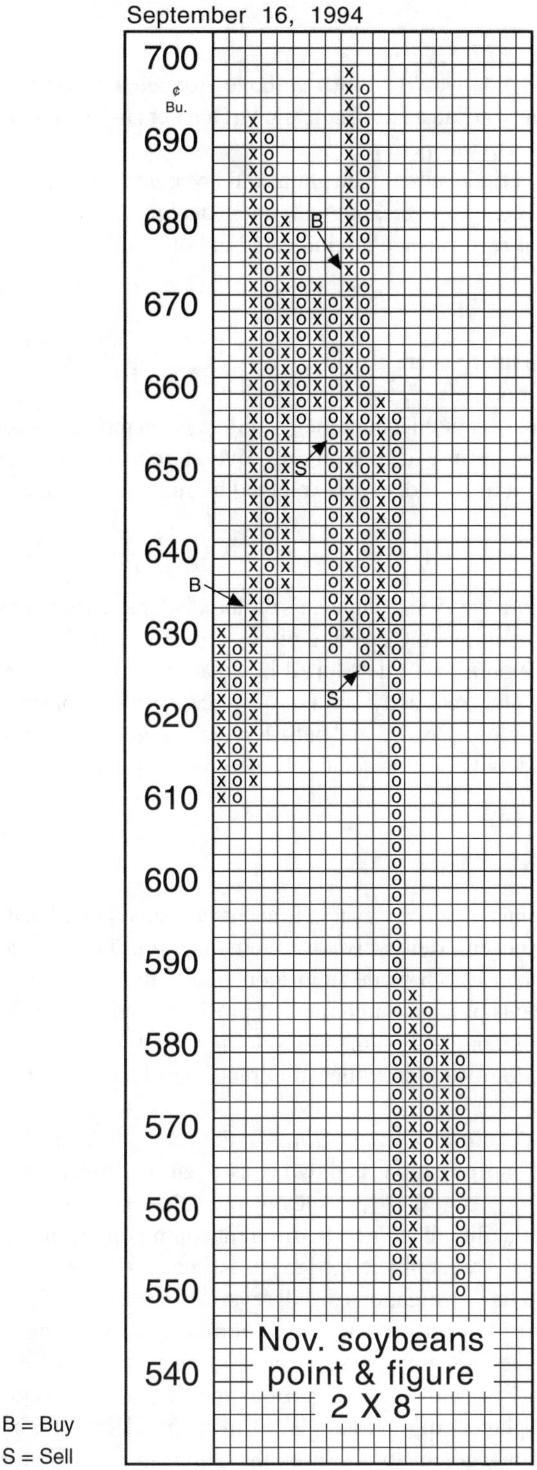

*Chart reprinted by permission from *Commodity Price Charts*, 219 Parkade, P.O. Box 6, Cedar Falls, IA 50613, a weekly publication.

in Figure 17-18, you would not buy at the low or sell at the top of the market. The system insisted that you had a clear indication of a reversal. Even so, the system would have generated profits in this period.

The point and figure charting method could be computerized with somewhat more difficulty than moving averages, but with questionable advantages. A disadvantage is that specific dates of reversals are not indicated in point and figure charting.

Cycles

Many technical analysts are ardent cyclists, believing that the ups and down in futures can be traced to periods of, say, 21 to 35 days. However, departures from such patterns are such that this author questions their validity. Even more, this author has difficulty accepting that long-term cycles spanning several years can be useful forecasting tools other than the cyclical tendencies explained by fundamental analysis.

Japanese Candlesticks

A recent entry into the U.S. technician's toolbox is Japanese candlesticks. This is the only procedure that employs the opening price as well as the close. As described by Steve Nison, this technique was "developed in Japan and honed by centuries of evolution" (Nison, 1990). The "real body" of a day's price action is considered to be between the opening and the close. Bearish and bullish reversals are similar to bearish and bullish key reversals. For details on this relatively new procedure, consult books written on the subject.

EVALUATION

Many other technical tools are available and used than reported in this chapter. Some such techniques have been extensively covered in numerous books on technical analysis. The role of this chapter is to provide an introduction to the general procedures involved.

Advertisements proclaim high rates of profits for selected schemes, yet many objective analysts of commodity markets claim that day-to-day movements in futures approach a random walk providing minimal opportunity for strictly empirical trading systems.

An article appearing in *Commodities* in the early 1970s evaluated eight bottom and six top vertical bar formations and two consolidation formations over unspecified periods (*Commodities,* August 1972). They were evaluated on the basis of frequency of occurrence and reliability relative to 18 different commodities. In only two or three percent of the cases was the reliability judged to be less than 50 percent. In two-thirds of the cases the reliability of these formations to call reversals was evaluated at 70 percent or greater.

An analysis of the performance of point and figure charting that appeared in *Commodities* about the same time revealed another aspect of technical trading (*Commodities,* July 1974). On 15 commodities in periods ranging across five to ten years during the 1960s, only 53 percent of the trades were profitable. However, because the system lets the profits run and cuts the losses short, the net profit per trade for all trades (profitable or not) amounted to $311.

Whether these results are applicable today may be questioned as technical trading has expanded. Some empirical analysis supports the random walk theory as applied to futures markets over the years.

In a review of the literature, Stevens reported that:

Samuelson (1965) introduced the theoretical relationships between random walk and expected returns models in the theory of efficient markets. Previous and subsequent empirical investigation of the market efficiency literature, for the most part, concludes that the futures markets are, in most cases, efficient as measured by serial dependence in a time series. (Stevens, 1991)

On the other hand, Stevens also mentions studies that cast serious doubts on the efficient market or random walk hypothesis and he proceeds to describe his own analysis on corn, soybeans, and wheat futures over the 1972–1989 period (Stevens, 1991). He selected the nearby contracts on corn, soybeans, and wheat at the Chicago Board of Trade and tested daily changes in the closing prices with the following linear regression equation:

$$P(t, k) = \alpha + \beta P(t-1, k) + E$$

where: P (t, k) = change in futures price on day "t" during season "k"

t = ranges from October 1, 1972 through September 30, 1989

k = ranges across 48 time periods in each year

E = randomly distributed error

The estimates of β were significant at the .05 level for the three commodities during their respective growing seasons, but not outside of those growing seasons. The growing seasons were defined as May 24 through August 23 for corn and soybeans and March 24 through June 23 for wheat. The growing season t-values on β were 5.71 for corn, 8.58 for soybeans, and 2.34 for wheat. The lower significance on wheat was due to a more diverse growth period, geographically and over time.

Stevens attributed this non-random pattern on corn, soybean, and wheat futures during the growing season to persistent weather patterns, particularly in North America during the summer months. The implication to speculators and commercials is that they could benefit from strategies that are based on a continuation of price trends during those periods.

If futures markets are efficient, they should exhibit no pronounced seasonal patterns as do cash markets. Yet, seasonal tendencies have been detected in futures that are similar to cash markets. This was established by an analysis of new crop corn, soybean, and wheat futures at the CBT for the crop years 1973 to 1992 (Ferris, 1996).

December corn futures were below average in September through December and above average during the other months. November soybeans were below average in October to March and above average in the other months. September wheat futures were below average in March through September and above average in the other months. While the departures of the monthly averages on these futures from the annual averages were not statistically significant, the consistency with the cash price seasonals merits attention.

One explanation is that hedging pressure from short selling at and around harvest tends to depress futures at that time. On the other hand, evolving patterns such as this should draw speculator interest and counter this hedging pressure.

Probably the best evidence that technical analysis and charting are valid forecasting tools is their widespread and continuing use. By following technical signs and applying stops appropriately, speculators can develop disciplined trading schemes. This helps remove emotion, ego, greed, fear, and other psychological influences that scuttle many entrants in this fast moving game. The techniques are easy to learn and do not require formal training in economics, statistics, or mathematics. This is not to say that such background is irrelevant because some technicians do apply some very sophisticated empirical techniques.

Possibly, technical analysis has gained more respectability as econometricians have turned their attention in recent years to a companion analytical procedure called "time series" to be covered in Chapter 18.

SUMMARY

Technical analysis emerged because fundamental analysis failed to explain adequately short-term fluctuations in commodity prices. While devoid of economic theory, technical analysis (or charting) does draw from psychology and ideas about typical behavior of buyers and sellers. A testimony to its value is its popularity even with many who are mostly fundamentalists. To the extent that technical analysis can add discipline to speculating, devoted technicians may be able to outperform those who allow emotion to dictate their trading schemes.

QUESTIONS FOR STUDY

1. Explain technical analysis, its rationale, and the contrast relative to fundamental analysis.
2. What is "price discovery"?
3. Explain the saying, "The trend is your friend."
4. Why don't technical forecasting procedures prompt you to buy at a market low and sell at a market high?
5. The longer the market is in a consolidation, the greater the move up or down when prices break out of the consolidation, as a rule. Why?
6. How would you interpret a gap in a vertical bar chart in terms of a trading strategy?
7. What is a major advantage in using moving averages to buy or sell relative to interpretation of vertical bar charts?
8. The combination of declining open interest and volume in a period of rising prices is considered to be "bearish." Explain.
9. For what reason would you follow the net positions of large speculators, small speculators, and commercials in futures markets?
10. How could your technical systems result in more losing trades than winning trades and yet be profitable overall?

18

TIME SERIES MODELS[1]

POINTS:

1 Rationale for time series models.
2 Meaning of "white noise."
3 Tests for stationarity.
4 Autoregressive and moving average models and their combinations applied to correcting errors in residuals.
5 Forecasting with time series models.

While technical analysis has a relatively long history as an approach in forecasting stock market and commodity prices, procedures with parallel purposes called "modern time series," or just "time series," emerged in the 1970s and captured growing attention of econometricians in the 1980s and 1990s. Similar to technical analysis, the process of time series analysis has been very empirical with minimal attention to economic theory.[2] In recent years, however, a number of approaches have been developed for imposing and testing economic theories within the context of time series models.

[1]Robert Myers, colleague in the Department of Agricultural Economics at Michigan State University, provided some helpful comments and suggestions in this chapter.

[2]Curiously, major texts that cover time series analysis give no recognition to technical analysis as a common empirical forecasting tool.

A rationale for time series analysis, like technical analysis, is that structural parameters are often difficult to measure and apply to short-run forecasting. While supply and demand are recognized as the fundamental forces undergirding markets, the process of monitoring these forces is often slow and subject to error. Price behavior provides some indications of what these unknown market fundamentals may be, so time series analysts closely inspect past prices in an effort to discern any patterns that may have implications for the future.

Another reason for time series analysis is that it is much easier and less time consuming than constructing structural models. If structural coefficients are not needed, or if the price (or any variable) being forecast is not critical to the overall project, time series provides a quick way to generate forecasts.

Possibly, the most valuable application of time series procedures is to map the error term from regression equations or even the errors from the forecasts of econometric structural models. Incorporating time series processes in regression analysis can also improve the estimation of the structural parameters.

For more depth on this subject, you should refer to several texts on this subject (Granger, 1989; Pindyck and Rubinfeld, 1991; Griffiths, Hill, and Judge, 1993; and Greene, 1993) and a journal article by Myers (Myers, 1994). Some of the earliest research in this area is credited to Box and Jenkins (Box and Jenkins, 1970). This chapter will focus on providing a conceptual view of time series models, with four examples of their application:

1 Testing for "stationarity" on selective variables.
2 Combining fundamental analysis with time series procedures to generate an error term approaching "white noise."
3 Demonstrating how time series models could be employed to project exogenous variables over the forecast period.
4 Developing dynamic forecasts on a price variable with time series.

STATIONARITY

Some elements of time series analysis have already been covered in this book. In Chapter 7, the dynamics of models with geometric and more complex lag structures were examined. Conditions for stability in first- and second-order difference equations involving current and lagged values of single variables were presented. As was concluded for the more complex difference equations, "Stability and convergence would be indicated if there is no root in the characteristic equation, real or complex, with an absolute value greater than or equal to one."

Because time series analysts concentrate on processes with current values regressed on past values, they worry about the possibility that the resulting forecasts would be divergent. If so, the forecast error would become larger over time and the series would be termed "non-stationary." In order to identify a stochastic process that is invariant with respect to time, procedures are followed in an attempt to convert a "non-stationary" series into "stationary."

Many economic variables in their raw form may be non-stationary. A series that follows a random walk is non-stationary. Variables, such as the Gross Domestic Product, which tend to increase over time, carry, with this trend, changing means and standard deviations. From quarter-to-quarter or year-to-year, the trend will deviate from the norm by some unpredictable random amount. Because of this random component, the Gross Domestic Product (and other such variables) follows a stochastic trend. However, if trending economic variables are converted to first differences, they usually can be transformed into a stationary series. If not, second differences or higher orders of differences can be explored in the process. First differences of random walks are, by definition, stationary and "white noise."

White Noise

"White noise" is the Holy Grail in time series analysis. The search is for some univariate equation or combination of equations that will generate an error term which has no discernable structure or pattern. Such an error term, called "white noise," confirms that the equation (or equations) has captured all the information from past data relevant for forecasting.

Specifically, (1) the expected values or mean for a white noise variable (ε) is constant for all periods, and is usually considered to equal zero, and (2) the correlation of the variable ε at any time t and any other time period is zero, or:

$$E(\varepsilon_t) = 0$$

$$\text{Correlation } (\varepsilon_t \varepsilon_s) = 0 \text{ for all } t \neq s$$

A random walk on the variable P is:

$$P_t = P_{t-1} + \varepsilon_t$$

The first difference is white noise, i.e.,

$$P_t - P_{t-1} = \varepsilon_t$$

If, as commonly believed, many economic variables contain random walks, using them in OLS equations can cause problems unless converted to a stationary form. As stated by Pindyck and Rubinfeld,

> First, if these variables follow random walks, a regression of one against the other can lead to spurious results. [The Gauss-Markov theorem would not hold, for example, because a random walk does not have a finite variance. Hence, ordinary least squares (OLS) would not yield a consistent parameter estimator.] Detrending the variables before running the regression will not help; the detrended series will still be non-stationary. Only first-differencing will yield stationary results. Second, the answer has implications for our understanding of the economy and for forecasting. If a variable like GNP follows a random walk, the effects of a temporary shock (such as an increase in oil price or a drop in government spending) will not dissipate after several years, but instead will be permanent (Pindyck and Rubinfeld, 1991).

For example, consider the following equation on P, an economic variable:

$$P_t = \alpha + \beta\, P_{t-1} + \delta\, T + \varepsilon_t$$

where: T = serial time

ε_t = white noise

If δ is positive, this signifies that P_t has been increasing over time. As long as $\beta < 1$, this series would remain stationary after detrending. The variable P_t could be employed in a regression equation. However, if $\beta = 1$, $\delta = 0$, and $\alpha > 0$, this indicates that P_t has been increasing as a random walk with a positive drift, and detrending would not generate a stationary variable.

Dickey-Fuller Test

If stationarity is a concern, a test called Dickey-Fuller is available to check for random walk components, involving the likelihood that $\beta = 1$ and $\delta = 0$ (Dickey and Fuller, 1981). This is a test for a unit root. While easy to perform, this test provides only weak evidence, allowing the analyst to reject (or fail to reject) the null hypothesis that a variable does have a random walk component. The rejection of the existence of a unit root points to stationarity.[3]

MicroTSP software employs an "Augmented Dickey-Fuller" test described in the MicroTSP manual as "running a regression of the first difference of the series against the series lagged once, lagged difference terms, and optionally, a constant and a time trend." To demonstrate the application of this test, five variables were selected that will be used in examples later in this chapter. These variables are quarterly and defined as follows:

PBGD — Price of barrows and gilts at 6 to 7 markets deflated by the CPI (1982–1984 = 1.00) for 1963.1 to 1993.4 ($/cwt.)

QPKC — Production of pork, in carcass weight per capita, in 1963.1 to 1993.4 (lbs.)

DICD — Disposable income per capita deflated by the CPI (1982–1984 = 1.00) for 1963.1 to 1993.4 ($)

SPKSUBC — Availability of beef, broilers, and turkeys, in edible weight per capita, in 1963.1 to 1993.4 (lbs.)

FPOND — Farm price of onions deflated by the CPI (1982–1984 = 1.00) in 1970.1 to 1993.4 ($/cwt.)

To demonstrate the procedure, the variable SPKSUBC was selected. As a starting point, the MicroTSP command UROOT(T,2) is suggested. This runs a regression of the first difference of SPKSUBC against SPKSUBC lagged once, the first difference of SPKSUBC lagged once and twice plus a constant and a time trend. The results of this procedure to test the unit root are presented in the top half of Table 18-1.

According to this test, the augmented Dickey-Fuller t-statistic must be above the indicated "MacKinnon critical values" to reject the hypothesis of a unit root. Such a

[3]Myers points out that a new test has been developed by Kwiatkowski, Phillips, Schmidt, and Shin that tests the null hypothesis of stationarity against the alternative that the series has a stochastic trend (Myers, 1992).

TABLE 18-1 AUGMENTED DICKEY-FULLER TEST ON SPKSUBC

Augmented Dickey-Fuller:	**UROOT(T,2)**	**SPKSUBC**
Dickey-Fuller t-statistic		−3.3131
MacKinnon critical values:	1%	−4.0342
	5%	−3.4463
	10%	−3.1479

SMPL Range: 1963.1–1993.4
Number of Observations: 124
Augmented Dickey-Fuller: UROOT(T,2) SPKSUBC

Variable	Coefficient	Std. Error	T-Stat.	2-Tail Sig.
D(SPKSUBC(−1))	−0.0088455	0.0695602	−0.1271630	0.8990
D(SPKSUBC(−2))	−0.6570010	0.0658298	−9.9802981	0.0000
SPKSUBC(−1)	−0.2628876	0.7934699	−3.3131436	0.0012
C	7.1580508	2.0719464	3.4547471	0.0008
TREND	0.0138607	0.0055914	2.4789060	0.0146

R-squared	0.632075	Mean of dependent var	0.082824
Adjusted R-squared	0.619708	S.D. of dependent var	1.781179
S.E. of regression	1.098414	Sum of squared resid	143.5751
Log likelihood	−185.0361	F-statistic	51.10898
Durbin-Watson stat	2.773354	Prob (F-statistic)	0.000000

Augmented Dickey-Fuller:	**UROOT(T,1)**	**SPKSUBC**
Dickey-Fuller t-statistic		−7.4989
MacKinnon critical values:	1%	−4.0342
	5%	−3.4463
	10%	−3.1479

SMPL Range: 1963.1–1993.4
Number of Observations: 124
Augmented Dickey-Fuller: UROOT(T,1) SPKSUBC

Variable	Coefficient	Std. Error	T-Stat.	2-Tail Sig.
D(SPKSUBC(−1))	0.2485134	0.0871966	2.8500363	0.0051
SPKSUBC(−1)	−0.6816336	0.0908979	−7.4988907	0.0000
C	17.909712	2.3888020	7.4973616	0.0000
TREND	0.0404602	0.0066343	6.0985879	0.0000

R-squared	0.324112	Mean of dependent var	0.082824
Adjusted R-squared	0.307215	S.D. of dependent var	1.781179
S.E. of regression	1.482541	Sum of squared resid	263.7515
Log likelihood	−222.7414	F-statistic	19.18143
Durbin-Watson stat	1.636171	Prob (F-statistic)	0.000000

rejection would support the contention that the series is stationary. This form of the test rejected the unit root test at the 10-percent level, but not at the lower levels. The OLS representation of this test revealed t-statistics significant on each coefficient except D(SPKSUBC(–1)), the first difference of SPKSUBC lagged one period (Table 18-1). Note that the t-value on SPKSUBC(–1) is the Dickey-Fuller t-statistic.

Since the test does not provide for an exclusion of D(SPKSBC(–1)) and an inclusion of D(SPKSBC(–2)), the alternative UROOT(T,1) was tried with the results printed out in the bottom half of Table 18-1. Note that the Dickey-Fuller t-statistic was clearly above the MacKinnon critical values at all three levels of significance.

The same procedure was applied to the other variables with the final results shown in Table 18-2. For DICD, PBGD, and QPKC, the test with the strongest statistical properties was UROOT (T,0), involving only the lagged variable, a constant, and a trend variable. For FPOND, the test with the strongest statistical properties was UROOT (T,1). The DICD variable was clearly non-stationary, PBGD was stationary with the probability of only 10 percent, and both QPKC and FPOND passed the stationarity test at even the 1-percent level. When DICD and PBGD were converted to first differences, the t-statistic was clearly above the MacKinnon critical values at all three levels.

TABLE 18-2 AUGMENTED DICKEY-FULLER TEST ON SELECTED VARIABLES

Augmented Dickey-Fuller: UROOT(T,0) DICD		
Dickey-Fuller t-statistic		–2.4189
MacKinnon critical values:	1%	–4.0342
	5%	–3.4463
	10%	–3.1479
Augmented Dickey-Fuller: UROOT(T,0) PBGD		
Dickey-Fuller t-statistic		–3.2294
MacKinnon critical values:	1%	–4.0342
	5%	–3.4463
	10%	–3.1479
Augmented Dickey-Fuller: UROOT(T,0) QPKC		
Dickey-Fuller t-statistic		–6.7570
MacKinnon critical values:	1%	–4.0342
	5%	–3.4463
	10%	–3.1479
Augmented Dickey-Fuller: UROOT(T,1) FPOND		
Dickey-Fuller t-statistic		–6.1685
MacKinnon critical values:	1%	–4.0580
	5%	–3.4576
	10%	–3.1545

Engle-Granger Co-integration Test

The implication is that if DICD is an explanatory variable for PBGD in a regression equation, both should probably be differenced. A caveat is, however, a linear combination of these two variables (which individually may display random walks) may be stationary. This could be checked by regressing PBGD on DICD and subjecting the error term to a Dickey-Fuller test. The term used to describe random walk variables with linear combinations displaying stationarity is called "co-integration," which also can be established by a procedure known as the "Engle-Granger Co-integration Test" (Engle and Granger, 1987). This test on PBGD and DICD rejected the hypothesis of a unit root only at the 10-percent level, which left the analyst in some doubt as to how to proceed. Had the test clearly rejected the unit root hypothesis, the analyst would have proceeded without differencing the data.

Even without co-integration, the decision of whether or not to enter differenced variables into a regression equation is subject to other considerations. The variable QPKC is stationary and much more important in explaining PBGD than is DICD. Generally, a decision to use differenced data would extend to all variables. Unless all variables were clearly non-stationary, this author would question wholesale differencing. At least in equations related to agriculture, non-differenced data tend to provide better fits than differenced variables. As mentioned by Pindyck and Rubinfeld, "differencing may result in a loss of information about the long-run relationship between two variables" (Pindyck and Rubinfeld, 1991).

To verify that non-differenced data might be appropriate for the more encompassing equation in which PBGD was regressed on QPKC, SPKSUBC, and DICD, the combination of all four variables was subjected to the Engle-Granger Co-integration Test (Table 18-3). The UROOT(T,2) formulation did not reject the unit root, but the UROOT(C,1) did reject the unit root at the 5-percent level. The UROOT(C,1) command in MicroTSP deletes the trend and confines the differenced residuals to the previous period only.

APPLYING AR, MA, AND ARMA MODELS TO A DEMAND EQUATION ON HOGS

A promising application of time series techniques is to improve the predictive power of fundamental type equations and models. This is particularly relevant for quarterly or monthly models. Such procedures will likely be of limited value for annual models except for the application of AR(1) to be discussed later in this chapter. Problems of serial correlation in annual models tend to be less serious than for models with variables of higher frequency.

As an example of a quarterly equation to predict hog prices (PBGD), Table 18-4 presents the printout of the OLS results. Variables not defined previously are:

DVQ_i	Quarterly constant dummies assuming the value of one in the given quarter and zero in other quarters.
$QPKC_i$	Production of pork in carcass weight per capita in the given quarter and zero otherwise.
TO76	Linear trend up to 1976 and zero after.

TABLE 18-3 APPLICATION OF ENGLE-GRANGER CO-INTEGRATION TEST ON FOUR KEY VARIABLES IN A DEMAND EQUATION ON HOGS

Engle-Granger Co-integration Test: UROOT(T,2)

—Co-integrating Vector—	
PBGD	1.000000
QPKC	5.445574
SPKSUBC	–1.379354
DICD	–0.009984
TREND	0.870739

Dickey-Fuller t-statistic		–2.9555
MacKinnon critical values:	1%	–5.1589
	5%	–4.5506
	10%	–4.2403

SMPL Range: 1963.4–1993.4
Number of Observations: 121

Engle-Granger Co-integration Test: UROOT(T,2)

Variable	Coefficient	Std. Error	T-Stat.	2-Tail Sig.
D(RESID(–1))	–0.0683035	0.0882559	–0.7739254	0.4405
D(RESID(–2))	–0.3719932	0.0838918	–4.4342022	0.0000
RESID(–1)	–0.2232365	0.0755315	–2.8555423	0.0038

R-squared	0.294203	Mean of dependent var	0.063408
Adjusted R-squared	0.282241	SA.D. of dependent var	6.890998
S.E. of regression	5.838100	Sum of squared resid	4021.843
Log likelihood	–383.6657	F-statistic	24.59347
Durbin-Watson stat	2.099596	Prob (F-statistic)	0.000000

Engle-Granger Co-integration Test: UROOT(C,1)

—Co-integrating Vector—	
PBGD	1.000000
QPKC	6.068559
SPKSUBC	–1.860303
DICD	–0.011407

Dickey-Fuller t-statistic		–4.5976
MacKinnon critical values:	1%	–4.7942
	5%	–4.1895
	10%	–3.8795

SMPL Range: 1963.4–1993.4
Number of Observations: 121

Engle-Granger Co-integration Test: UROOT(C,1)

Variable	Coefficient	Std. Error	T-Stat.	2-Tail Sig.
D(RESID(–1))	0.0673971	0.0897440	0.7509934	0.4541
RESID(–1)	–0.3171680	0.0689858	–4.5975856	0.0000

R-squared	0.157074	Mean of dependent var	0.074204
Adjusted R-squared	0.150050	S.D. of dependent var	8.058608
S.E. of regression	7.429451	Sum of squared resid	6623.610
Log likelihood	–416.7674	F-statistic	22.36129
Durbin-Watson stat	1.972095	Prob (F-statistic)	0.000006

TABLE 18-4 ORDINARY LEAST SQUARES EQUATION FOR PREDICTING QUARTERLY PRICES OF BARROWS AND GILTS AT 6-7 MAJOR MARKETS, DEFLATED BY THE CPI (1982–1984 = 1.00)

SMPL Range: 1963.1–1993.4
Number of Observations: 124

Variable	Coefficient	Std. Error	T-Stat.	2-Tail Sig.
C	198.97879	25.719720	7.7364291	0.0000
DVQ2	23.489371	13.979180	1.6803111	0.0957
DVQ3	43.434342	14.371437	3.0222685	0.0031
DVQ4	5.0854734	12.697155	0.4005207	0.6895
QPKC1	–5.4775223	0.5974971	–9.1674464	0.0000
QPKC2	–7.0606681	0.6878434	–10.264935	0.0000
QPKC3	–8.1313802	0.7446760	–10.919353	0.0000
QPKC4	–5.1499654	0.5435478	–9.4747232	0.0000
SPKSUBC	–2.4675263	0.5763245	–4.2814877	0.0000
DICD	0.0038355	0.0018183	2.1094222	0.0372
TO76	0.2098835	0.1083480	1.9371229	0.0553
AFT76	–1.4987545	0.1096944	–13.662999	0.0000
AFT76SQ	0.0123714	0.0017091	7.2383541	0.0000

R-squared	0.916694	Mean of dependent var	55.39483
Adjusted R-squared	0.907688	S.D. of dependent var	17.06329
S.E. of regression	5.184315	Sum of squared resid	2983.360
Log likelihood	–373.1409	F-statistic	101.7867
Durbin-Watson stat	1.052539	Prob (F-statistic)	0.000000

AFT76 Zero to 1976 and linear trend after.

AFT76SQ $AFT76^2$

The variables TO76 and AFT76 indicate a reversal from a positive trend before 1976 to a negative trend afterward. The highly significant, positive coefficient on AFT76SQ indicates the negative trend since 1976 has been leveling off. This equation represents a priori beliefs about the major variables affecting the price of hogs and reflects reasonable statistical properties.

Correcting for Serial Correlation in Residuals with AR(1)

While the signs on the independent variables in the equation shown in Table 18-4 are as expected and significant at the 5-percent level or less (excluding the dummies for the quarterly constants), and while the equation explains over 90 percent of the variation in PBGD, the Durbin-Watson statistic indicates serial correlation in the residuals.

The first step a modeler should take is to respecify the equation to correct this fundamental problem. If such a respecification fails to correct for serial correlation in the residuals, the next step is to attempt to obtain more efficient estimates by a first-order autocorrelation procedure. This simply assumes that the residual in time t is generated as a correlation with the residual in time t-1 plus an error term that displays white noise, i.e.,

(1) $\mu_t = k\, \mu_{t-1} + \varepsilon_t$

An example of an equation with such a residual would be:

(2) $Y_t = a + b\, X_t + (k\, \mu_{t-1} + \varepsilon_t)$

with the previous period as:

(3) $Y_{t-1} = a + b\, X_{t-1} + \mu_{t-1}$

By transposition,

(4) $\mu_{t-1} = Y_{t-1} - a - b\, X_{t-1}$

and by substitution,

(5) $Y_t = a + b\, X_t + k\, (Y_{t-1} - a - b\, X_{t-1}) + \varepsilon_t$

(6) $Y_t = (1 - k)\, a + k\, Y_{t-1} + b\, (X_t - k\, X_{t-1}) + \varepsilon_t$

The latter equation is non-linear and, in MicroTSP, the coefficients are estimated by applying a Marquardt non-linear least squares algorithm to the transformed equation (Hall, Jackson, and Lilien, 1990). Other techniques are available such as Hildreth-Lu (HI-LU) in which alternative values for k are tried. The value that results in the lowest sum of squared residuals is the one selected (Hildreth and Lu, 1960).

The application of the technique in MicroTSP, which simply involves adding "AR(1)" to the least squares equation designation, increased the Durbin-Watson statistic to 1.83 (Table 18-5). This value is in the indeterminant range of the Durbin-Watson 5-percent significance level. While the AR(1) procedure raised the $\bar{R}^2$ to .936 and reduced the standard error of the regression, *t* values on all the independent variables were diminished and the sign was changed on TO76.

Autoregressive Models (AR)

The application of AR(1) to correct for serial correlation in the residuals of a regression equation is an example of an autoregressive model of order one. The residual for the current period is assumed to be correlated to the residual in the immediate past period plus an error term. Since the residual in the immediate past period is also correlated with the residual in two periods back, etc., the relationship technically extends back to infinity.

Recall in Chapter 6, in the section on geometric distributed lags, that an equation of the form,

(7) $Q_t = (1 - \lambda)\, \alpha + \lambda\, Q_{t-1} + \beta\, \lambda\, P_{t-1}$

would represent an infinite series in P_{t-1}. Stability in this series would be indicated if $0 < \lambda < 1$. Equation (7) is similar to equation (6) except that the X variable in equation (6)

TABLE 18-5 ORDINARY LEAST SQUARES EQUATION FOR PREDICTING HOG PRICES WITH THE PRICE OF BARROWS AND GILTS AT 6-7 MAJOR MARKETS DEFLATED BY THE CPI (1982–1984 = 1.00) WITH SERIAL CORRELATION IN RESIDUALS CORRECTED BY AR(1)

SMPL Range: 1963.1–1993.4
Number of Observations: 124
Convergence Achieved After 6 Iterations

Variable	Coefficient	Std. Error	T-Stat.	2-Tail Sig.
C	107.37445	37.770171	2.8428373	0.0053
DVQ2	26.637889	8.6781235	3.0695448	0.0027
DVQ3	38.884377	9.9605639	3.9038329	0.0002
DVQ4	0.3829311	7.5883400	0.0504631	0.9598
QPKC1	−4.6858514	0.5337551	−8.7790285	0.0000
QPKC2	−6.5240618	0.6299090	−10.357150	0.0000
QPKC3	−7.3007128	0.6767708	−10.787571	0.0000
QPKC4	−4.4404904	0.4980739	−8.9153249	0.0000
SPKSUBC	−0.2904198	0.5755749	−0.5045734	0.6149
DICD	0.0049343	0.0032520	1.5173158	0.1321
TO76	−0.0721943	0.1924104	−0.3752097	0.7082
AFT76	−1.3120073	0.2219082	−5.9123877	0.0000
AFT76SQ	0.0076159	0.0034008	2.2394614	0.0271
AR(1)	0.6521734	0.0750718	8.6873268	0.0000

R-squared	0.943160	Mean of dependent var	55.39483
Adjusted R-squared	0.936442	S.D. of dependent var	17.06329
S.E. of regression	4.301772	Sum of squared resid	2035.576
Log likelihood	−349.4400	F-statistic	140.4035
Durbin-Watson stat	1.830849	Prob (F-statistic)	0.000000

enters as a difference rather than the absolute level represented by P_{t-1} in equation (7). With $|\lambda| < 1$, the process would be stationary.

Autoregressive models may be of orders greater than 1 with the general form,

$$(8) \quad Y_t = a + k_1 Y_{t-1} + k_2 Y_{t-2} \ldots + k_j Y_{t-j} + \varepsilon_t$$

which would be described as an autoregressive model of order j. The sum of the weights, k_i, must be less than one for the process to be stationary.[4] Substituting a term for residuals (μ_i) for Y_i, equation (8) would simply become:

$$(9) \quad \mu_t = a + k_1 \mu_{t-1} + k_2 \mu_{t-2} \ldots + k_j \mu_{t-j} + \varepsilon_t$$

[4]This is a necessary, but not sufficient condition (Pindyck and Rubinfeld, 1991).

The point is that the autoregressive process could be applied to forecast any variable for which current values correlate with past values of that variable.

Moving Average Models (MA)

Rather than correlation of a given variable with past values of that variable as in autoregression models, moving averages relate to correlation of a given variable with past random disturbances, i.e., the white noise term. A moving average model of order m would be:

$$(10)\quad Y_t = c + \ell_1\,\varepsilon_{t-1} + \ell_2\,\varepsilon_{t-2} + \ldots + \ell_m\,\varepsilon_{t-m} + \varepsilon_t$$

where: the mean, $E(\varepsilon_t) = 0$

with variance, $E(\varepsilon_t^2) = \sigma^2\,\varepsilon_t$

and with covariance, $E(\varepsilon_t\,\varepsilon_{t-i}) = 0$ for $i \neq 0$.

These are the conditions for white noise.

Applied to residuals, μ, in a regression equation, the formulation would be:

$$(11)\quad \mu_t = c + \ell_1\,\varepsilon_{t-1} + \ell_2\,\varepsilon_{t-2} + \ldots + \ell_m\,\varepsilon_{t-m} + \varepsilon_t$$

since $E(\varepsilon_t) = 0$, $E(\mu_t) = c$.

The signs on ℓ_i may be positive or negative and are often represented as negative. In contrast to the autoregressive model, the moving average process has finite memory. What happened before t-m would have no affect on the current value of the variable.

The formula in equation (11) also generalizes into processes of infinite order, and stationary conditions can be established. The converse is demonstrated in Wold's decomposition theorem that indicates the non-deterministic part of any stationary stochastic process can be represented in the form of an infinite MA process. This means that any stationary stochastic process can be decomposed into a deterministic part and a non-deterministic part. These parts are uncorrelated and the non-deterministic component can be represented by an MA process. A process is termed "deterministic" if it can be predicted without error. The implication of Wold's decomposition theorem is that a stationary AR process has an MA representation (Judge et al., 1985).

Also, many MA processes have AR representations. These relationships provide support for the application of ARMA and ARIMA models which are described in the following sections.

Autoregressive Moving Average Models (ARMA)

The patterns of random processes, such as the residuals from a regression equation, may not be captured strictly by an autoregressive model nor by a moving average model. What might be required is a combination of the two, called an autoregressive-moving average (ARMA) model as follows:

$$(12)\quad Y_t = d + k_1 Y_{t-1} + k_2 Y_{t-2} + \ldots + k_j Y_{t-j} + \ell_1 \varepsilon_{t-1} + \ell_2 \varepsilon_{t-2} + \ldots + \ell_m \varepsilon_{t-m} + \varepsilon_t$$

Assuming this process is stationary, the model would be designated as ARMA (j, m), meaning an order of j on the autoregressive portion and order of m on the moving average portion. For residuals in a regression equation, the format would be:

$$(13)\quad \mu_t = d + k_1 \mu_{t-1} + k_2 \mu_{t-2} + \ldots + k_j \mu_{t-j} + \ell_1 \varepsilon_{t-1} + \ell_2 \varepsilon_{t-2} + \ldots + \ell_m \varepsilon_{t-m} + \varepsilon_t$$

Application of ARMA to Residuals in OLS Equations

The application of AR(1) to correct for serial correlation in residuals, as illustrated in Tables 18-4 and 18-5 on hog demand, is a common procedure, but represents only one treatment of the residuals. The residuals can be tested using ARMA that includes some combination of AR and MA of varying degrees.

Autocorrelations and partial autocorrelations on the residuals to the hog demand equation in Table 18-4 are displayed in Table 18-6. These figures represent the pattern of correlation between current and past residuals over a sixteen-quarter lag period, i.e., four years. The selection of the 16-quarter lag period was arbitrary and partly based on the tendency for hog production and prices to follow a four-year cycle. The

TABLE 18-6 DIRECT AND PARTIAL AUTOCORRELATIONS ON THE RESIDUALS OF THE HOG DEMAND EQUATION IN TABLE 18-4

SMPL Range: 1963.1–1993.4
Number of Observations: 124

Autocorrelations	Partial Autocorrelation		ac	pac
. |******	. |******	1	0.457	0.457
. |**	.*| .	2	0.139	−0.089
. |**	. |**	3	0.162	0.170
. |***	. |*.	4	0.210	0.096
**| .	*****| .	5	−0.165	−0.404
***| .	. | .	6	−0.257	−0.019
**| .	. | .	7	−0.116	0.011
. | .	. | .	8	−0.029	0.026
**| .	. | .	9	−0.123	0.033
**| .	.*| .	10	−0.138	−0.109
.*| .	**| .	11	−0.107	−0.139
.*| .	. | .	12	−0.076	−0.031
.*| .	. | .	13	−0.071	0.030
**| .	**| .	14	−0.138	−0.118
**| .	.*| .	15	−0.157	−0.070
.*| .	. | .	16	−0.047	0.027

Box-Pierce Q-Stat 63.09 Prob 0.0000 SE of Correlations 0.090
Ljung-Box Q-Stat 66.73 Prob 0.0000

autocorrelations are the direct measurement of the correlation between the current and lagged quarters. The partial autocorrelations measure the *additional* predictive power of each of the 16 lagged residuals in explaining the current residual. The –.089 for the lagged second quarter, for example, is the relatively small (and negative) contribution of adding that lagged quarter.

The Box-Pierce and Ljung-Box Q-Statistics at the bottom of Table 18-6 indicate the probability of observing a Q-value equal to or greater than the calculated value, given that the null hypothesis of white noise is true. In this case, the probability is very low. The Ljung-Box Q-Statistic has the same large sample properties as the Box-Pierce Q-Statistic, but is said to have better small-sample properties.

Realizing that the error term in this equation is not white noise, the analyst would inspect the autocorrelations in Table 18-6 for clues about what type of ARMA model might be appropriate. Candidates would be lags of 1, 4, 5, and 6. Not knowing whether these would be AR or MA functions, a first attempt might be to apply both.

The results of the OLS procedure with MA(1), MA(4), MA(5), MA(6), AR(1), AR(4), AR(5), and AR(6) are shown in Table 18-7. Checking the *t* statistics on these formulations, only coefficients on MA(5), MA(6), AR(1), AR(4), and AR(5) were significant at the 5-percent level or below. The pattern on the direct and partial autocorrelations at the bottom of Table 18-7 indicates that lags of 12 and 15 quarters would also be candidates for inclusion. Adding MA(12), MA(15), AR(12), and AR(15) to the significant operators listed above, another OLS equation was estimated. The coefficients on MA(12) and MA(15) were significant, but those on AR(12) and AR(15) were not. This indicated that the correlation with the longer-term lags were better captured by the MA process. Also apparent was that the correlations with shorter lags were better represented by the AR process.

The final OLS equation on hog demand is presented in Table 18-8. The ARMA procedure on the residuals included MA(6), MA(12), MA(15), AR(1), AR(4), and AR(5). The coefficients on the ARMA components were all statistically significant except the *t* value of –1.67 on MA(6). The Box-Pierce and Ljung-Box Q-Statistics indicated a relatively high probability of white noise.

Comparing the equation in Table 18-8 with the one in Table 18-4, the $\bar{R}^2$ was increased from .907 to .956; the standard error of the regression was reduced from \$5.18/cwt. to \$3.58/cwt, and the sum of squared residuals was reduced from 2983 to 1343. The Durbin-Watson statistic was increased from 1.05 to 1.82. The *t* values increased on the coefficients on the quantity of pork per capita ($QPKC_i$), but were diminished on the other independent variables.

This process to generate residuals with white noise may appear a bit ad hoc—and it is. However, even with the most carefully crafted fundamental model, errors in the data and in specification remain and some explanatory variables are excluded. Introducing time series analysis into the fundamentally based models to help capture those nonrandom errors can be legitimized.

INTEGRATED AUTOREGRESSIVE MOVING AVERAGE MODELS (ARIMA)

If the original data is non-stationary and must be differenced before applying the ARMA model, the resulting model is called the integrated autoregressive moving average (ARIMA) process. To illustrate this process, assume that an analyst wished to project real

TABLE 18-7 ORDINARY LEAST SQUARES EQUATION FOR PREDICTING QUARTERLY PRICES OF BARROWS AND GILTS AT 6-7 MAJOR MARKETS, DEFLATED BY THE CPI (1982–1984 = 1.00); INITIAL FORMULATION INCORPORATING AN ARMA PROCESS ON THE RESIDUALS

SMPL Range: 1963.1–1993.4
Number of Observations: 124
Convergence Achieved After 10 Iterations

Variable	Coefficient	Std. Error	T-Stat.	2-Tail Sig.
C	125.21279	40.708327	3.0758520	0.0027
DVQ2	20.369708	9.8764429	2.0624539	0.0417
DVQ3	30.981712	10.625206	2.9158692	0.0044
DVQ4	−3.4490169	9.2473519	−0.3729735	0.7099
QPKC1	−5.2340459	0.6594372	−7.9371412	0.0000
QPKC2	−6.6731223	0.7188626	−9.2828895	0.0000
QPKC3	−7.3158705	0.6970816	−10.494999	0.0000
QPKC4	−4.7113225	0.5490419	−8.5809893	0.0000
SPKSUBC	−0.6149854	0.6197371	−0.9923327	0.3234
DICD	0.0050844	0.0035675	1.4252113	0.1571
TO76	−0.0265294	0.2317985	−0.1144503	0.9091
AFT76	−1.3611759	0.3127815	−4.3518426	0.0000
AFT76SQ	0.0082484	0.0047265	1.7451568	0.0839
MA(1)	0.0350862	0.1219675	0.2876687	0.7742
MA(4)	−0.1285394	0.1359339	−0.9456022	0.3466
MA(5)	−0.2505056	0.1235407	−2.0277182	0.0452
MA(6)	−0.4080057	0.1126249	−3.6226967	0.0005
AR(1)	0.6381979	0.0924585	6.9025299	0.0000
AR(4)	0.3821801	0.1319672	2.8960233	0.0046
AR(5)	−0.3288324	0.1603313	−2.0509562	0.0428
AR(6)	0.1185656	0.1331443	0.8905047	0.3753

R-squared	0.955836	Mean of dependent var	55.39483
Adjusted R-squared	0.947260	S.D. of dependent var	17.06329
S.E. of regression	3.918610	Sum of squared resid	1581.617
Log likelihood	−333.7955	F-statistic	111.4602
Durbin-Watson stat	1.920142	Prob (F-statistic)	0.080000

SMPL Range: 1963.1–1993.4
Number of Observations: 124

Autocorrelations	Partial Autocorrelation		ac	pac
. | .	. | .	1	0.030	0.030
.*| .	.*| .	2	−0.045	−0.046
.*| .	.*| .	3	−0.060	−0.057
. | .	. | .	4	0.029	0.031
. | .	. | .	5	0.021	0.014
. |*.	. |*.	6	0.054	0.053
.*| .	.*| .	7	−0.062	−0.061
.*| .	.*| .	8	−0.055	−0.046
.*| .	.*| .	9	−0.075	−0.073
. |*.	. |*.	10	0.085	0.076
.*| .	.*| .	11	−0.051	−0.068
**| .	**| .	12	−0.160	0.160
. | .	. | .	13	−0.037	0.013
. |*.	. | .	14	0.047	0.031
**| .	***| .	15	−0.171	−0.201
. |*.	. |*.	16	0.066	0.070

Box-Pierce Q-Stat	11.88	Prob	0.7521	SE of Correlations	0.090
Ljung-Box Q-Stat	13.33	Prob	0.6487		

TABLE 18-8 ORDINARY LEAST SQUARES EQUATION FOR PREDICTING QUARTERLY PRICES OF BARROWS AND GILTS AT 6-7 MAJOR MARKETS, DEFLATED BY THE CPI (1982–1984 = 1.00); FINAL FORMULATION INCORPORATING AN ARMA PROCESS ON THE RESIDUALS

SMPL Range: 1963.1–1993.4
Number of Observations: 124
Convergence Achieved After 16 Iterations

Variable	Coefficient	Std. Error	T-Stat.	2-Tail Sig.
C	147.99931	33.114030	4.4693838	0.0000
DVQ2	9.9131984	9.5909630	1.0335978	0.3037
DVQ3	23.165054	9.8332126	2.3557971	0.0203
DVQ4	−3.9226863	8.4452354	−0.4644851	0.6433
QPKC1	−6.4078489	0.5506376	−11.637144	0.0000
QPKC2	−7.2103736	0.6190738	−11.647034	0.0000
QPKC3	−7.9969691	0.6026368	−13.269964	0.0000
QPKC4	−5.7374106	0.4694797	−12.220785	0.0000
SPKSUBC	−0.9115811	0.5569426	−1.6367595	0.1047
DICD	0.0055407	0.0029285	1.8919944	0.0612
TO76	−0.0868676	0.1690526	−0.5138495	0.6084
AFT76	−1.2919282	0.1568895	−8.2346399	0.0000
AFT76SQ	0.0066948	0.0027284	2.4537414	0.0158
MA(6)	−0.1321241	0.0790904	−1.6705451	0.0978
MA(12)	−0.3534549	0.0718774	−4.9174719	0.0000
MA(15)	−0.4514368	0.0688332	−6.5584123	0.0000
AR(1)	0.6015841	0.0693047	8.6802782	0.0000
AR(4)	0.4209480	0.0831606	5.0618683	0.0000
AR(5)	−0.4725625	0.0814783	−5.7998550	0.0000

R-squared	0.962511	Mean of dependent var	55.39483
Adjusted R-squared	0.956085	S.D. of dependent var	17.06329
S.E. of regression	3.575779	Sum of squared resid	1342.551
Log likelihood	−323.6352	F-statistic	149.7693
Durbin-Watson stat	1.823803	Prob (F-statistic)	0.080000

SMPL Range: 1963.1–1993.4
Number of Observations: 124

Autocorrelations	Partial Autocorrelation		ac	pac
. |*.	. |*.	1	0.075	0.075
. | .	. | .	2	−0.005	−0.011
.*| .	.*| .	3	−0.075	−0.074
.*| .	.*| .	4	−0.099	−0.089
.*| .	.*| .	5	−0.053	−0.041
.*| .	.*| .	6	−0.044	−0.045
. |*.	. |*.	7	0.062	0.055
. | .	. | .	8	0.031	0.007
. | .	. | .	9	−0.008	−0.025
. |*.	. |*.	10	0.058	0.059
**| .	**| .	11	−0.139	0.142
. |*.	. |*.	12	0.048	0.076
. | .	. | .	13	0.036	0.038
. | .	.*| .	14	−0.022	−0.042
. |*.	. |*.	15	0.105	0.104
. |*.	. |*.	16	0.094	0.092

Box-Pierce Q-Stat	9.60	Prob	0.8869	SE of Correlations	0.090
Ljung-Box Q-Stat	10.57	Prob	0.8352		

disposable income per capita (DICD) three years into the future with a time series model. In Table 18-2, the Augmented Dickey-Fuller test failed to reject the existence of a unit root, suggesting that DICD was non-stationary—but the first difference of DICD did appear stationary from the test. The first difference of DICD became the variable subjected to a check on its autocorrelations.

In the judgment of this author, one might want to look back as far as 10 years (40 quarters) to discern patterns in macroeconomic variables such as consumer income to pick up cyclical effects. An examination of the direct and partial autocorrelations indicated significant relationships at 26 to 28 quarter lags. Not knowing whether this was an autoregressive process or a moving average process, the following least squares equations were estimated for the period 1963.1 to 1993.4:

$$(14) \quad D(DICD) = 39 + \underset{(.286)}{.00476}\, AR(28) \qquad \bar{R}^2 = -.00874$$

$$(15) \quad D(DICD) = 41 + \underset{(37.835)}{.87092}\, MA(28) \qquad \bar{R}^2 = .21623$$

where: D(DICD) = the first difference of DICD

AR(28) = an autoregressive process of order 28

MA(28) = a moving average process of order 28

Numbers in parentheses are *t* values.

Obviously, the autocorrelation reflected a moving average process. When the residuals from equation (15) were subjected to the autocorrelation test, a significant relationship remained for a one-quarter lag. The next step was to add AR(1) to equation (15) which formed an ARIMA (1,1,28) model. The first term is the order of the autoregressive component, the second term is the number of times DICD was differenced, and the 28 is the order of the moving average component. The results were as follows:

$$(16) \quad D(DICD) = 41 + \underset{(37.121)}{.872}\, MA(28) + \underset{(2.635)}{.205}\, AR(1) \qquad \bar{R}^2 = .26147$$

For the 28-quarter lag period, the probability of observing a Q-value equal to or greater than the calculated value, given the null hypothesis of white noise being true, is .569 by the Box-Pierce Q-Statistic and .354 by the Ljung-Box Q-Statistic. Further refinement of this time series analysis could be pursued, but this illustrates the essence of the procedure. Figure 18-1 compares the estimated values with actual values for DICD in 1963.1 to 1993.4 and shows the forecast for 1994.1 to 1996.4.

In modeling efforts when the analyst needs to project an exogenous variable, but has no alternatives, ARMA or ARIMA procedures may suffice. Obviously, such methods should be used with care and normally secondary to or in conjunction with existing fundamentally based forecasts from authoritative sources.

FIGURE 18-1 Real disposable income per capita (1982–1984 $) estimated and projected by an ARIMA Model (1,1,28).

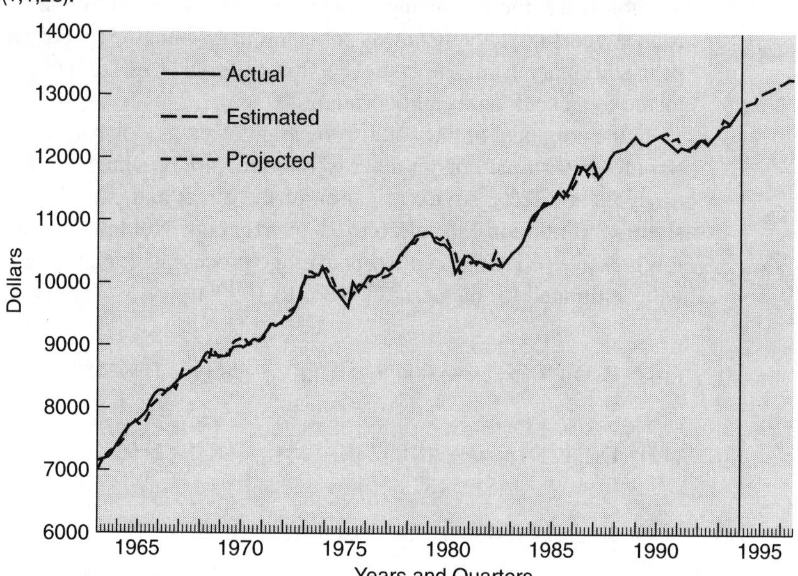

UNIVARIATE FORECASTING WITH TIME SERIES MODELS

As demonstrated with DICD, time series models can be quite useful in capturing past patterns in economic variables and projecting those variables into the future. By necessity, modelers must resort to ad hoc methods to project exogenous variables when fundamental models incorporating these variables are missing. In the very short-run, even fundamental analysis is often deficient in providing accurate forecasts.

Frequent reference to the use of the variable TIME as an independent variable in regression analysis embodies the acceptance that simple trends can contribute useful information to forecasting. In Chapter 9, the value of double exponential smoothing was featured as a means to track non-linear trends and extend them into the future (linearly) with heavier weights on recent changes. Chapter 14 on seasonals is basically time series analysis incorporating some techniques not generally covered in texts on time series. Chapter 17 on technical analysis carried the same philosophy behind time series analysis—how to extract information from price behavior in the past to generate forecasts.

In addition, time series analysis can provide some new dimensions into forecasting in which fundamental analysis is implicit, but not explicit. Suppose, for example, that the only data available were quarterly averages on the farm price of onions (FPON) and the Consumer Price Index (CPI). You need to forecast FPON 10 quarters into the future. You have very limited time and resources to generate these forecasts and therefore cannot construct a fundamental supply-demand model. What might you do drawing on the basics of time series analysis?

You would not necessarily ignore what you know about the onion industry. First of all, you would incorporate the fact that onion production is very seasonal with peak production in the late summer and early fall. Second, you might presume that onion growers will respond with their plantings directly related to prices received the year before. With this knowledge you might first construct a model with dummy constants for each quarter, expecting negative signs on the third and fourth quarters relative to the constant for the equation that represents the first quarter. Second, you would deflate FPON by the CPI to form the deflated variable FPOND as the dependent variable and FPOND(−4) as an independent variable, i.e., the deflated farm price of onions four quarters earlier. You would expect the sign on FPOND(−4) to be negative, indicating the price impact of the direct relationship between plantings in the current quarter and FPOND a year earlier.

The results of the regression with this formulation for 1972.1 to 1991.4 are presented in Table 18-9. The signs on the coefficients were as expected, but only on DVQ4 (dummy variable for the fourth quarter) was the effect significant at the five percent level. The $\bar{R}^2$ was quite low and the Durbin-Watson (D-W) statistic indicated serious serial correlation

TABLE 18-9 EQUATION 1 FOR PREDICTING QUARTERLY AVERAGE FARM PRICES ON ONIONS DEFLATED BY THE CPI (1982–1984 = 1.00), WITH MEASUREMENT OF AUTOCORRELATION ON THE RESIDUALS

SMPL Range: 1972.1–1991.4
Number of Observations: 80

Variable	Coefficient	Std. Error	T-Stat.	2-Tail Sig.
C	16.228824	1.9938370	8.1394938	0.0000
DVQ2	0.8138510	1.6881781	0.4820884	0.6311
DVQ3	−1.6492018	1.6940531	−0.9735243	0.3334
DVQ4	−3.7669986	1.7232884	−2.1859363	0.0319
FPOND(-4)	−0.1537530	0.1137478	−1.3517009	0.1805

R-squared	0.101247	Mean of dependent var	13.06819
Adjusted R-squared	0.053314	S.D. of dependent var	5.482708
S.E. of regression	5.334554	Sum of squared resid	2134.310
Log likelihood	−244.8700	F-statistic	2.112245
Durbin-Watson stat	0.727915	Prob (F-statistic)	0.087591

SMPL Range: 1972.1–1991.4
Number of Observations: 80

<table>
<tr><th>Autocorrelations</th><th>Partial Autocorrelation</th><th></th><th>ac</th><th>pac</th></tr>
<tr><td>.|********</td><td>. |********</td><td>1</td><td>0.627</td><td>0.627</td></tr>
<tr><td>.|****</td><td>.**|</td><td>2</td><td>0.294</td><td>−0.165</td></tr>
<tr><td>.|** .</td><td>. |**.</td><td>3</td><td>0.191</td><td>0.135</td></tr>
<tr><td>.| .</td><td>****| .</td><td>4</td><td>−0.022</td><td>−0.300</td></tr>
<tr><td>.| .</td><td>. |*****</td><td>5</td><td>0.021</td><td>0.354</td></tr>
<tr><td>.| .</td><td>. | .</td><td>6</td><td>0.176</td><td>0.006</td></tr>
<tr><td>.| .</td><td>. *| .</td><td>7</td><td>0.096</td><td>−0.080</td></tr>
<tr><td>.| .</td><td>. | .</td><td>8</td><td>0.063</td><td>0.003</td></tr>
</table>

Box-Pierce Q-Stat	44.91	Prob	0.0000	SE of Correlations	0.112
Ljung-Box Q-Stat	47.06	Prob	0.0000		

problems in the residuals. The section of the table on direct and partial autocorrelations pointed to high correlations in one quarter lagged and to the likely absence of white noise in the residuals.

This being the case, first-order autoregression and moving average procedures were incorporated with the results shown in Table 18-10. Both MA(1) and AR(1) were highly significant and they enhanced the *t* values on the independent variables. The $\bar{R}^2$ was raised to .483, and the D-W statistic suggested that the serial correlation problem was eliminated. However, the residuals still did not display white noise, and the autocorrelations, at lags 3 and 6, need to be examined.

These lag terms were included in equation (3), presented in Table 18-11, by adding

TABLE 18-10 EQUATION 2 FOR PREDICTING QUARTERLY AVERAGE FARM PRICES ON ONIONS DEFLATED BY THE CPI (1982–1984 = 1.00), WITH MEASUREMENT OF AUTOCORRELATION ON THE RESIDUALS

SMPL Range: 1972.1–1991.4
Number of Observations: 80
Convergence achieved after 7 iterations

Variable	Coefficient	Std. Error	T-Stat.	2-Tail Sig.
C	19.667930	1.7944328	10.960528	0.0000
DVQ2	0.9701368	1.0318569	0.9401854	0.3502
DVQ3	−1.9725261	1.1640135	−1.6945904	0.0944
DVQ4	−4.4968808	1.0804285	−4.1621272	0.0001
FPOND(-4)	−0.4009825	0.1068436	−3.7529863	0.0003
MA(1)	0.5720703	0.1011541	5.6554334	0.0000
AR(1)	0.4036283	0.0907364	4.4483609	0.0000

R-squared	0.522134	Mean of dependent var	13.06819
Adjusted R-squared	0.482857	S.D. of dependent var	5.482708
S.E. of regression	3.942761	Sum of squared resid	1134.812
Log likelihood	−219.6029	F-statistic	13.29373
Durbin-Watson stat	2.152888	Prob (F-statistic)	0.080000

SMPL Range: 1972.1–1991.4
Number of Observations: 80

Autocorrelations	Partial Autocorrelation		ac	pac
. *| .	. *| .	1	−0.086	−0.086
. | .	. | .	2	−0.016	−0.024
. |****	. | ***	3	0.270	0.268
. *| .	. | .	4	−0.053	−0.008
. *| .	. *| .	5	−0.072	−0.079
. |****	. | ***	6	0.323	0.261
. | .	. | * .	7	0.008	0.078
.**| .	. **| .	8	−0.182	−0.179

Box-Pierce Q-Stat	18.06	Prob	0.0208	SE of Correlations	0.112
Ljung-Box Q-Stat	19.79	Prob	0.0112		

TABLE 18-11 EQUATION 3 FOR PREDICTING QUARTERLY AVERAGE FARM PRICES ON ONIONS DEFLATED BY THE CPI (1982–1984 = 1.00)

SMPL Range: 1972.3–1991.4
Number of Observations: 78
Convergence Achieved After 7 Iterations

Variable	Coefficient	Std. Error	T-Stat.	2-Tail Sig.
C	17.087618	1.8793860	9.9091278	0.0000
DVQ2	0.9633731	0.9909674	0.9721541	0.3345
DVQ3	−1.7162039	1.1515875	−1.4902939	0.1408
DVQ4	−3.6994212	1.0429486	−3.5470790	0.0007
FPOND(-4)	−0.2470986	0.1183796	−2.0873405	0.0407
MA(1)	0.3705730	0.0581540	6.3722683	0.0000
MA(3)	0.2088206	0.0696513	2.9980856	0.0038
MA(6)	0.6867436	0.0481503	14.262509	0.0000
AR(1)	0.4789521	0.0858198	5.5809029	0.0000
AR(3)	−0.0501977	0.1084317	−0.4629430	0.6649
AR(6)	−0.1338994	0.0837706	−1.3596588	0.1785

R-squared	0.625560	Mean of dependent var	13.10133
Adjusted R-squared	0.569673	S.D. of dependent var	5.543940
S.E. of regression	3.636787	Sum of squared resid	886.1567
Log likelihood	−205.4544	F-statistic	11.19337
Durbin-Watson stat	2.055647	Prob (F-statistic)	0.000000

SMPL Range: 1972.1–1991.4
Number of Observations: 80

Autocorrelations	Partial Autocorrelation		ac	pac
. | .	. | .	1	−0.018	−0.018
. |* .	. |* .	2	0.050	0.050
. | .	. | .	3	0.003	0.004
***| .	***| .	4	−0.209	−0.212
. | .	. | .	5	−0.010	−0.018
***| .	***| .	6	−0.231	−0.219
. |** .	. |** .	7	0.155	0.163
.**| .	***| .	8	−0.156	−0.206

Box-Pierce Q-Stat	11.88	Prob	0.1566	SE of Correlations	0.112
Ljung-Box Q-Stat	13.14	Prob	0.1071		

MA(3), MA(6), AR(3), and AR(6) to equation (2). The *t* values were generally reduced, but the $\bar{R}^2$ was increased. However, the impacts of AR(3) and AR(6) were not significant. Therefore, in equation 4, as shown in Table 18-12, AR(3) and AR(6) were dropped. The *t* values improved and the $\bar{R}^2$ remained about the same at .565. The probability of white noise was enhanced. The remaining notable autocorrelation was at a lag of eight quarters.

After exploring additional combinations of AR and MA, the conclusion was reached that the AR processes were more effective in capturing the shorter-term lags, and the MA

TABLE 18-12 EQUATION 4 FOR PREDICTING QUARTERLY AVERAGE FARM PRICES ON ONIONS DEFLATED BY THE CPI (1982–1984 = 1.00), WITH MEASUREMENT OF AUTOCORRELATION ON THE RESIDUALS

SMPL Range: 1972.1–1991.4
Number of Observations: 80
Convergence Achieved After 6 Iterations

Variable	Coefficient	Std. Error	T-Stat.	2-Tail Sig
C	18.052761	1.6866315	10.703442	0.0000
DVQ2	0.8183544	0.9280454	0.8818043	0.3809
DVQ3	–1.8949574	1.0519539	–1.8005137	0.0760
DVQ4	–4.0238664	0.9769720	–4.1187119	0.0001
FPOND(-4)	–0.3053830	0.1010900	–3.0209015	0.0035
MA(1)	0.4243286	0.1001702	4.2360782	0.0001
MA(3)	0.2861192	0.1035431	2.7632849	0.0073
MA(6)	0.4395443	0.0907299	4.8445377	0.0000
AR(1)	0.4504124	0.0850143	5.2980751	0.0000

R-squared	0.608685	Mean of dependent var	13.06819
Adjusted R-squared	0.564593	S.D. of dependent var	5.482708
S.E. of regression	3.617786	Sum of squared resid	929.2746
Log likelihood	–211.6102	F-statistic	13.80492
Durbin-Watson stat	1.880596	Prob (F-statistic)	0.080000

SMPL Range: 1972.1–1991.4
Number of Observations: 80

Autocorrelations	Partial Autocorrelation		ac	pac
| • | • |	• | • |	1	0.035	0.035
| • |* • |	• |* • |	2	0.046	0.045
| • *| • |	• *| • |	3	–0.067	–0.071
| •**| • |	•**| • |	4	–0.162	–0.161
| • *| • |	• *| • |	5	–0.109	–0.096
| • *|* • |	• | • |	6	–0.040	–0.026
| • | • |	• | • |	7	0.046	0.038
| ***| • |	***| • |	8	–0.197	–0.244

Box-Pierce Q-Stat	7.09	Prob	0.5274	SE of Correlations	0.112
Ljung-Box Q-Stat	7.84	Prob	0.4491		

the longer-term lags. The end product is presented as equation 5 in Table 18-13. The signs on the independent variables are as expected with the coefficient on FPOND(–4) highly significant. The $\bar{R}^2$ improved to .614 and the D-W indicates no serial correlation problem. None of the autocorrelations were highly significant and the probability of white noise was further increased.

The equations on FPOND were based on data for 1972.1 to 1991.4, allowing for a test period in 1992.1 to 1994.2 to check the ability of the model to forecast. The performance

TABLE 18-13 EQUATION 5 FOR PREDICTING QUARTERLY AVERAGE FARM PRICES ON ONIONS DEFLATED BY THE CPI (1982–1984 = 1.00), WITH MEASUREMENT OF AUTOCORRELATION ON THE RESIDUALS

SMPL Range: 1972.1–1991.4
Number of Observations: 80
Convergence Achieved After 6 Iterations

Variable	Coefficient	Std. Error	T-Stat.	2-Tail Sig.
C	23.381927	2.7182415	8.6018578	0.0000
DVQ2	1.3041331	2.6822309	0.4862121	0.6283
DVQ3	−2.0979536	1.2516534	−1.6761458	0.0982
DVQ4	−5.2171316	2.5470134	−2.0483330	0.0443
FPOND(-4)	−0.6615374	0.1095561	−6.0383437	0.0000
MA(6)	0.3328476	0.0910989	3.6536975	0.0005
MA(8)	−0.6181557	0.0955023	−6.4726768	0.0000
AR(1)	0.8516921	0.0949442	8.9704453	0.0000
AR(2)	−0.3223319	0.1265474	−2.5471247	0.0131
AR(3)	0.2936599	0.1126834	2.6060629	0.0112

R-squared	0.658145	Mean of dependent var	13.06819
Adjusted R-squared	0.614193	S.D. of dependent var	5.482708
S.E. of regression	3.405496	Sum of squared resid	811.8183
Log likelihood	−206.2051	F-statistic	14.97393
Durbin-Watson stat	1.873489	Prob (F-statistic)	0.000000

SMPL Range: 1972.1–1991.4
Number of Observations: 80

Autocorrelations	Partial Autocorrelation		ac	pac
| . |* .	| . |* .	| 1	0.062	0.062
| . |* .	| . |* .	| 2	0.066	0.062
| . | .	| . | .	| 3	0.035	0.028
| . | .	| . | .	| 4	0.028	0.021
| . *| .	| . *| .	| 5	−0.091	−0.099
| . *| .	| . *| .	| 6	−0.054	−0.048
| . | .	| . | .	| 7	−0.025	−0.009
| . |** .	| . |** .	| 8	0.144	0.162

Box-Pierce Q-Stat	3.43	Prob	0.9046	SE of Correlations	0.112
Ljung-Box Q-Stat	3.79	Prob	0.8752		

of equation 5 in tracking the historical period and forecasting in 1992.1 to 1994.2 is charted in Figure 18-2. The tracking over 1973.1 to 1991.4 was credible and reasonable for the forecast period except for the final quarter in which prices touched an extreme low.

The conclusion from this example is that formulations of univariate equations should incorporate as much information about the market as can be assembled. Once this is done, exploration with AR, MA, ARMA, or ARIMA models can appreciably enhance the predictive power of such equations.

FIGURE 18-2 Real farm price of onions (1982–1984 $) estimated by a univariate equation with ARMA (1,2,3; 6,8).

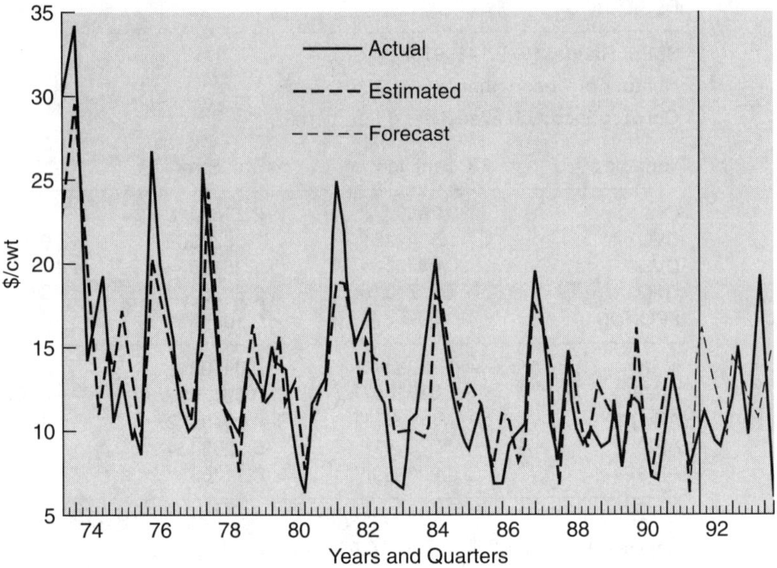

SUMMARY

Time series analysis is a tool that is most appropriate for short-term forecasting. The most promising role for this technique is to improve the forecasting performance of quarterly structural models or those with a database of even a higher frequency, i.e., monthly or weekly models. While the approach is somewhat ad hoc, time series analysis provides a convenient means to capture information from historical data not measured by traditional regression equations. Alternatively, pure time series models have value themselves for forecasting and providing a standard to evaluate fundamental econometric/simulation models.

QUESTIONS FOR STUDY

1 What is the similarity between technical analysis and time series models?
2 How would you define "white noise"?
3 What is the relationship between the Dickey-Fuller and Engle-Granger Co-integration tests?
4 Do you perceive lack of "stationarity" to be a major problem with variables used in econometric analysis? Why or why not?
5 An equation exhibiting an AR(1) relationship in the residuals is non-linear and presents problems for OLS estimation. Explain. Describe the Hildreth-Lu technique for handling this problem.
6 Describe the difference between autoregressive models and moving average models.
7 Describe the difference between ARMA and ARIMA models.

8 Why is the procedure for determining the appropriate model for mapping the error term in a structural equation called "ad hoc"?

9 Discuss how to use strictly time series analysis to generate projections of exogenous variables to be included in an econometric model.

10 Assume that the only data you have about a product are quarterly average prices. You know that the production is highly seasonal and that the lag between farmers' decisions on how much to produce and when the product is on the market is one year. How would you develop a model to predict prices using what you know about the industry?

19

SOURCES OF AGRICULTURAL DATA AND MARKET ANALYSIS

POINTS:

1. Data and analysis in the context of a decision-making framework.
2. How the USDA collects data; their sampling error.
3. How census data and other non-annual data can be interpolated for annual models.
4. Differences between USDA's "crop and livestock estimates" and "market news."
5. Major sources of agricultural market analysis and outlook.
6. Role of private sector in monitoring and analyzing agricultural data.
7. Potential for electronic transmission.

No matter how sophisticated the tools for agricultural commodity market analysis may become—from ordinary least squares to time series techniques—accuracy of the basic data is paramount. But even accurate data without the input of those who can interpret the statistics can be sterile. The extensive database for U.S. and world agriculture, in combination with professional analysts and other users of this information, can be viewed as components of a large system. A schematic of such a system is illustrated in Figure 19-1.

The focal point is the decision maker (person or group) who establishes goals and objectives for a firm, institution, or government agency. The decision maker has the means to take action to achieve those goals and objectives. But for the system to operate efficiently, the results of those actions need to be monitored and interpreted for the decision

FIGURE 19-1 Schematic for a decision-making framework.

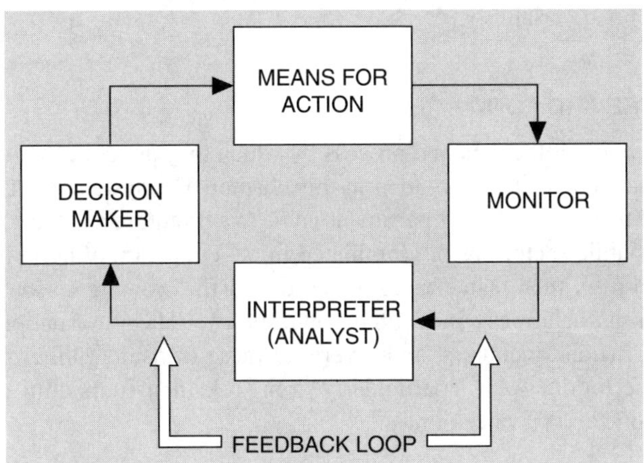

maker, if not *by* the decision maker. This "feedback loop" enables the decision makers to take corrective action in a timely fashion if necessary. The combination of monitor and interpreter (analyst) should provide advance warning to the decision maker if the unit is not heading toward the goals and objectives.

This system approach highlights the importance of developing databases with analysts and ultimate users in mind. Recognizing this, the USDA has solicited recommendations from users over the years (Good et al., 1985). Agriculture and the food sector have somewhat unique demands on information systems because of the biological lag; dominating influences from weather, pests and diseases; the perishable nature of the product; and the large number of decision makers involved, particularly the farmers.

Action of an individual farmer, who would typically represent only a minuscule portion of total output, will not affect the market, but the collective action will. This is an example of why the government has played a central role in collecting, analyzing, and disseminating agricultural data and information. Each farmer needs to know what other farmers are doing, but lacks the resources to collect and analyze such information.

Data that are particularly valuable are those that can be classified as leading indicators. An example of such statistics is cow slaughter. This is a key indicator of whether cattle producers are building or liquidating herds. Farmers' intentions are also being monitored for such activities as planting, having sows farrow, marketing cattle from feedlots, etc. During the growing season, yield projections on crops are generated from objective techniques and subjective input as well.

A purpose of such information is to provide advance warning of possible over- or under-production in time for some decision makers to modify their plans to dampen the prospective change. In doing so, the final result may differ from the earlier intentions, which is one of the purposes of leading indicators. Another purpose is to help decision makers prepare for an eventuality that cannot be dodged. For example, processors may need to plan ahead for over- or under-production in a way that may help dampen the upcoming price variability.

MONITORS IN AGRICULTURE AND FOOD

A description of the data and process by which they are collected is complex and only a brief treatment will be provided in this chapter. The system itself is continually evolving. The focus is on data of particular value to agriculture and the food system in the U.S.

The public sector has predominated in the collection of agricultural data. However, in some areas, such as in crop estimates during the growing season, several private firms and trade associations conduct their own surveys. This information is made available to their clients and members, and several of these firms do publicize their estimates. The private sector does play a particularly strong role in disseminating agricultural data from both public and private sources.

Crop and Livestock Estimates, General Farm Statistics

Initially, federal and later state governments were primarily responsible for collecting agricultural data. Congress gave the U.S. Patent Office $1,000 in 1839 to "collect statistics and distribute seeds" (Caudill, 1988). In 1863, the U.S. Department of Agriculture (USDA) issued its first crop report. Since the early part of the twentieth century, most of the states have cooperated with the federal government in the monitoring function.

Most crop and livestock estimates originate with the USDA and 44 field offices serving all the states. The federal unit has been the National Agricultural Statistics Service (NASS). Sample surveys provide the information for most of the estimates. Survey contacts are made by mail, personal interviews, and in-the-field counts and measurements of growing crops (Caudill, 1988). Estimates are obtained by various combinations of:

1 Mail questionnaires to farmers and others close to the industry.
2 Probability sampling, using area frames, list frames, and multiple frames.
3 Enumerative surveys in June and December.
4 Objective yield measurements.
5 Remote sensing by satellites.

In the area frames, farmers living in randomly selected land segments (averaging about a mile square) are surveyed. While such segments represent less than one percent of all the land area in the 48 contiguous states, representative information on the nation's agriculture can be obtained. The sampling from list frames simply involves randomly selecting names from a list of known producers. The multiple frame is a combination of the application of area and list frames.

Using area frames, NASS conducts a major survey each June at which time field interviewers contact all farmers in about 11,600 area segments for a first-hand view of their activities. Sampling errors on major items average about 4 to 8 percent on a state basis and 1 to 2 percent at the national level. A sampling error of 2 percent implies that there is a 95-percent probability that the estimate is within 2 percent of the result obtained from a survey of the entire population (Caudill, 1988).

The June enumeration collects data on crop acreages, number of farms and land in farms, livestock inventories, pigs farrowed, calves born, economic data, farm labor, and other agricultural items for state, regional, and national estimates. The December survey covers a sub-sample of the area frame farms visited in June, combined with extensive list samples to estimate livestock inventories and production, and acres seeded to fall grain crops.

Objective yield measurements are taken monthly through the growing season on most crops. In a recent season, sample plots were monitored in 1,900 typical corn and soybean fields in major producing states.

Information gathered from satellites complements that collected by enumerators on the ground. With reasonable accuracy, the equipment can identify crops and planted acreage.

Surveys of agribusinesses also contribute to the fund of information in the federal–state system. For example, questionnaires are distributed monthly to grain elevators to obtain prices they pay farmers. This provides a base for calculating the average price received by farmers for crops for each month in each state. This information, in combination with sales data, enables NASS to estimate gross income from marketings.

NASS regularly checks estimates against subsequent information and will revise the estimates if necessary. For example, data on federally inspected slaughter of livestock are regarded as very accurate statistics. This provides a means for revising estimates of livestock on farms and marketings. Also, the Census of Agriculture conducted about every five years by the U.S. Department of Agriculture provides benchmark numbers.

The major series generated by NASS include area planted, area harvested, yield, production, and stocks on crops; and inventory, births, and marketings on livestock. Inventories on livestock are mainly estimated once or twice per year with some species in some states on a more frequent basis (hogs and cattle on feed). Production figures on milk and eggs are tabulated monthly. Livestock slaughter numbers are actually available on a daily basis and normally published as weekly and monthly totals.

The USDA also collects and publishes a substantial amount of other statistics. This includes farm financial data; prices paid as well as received by farmers; land values; enterprise costs of production; land in farms and number of farms; farm employment and wage rates; food consumption, prices and expenditures; and foreign agricultural trade.

For many years the USDA adjusted their crop and livestock estimates to the Census of Agriculture taken approximately at five-year intervals by the USDC. This was because the Census took a complete enumeration until 1969 providing detailed information as localized as townships. Since 1969, each Census has been primarily conducted by mail and has continued to tabulate even very localized township data. While coverage is broad in the Census, NASS has not revised their estimates to the Census in an identical fashion. The Census data has become one piece of information in the revision process.

Applying the Census and Other Non-Annual Data

The Census of Agriculture provides a snapshot of U.S. agriculture at points in time that can be very valuable for analysts who rely heavily on annual data. For one, the Census provides much more detail on the structure of agriculture than do annual estimates—information such as the concentration of production by size of unit, characteristics of operator in terms of age, employment off the farm, equity position, ethnic background, etc. Second, procedures are available to incorporate Census data in time series analysis requiring annual numbers.

For example, an analyst feels strongly that structural change has affected supply relationships in an agricultural industry and wants to capture this change in an OLS equation. The U.S. hog industry is a case in point. The Censuses of Agriculture in 1978, 1982, 1987, and 1992 indicated a rapid shift to fewer farms with hogs but with much larger volumes being sold from the remaining farms. Also, the hog industry has shifted dramatically to mega-operations in North Carolina (Figures 19-2 and 19-3). Note that North Carolina became the number two hog state in 1994, second to Iowa (Figure 19-2). Also note that in 1992, over 80 percent of hogs sold in North Carolina were from farms selling 5,000 or more head per farm (Figure 19-3).

For the period from 1978 to 1992, an analyst could generate an annual variable "percent of hogs sold from farms marketing 5,000 or more hogs per year" by a linear (or nonlinear) interpolation between the Census years. Structural change tends to be monotonic and does not require "heroic assumptions" to estimate for the intercensal years. For the period prior to 1978, the analyst would have to explore other sources for this variable, since the breaking point in the earlier Census was "farms selling 1,000 and over." However, the percent of hogs from farms selling 5,000 or more hogs per year prior to 1978 was nominal and not likely a major challenge to estimate.

FIGURE 19-2 Hog production in selected states 1960 to 1994.

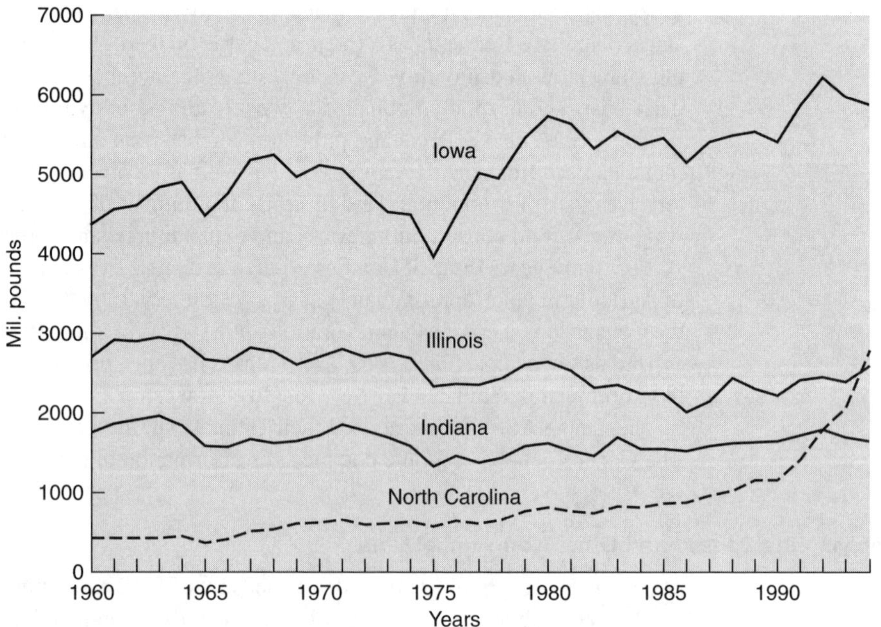

FIGURE 19-3 Percent of hogs sold from farms marketing 5,000 or more head per year.

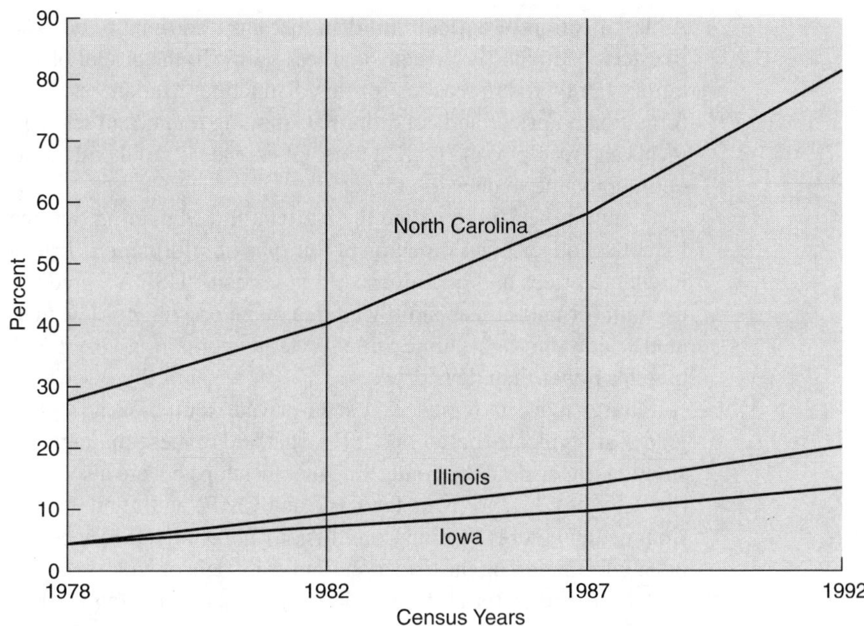

The point being made with this example on hogs is that analysts developing models with annual (or even quarterly or monthly) data should not omit key indicators just because they are not available on an annual basis. Certainly, judgment is required in the interpolation procedure but the information gained may well offset the measurement errors in the interim years.

Another example is monitoring technical change in which only sporadic surveys are available. Like structural change, technological advancement and/or its adoption tends to follow predictable patterns between observation points and can be reasonably charted.

The USDA has been maintaining a series of annual estimates of enterprise costs of production beginning in the mid 1970s on major field crops and livestock. Prior to then, such cost data were available sporadically from the USDA and Land Grant universities that would require analysts to apply interpolation procedures to construct a long time series on such costs. Also, the USDA has not estimated costs of production on fruit and vegetables and a number of minor crops. Those analysts researching such enterprises would have to generate their own time series. Some Land Grant universities have data sets on costs that are fairly complete year-by-year, but in most cases, gaps of several years exist.

Some components of production costs could be interpolated between data sets. However, inputs related to energy (fertilizer, fuels, pesticides) might require a refined procedure in which the USDA's series on "Prices Paid by Farmers" or other price indexes be incorporated in the interpolation procedure. Similarly, such costs as feed, seed, and replacement livestock should be related to the relevant price series on these inputs that, along with energy-related inputs, tend to fluctuate over time.

Market News

A classification of agricultural data that has traditionally been set apart from crop and livestock estimates is termed "market news." To the casual observer, this may seem arbitrary but there are reasons for this distinction. Market news relates to very timely information on prices and conditions at shipping points and wholesale markets, total shipments and receipts, and market tone. Of essence is rapid collection and dissemination for optimum value to decision makers.

A unit in the USDA called the Agricultural Marketing Service has been responsible for collection and dissemination of this type of information. Trained market reporters differentiate prices and quantities sold in terms of USDA's grades, providing much more useful information than simply a price range or average. The market reports are distributed widely through public and private networks in a very timely fashion, in terms of minutes rather than days or weeks.

Futures markets represent a semi-private source of agricultural prices. Deliverable grades are typically based on USDA standards. These markets are essentially private institutions in terms of the controlling memberships but are also owned by government units (the City of Chicago owns the CBT and CME) and regulated by a federal agency (the Commodity Futures Trading Commission). Other private services provide up-to-the-minute price information on these markets and daily data on volume and open interest.

The private sector performs a key role in disseminating market news, along with crop and livestock estimates, market analysis, and other agricultural information. This includes printed material and increasingly electronic transmission.

Macro-Economic, Other Data Related to Agriculture and Food

While the Census of Agriculture is a specialized source of data on agriculture, other Census reports contain information directly related to the total food and fiber system. These reports include the enumerations on population, manufacturing, wholesale trade, retail trade, and services conducted every five years or so. Of particular importance is the information on food processing contained in the Census of Manufacturers.

The USDC collects information in the interim years and publishes "County Business Patterns." This provides annual estimates on a subset of the series collected in the regular censuses.

Another function of the USDC vital to agriculture is weather monitoring and forecasting. A number of private firms are also active in this arena and provide services to customers.

Of particular value to analysts are the national income and product accounts, and other macro-economic data gathered and published regularly by the USDC in their *Survey of Current Business.* They also publish business cycle indicators, some of which are leading, some coincident, and some lagging.

In addition to USDC, the U.S. Department of Labor contributes to the database for agriculture and food, along with other sectors of the economy. This department collects both consumer and producer prices and publishes monthly indices on a large number of these items. These are known as the Consumer Price Indices and the Producer Price

Indices. For analysts concentrating on wholesale and retail market levels, these price series would be standard data sets.

International Statistics

International institutions and agencies such as the Food and Agricultural Organization (FAO) of the United Nations, the World Bank (International Monetary Fund), and the Organization for Economic Cooperation and Development (OECD) are monitoring the global scene. FAO collects balance-sheet-type information and producer prices on a large number of agricultural and food products from individual nations. The Foreign Agricultural Service (FAS) of the USDA draws from the FAO data but also screens the information. FAS has offices in many countries of the world and is in a position to evaluate the data that FAO receives from their member nations.

The International Monetary Fund maintains a substantial database on individual nations and publishes *International Financial Statistics,* which provides monthly updates on major macro-economic variables. Among other information related to agriculture, OECD has developed a set of measures of subsidization in agriculture and food. Called producer subsidy equivalents (PSE's) and consumer subsidy equivalents (CSE's), these series have provided a basis for understanding domestic farm and consumer subsidy programs and restrictions to international trade as well. This is an attempt to develop consistent measures of these subsidies that have been used in GATT negotiations and can be a basis for further efforts to remove barriers to trade.

INTERPRETERS (ANALYSTS) IN AGRICULTURE AND FOOD

While the monitoring function is almost exclusively in the public sector, the interpretation and analysis of agricultural data have been more evenly distributed between the public and private sectors. In the USDA, the analysis is concentrated in the Economic Research Service (ERS), the largest such unit for agriculture in the world. Much of the regular forecasting, however, resides with an inter-agency committee known as the World Agricultural Outlook Board (WAOB). Each month following major reports from NASS, the WAOB releases a set of balance sheets on major crops and livestock for the U.S. and for major nations outside of the U.S. Forecasts of production, utilization, and prices for the coming year are also included in these reports.

Many Land Grant universities also have extension programs in the outlook area. Agricultural economists on these faculties regularly prepare forecasts on major products, normally for a year or two into the future.

A substantial number of private firms specialize in commodity market analysis and provide outlook services to clientele for a fee. Such activities may be for very short-run time horizons, as is usually the case, or for several years into the future. Of course, agribusiness and food firms and trade associations have their own economists engaged in forecasting.

In the international arena, FAO, OECD, and the World Bank also analyze agriculture data extensively. Their forecasts and projections tend to be long-range or intermediate-range. The large-scale econometric models listed in Chapter 8, representing both public and private sources, also generate long-term forecasts.

ELECTRONIC TRANSMISSION

A large portion of U.S. agricultural sales is on farms with electronic access to very current information on markets, market outlook, weather, NASS reports, pest problems and general news related to agriculture. Data Transmission Network, an early private provider of such service (since 1984), expanded in 20 years to 75,000 subscribers with major presence in the Midwest. For example, in 2004, well over 90 percent of corn and soybean growers in the U.S. were subscribers (Data Transmission Network, 2004).

The World Wide Web has also become a predominant source of such information for farmers as well as for commodity analysts. A USDA survey in 2003 indicated that nearly half of U.S. farms in total and about three-fourths of the larger farms (sales and government payments of $250,000 or more) had access to the internet (USDA, NASS, 2003). Farms with internet access represented about two-thirds of the value of sales and governments payments. Analysts can tap into government reports as they are released and quickly interpret them for clientele. The need to obtain and retain hard copies of government reports has been diminished as archives are maintained on websites.

SUMMARY

The information system in U.S. and world agriculture is very extensive and has become more accessible through electronic transmission. Accurate and timely data are crucial to effective analysis and ultimate decision making. Information systems, including both monitoring and interpretation, need to develop with the user or decision maker in mind. The nature of agriculture poses special challenges in terms of establishing such a system that will facilitate response to consumer demands and dampen the perennial instability.

QUESTIONS FOR STUDY

1 Discuss the role of "monitors" and "interpreters" in the feedback loop of a decision-maker framework.
2 In probability sampling by the USDA, what is the difference between list frames and area frames?
3 What is meant by a sampling error of 2 percent?
4 Why doesn't NASS adjust their estimates to match the Census data?
5 What are "leading indicators" in agricultural data and why are they so labeled?
6 Why does NASS calculate average prices received by farmers?
7 The Census of Agriculture is taken about every five years. If you want to use Census data in an annual model, how would you proceed?
8 Data emanating from the USDA can be classified as "crop and livestock estimates" and "market news." In essence, what are the differences?
9 What publication or source would you check for the following information?
  a Prices received by farmers (U.S.).
  b Indices of consumer prices (U.S.).
  c Indices of general producer (wholesale) prices (U.S.).
  d Disposable personal income (U.S.).
  e Gross domestic product of individual foreign nations.
  f Producer and consumer subsidy equivalents.

g Balance sheets for agricultural commodities by nations.
h Outlook for farm prices.
i Long-term outlook for global food supplies and demands.

10 Select a commodity with which you are familiar. Can you describe the information system and how effective it is in matching supplies with demands? When is data collected on prospective production, who analyzes it in terms of implication to prices, and how and when are the forecasts relayed to producers? How do you evaluate the effectiveness of the system?

APPENDIX A

GLOSSARY OF STATISTICAL TERMS

Adjusted (corrected) coefficient of determination ($\bar{R}^2$) The coefficient of determination adjusted for degrees of freedom. This involves modifying R^2 by the number of observations less restrictions placed on the data set. These restrictions would take into account the number of independent variables as follows:

$$\bar{R}^2 = (1-R^2) * \frac{N-1}{N-k}$$

where: N = number of observations
k = number of independent variables.

Coefficient of determination (R^2) The ratio of the total variation in the dependent variable "explained" by the regression (OLS) equation. Values range from 0 to 1 with 1 denoting a perfect fit of the regression to the observations.

Degrees of freedom Such a number refers to the unrestricted data points in a set of observations being analyzed. For a regression equation with a constant and one independent variable, the degrees of freedom would equal the number of observations less two. For a regression equation with a constant and two independent variables, the degrees of freedom would be equal to the number of observations less three, etc. Consider a trivial case of an equation with a constant and a single independent variable being fit to two observations, providing no degrees of freedom.

Dependent variables Variables appearing on the left side of regression equations which register the effects of other variables in the equation called independent variables.

Durbin-Watson (dw) A popular test for serial correlation in the residuals of a regression equation. Values around 2 generally are desired in order to accept the null hypothesis of no serial correlation. Unfortunately, there are ranges of the dw statistic in which the test is indeterminant. The statistic does not apply to equations in which the lagged value of the dependent variable is an independent variable.

Heteroscedasticity A situation in which the variance of the estimated values of the dependent variable relative to actual values is not constant throughout the range of the dependent variable. The problem is that ordinary least squares places more weight on the observations with large error variances than those with small error variances. A technique to handle this problem is "weighted least squares" in which the logarithm of the squared values of the residuals is regressed on variables that may be associated with heteroscedasticity.

Independent variables Variables appearing on the right side of regression equations which are designed to explain "variation in the dependent variable."

Kurtosis A characteristic of a frequency distribution denoting the extent to which the curve is "peaked" in the neighborhood of the mode. This also translates to thickness of the tails of the distribution. While difficult to measure, a "moment-ratio" has been applied with the value of 3 as standard for a normal distribution.

Multicollinearity A situation in which a linear relationship exists between independent variables in a regression equation. The coefficients on these variables are indeterminant. Properly, a single example of a correlation between two independent variables would be called collinearity and the presence of several would be multicollinearity.

Normality A term associated with the characteristics of a "normal distribution." A normal distribution is generated from a series of observations of a variable influenced only by a large number of random events, each of which represents a small portion of the total observations.

Ordinary Least Squares (OLS) regression equation A popular analytical tool for relating a variable (called dependent) to one or more independent (explanatory) variables. A line representing that relationship is positioned so that the sum of squares of the differences between the line and actual observations of the dependent variable is minimized. The line is expressed as an equation, i.e.,

$$y = a + b_1 x_1 + b_2 x_2 + \ldots b_k x_k$$

where: y is the dependent variable, the x_is are independent variables, a is the constant, and b_is are the coefficients being estimated.

Regression equation Equations fitted statistically to data. Ordinary least squares is the common technique in estimating regression equations.

Serial correlation in the residuals A situation in which the residuals in a regression equation for a given time period (i.e., year, quarter, month) are related to the residuals in the previous time period. The Durbin Watson (dw) statistic is employed to test for the existence of serial correlation.

Skewness A characteristic of a frequency distribution displaying a lack of symmetry about its mean. A normal distribution would have zero skewness.

Specification errors Problems associated with the design of a regression equation which may be attributed to the choice of independent variables, omission of independent variables, or choice of the functional form of the equation.

Standard error of the regression The square root of the sum of squares of the residuals in a regression equation divided by the number of observations less the number of restrictions on the data set. The number of restrictions would include the constant and the number of independent variables. To compare performance of different equations, dividing the standard error of the regression by the mean of the dependent variable provides a common measure.

Structural parameters The framework of supply-demand models. Econometric analysis is applied in estimating such parameters which measure behavioral relationships in supply and demand.

t values These numbers refer to the "t" distribution used to test whether the value for a coefficient in a regression equation is significantly different than zero (or some prescribed number). The "t" distribution approaches the normal distribution for large sample sizes, but has fatter tails than the normal for samples of around 30 or less. For a 5 percent significance test, absolute values of around 2 are standard.

APPENDIX **B**

A NOTE ON INDEXES

As mentioned several times in the book, particularly chapters 2 through 6, indices are important variables for econometricians, particularly for deflation purposes. For this reason, a brief review and commentary on their construction and use is appended here. As described in Chapter 3, the Consumer Price Index (CPI) is weighted by a fixed bundle of goods and services in some base period—at this writing, 1982–1984. This is known as the Laspeyres Index, with the following formula:

$$\text{Laspeyres Index} = \left(\frac{\sum_{i=1}^{n} p_{ti} q_{bi}}{\sum_{i=1}^{n} p_{bi} q_{bi}} \right) * 100$$

where: p_{ti} = price of item i in time t

q_{bi} = quantity of item i in base period b

p_{bi} = price of item i in base period b

The Laspeyres Index is also used to calculate the U.S. Department of Labor's Producer Price Index (PPI) which covers a broad range of products at the wholesale level. The indexes of real exchange rates described in Chapter 4 also incorporate this formula. The USDA's Index of Prices Paid By Farmers used to compute "parity" prices is a Laspeyres Index.

By holding weights constant, the index purports to reflect true price changes over time taking into account the relative importance of each component. However, since consumers, or other participants in the realm of the particular index, tend to respond by shifting from higher priced items to lower priced items, Laspeyres' procedure places too much weight on prices that have increased and too little weight on items declining in price (Mendenhall et al., 1989).

To correct for this problem, an alternative is the Paasche Index calculated as follows:

$$\text{Paasche Index} = \left(\frac{\sum_{i=1}^{n} p_{ti} q_{ti}}{\sum_{i=1}^{n} p_{bi} q_{bi}} \right) * 100$$

where: q_{ti}=quantity of item i in time t

The difference from the Laspayres Index is that the weights change in each period over time. Unfortunately, this index understates the price change on products increasing in price and overstates price changes on items and services declining in price. The obvious solution is an index that compromises these extremes, which was the rationale for the Fisher's "ideal index," calculated as follows:

$$\text{Fisher's "Ideal Index"} = \sqrt{(\text{Laspeyres Index})\ (\text{Paasche Index})}$$

The reason neither the Paasche Index nor the Fisher's "ideal index" has been very popular is that they require an estimate of the quantities used in each year. However, if an analyst is constructing an index or a variable of averages and can easily generate the weights, why not apply a procedure similar to Paasche or Fisher?

Actually, the U.S. Department of Commerce in 1995 did adopt Fisher's "ideal index" in a major revision on how to calculate national income and product accounts in real terms (U.S. Department of Commerce, Bureau of Economic Analysis, 1995). In a year-to-year framework, they simply calculated a geometric average of the Laspeyres Index and the Paasche Index as Fisher did, applying this to quantities (q) rather than price (p). This revision was prompted by the overestimation of growth in a period when prices on personal computers dropped sharply while sales accelerated. This year-to-year application of Fisher's "ideal index" is called a chain-type annual weighted index. With these revisions, the implicit deflator for consumer expenditures should become even more reliable in demand analysis on food as a replacement for the CPI.

REFERENCES

Aradhyula, Satheesh and Matthew Holt, "Risk Behavior and Rational Expectations in the U.S. Broiler Market," *American Journal of Agricultural Economics,* 79, November 1989.

Armington, P.S., "A Theory of Demand for Products Distinguished by Place of Production," IMF Staff papers, Vol. 16, 159–178, 1969.

Armstrong, J. Scott, *Long-range Forecasting: From Crystal Ball to Computer,* 2nd ed. (New York: John Wiley and Sons, 1985).

Ascher, William, *Forecasting: An Appraisal for Policymakers and Planners* (Baltimore, MD: Johns Hopkins University Press, 1978).

Baker, C.B., "Interpretation of Regional and Spatial Models," Chapter 13, *Agricultural Supply Functions—Estimating Techniques and Interpretation,* Heady, Earl O., et al., eds. (Ames: Iowa State University Press, 1961).

Baumol, William J., *Economic Dynamics—An Introduction,* 3rd ed. (New York: Macmillan Publishing Co., Inc., 1970).

Behrman, Jere R., *Supply Response in Underdeveloped Agriculture* (Amsterdam: North Holland Publishing Co., 1968).

Bell, Daniel, *Toward the Year 2000, Work in Progress,* Commission on the Year 2000, American Academy of Arts and Sciences, Beacon Press, 1970.

Bera, A. and C. Jarque, "Efficient Tests for Normality, Heteroscedasticity and Serial Independence of Regression Residuals," *Economics Letters,* 6, 1980.

Bessler, David A. and Charles V. Moore, "Use of Probability Assessments and Scoring Rules for Agricultural Forecasts," *Agricultural Economic Research,* 13(4), U.S. Department of Agriculture, October 1979.

Blakeslee, Leroy L., Earl O. Heady, and Charles F. Framingham, *World Food Production, Demand and Trade,* (Ames: Iowa State University Press, 1973).

Boehlje, Michael and Vernon R. Eidman, *Farm Management* (New York: John Wiley and Sons, 1984).

Bowerman, B. and R. O'Connell, *Forecasting and Time Series* (North Scituate, MA: Duxbury Press, 1979).

Box, G.E.P., and G.M. Jenkins, *Time Series Analysis, Forecasting and Control,* (San Francisco, Holden Day, 1970).

Bressler, Jr., Raymond G. and Richard A. King, *Markets, Prices and Interregional Trade,* (New York: John Wiley and Sons, 1970).

Bretschneider, Stuart, "Forecasting: Some New Realities," Metropolitan Studies Program, Syracuse University, Syracuse, NY, December 1985.

Brock, Richard A., *Charting Farm Markets,* Top Farmers of America Associates, Milwaukee, WI, 1981.

Brokken, Ray F. and Earl O. Heady, *Interregional Adjustments in Crop and Livestock Production,* Technical Bulletin No. 1396, Economic Research Service, U.S. Department of Agriculture in cooperation with Iowa State University, July 1968.

Caudill, Charles E., "Getting Facts and Figures for Farming," *Marketing of Agriculture, 1988 Yearbook of Agriculture,* U.S. Department of Agriculture.

Center for Farm Financial Management, *FINPACK User's Manual,* University of Minnesota, St. Paul, MN, 1993.

Chance, Don M., *An Introduction to Options and Futures,* 2nd ed. (Orlando, FL: Dryden Press, 1991).

Chicago Board of Trade, *Wheat Options Trading Manual,* 1987.

Chicago Board of Trade, *Commodity Trading Manual,* 1985.

Commodities, 219 Parkade, Cedar Falls, IA, July 1974.

Commodities, "Technical Personalities of Major Commodities" (Columbia, MD: Investor Publications, Inc., August 1972).

Conway Data, Inc., *Site Selection Handbook, 1986,* 40 Technology Park, Atlanta/Norcross, Georgia.

Croxton, Frederick E. and Dudley J. Cowden, *Practical Business Statistics,* 3rd ed. (Englewood Cliffs, NJ: Prentice Hall, 1960).

Data Transmission Network, http://www.dtnag.com/foradvert.htm, September 2004.

Delbecq, Andre L., Andrew H. Van De Ven, and David Gustafson, *Group Techniques for Program Planning: A Guide to Nominal Group and Delphi Processes* (Glenview, IL: Scott Foresman, 1975).

Dickey, D.A. and W.A. Fuller, "Distribution of the Estimators for Autoregressive Time-Series with a Unit Root," *Journal of the American Statistical Association,* Vol. 74, 1979.

Eggert, Robert, *Blue Chip Economic Indicators,* various issues, Capitol Publications, Inc., Alexandria, VA.

Engle, R. and C. Granger, "Co-integration and Error Correlation: Representation, Estimation and Testing," *Econometrica,* 35, 1987.

Ensminger, M.E. and C.G. Olentine, Jr., *Feeds and Nutrition—Complete,* 1st ed. (Clovis, CA: Ensminger Publishing Co., 1980).

Enzer, Selwyn, *Delphi and Cross-impact Techniques: An Effective Combination for Systematic Futures Analysis,* WP-8, Institute for the Future, Middletown, CT, June 1970.

Ferris, John N., "Analysis of Past and Future Impacts of the Wheat, Feed Grain and Conservation Reserve Provisions of the Food Security Act of 1985 on U.S. Agriculture," Selected Paper, American Agricultural Economics Association, 1990.

Ferris, John N., "A Description of 'AGMOD'—An Econometric Model of U.S. and World Agriculture," Agricultural Economics Staff Paper No. 89-19, Michigan State University, February 1989.

Ferris, John N., *Developing Marketing Strategies and Keeping Records on Corn, Soybeans and Wheat,* North Central Region Extension Publication No. 217, Producer Marketing Management Fact Sheet No. 4, Michigan State University, December 1985.

Ferris, John N., "Forecasting Corn Producers' Response to the 1986 Feed Grain Program," Selected Paper, American Agricultural Economics Association, 1986.

Ferris, John N., "Generation of Probability Distributions on Farm Prices and Supply/Utilization Balances on Corn, Soybeans and Wheat for the Crops of 1989–91," NCR-134 Conference on *Applied Commodity Price Analysis, Forecasting and Market Risk Management,* April 20–21, 1989.

Ferris, John N., *Highlights, Status and Potential of Michigan Agriculture,* Special Report 32, Michigan State University Agricultural Experiment Station, January 1993.

Ferris, John N., *Highlights and Summary of Project '80 & 5, A Look at Michigan Rural Potential in 1985,* Research Report 180, Michigan State University Agricultural Experiment Station and Cooperative Extension Service, February 1973.

Ferris, John N., *Highlights and Summary of Project '80, Rural Michigan Now And in 1980,* Research Report 37, Michigan State University Agricultural Experiment Station and Cooperative Extension Service, 1966.

Ferris, John N., *Rural Michigan and the Year 2000: A Delphi Analysis,* Research Report 194, Michigan State University Agricultural Experiment Station and Cooperative Extension Service, April 1973.

Ferris, John N., *Using Seasonal Cash Price Patterns for Selling Decisions on Corn, Soybeans and Wheat,* North Central Region Extension Publication No. 217, Producer Marketing Management, Fact Sheet #3, Michigan State University, June 1996 (revision).

Food and Agricultural Policy Research Institute, "Policy Options for the 1995 Farm Bill," University of Missouri-Columbia/Iowa State University, April 27, 1995.

Foote, Richard and Karl A. Fox, *Seasonal Variation: Methods of Measurement and Tests of Significance,* U.S. Department of Agriculture Handbook No. 48, 1952.

Fulton, George and Donald R. Grimes, *The REMI Resource Package for Michigan: Capabilities, Products and Information Base,* the University of Michigan, January 1988.

Good, Darrel, et al., "USDA Economic and Statistics Review Panel, Report to Secretary of Agriculture John R. Block," unnumbered publication, U.S. Department of Agriculture, June 28, 1985.

Gordon, T.J. and Olaf Helmer, *Report on a Long-range Forecasting Study,* the Rand Corporation, U.S. Department of Commerce, Office of Technical Services, September 1964.

Granger, C.W.J., *Forecasting in Business and Economics,* 2nd ed. (Orlando, FL: Academic Press, Inc., 1989).

Green, E.I., "Creative Thinking in Scientific Work," *Electrical Engineering,* Vol. LXIII, June 1954.

Greene, William H., *Econometric Analysis,* 2nd ed. (New York: Macmillan Publishing Co., 1993).

Greig, Smith, *Economics and Management of Food Processing* (Westport, CT: Avi Publishing Co., Inc., 1984).

Griffiths, William E., R. Carter Hill, and George G. Judge, *Learning and Practicing Econometrics* (New York: John Wiley and Sons, 1993).

Halcrow, Harold G., Robert G. F. Spitze, and Joyce E. Allen-Smith, *Food and Agricultural Policy, Economics and Politics* (New York: McGraw-Hall, 1994).

Hall, Robert E., Jack Jackson, and David M. Lilien, *MicroTSP User's Manual* (Irvine, CA: Quantitative Micro Software, 1990).

Hannan, E.J., "The Estimation of Seasonal Variation in Economic Time Series," *Journal of the American Statistical Association,* 58:31–44, March 1963.

Harsh, Stephen B., J.W. Lloyd, and A.S. Go, "Model for Financial Evaluation of Alternative Production Strategies for Michigan Dairy Farms," Proceedings of *FACTs95: Farm Animal Computer Technologies Conference,* Orlando, FL, March 1995.

Harsh, Stephen B., Larry J. Connor, and Gerald D. Schwab, *Managing the Farm Business* (Englewood Cliffs, NJ: Prentice-Hall, Inc., 1981).

Heady, Earl O., et al., eds., *Agricultural Supply Functions—Estimating Techniques and Interpretations* (Ames: Iowa State University Press, 1961).

Heien, Dale J., J. Matthews, and A. Womack, "A Methods Note on the Gauss-Seidel Algorithm for Solving Econometric Models," *Agricultural Economics Research,* Vol. 25, No. 3, U.S. Department of Agriculture, 1973.

Hildreth, C. and J. Lu, *Demand Relations with Autocorrelated Disturbances,* Technical Bulletin No. 276, Michigan State University Agricultural Experiment Station, 1960.

Hill, Lowell, et. al., *Economic Evaluations of Quality Characteristics in the Dry Milling of Corn,* Bulletin 804, University of Illinois at Urbana-Champaign, College of Agriculture, Agricultural Experiment Station, North Central Regional Research Publications 330, November 1991.

Huang, Kuo S., *A Complete System of U.S. Demand for Food,* Technical Bulletin No. 1821, Economic Research Service, U.S. Department of Agriculture, September 1993.

Huang, Kuo S., *U.S. Demand for Food: A Complete System of Price and Income Effects,* Technical Bulletin No. 1714, National Economic Division, Economic Research Service, U.S. Department of Agriculture, December 1985.

Hurt, Christopher and Philip Garcia, "The Impact of Price Risk on Sow Farrowings, 1967–78," *American Journal of Agricultural Economics,* Vol. 64, No. 3, August 1982.

Ikerd, John, "Using Probability Estimates in Outlook Work," Discussion Paper for the Southern Region Outlook Conference, Atlanta, GA, September 1979.

Jantsch, E., *Technological Forecasting in Perspective,* OECD, Paris, 1967.

Johnson, Glenn L. and C. Leroy Quance, *The Overproduction Trap in U.S. Agriculture,* Resources for the Future, Inc. (Baltimore, MD: Johns Hopkins University Press, 1972).

Judge, George G., et al., *The Theory and Practice of Econometrics,* 2nd ed. (New York: John Wiley and Sons, 1985).

Judge, G.G., J. Havlicek, and R.L. Rizek, *Spatial Structure of the Livestock Economy, I., Spatial Analysis of the Meat Marketing Sector in 1955 and 1960,* Regional Research Bulletin No. 157, Experiment Station Bulletin No. 520, South Dakota State University, May 1964.

Just, Richard E., "Risk Response Models and Their Use in Agricultural Policy Evaluation," *American Journal of Agricultural Economics,* Vol. 57, No. 5, December 1975.

Kalbacher, Judith Z., "Shift-Share Analysis: A Modified Approach," *Agricultural Economics Research,* Vol. 31, No. 1, January 1979.

Kalter, Robert J. and Robert Milligan, "Emerging Agricultural Technologies: Economic and Policy Implications for Animal Production," Cornell University, 1986.

Kastens, Terry L., Ted C. Schroeder, and Ron Plain, "Evaluation of Extension and USDA

Price and Production Forecasts," Proceedings of NCR-134 Conference, Applied Price Analysis, Forecasting and Market Risk Management, Chicago, IL, April 22–23, 1996.

Keisling, Jill D. and Vincent F. Bralts, *SAPMINR Highlights,* Status and Potential of Michigan Natural Resources, Special Report No. 67, Michigan State University Agricultural Experiment Station, January 1995.

Koyck, L. *Distributed Lags and Investment Analysis,* (Amsterdam: North Holland Publishing Co., 1954).

Lerohl, Milburn L., "Expected Prices for U.S. Agricultural Commodities, 1917–62," unpublished Ph.D. thesis, Michigan State University, pp. 32–49, 1965.

Leuthold, Raymond M., "On the Use of Theil's Inequality Coefficients," *American Journal of Agricultural Economics,* Vol. 57, May 1975.

Mabbs-Zeno, Carl and Arthur Dommen, *Subsidy Equivalents, Yardsticks of Government Intervention in Agriculture for the GATT,* Agriculture Information Bulletin No. 558, Economic Research Service, U.S. Department of Agriculture, January 1989.

Makridakis, Spyros, et al., *The Forecasting Accuracy of Major Time-Series Methods* (New York: John Wiley and Sons, 1984).

Marshall, Alfred, *Principles of Economics,* 8th ed. (New York: Macmillan Publishing Co., 1920).

McKissick, John C., George A. Shumaker, and F.W. Williams, *Agricultural Commodity Options: A Teacher's Guide, Section I—Basic Concepts,* project entitled "Commodity Options as a Risk Management Alternative," financed by Extension Service, U.S. Department of Agriculture, Agricultural Economics Department, University of Georgia, August 1984.

Mendenhall, William, James E. Reinmuth, and Robert Beaver, *Statistics for Management and Economics,* 6th ed. (Boston: PWS–Kent Publishing Company, 1989).

Minnesota IMPLAN Group, Inc., *IMPLAN Professional*, 1996, 1940 South Greeley St., Suite 101, Stillwater, MN 55082.

Mundlak, Yair and Donald F. Larson, "On the Relevance of World Agricultural Prices," WPS 383, Policy, Research and External Affairs, International Economics Department, the World Bank, March 1990.

Muth, J.F., "Rational Expectations and the Theory of Price Movements," *Econometrica,* 29, 1961.

Myers, Robert, "Time-Series Econometrics and Commodity Price Analysis: A Review," *Review of Marketing and Agricultural Economics,* Vol. 62, No. 2, Australian Agricultural Economics Society, Inc., August 1994.

Myers, Robert J. and Steven Hanson, "Pricing Commodity Options When the Underlying Futures Price Exhibits Time-Varying Volatility," *American Journal of Agricultural Economics,* Vol. 75, No. 1, February 1993.

Myers, Robert J., "Time-Series Econometrics and Commodity Price Analysis," Invited Paper at the 36th Annual Conference of the Australian Agricultural Economics Society, Australian National University, Canberra, February 1992.

Myers, Robert J. and Stanley R. Thompson, "Generalized Optimal Hedge Ratio Estimation," *American Journal of Agricultural Economics,* Vol. 71, No. 4, pp. 858–868, November 1989.

Naisbitt, John and Patricia Aburdene, *Megatrends 2000* (New York: William Morrow and Co., Inc., 1990).

Naisbitt, John, *Megatrends: Ten New Directions Transforming Our Lives* (New York: Warner Books, 1982).

Nelson, Gene A., "The Case for Probabilistic Outlook Information for Agricultural Commodities," Paper presented at the Great Plains and Western States outlook Conference, Moscow, ID, 1979.

Nerlove, Marc, *The Dynamics of Supply: Estimation of Farmers' Response to Price* (Baltimore, MD: Johns Hopkins University Press, 1958).

Nison, Steve, "Trading Insight," *The Commodity Futures Professional,* Chicago Board of Trade, September 1990.

Nott, Sherrill, et al., "Michigan 1992 Estimates for Crop and Livestock Budgets," Agricultural Economics Report No. 556, Department of Agricultural Economics, Michigan State University, 1992.

Organization for Economic Cooperation and Development, *Tables of Producer Subsidy Equivalents and Consumer Subsidy Equivalents, 1979–1990,* OCDE/GE (91)128, Paris, 1991.

Oster Communications, Inc., *Commodity Price Charts,* 219 Parkade, P.O. Box 6, Cedar Falls, IA, 50613.

Pindyck, Robert and Daniel Rubinfeld, *Econometric Models and Economic Forecasts,* 3rd ed. (New York: McGraw-Hill, 1991).

Porter, Michael, *The Competitive Advantage of Nations* (New York: The Free Press, 1990).

Rao, D., *Intercountry Comparison of Agricultural Output and Productivity,* FAO Economic and Social Development Paper, No. 112, Rome, 1993.

Richardson, James W., "Description of FLIPSIM: The Farm Level Income and Policy Simulation Model," Paper presented at the Forum on Risk Management Education, Kansas City, MO, December 16–17, 1996.

Roberts, Donna and Martin Johnson, *Estimates of Producer and Consumer Subsidy Equivalents, Government Interventions in Agriculture, 1982–92,* Statistical Bulletin No. 913, Economic Research Service, USDA, December 1994.

Robinson, Sherman, Maureen Kilkenny, and Kenneth Hanson, *The USDA/ERS Compatable General Equilibrium (CGE) Model of the United States,* Staff Report No. AGES 9049, Economic Research Service, U.S. Department of Agriculture, June 1990.

Rojko, Anthony, Patrick O'Brien, Donald Regier, Arthur Coffing, and Linda Bailey, *Alternative Futures for World Food in 1985,* Foreign Agricultural Economics Report No. 149, Economic Research Service, U.S. Department of Agriculture, May 1978.

Roningen, Vernon, *Documentation of the Dynamic World Policy Simulation (DWOPSIM) Model Building Framework,* Staff Report No. AGES 9226, Economic Research Service, U.S. Department of Agriculture, October 1992.

Roningen, Vernon, John Sullivan, and Praveen Dixit, *Documentation of the State World Policy Simulation (SWOPSIM) Modeling Framework,* Staff Report No. AGES 9151, Economic Research Service, U.S. Department of Agriculture, September 1991.

Roningen, V.O. and Praveen M. Dixit, *How Level Is the Playing Field?,* Foreign Agricultural Economics Report No. 239, Economic Research Service, U.S. Department of Agriculture, December 1989.

Salathe, Larry E., J. Michael Price, and Kenneth E. Gadson, "The Food and Agricultural Policy Simulator," *Agricultural Economics Research,* Vol. 34, No. 2, April 1982.

Samuelson, P.A., "Proof That Properly Anticipated Prices Fluctuate Randomly," *Industrial Management Review,* 6:41–49, 1965.

Seitz, Wesley D., Gerald C. Nelson, and Harold G. Halcrow, *Economics of Resources, Agriculture, and Food* (New York: McGraw-Hill, 1994).

Smith, Edward G., et al., *Representative Farms Economic Outlook: FAPRI/AFPC April 1996 Baseline,* AFPC Working Paper No. 96-1, Agricultural and Food Policy Center, Texas A&M University, April 1996.

Sorenson, Vernon L., ed., *Agricultural Market Analysis,* Bureau of Business and Economic Research, Graduate School of Business Administration, Michigan State University, 1964.

Stapleton, James H., *Linear Statistical Models* (New York: John Wiley & Sons, Inc. 1995)

Stevens, Stanley C., "Evidence for a Weather Persistence Effect on the Corn, Wheat and Soybean Growing Season Price Dynamics," *The Journal of Futures Markets,* Vol. 11, No. 1, 1991.

Stevens, Stanley C., "Weather Markets: U.S. Corn and Soybeans," Staff Paper No. P88-27, Department of Agricultural and Applied Economics, University of Minnesota, Institute of Agriculture, Forestry and Home Economics, St. Paul, MN, August 1988.

Stillman, Richard, *A Quarterly Model of the Livestock Industry,* Technical Bulletin No. 1711, Economic Research Service, U.S. Department of Agriculture, December 1985.

Stoll, Hans R. and Robert E. Whaley, *Futures and Options, Theory and Application,* (Cincinnati, OH: South-Western Publishing Co., 1993).

Stollsteimer, John F., "A Working Model for Plant Numbers and Locations," *Journal of Farm Economics,* Vol. 45, No. 36, August 1963.

Taylor, Robert, Katherine H. Reichelderfer, and Stanley R. Johnson, *Agricultural Sector Models for the United States* (Ames: Iowa State University Press, 1993).

Teigen, Lloyd D. and Thomas Bell, "Confidence Intervals for Corn Price and Utilization Forecasts," *Agricultural Economic Research,* 30(1), U.S. Department of Agriculture, January 1978.

Theil, Henri, *Applied Economic Forecasting* (Amsterdam: North Holland Publishing Co.; Chicago: Rand McNally and Co., 1966).

Tomek, William G. and Kenneth L. Robinson, *Agricultural Product Prices,* 3rd ed. (Ithaca, NY: Cornell University Press, 1990).

Traill, Bruce, David Colman, and Trevor Young, "Estimating Irreversible Supply Functions," *American Journal of Agricultural Economics,* Vol. 60, No. 3, August 1978.

Tweeten, Luther, *Agricultural Trade, Principles and Policies* (Boulder, CO and San Francisco: Westview Press, 1992).

Uhrig, J. William, *Cost of Grain Storage,* North Central Region Extension Publication No. 217, Producer Marketing Management Fact Sheet No. 19, Purdue University Cooperative Extension Service.

Uhrig, J. William, *Technical Analysis,* North Central Region Extension Publication No. 217, Producer Marketing Management Fact Sheet No. 20, Purdue University Cooperative Extension Service.

United Nations, Food and Agriculture Organization, *Agricultural Commodity Projections for 1975 and 1985,* Vol. II, 1967.

United Nations, Food and Agriculture Organization, *World Agriculture: Towards 2000,* (John Wiley and Sons, 1995).

United Nations, Food and Agriculture Organization, *A World Price Equilibrium Model,* 1968.

U.S. Department of Agriculture, *Agricultural Outlook,* various issues.

U.S. Department of Agriculture, *Agricultural Outlook,* October 1988.

U.S. Department of Agriculture, *Costs of Production—Major Field Crops and Livestock and Dairy, 1992,* ECIFS 12-3, Economic Research Service, August 1994.

U.S. Department of Agriculture, *Embargoes, Surplus Disposal, and U.S. Agriculture,* Agricultural Economic Report No. 564, Economic Research Service, December 1986.

U.S. Department of Agriculture, *Farm Computer Usage and Ownership*, Sp.Sy 9 (7-03), National Agricultural Statistics Service (NASS), July 2003.

U.S. Department of Agriculture, *Feed Situation and Outlook Report,* various issues.

U.S. Department of Agriculture, *Food Cost Review, 1995,* Agricultural Economics Report No. 729, Economic Research Service, June 1996.

U.S. Department of Agriculture, *Food Marketing Review,* Agricultural Ecomonics Report No. 743, September 1996.

U.S. Department of Agriculture, *State Financial Summary, 1993,* Economic Indicators of the Farm Sectors, ECIFS-13-2, Economic Research Service, January 1995.

U.S. Department of Agriculture, *Weights, Measures and Conversion Factors for Agricultural Commodities and Their Products,* Agricultural Handbook No. 697, Economic Research Service, June 1992.

U.S. Department of Agriculture, World Agricultural Outlook Board, *World Agricultural Supply and Demand Estimates,* WASDE-302, May 11, 1995.

U.S. Department of Commerce, "Tests and Revisions of Bureau of the Census Methods of Seasonal Adjustments," Bureau of the Census Technical Paper No. 5, 1960.

U.S. Department of Commerce, Bureau of Economic Analysis, *BEA Regional Projections to 2040, Vol. I: States, Washington, D.C.,* U.S. Government Printing Office, June 1990.

U.S. Department of Commerce, Bureau of Economic Analysis, *Survey of Current Business,* Vol. 75, No. 7, July 1995.

U.S. General Accounting Office, *USDA Commodity Forecasts,* GAO/PEMD-91-24, August 1991.

Webb, Alan J., Michael Lopez, and Renata Penn, *Estimates of Producer and Consumer Subsidy Equivalents,* Statistical Bulletin No. 803, Economic Research Service, U.S. Department of Agriculture, April 1990.

Wilder, J. Welles, *New Concepts in Technical Trading Systems* (Trend Research, 1978).

Wisner, Robert N., *An Evaluation of Pre-harvest Corn Futures and Option Marketing Strategies in Selected Iowa and Nebraska Locations,* Report No. 167, Department of Agricultural Economics, the Agricultural Research Division, University of Nebraska-Lincoln, Institute of Agriculture and Natural Resources, June 1991.

AUTHOR INDEX

Aburdene, Patricia, 184
Allen-Smith, Joyce E., 44
Aradhyula, Satheesh, 84
Armington, P.S., 196
Armstrong, J. Scott, 142
Ascher, William, 142

Bailey, Linda, 352
Baker, C.B., 192
Baumol, William J., 108, 110
Beaver, Robert, 351
Behrman, Jere R., 86
Bell, Daniel, 184
Bell, Thomas, 155
Bera, A., 158, 159
Bessler, David A., 155
Blakeslee, Leroy L., 179
Boehlje, Michael, 209
Bowerman, B., 348
Box, G.E.P., 306
Bralts, Vincent F., 186
Bressler, Raymond G., Jr., 191, 192, 202
Bretschneider, Stuart, 142
Brock, Richard A., 299
Brokken, Ray F., 196, 197

Caudill, Charles E., 332
Chance, Don M., 234, 246
Coffing, Arthur, 352
Coleman, David, 353
Connor, Larry J., 209
Cowden, Dudley J., 221
Croxton, Frederick E., 221

Delbecq, Andre, 186
Dickey, D.A., 308
Dixit, Praveen, 212, 252
Dommen, Arthur, 214

Eggert, Robert, 133
Eidman, Vernon R., 209
Engle, R., 311
Ensminger, M.E., 66
Enzer, Selwyn, 186

Ferris, John N., 85, 162, 185, 186, 213, 228, 303
Foote, Richard, 221
Fox, Karl A., 221
Framingham, Charles F., 348
Fuller, W.A., 308
Fulton, George, 215

Gadson, Kenneth E., 352
Garcia, Philip, 350
Go, A.S., 350
Good, Darrel, 331
Gordon, T.J., 184
Granger, C.W.J., 306, 311
Green, E.I., 182
Greene, William H., 306
Greig, Smith, 205
Griffiths, William E., 306
Grimes, Donald R., 215
Gustafson, David, 348

Halcrow, Harold G., 8, 44
Hall, Robert E., 121, 149, 314
Hannan, E.J., 221
Hanson, Kenneth, 352
Hanson, Steven, 247, 248
Harsh, Stephen B., 209
Havlicek, J., 196
Heady, Earl O., 196, 197, 348
Heien, Dale J., 122
Helmer, Olaf, 184
Hildreth, C., 314
Hill, Lowell, 61
Hill, R. Carter, 306
Holt, Matthew, 84
Huang, Kuo S., 36
Hurt, Christopher, 86

Ikerd, John, 155

Jackson, Jack, 314
Jantsch, E., 183
Jarque, C., 158, 159
Jenkins, G.M., 306
Johnson, Glenn L., 15
Johnson, Martin, 214
Johnson, Stanley R., 353

Judge, George G., 196, 306, 316
Just, Richard E., 86

Kalbacher, Judith Z., 201
Kalter, Robert J., 215
Kastens, Terry L., 147
Keisling, Jill D., 186
Kilkenny, Maureen, 352
King, Richard A., 191, 192, 202
Koyck, L., 75

Larson, Donald F., 49
Lerohl, Milburn L., 83
Leuthold, Raymond M., 146
Lilien, David M., 314
Lloyd, J.W., 350
Lopez, Michael, 354
Lu, J., 314

Mabbs-Zeno, Carl, 214
Makridakis, Spyros, 142
Marshall, Alfred, 8, 9, 48
Matthews, J., 350
McKissick, John C., 241
Mendenhall, William, 346
Milligan, Robert, 215
Moore, Charles V., 155
Mundlak, Yair, 49
Muth, J.F., 82
Myers, Robert J., 247, 248, 279, 305, 306, 308

Naisbitt, John, 184
Nelson, Gene A., 155
Nelson, Gerald C., 8
Nerlove, Marc, 75
Nison, Steve, 302
Nott, Sherrill, 91

O'Brien, Patrick, 352
O'Connell, R., 348
Olentine, C.G., Jr., 66

Penn, Renata, 354
Pindyck, Robert, 78, 149, 306, 307, 311, 315
Plain, Ron, 350
Pool, Ithiel De Sola, 184
Porter, Michael, 198
Price, J. Michael, 352

Quance, C. Leroy, 350

Rao, D., 352
Regier, Donald, 352
Reichelderfer, Katherine H., 353
Reinmuth, James E., 351
Richardson, James W., 210
Rizek, R.L., 196
Roberts, Donna, 214
Robinson, Kenneth L., 26, 35, 192
Robinson, Sherman, 134
Rojko, Anthony, 179
Roningen, Vernon, 134, 212
Rubinfeld, Daniel, 78, 149, 306, 307, 311, 315

Salathe, Larry E., 128
Samuelson, P.A., 303
Schroeder, Ted C., 350
Schwab, Gerald D., 209
Seitz, Wesley, D., 8, 15, 197
Shumaker, George A., 241
Smith, Edward G., 210
Sorenson, Vernon L., 16
Spitze, Robert G.F., 44
Stapleton, James H., 161
Stevens, Stanley C., 298, 303
Stillman, Richard, 113
Stoll, Hans R., 234, 279
Stollsteimer, John F., 203
Sullivan, John, 352

Taylor, Robert, 133, 138
Teigen, Lloyd D., 155
Theil, Henri, 145
Thompson, Stanley R., 279
Tomek, William G., 26, 35, 192
Traill, Bruce, 86
Tweeten, Luther, 196

Uhrig, J. William, 231, 283

Van De Ven, Andrew, 348

Webb, Alan J., 214
Whaley, Robert E., 234, 279
Wilder, J. Welles, 300
Williams, F.W., 241
Wisner, Robert N., 247, 271
Womack, A., 350

Young, Trevor, 353

SUBJECT INDEX

Add factors, 143, 149
AGMOD, 131, 133, 136–40, 213
Agriculture and Consumer Protection Act of 1973, 90
AGSIM, 133
Arbitrage, 190, 192, 245, 273
Autoregression error specification of the first order [AR(1)], 60, 311, 313–14
Autoregressive models (AR), 314–16
Autoregressive Moving Average models (ARMA), 316–18

Balance sheet, 68, 128
Base acre, 93
Basic Linked System (BLS), 133
Basis, 43, 84, 249, 255–78
  break-even, 276–78
  calculation, 254
  continuation, 274–75
  contract, 249, 260–270, 272–73
  forecasting, 43, 273–74
  new crop, 259–71, 274–75
  risk, 249, 270–71, 272, 273, 279
  storage, 254–59, 275–78
  strong, 263–64, 267–68
  weak, 259–62, 265–67
Bear, bearish, 240, 250
Beef, wholesale prices by grade, 63–65
Biological lag, 100, 111–14
Black/Scholes formula. *See* Options on commodity futures
Blue Chip Economic Indicators, 133
Border protection policy, 45, 50
Box-Pierce Q-Statistic, 318, 321
Bull, bullish, 240, 250
Bureau of Economic Analysis, U.S. Department of Commerce, 67, 201, 346

Capital gains effect on farm input demand, 68
Carrying costs, "carry", 44, 274, 278
Census of Agriculture, 2, 333–35
Census of Manufacturers, 336
Center for Agricultural and Rural Development (CARD), 133
Centre for World Food Studies (SOW), 133
Charting. *See* Technical analysis
Chicago Board of Trade (CBT), 62, 233–35, 240, 251, 275–77, 279, 336
Chicago Mercantile Exchange (CME), 234, 235, 250, 336
Cobweb Theorem, 100–112
  convergent, 100–107
  divergent, 100–107
  stable, 100–107
  stable at extremes, 102, 103
Coefficient of determination unadjusted (R^2) and adjusted ($\bar{R}^2$), 13, 14, 95, 341
Coffee, Sugar and Cocoa Exchange, 250
COMGEM, 133
Commission on the Year 2000, 184
Commodity Futures Trading Commission (CFTC), 234, 251, 300, 336
Commodity Price Charts (Oster Communications, Inc.), 297, 299–301
Computable General Equilibrium models (CGE), 134, 135
Conditional regression, 39, 40
Congressional Budget Office, 133, 134
Consensus forecasts, 146, 147, 184–87
Consumer income, 10, 11, 22, 25, 173
  discretionary, 22, 25
  disposable, 22, 25
Consumer Price Index (CPI), 12, 23, 26, 54, 55, 59–61, 69, 70, 88, 92, 93, 129, 131, 136, 220, 322, 336, 345, 346
Consumer Subsidy Equivalents (CSE), 134, 214, 337
Corn gluten feed and meal, 66
Cost curves, 15, 18
Cost of production by enterprise, 87–95
  fixed, 15, 91, 92
  total, 15, 16, 18
  variable cash, 15, 18, 91, 92
County Business Patterns, 336
Crop and livestock estimates, 332, 333
  area frames, 332
  list frames, 332

Crop and livestock estimates, (*Cont.*)
multiple frames, 332
Cycles, 111–14, 219–21

Data Resources, Inc. (DRI), 133
Data Transmission Network, FarmDayta, 338
Decision support systems
Agriculture and Food Policy Center, 210
FINPACK, 209
Strategic Financial Planning Model (SFPM), 209
Deficiency payments, 93
Deflation, 22, 26, 88, 220, 345, 346
farm income, 69, 70
Degrees of freedom, 14, 23, 25, 35, 75, 95, 341
Delphi, 184–86
Demand
derived, 16–18
farm level, 16–19
law of, 8
retail level, 12–14, 16–19
Demand, impact multipliers, 30, 31
Demand curves
irreversible, 10, 11, 22, 28
reversible, 10
Demand elasticity, 18, 19, 30–40, 173–82
cross-price, 31, 33–40
farm versus retail, 18, 19
income, 31, 35–40, 173–82
own-price, 31–40
point, 31–33
Demand flexibility. *See* Price flexibility of demand
Demand for agricultural inputs, 67–69
Demand for domestic consumption, 8–14, 16–19, 21–40
Demand for exports, 8–11, 44–51
Demand for marketing services and materials, 16–18
Demand for storage and speculation, 8–11, 42–44
Demand shifters, 10, 173–82
Demand shifters (*Cont.*)
domestic consumption, 10–14, 22–29, 31, 34, 173–82
exports, 10, 45–51
storage and speculation, 10, 43, 44
Demand systems, 35–39
Dependent variables, 341
Derivatives, 233
Dickey-Fuller test, 308–10
Distillers' dried grain (DDGS), 66
Distributed lags, 16, 74–82, 95, 96
geometric, 75–78
polynomial, 78–82
Double Exponential Smoothing (DES), 74, 146, 149–52, 154–57, 172
Dummy variables, 22, 27–30, 63, 67, 73, 74, 211
Durbin-Watson statistic, 313, 314, 318, 323, 324, 326, 341, 342
Dynamic versus static models, 212, 213
Dynamic World Policy Simulation (DWOPSIM), 134

Econometric/simulation modeling
building guidelines, 124–32
dairy, 131, 132
livestock, 129–31
Econometric/simulation models, 133–40
Economic Research Service (ERS), USDA, 1, 337, 338
Elasticities and flexibilities from AGMOD, 138–40
Endogenous variables, 111
Engle aggregation, 35
Engle-Granger Co-integration test, 311, 312
European Community (EC), 45, 49
European Currency Unit (ECU), 45, 46
European Union (EU), 10, 158–61, 211, 212
Exchange rates, 45–49
Exogenous variables, 111, 150, 152, 172, 321
Expectations, 8, 9, 73–85
Expected prices, 9, 15, 43, 72–85, 95
Export earnings, 45
Export Enhancement Program, 10
Export subsidies, 10, 45, 50, 212

FAPSIM, 133
Farm income
net, 67, 68
net cash, 67, 68
Farm-retail price spreads. *See* Price spreads, farm-retail
Farm supply. *See* Supply, farm level
Farm supply elasticity. *See* Supply elasticity, farm level
Farm supply shifters. *See* Supply shifters, farm level
Federal Agricultural Improvement and Reform Act of 1996 (FAIR), 93, 94, 171, 209, 211, 213
Federal Reserve Board, 119
Feedback in livestock cycles, 112, 114
Feed Grain Program, 92–94, 210
FINPACK. *See* Decision support systems
Fisher's "Ideal Index," 346
Food, Agriculture, Conservation and Trade Act of 1990 (FACTA), 210, 211, 213
Food and Agricultural Policy Research Institute (FAPRI), 133, 210, 212
Food and Agriculture Organization (FAO), United Nations, 2, 133, 173–76, 178, 179, 182, 185, 337
Forecast errors, 142–53
adjusted mean absolute percentage error, 144
asymmetric, 143, 144
bias, 143, 145
mean absolute percentage error, 144
mean percentage error, 145

Forecast errors (*Cont.*)
  random, 143, 152
  root mean squared error, percentage error, 87, 144
  standard, 142
  Theil's inequality coefficients, 145–47, 149
  total, 144–53
  trimmed mean percentage error, 145
  turning point, 142
  weighted mean percentage error, 145
Forecast evaluation, 142–52
  ex-ante and ex-post, 152
  exogenous variables, 150, 152
  long-range, 147–49
  short-range, 147, 148
Forecasts and predictions, 172, 182–87
Foreign Agriculture Service (FAS), USDA, 337
Foreign exchange, 45, 49
Forward contracts, 234, 250, 259–73
Forward pricing a cash purchase, 251, 271–73
Forward pricing a cash sale, 250, 251, 253–71
  basis contract, 249, 250–51, 260–71
  buy puts, 260–71
  delayed pricing, 250, 268, 269
  fence, 250, 271
  forward contract, 250, 259–71
  forward contract (or sell cash) and buy calls, 260–71
  forward contract (or sell cash) and buy futures, 270
  hedge, 251, 254–57, 259–71
  hedged-to-arrive contract, 251, 269
  minimum price contract, 252, 269
  minimum price hedged-to-arrive contract, 252, 269
  multiple crop year pricing, 280
  synthetic put, 252
Functional forms, 28, 172–81
Futures, 43, 233–40, 243, 244
  clearing house, 234
  contracts, 234–37, 251
  delivery, 234, 235, 240, 250, 275
  economic functions, 237–39
  long, 234, 239, 240, 251
  margin calls, 240, 251
  margins, 236, 240, 251
  markets, 234–37, 251
  offset, 234, 252
  open interest, 235, 252
  positions, 235
  price limits, 235
  short, 234, 239, 240, 252
  spreads, 236
  volume, 235, 252

GATT, 3, 200, 211, 212, 337
Gauss-Seidel algorithm, 111, 122–24, 127, 136
Georgia State, 133
Government loans, non-recourse marketing assistance loans, 43, 82, 93, 210, 251
Grades, government, 61–65
Grain-Oilseed-Livestock model (GOL), 179, 180
Gross Domestic Product, 25
Gross margins in supply equations, 87–95, 129–32, 136, 137

Hedge ratios, 248, 278–80
  multiple crop year pricing, 280
  optimal, 279, 280
Hedging, hedgers, 236, 251, 253–80
  cross, 250, 279, 280
  new crop, 259–71
  storage, 254–57
Heteroscedasticity, 26, 342
Hildreth-Lu (HI-LU) correction for serial correlation, 314
Hog price model, 311–20
Homogeneity, 35, 36
Household consumption survey, 2

Identification problem, 112, 114–19
Implicit Price Deflator for Personal Consumption Expenditures, 26, 346
Independent variables, 342
Index of Prices Paid by Farmers, 70, 335, 345
Index of Real Trade-Weighted Dollar Exchange Rates, 47, 48
Inferior good, 10, 174–76
Inflation, 26, 345, 346
Input-output analysis, 215
Integrated Autoregressive Moving Average models (ARIMA), 318, 321, 322
Interest rates, 2, 43, 44, 67
International Financial Statistics, 337
International Food Policy Research Institute (IFPRI), 133
International Institute for Applied Systems Analysis (IIASA), 133
Interregional analysis. *See* Spatial competition in agriculture

Jarque-Bera normality test, 158–60, 166

Kansas City Board of Trade (KCBT), 62
Kurtosis, 159, 160, 342

Land Grant universities, 1, 91, 133, 212, 214, 337
Laspeyres Index, 345, 346
Leading indicators, 331
Linear programming, 180, 181, 196, 197
Ljung-Box Q-Statistic, 318, 321
Log-log demand equation, 33, 39, 175, 176, 181
Long, 234, 239, 240, 251, 254, 259
Long run versus short run analysis, 171, 172

Marketing costs, 17, 18, 58, 59
Market news, 336
Market News Branch, Agricultural Marketing Service, USDA, 238, 336
Marquardt algorithm, 314
Meat Import Law, 211
MicroImplan, 215
MicroTSP, 79, 121, 122, 124, 136, 149, 150, 161, 166, 308
Minneapolis Grain Exchange (MGE), 62
Money illusion, 26
Moving average models (MA), 316
MSU Agriculture Model, 136
Multicollinearity, 14, 75, 87, 95, 342
Multiple crop year pricing, 280

National Agricultural Statistics Service (NASS), USDA, 238, 332, 333, 338
National Futures Association, 234
Nationwide Food Consumption Survey, 24, 25
Net present value estimates, 213
Nominal Group Technique (NGT), 186, 187
Normality, 158–60, 342
Normal profit, 190
North American Free Trade Agreement (NAFTA), 3, 212

Olympic average, 43, 211, 273, 277
Onion model, 12–14, 322–28
Options on commodity futures, 240–48
  Black/Scholes pricing model, 246–48, 250
  calls, 241–48, 250
  contracts, 240, 241, 252
  delta formulas, 248, 250
  exercise, 241, 250
  exercise price (*see* strike price)
  GARCH pricing model, 248
  intrinsic value, 241, 251
  markets, 240
  offset, 241
Options on commodity futures (*Cont.*)
  premiums, 241–48, 252
  puts, 241–48, 252
  strike price, 241–43, 245, 246, 252
  time value, 241, 252
  volatility, 241, 245–48, 252
Ordinary Least Squares (OLS), 12–14, 23, 59, 60, 65, 79, 116, 118, 119, 129, 172, 220, 222, 307, 311, 342
Organization for Economic Cooperation and Development (OECD), 2, 134, 214, 337
Outliers, 29

Paasche Index, 346
Perfect competition, conditions, 99, 100, 196
Pipeline carryover, 44, 126
Plant location analysis, 202–6
Policy analysis, 210–15
Policy insruments, 210, 211
POLYSIM, 133
Population, 23, 24, 45, 49, 172, 173
Population variable, adjusted, 24, 25
Predictions. *See* Forecasts and predictions
Price discovery, 100, 282, 283
Price flexibility of demand, 30–34
Price ratios in supply equations, 87, 94, 95
Prices
  farm, 17–19, 23, 57, 62
  farmland, 68
  paid by farmers (*see* Index of Prices Paid by Farmers)
  representative, 190
  retail, 17–19, 23, 57, 59–61
  wholesale, 23, 63–65
Price spreads, farm-retail, 16–19, 53–61
  by-product allowance, 55, 56
  conversion factors, 55, 56
  farmer's share of retail price, 56, 57
  gross farm value, 55, 56
  net farm value, 55–57
Price spreads related to quality and close substitutes, 62–66
Price transmission elasticities, 48, 49, 196
Processed feed market, 65, 66
Producer Price Index, 91, 336, 337, 345
Producer Subsidy Equivalents (PSE), 134, 214, 337
Production functions, 90
Productivity, 68, 69
Program evaluation for research and education, 215
Projections, long-run, 172–82
  demand, 173–82
  income elasticity, 173–81
  prices, 181, 182
  supply, 178–81
Project Link, 133

Quarterly models, 29, 30, 311–28

Random walk, 283, 284, 303, 304, 306–11
Rational expectations, 43, 44, 74, 82–85, 100
Recursive models, 100–112, 129–31
Reduced form of simultaneous models, 116, 118, 119
Regression equation, 343. *See also* Ordinary Least Squares
REMI (Regional Economic Models, Inc.), 215
Replacement demand for capital items, 69
Research Seminar in Quantitative Economics (RSQE), 133
Risk effects on supply, 69, 85–87
Roots of characteristic equations, 108–11, 306

Satellite models, 136, 209
Scale economies, 197
Scenario writing, 183, 184
Seasonal price patterns, 219–31, 303, 304

Seasonal price patterns (*Cont.*)
centered 12-month moving average, 221–25
corn prices, 228–31
decision making implications, 225–31
futures, 303, 304
hog prices, 222–28
trends, 222–27
Second order difference equations, 107
Serial correlation in the residuals, 342. *See also* Durbin-Watson statistic
Set-aside acreage, 93–95, 210, 211
Shift-share analysis, 200–202
Shocks to the system, 111
Short, 234, 239, 240, 252, 254
Simultaneous models, 112–19, 131, 132
Skewness, 158–60, 164
Slutsky's condition. *See* Symmetry
Sparks Companies, Inc., 133
Spatial competition in agriculture, 196–202
endowment resources, 198, 200
environment, 198, 200
government programs, 198, 200
supporting services, 198–200
Spatial market division, 191–93
Spatial price differences, 190–92
Specification errors, 14, 342
Speculators, 236, 238, 252
Standard error of the regression, 13, 342, 343
as a percent of the mean of the dependent variable, 142, 342, 343
Static World Policy Simulation model (SWOPSIM), 134, 135, 180, 212, 213
Stationarity, 306–11
Stochastic analysis, 154–66, 214
Stochastic forecasts of crop yields, 136, 154–66
Stochastic forecasts of crop yields (*Cont.*)
aggregation of countries or regions, 160, 161
correlations, 161, 162
distributions, 161, 162
generation by AGMOD, 161–66
normality tests, 158
Stollsteimer model, 203–5
Storage costs, 228, 230, 231, 254–59, 275–78
Structural parameters, 343
Supply, farm level, 15, 72–96
irreversible, 15, 16
reversible, 15
Supply, impact multipliers, 75–77, 87
Supply elasticity, farm level, 76, 77, 87
Supply of beef cows, 80, 129, 130
Supply of marketing services and materials, 16–18
Supply shifters, farm level, 16, 74, 83, 85–96
structural change, 89, 334
technical conversion rates, 74, 89–91, 171, 336
Survey of Current Business, 336
Symmetry, 35, 36

Technical analysis, 282–304
Technical analysis evaluation, 302–4
Technical analysis tools, 284–302
consolidation, 288–90
continuation formations, 290–92
cycles, 302
double bottom, 285–86
double top, 285, 286
gaps, 293–95
head and shoulders, 284, 285
Japanese candlesticks, 302
moving averages, 295–97
net trader positions, 300
objectives, 285–288, 292, 293
point and figure charts, 300–2
Technical analysis tools (*Cont.*)
relative strength index, 299, 300
reversals, 292–94
stochastics, 297, 298
trends, 287–90
vertical bar charts, 284–95
volume, open interest, and price, 298, 299
Theil's Inequality Coefficients, 145–47, 149
Time, serial (TIME), 13, 14, 22, 27, 28, 54, 65, 67, 69, 73, 74, 84, 89, 90, 91, 131, 201, 202, 222, 307, 308
Time series models, 30, 146, 305–28
Trade models, 192–96
Armington, 196
price discrimination, 196
Transportation, transfer costs, 45, 50, 190–92
Trends, 28, 54, 65, 67, 69, 89, 219–22
t values, 13, 14, 343
Two-stage least squares, 118, 119

Univariate forecasting, 322–28
USDA. *See* U.S. Department of Agriculture
U.S. Department of Agriculture (USDA), 1, 46, 47, 55, 56, 60, 65, 67, 68, 70, 185, 190, 214, 331–33, 335–38
U.S. Department of Commerce, 2, 25, 333, 336, 346
U.S. Department of Labor, 26, 60, 61, 92, 336, 345

WEFA, 133
White noise, 307–11
Wold's decomposition theorem, 316
World Agricultural Outlook Board, USDA, 1, 128, 190, 337
World Bank (International Monetary Fund), 2, 49, 337
World Wide Web, 338